1495/1

OPERATING SYSTEMS SURVEY

AUERBACH Computer Science Series

Ned Chapin, Ph.D., General Editor
 Flowcharts—Ned Chapin
 Compiler Techniques—Bary W. Pollack
 Operating Systems Survey—Comtre Corporation,
  edited by Anthony P. Sayers

OPERATING SYSTEMS SURVEY

by THE COMTRE CORP.
Anthony P. Sayers, Editor

AUERBACH publishers

princeton
philadelphia
new york
london

Copyright © 1971 by AUERBACH Publishers Inc.

Published simultaneously in Canada by Book Center, Inc.

All rights reserved. No part of this work covered by
the copyrights hereon may be reproduced or used in
any form or by any means—graphic, electronic, or
mechanical, including photocopying, recording, or
taping, or information storage and retrieval systems—
without written permission of the publisher.

Library of Congress Catalog Card Number: 76-166523
International Standard Book Number: 0-87769-095-2 Cloth
                                     0-87769-077-4 Paper

First Printing

Printed in the United States of America

CONTENTS

Preface / vii
1 Introduction and Background / 1
   History / 1
   Third-Generation Development / 4
   The Fourth Generation / 18
2 Job Management—Arranging the Environment / 20
   The Job / 20
   The Job Scheduler / 22
   The Queue Concept / 23
   Communications between the Operator/Programmer and
      the Operating System / 26
   Starting the Job / 29
   Implications for the User / 30
3 Task Management / 34
   The Interrupt Scheme / 34
   Resource Allocation / 37
   Task Supervision / 44
   System Error Recovery / 48
   Implications for the User / 52
4 Data Management / 55
   Data Sets and Records / 55
   Types of I/O Devices / 60
   Access Methods / 61
   Features / 64
   I/O Error Recovery / 66
   User Implications / 68

5 Telecommunications—The World of Now / 71
   Remote-Entry Concepts / 71
   Remote Data Entry / 72
   Remote Program Entry / 78
   User Implications / 81
6 An Overview of Contemporary Operating Systems / 85
   Operating System Features / 85
   Executive and Control Functions / 96
   System Management Functions / 120
   Data Manipulation Functions / 128
7 Operating Systems for Small Computers / 140
   Overview / 140
   SEL 810A/810B Operating System / 142
   DEC PDP-8 Time-Sharing System (TSS/8) / 146
   XDS Sigma 2 Real-Time Batch Monitor / 154
   IBM 1800 Multiprogramming Executive (MPX) Operating System / 159
8 Operating Systems for Large Computers / 167
   Overview / 167
   RCA Spectra 70 Tape-Disk Operating System (TDOS) / 168
   IBM System/360 and IBM System/370 Disk Operating
       System (DOS) / 175
   CDC 3300/3500 Master Operating System / 182
   Honeywell Series 200 Mod 4 Operating System / 191
   IBM System/360 Operating System (OS)—MFT/MVT / 201
   CDC 6400/6500/6600 Scope 3 Operating System / 211
9 Time-Sharing Operating Systems / 229
   Overview / 229
   XDS Sigma 5/7 Batch Time-Sharing Monitor (BTM) / 229
   Honeywell 600 Systems (615/625/635) General Electric
       Comprehensive Operating Supervisor (GECOS III) / 238
   Univac 1108 Exec 8 Operating System / 247
   Burroughs B6500 Master Control Program / 261
Appendix A Operating System Functional Classification Scheme / 278
Appendix B Glossary of Operating System Terminology Addendum / 294
Bibliography / 327
Index / 329

PREFACE

The rapid growth of computer technology has thrust into prominence the executive and supervisory software that we refer to as "computer operating systems." This book is a direct result of the increased importance of operating systems to users of computers.

For both the student and the professional, this book provides a broad background for the concepts, facilities, and characteristics of contemporary operating systems. For the student, it surveys at a conceptual level, and offers examples of the role, scope, and complexity of operating systems. The student needs this knowledge as he goes on in the process of developing computer system skills, such as in the implementation, modification, design, or development of system programs.

For the professional, this book offers a general operating system survey and reference source useful for such activities as the selection, evaluation, adaptation, and implementation of operating systems. Throughout, the emphasis is on clarification of concepts, often by means of useful distinctions.

The first part covers basic concepts and functions of operating systems. It is oriented toward the student who has attained the level of knowledge normally conveyed in an introductory data processing course. Chapter 6 serves as a transition chapter to the second part, which is a comprehensive survey of operating systems currently in wide use. It is organized for convenience of reference and should be used in conjunction with the appendices. Appendix A should be referenced by all readers as a consolidated statement of operating system functions. The glossary and its addendum presented in Appendix B are quite important in view of the semantic difficulties associated with computer technology, and the typically weak coverage of operating system terminology given in most glossaries (such as, for example, the otherwise comprehensive *Standard Dictionary of Computers and Information Processing* by Martin H. Weik).

Many of the headings in the first five chapters are followed by reference numbers, for example, "Direct Access Space Management III (1.3.2.2)." "III (1.3.2.2)" refers to the appropriate section in Appendix A and thereby to Chapter 6, which has a functional outline of operating system facilities. This, in turn, has been designed to serve as a guide to the surveys of individual operating systems that are found in Chapters 7, 8, and 9. These surveys should be of great value to the systems programmer desiring an overview of the various operating systems now in use, and especially to their job management facilities. Since the operating system surveys are functionally oriented on a consistent basis, the systems programmer can easily compare the various operating systems in terms of the specific function with which he is concerned.

This book is based in part on contractual studies of contemporary operating systems conducted by the COMTRE Corporation, La Mesa, California, for the Electronic Systems Division of the Air Force Systems Command, USAF. Air Force permission to adapt from these studies does not constitute or imply endorsement of any part of this book.

This book is based partly on the experience of the editor, Anthony P. Sayers, in maintaining operating systems in the field and in teaching professionals and students about operating systems. To his colleagues and students, the editor offers his thanks. The editor wishes to state that no part of this book necessarily reflects the position, whether official or unofficial, of International Business Machines, his employer. Any value judgments herein contained are solely those of the author and/or the editor.

The COMTRE Corporation acknowledges the considerable efforts of all its staff members who participated on the various operating system projects leading up to this book. Mr. Sayers would like to thank particularly Roxy Ashline and Dorcy Cahorshak for their typing assistance, Phillip Janikowski and Ned Chapin for their counsel, and his wife Susan for her assistance.

The COMTRE Corporation
Anthony P. Sayers

OPERATING SYSTEMS SURVEY

1
INTRODUCTION AND BACKGROUND

HISTORY

Early Developments

To use the early computers required an intimate knowledge of the workings of the machine on the part of the programmer. He would write a program, feed it into the computer, and sit in front of the console while the machine processed the data. Since he was the only person who knew the way that the computer would react while his program was running, his presence was necessary. If the unexpected occurred, the programmer could stop the machine and make corrections in his data or his program. He could then restart the computer to finish his run.

Since each programmer was concerned only with his program and since applications were still quite limited, there was little standardization between programs. Most programs had little in common, and programmers did not see the need for standardization. Documentation and console directions were rare. In their absence, the programmer had to be quickly available—or had to serve as his own computer operator!

As programmers gained experience, they and their installations attempted to make the running requirements for their programs more similar. Documentation improved, and eventually program libraries developed. These consisted of a number of programs, most of which could be executed in the same manner. These made it possible for one person, a console operator, to set up the computer and run the various programs for the programmers. The programmers, thus relieved of the necessity of waiting at the computer while their program ran, could do more programming. This was accomplished only by standardizing and documenting the operational aspects of the programs so that a console operator could reasonably be expected to handle the various unusual events as well as the routine ones and continue the run as they came up.

In the early days of computers, mathematical computation was the big application. The paper tape and typewriter equipment used for input/output was not sufficiently sophisticated to allow anything much more complicated than handling mathematical computations.

Business and government could only minimally utilize the computer (except for computation) until the standardization was effective, along with improvements in input/output equipment. The combination extended the range of computer applications far beyond mathematical computation. The combination also enabled the console operator and the programmer to become specialists, each going his separate way. Also, the combination allowed a manager or supervisor to keep closer track of the operations of the computer. A manager could now better forecast what time would be needed in writing a given program and how much time would be taken to run this program when it was developed.

One of the things that helped the standardization of programs was the advent of the high-level language. Two examples of high-level languages are FORTRAN and COBOL. COBOL, particularly, is written for business, as its acronym suggests (Common Business Oriented Language). FORTRAN (derived from "Formula Translation") is popular for computational applications. Since using COBOL or FORTRAN or other high-level languages requires using the computer to translate the programs written by the programmer, the result is more standardization. The programs that direct the translation work provide their results in the form of operationally standardized programs. These standardized programs make possible more operator control of the computer and decrease the need for the programmer to do it.

As will be seen later, there have been many developments in computer systems, which allow more and more operational standardization and at the same time allow the programmer to devote more of his time to programming. The programmer, at the present time, has little worry about computer operation, scheduling input/output operations, allocating external storage space for data, determining the amount of internal storage needed, or, in short, about the environment his programs operate in.

Today, the console operator and the computer itself, using specialized programs called operating systems, handle these duties for the programmer. In brief, all he needs to do when using a computer with an operating system is to write a program and give it, with the test data; to the operator. First the computer compiles the program, then it attempts a trial run. After "debugging," recompilation, and further test runs, the program takes its place in the program library. From then on, the programmer will see no more of it except for possible implementation of changes. The operator is the only person directly concerned with the programs as they are executed in today's computers.

The operating system controls the total computer environment. The programer no longer tells the computer what to do in a total sense; rather he submits a request to the operating system (control program) to *allow* his program (problem program) to execute as but one of many distinct tasks *all* functioning under control of the operating system and vying for the various system resources. The console operator, in turn, only monitors the operation of the computer and takes action when directed to do so by the operating system.

Problems Encountered in Operating Systems Development

Many problems were encountered before present-day operating systems were developed. One of the main problems was the amount of operator time needed to prepare the computer for a program to be executed, usually called "set up" time. Operator set up time in the first-generation computers was trivial compared to the amount of computing time. The computers were slow; a job might take two hours and the operator might take only five minutes to set up the computer. In the second generation, however, computers became much faster, increasing their internal processing speed at least one hundred times over the first generation. Although it still took five minutes for the operator to set up the same job, it now needed only 15 or 20 minutes to run to completion. As this percentage of set up time increased, management began to look for ways to reduce it. The operating system was developed, to a large degree, because of the increased percentage of operator set up time that characterized the faster second-generation computers.

Another stride made in the second generation, was the idea of a supervisor or control state, and of a user or problem state. The computer would reserve certain functions for its operating system, or "control program," as the early operating systems were occasionally called. The control program would want to reserve, for instance, certain input/output operations to itself. It could not allow the programmer's program to direct an input/output operation when the control program itself needed to use the same data set, or data file.*[1]

Another example of a reserved operation is clock manipulation. Many computers have clocks, and any manipulations of the internal clock in a computer have to be in the province of the control program, because the computer keeps track of some of its operations by using the clock. If it is using the clock to control itself, it cannot allow the user's program to manipulate the clock.

Supervisor and user states allow the operating system, or control program, to reserve certain operations and functions for itself. By using a control program, we attain more standardization, less operator set up time, and many other advantages. But, we must pay a price: the programmer who works in an operating system environment must be restricted from the operations the control program must reserve for itself. For instance, if the control program is scheduling input/

---

* Whenever the reader is referred to the Glossary for an unfamiliar term, an asterisk appears beside the term.

[1] A data set or file is a collection of related records treated as a unit.

output, it cannot have a user program running under it trying to do the same function. If it did, the result would be chaos. One must be in control at all times.

Only by being in control during all crucial functions can an operating system know where the data it needs to retain for future reference is located in the computer. For instance, the operating system may want to keep certain facts about a data set in a given location in internal storage. If we allow the user (problem programmer) to access this storage, the problem program could write over the data that was being saved and destroy it. In order to achieve the manifest advantages of an operating system, the programmer and the operator must give up some privileges. In practice, however, the advantages a computer installation gains by using an operating system far outweigh the disadvantages of the loss of the privileges.

THIRD-GENERATION DEVELOPMENT

Hardware-Software Interaction

Designers of the third generation of computers took into account certain shortcomings that were noted in all but the most advanced second-generation equipment of the time. The third generation appeared in the mid-1960's. The features of the third generation are: even less operator set up time, relocatability and reenterability, channels and input/output queues, the interrupt concept, dual state computers with problem and supervisor states, and tailoring a system for an individual user (otherwise known as system generation). Less operator set up time is a huge benefit to the computer user. One obvious reason is more efficiency, which has already been commented on. Another less obvious advantage is that the operator has less opportunities to make mistakes.

Although many of the above hardware features—for example, relocatability, channels, interrupt capability, and dual state CPU's, were available on later second-generation computers, it remained for the third generation to *integrate* them. Although these hardware features were available in many second-generation computers, there remained a great need for a master program to utilize them most effectively *with each other*. The operating system fulfilled this need. It was, after all, designed with the hardware features in mind.

In addition to integrating hardware functions, the operating system brought about a heretofore unrealized degree of standardization. The programmer, when using a hardware feature, had to request it in a standard manner no matter what his program was designed to do, because the operating system itself was designed to accept only requests that conformed.

Features of the Third Generation

Operator Set Up Time

In pre-operating system days, many situations would come up which were not in an operator's realm of experience. He did not know what to do if an unusual situation developed; but, faced with the necessity of making a decision, he would try some action or some modification of the program while it was running. Since it was largely guesswork, it resulted in many aborted program runs, more inefficiency in operation, and generally more data processing cost. This unreliability in operation kept some potential users away. Only users who needed the computer's speed of calculation found it profitable to use the computer. As an example, calculations of satellite orbits, speeds, directions, distances, and so forth, might have taken years using a slide rule, an adding machine, or a calculator—and not yielded accurate results. These years of effort could be, with the help of the computer, reduced to weeks or even days, and the results made more accurate.

For these users, the speed of the computer was the important thing, not its efficiency. But even for these users, the growing percentage of operator set up time, in relation to reduced computational time as computer speeds improved, pointed out the need for standardization and I/O control that an operating system provides. When these two features are artfully utilized, the operator set up time factor can be reduced to near negligibility. As this reduction was provided, computers became more widely attractive, because the amount of computer output could be more reliably forecast. With the advent of the third generation and its lessened proportion of operator set up time and resultant efficiency, along with other improvements, computer users could greatly broaden their use of computers.

Relocatability I (1.1.5.3), I (1.1.3.2)

The second new feature is relocatability, also a very significant advance, because it allowed the interrupt concept to evolve into multiprogramming (which will be discussed later). In the early computers, a program was punched on cards or tape and fed into the storage unit in the central processing unit (CPU) or main frame.* The program was loaded in at the beginning of main internal storage and took as much storage as it needed to run. Every time the program was loaded, it went in at the beginning of internal storage because there was only one program at a time. Consequently, much of the remainder of main storage in the computer was wasted, or at best, inefficiently used.

With relocatability we found the capability of being able to load the program in at any place in internal storage. Perhaps we would have the primitive control program of the second generation loaded into the lower portion of internal storage. It would only schedule input/output (I/O) operations. Higher, or above the control program in internal storage, would be the problem (user) program. These two programs communicated with each other in the following manner: the user program indicated to the control program that it required input/output operations. The control program asked the user program to wait while it scheduled the input/output operation. The input/output operation then took place. Upon completion of the input/output operation, the control program notified the problem program that I/O was completed and where the input data or space for the output data was available. It would then give control of the system (in problem state) back to the user program. Thus the user program was then able to take the input data it had obtained and perhaps do calculations with them or modify them, and finally output them on the printer via the control program. To produce the output, the control program, after having acquired control, would take the data and schedule the output operations, then write the data on a printer in the desired format.

With relocatability we were able to store our problem program anywhere outside the storage range of the control program, which provides an important assist in multiprograming. (Multiprograming, simply stated, is concurrent operation of more than one user program.) With relocatability we have the facility to place a user program anywhere in storage outside the place occupied by the control program. The control program keeps track of the location of the problem program and then allows other user programs to come in outside the area taken up by the programs already loaded. (See Figure 1-1.) Relocatability frees us from having to use the same area for each specific program each time it is loaded.

Reenterability

Reenterability allows us to reexecute a program before it has completed its first execution. While a program is in the middle of execution, another job may want the same program executed, and could start executing the program at its beginning. This is important to an operating system; indeed, it is one of the enabling characteristics.

As an example, let us assume that a system is using multiprogramming. If all programs in concurrent execution want to print their output, they will all want to use the operating system I/O module* for the printer. With reenterability, the printer module can be used by a number of the programs concurrently. In fact, each program may branch (send control) to the printer module, and all can execute at different points in that program at the same time. The operating system makes much use of this feature in its more frequently used supervisor call modules.

The Interrupt Concept

The interrupt concept, which was another concept mentioned as a second- and third-generation advance, allows us to execute these programs concurrently. As an example, the problem program "A" is executing in problem state. It tells the control program to schedule input/output for it. The control program gains control in supervisor state, schedules the input/output, returns control of the com-

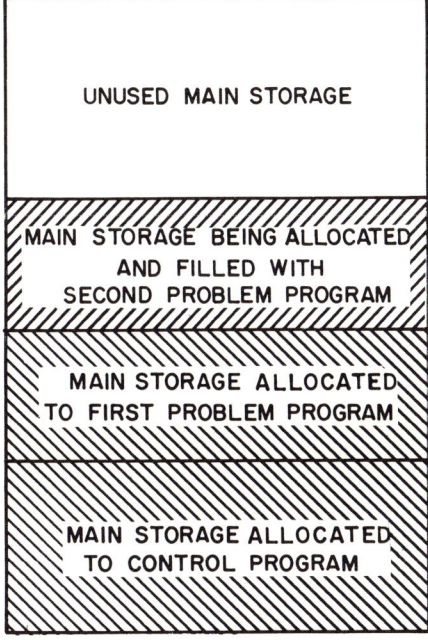

Figure 1-1. Internal Storage with Program Relocation

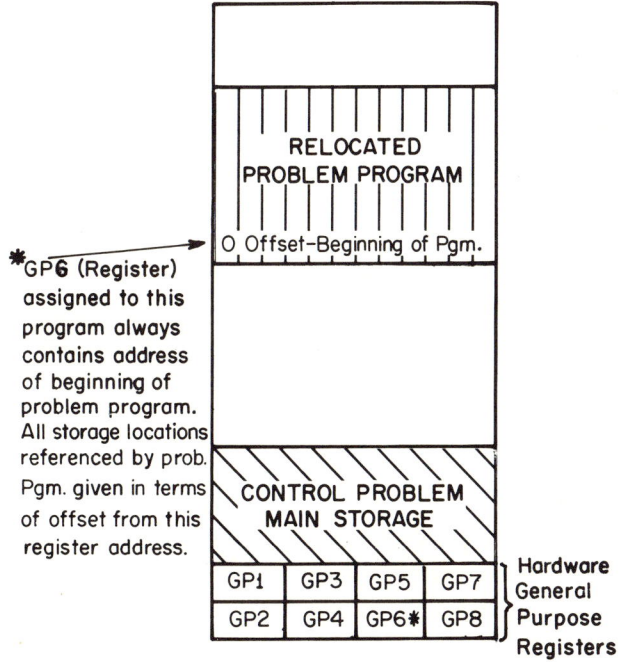

Figure 1-3. Problem Program and Base Registers

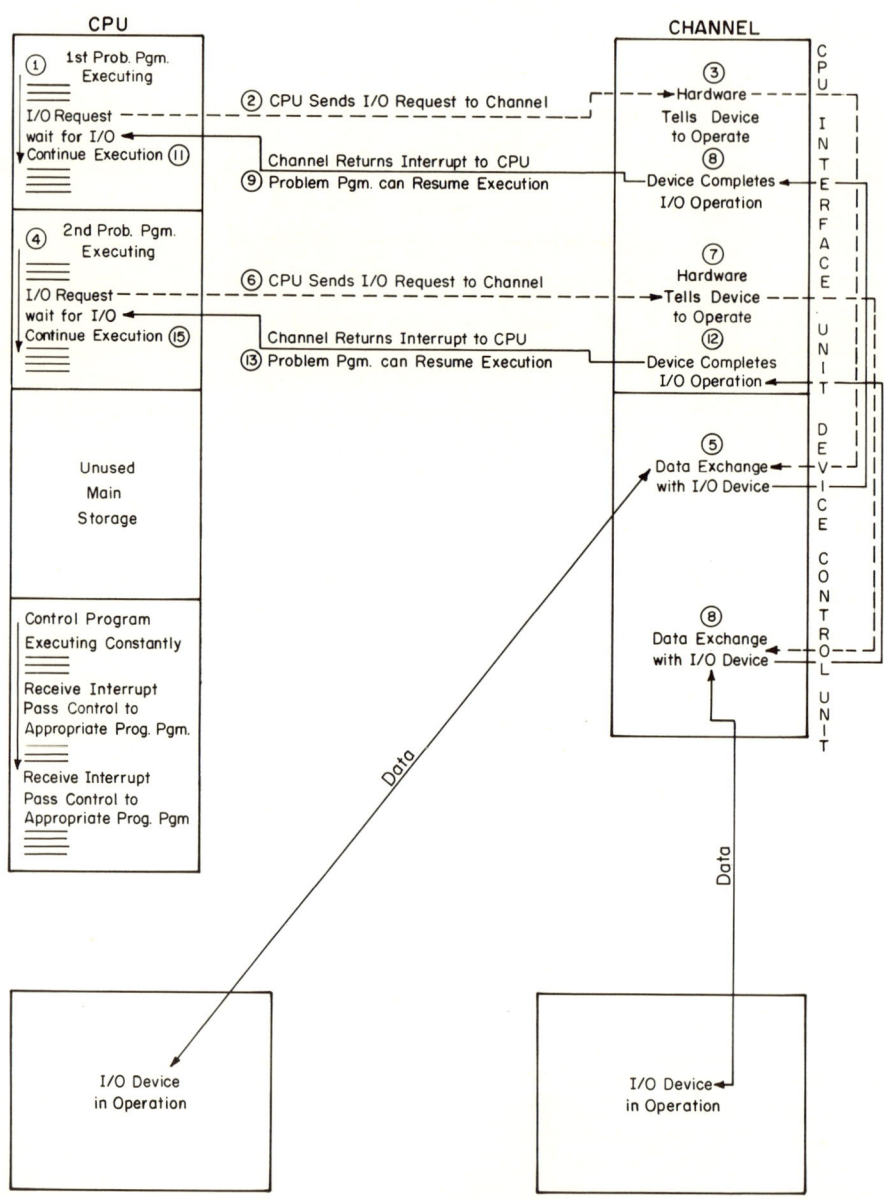

Figure 1-2. Input/Output Operation with Channel and Multiprogramming

puter to the problem program after taking the input/output request and executing it. This input/output request, therefore, was made by problem program "A." As soon as the control program received the request, it scheduled the input/output equipment and started the input/output operation.

Since input/output takes many times as long as a central processing unit (CPU) operation, it stands to reason that it would be rather inefficient to have a program waiting for the input/output operation to finish. To compensate for this speed differential, multiprogramming was developed. The control program with multiprogramming takes the I/O request from the user program and, having started the input/output operation, passes control to a second user program in the computer, "B," which has been waiting for CPU time. Program "A" is now awaiting completion of I/O, while Program "B" is now executing. Program "B" executes for some time. The input/output operation started for program "A" completes. The control program is informed of the completion of the input/output operation, stops the execution of program "B," and hands control back to program "A." It does this by means of an interrupt.

The control program is sensitive to many sources of interrupt. The input/output interrupt in the example is only one. When the input/output operation finishes, an *interrupt* occurs in the I/O device or channel.* The control program recognizes the interrupt and acts upon it. It determines that the input operation is being waited on by program "A," so it passes control back to program "A" to continue processing. When program "A" is ready for its next input/output operation, it tells the control program that it wants another input/output operation to occur. The control program schedules and starts the input/output operation and hands control back to program "B," which now continues running from where it was interrupted previously.

In many multiprogramming operating systems at the present time, large numbers of programs can run concurrently. Up to 15, for example, are allowed in the IBM Priority Scheduler Operating Systems (MFT and MVT).

Channels and Input/Output Queues

Multiprogramming also depends on another third-generation feature, the channel and the input/output queue. The channel, in effect, takes over the details of the hardware scheduling of the input/output operation from the central processing unit. It is a specialized computer which has one function—to keep track of the input/output operations. It handles data transfer and scheduling via hardware. Since the channel is handling the actual input/output operation, the control program is only required to handle interrupts. This frees the central processing unit to perform the data manipulation called for in this or other problem programs. (See Figure 1-2.) The input and output queues will be examined in detail later in the text.

Linkage Editor/Loader

Relocatability and reenterability are accomplished in part by the use of a type of service program* called a linkage editor, or a loader. The linkage editor analyzes the source programs to be executed and specifies the absolute addresses for all symbolic names, data locations, and so on, after which the converted source program is called a load module. Since we do not know where the load module is going to go (reside) in internal storage, these linkage editors or loaders operate on the principle of taking a symbolic address and giving it an offset (displacement) from the beginning of the load module. The load module may use a base register to provide a basis of addressability. That is, a base register may have as its contents a "base address" to serve as the basis of all addresses within the load module. (See Figure 1-3.) If the computer is executing somewhere in the load module and one of the commands is a branch command (transfer of control), the branch is to a specific address location. The linkage editor may have translated the symbolic name for that location and assigned a specific offset or displacement from the base address.

The base register contains an absolute storage address, which will be determined at the time the program is loaded into internal storage. Relocatability, then, is enhanced by the linkage editor, which makes possible references between the potentially relocated parts of a program. Thus a load module may try to communicate with another load module which will, in turn, try to communicate back. The computer may be executing within a load module which will encounter a branch instruction, which is an external reference to a location in another load module (to an address outside the range of the original load module). When the linkage editor loads the relocatable modules, it resolves the external symbolic references by providing the current correct absolute address equivalents. Thus control and data can go back and forth between load modules, wherever they be located in internal storage.

Summary of the Main Third-Generation Features

The channel(s) takes the responsibility from the CPU for scheduling the details of input and output operations and allows I/O to happen as a normal operation apart from CPU execution. The CPU, however, still calls for the initiation of all input and output operations.

The interrupt concept is useful for telling the operating system or control program that an event has occurred and needs attention. It also helps facilitate concurrent running of jobs. Since one job can execute while others wait for certain slow operations, mainly I/O events, multiprogramming is possible.

The problem (and supervisor or privileged) state allows the operating system or control program to reserve certain functions for itself, which allows certain constant system information to be maintained and certain data areas to be preserved. This helps the operating system keep track of all operations the computer undertakes.

Characteristics of Operating Systems

Flow of Work

The operating system is useful to many people. The computer manager primarily uses the operating system to monitor the flow of jobs* in and out of his computer installation. This allows him to maintain close surveillance of the efficiency with which his computer installation is operating (and consequently, the profitability). He is aided in his management by the fact that many operating systems today log all machine activities or are at least capable of doing so. These activities include items such as the level of data set usage, the amount of CPU time utilized, and the amount of storage used. Such information, taken together with some cost factors and operating practices, can be used to estimate the cost of providing computer services.

An organization might have a data processing department at the disposal of all other departments for handling data processing work such as inventories, payroll, and accounting. The organization may transfer funds between departments on the basis of computer time used or may allocate time on the computer to departments. When a department uses up its allocated time for a fiscal period, for example a month, it might not be allowed any more use of the computer that month, or it might be charged extra for excess usage. In many operating systems the computer itself keeps track of the computer system resource usage and maintains a log of this information. Even if it is used only for measuring the efficiency of the data processing application, this log is a necessity for most computer management.

Priorities

Job control is another major aid to the manager. Some jobs are urgent, some must be run within a week, some are run every day but are not tightly scheduled within the day. Hierarchies of priorities can and have been established with operating systems to deal with the varying degrees of urgency. These priorities allow the computer operations manager to schedule his jobs by priority, which greatly simplifies the job of the operator. Again, less operator intervention is necessary.

Some jobs are heavily weighted with CPU usage, while others are heavily weighted with input/output activity. A scientific program may do many calculations. A program to put out payroll checks would do many input/output operations. It is to the advantage of the user to achieve a balance so that the computer does not wait too long for input/output operations, since they will, as previously indicated, be on the order of a thousand times as slow as CPU operations. Nor does the user want the computer to be tied up by a computational program that will tie up the CPU without concurrently accomplishing any input or output work. This condition is called "computer bound," while the opposite extreme is called "I/O bound." With the proper balance and proper assignment of priority, the operating system averages these two types of jobs together, resulting in an optimal job mix. That is, it is neither input/output bound nor CPU bound, which makes for the greatest efficiency of operation.

Use of Storage

Another operating system service performed for the data processing manager is ensuring that a job's allocated main storage and/or data sets not be accessed by another job. Again, a typical example is the payroll job. We would not want other programs modifying the data records which have to do with payroll. We want and have the facility for the data processing manager to exercise job protection or job security through data set protection and through storage protection hardware in the CPU. If we are multiprogramming and do not make protection features available, the first program could very easily access the internal storage occupied by the second program and modify it so as to destroy it or at least make it unpredictable. The manager must have protection for the programs and their data.

Restart

Another and final example of an aid for the data processing manager is called check and restart, or sometimes checkpoint restart. If this feature is used, then at various stages during the execution of a job, the program stops executing. The data it has accumulated up to this point are saved in secondary storage (as on magnetic tape), so that when the system resumes regular execution, it continues precisely from the location it left. By taking these checkpoints at intervals throughout the execution of a job, there is now the possibility of returning to the last time the checkpoint data were stored and restarting from that point. Thus if the computer suffers a hardware failure, this restart capability can avoid rerunning the entire job from the beginning.

Assistance to the Operator

Operating systems give aid to the computer operator, whose main interest is control of the computer's operation. The operating system can prompt the operator by notifying him what action is to be taken next. He does not have to guess at what he should do next. He is told the status of various input/output devices the computer might have. He can be told, for instance, that he will have to wait for a while because the disk drive on which he wants to mount a new pack is busy.

Another assistance the operating system gives the operator is requesting tapes or disks that will be needed. He will no longer have to, previous to the starting of a job, gather up all the input and output data sets to place them at the disposal of the system. Instead, as the computer needs them, the operating system informs the operator what it needs and requests that the operator place the data set in readiness. This is done so that the input/output activity is not taken up by one job at a time, but is anticipated by the system, which has the operator mount the tape or disk *before* the program in the system requires it, whenever possible.

If there are problems with jobs, the operator alone no longer has to diagnose these problems. The operating system tells the operator what has happened and how to correct it. Again, the operator is told what to do instead of having to guess. This takes more inadvertent human judgment errors out of computer operation.

Assistance to the Programmer

The programmer, as noted earlier, suffers the main disadvantages of an operating system: no longer can he do certain things he could do in the early history of computers. However, he gains three advantages which far outweigh the disadvantages.

First, the operating system provides some facilities for debugging programs. Operating systems presently contain many facilities for testing programs and telling the programmer what went wrong when the computer tried to execute his program, which is useful in preparing new programs.

Second, the programmer does not have to call or specify the input/output device. Operating systems provide device independence, so the programmer merely needs to say he is going to output a data set. Since the operating system takes over the job of finding space for the data set, a device for the data set, and scheduling the time on the device for the input/output operation, the programmer no longer must do this. This saves him much time and makes the input/output part of his programming job simpler.

Third, another useful facility of an operating system helping the programmer is the fact that in a given installation, certain basic instructions are done for many of the programs. Many different programs may use the same data in an installation. For example, assume that we have a stock inventory. The stock inventory data is used by a program to determine what amounts need to be ordered. Another program might use the inventory data to decide how efficiently parts are being used that were listed in the inventory. Another program might be used for cost effectiveness.

The function that all three programs have in common is the input and output of the inventory records. This small common portion of the programs could be pulled out of each and kept only once in a library or secondary storage, and link-edited in to any program which needed the function. The linkage editor can resolve the symbolic references and external names. If a number of programs need this common program from the library, each programmer has saved the time required to program the module. It is no longer necessary to write over and over again the instructions for the input/output operation for each program. This saves much programming time and at the same time encourages more standardization of programming, both of which we have seen are decided benefits.

Summary of Characteristics

Although there are many advantages to an operating system, the basic one is that the operating system provides the data processing user with automatic control over the computer. In effect, the operating system tells the user what he can use for input/output and how he can use it. This enables more standardization and more efficiency. The only disadvantage offered by the operating system is the loss of control over system resources, which is suffered by the user programmer.

Figure 1-4 gives one view of how an operating system fits into a computing system. A computing system can be divided into hardware and software. The hardware consists of the CPU, on the one hand, and the peripherals, including the input/output and channels, on the other. The software is the operating system and the problem programs. The operator is included for purposes of illustration.

We have seen some of the advantages of an operating system, along with a disadvantage. Another rather minor disadvantage is that the user has something less than the full amount of storage that he might have without an operating system. Obviously, the operating system must take up a certain portion of storage for itself. This is a type of overhead and in some operating systems it can take up 50% or more of the total main storage available in a given computer.

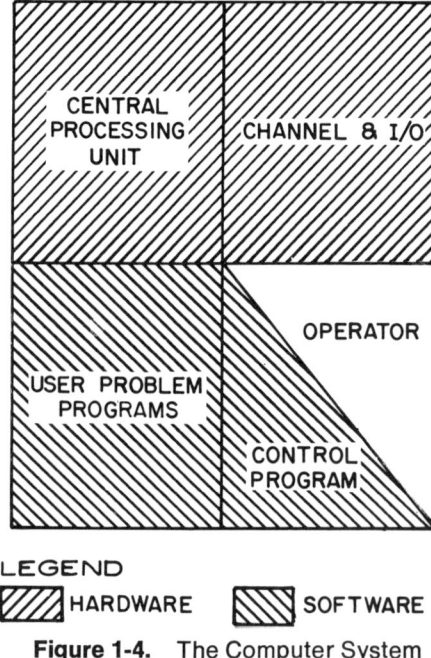

Figure 1-4. The Computer System

Surprisingly enough, even with this overhead ratio, it is usually still profitable for a data processing installation to use an operating system.

The two big disadvantages of an operating system are (a) the overhead of storage usage, and (b) less programmer control over the use of the computer's resources. There are a few installations that do not use operating systems. These are usually smaller computer users who do not have a large variety or number of programs to run and who are using small computers with very limited resources.

Types of Operating Systems Which Were Developed

Serial Batch Systems

There are four basic types of operating systems: (1) the serial batch system; (2) the multiprogramming system; (3) the time sharing system; and (4) the real time system. The serial batch system utilizes what is called sequential job scheduling. Jobs may come in from a card reader or may be stored on a faster intermediate device, usually direct access, and then be ready as they are needed by the operating system. The jobs will run one at a time. There is no multiprogramming and the operating system is primarily used for scheduling input/output.

It is still profitable and more efficient in certain installations to run an operating system and allow for its high overhead for the convenience of having the input/output operations scheduled for the programmers. Also, many users of simple batch systems are users that are growing from a small computing system to a larger one and eventually are going to go into the use of a more complex operating system. The simple batch system would then be used more to make the jobs acceptable for use under the operating system later planned for it. For instance, the files could be formatted while the customer was preparing to go to a more complex multiprogramming system. The programs could be link edited under this simple operating system so as later to be able to be executed under a multiprogramming system with a minimum of conversion at that time.

Multiprogramming

The serial batch system was the first type to be developed. Jobs were collected into groups called batches and then executed in a group. The operating system would process the jobs one at a time until all were done. This type of operating system is used mainly to operate the I/O. Examples are IBM's OS-PCP and DOS (early) and the SEL 810 A/B.

The multiprogramming system enables running two or more batch jobs running concurrently. In other words, 5 or 10 or maybe 15 jobs would be in the CPU at the same time contending for resources of the system. These jobs would, if run under batch processing, take much longer than running under multiprogramming because we do not have the inefficiency of waiting for input/output from one job under multiprogramming. While one job is waiting for an I/O event, another job has control of the CPU and is executing.

Multiprogramming is not simultaneous operation of two jobs, but is rather interleaved operation. At a casual glance it may look like there are 15 jobs running at the same time, but in reality only one job at a given time can be running, because only one program can have control of the CPU at any one time and only one instruction can be executed in the CPU at a given instant in time. (Computers capable of executing more than one instruction at a time in the CPU are termed "multiprocessing" computers.)

Computer speeds in the third generation, and even more so in the fourth, are astronomically fast. Certain modern computers have machine cycles of 80 nanoseconds (10^{-9} second) or faster. The input/output is done in the millisecond range. A fast input/output operation might take 5 or 6 milliseconds to accomplish an input/output operation. Given our 5 milliseconds I/O and 80 nanoseconds CPU time, and dividing I/O time by CPU time, we arrive at a figure of 16×10^6 (about 1.5 million) CPU operations which can be performed while one input/output operation is being done.

Therefore, it is easy to see why the input/output channel is useful and why multiprogramming can be accomplished. It is not at all unusual to see a system with 15 jobs running concurrently, and all of them waiting for input/output events. With this great disparity in speeds, it takes little longer for five jobs (assuming I/O activity in all the jobs) to run concurrently than it takes for one of them to run if it is by itself in the system), assuming sufficient input/output equipment is available on time. Obviously, multiprogramming offers a tremendous improvement over simple batch systems. Multiprogramming was the next advance in the operating system. The problem of time being wasted while I/O operations took place was one of the reasons for its development. There are many examples: IBM OS-MFT/OS-MVT, CDC MOS, GECOS, Honeywell Moon, RCA TDOS, XDS SIGMA 2 and 5/7, Univac EXEC-8, and others.

Time Sharing

Another type of operating system is the time sharing system. The time sharing system is a type of operating system where there are many users, each treating the computer as though each user had exclusive use of it. As an example, assume that there are 100 time sharing users on a computer. These 100 users are given some sort of a terminal, perhaps a teletypewriter or perhaps a video display unit with a keyboard. When the user types in a request to the system, again owing to the huge disparity between input/output and CPU time, the user gets an answer from the computer immediately, as far as he is concerned.

Introduction and Background   15

It seems then that he has exclusive use of the computer's resources. Actually though, 100 users are sharing that computer. Often these users are located across large geographical areas, perhaps an entire country. The request to the computer —and the reply from it—travel at nearly the speed of light. A user in Los Angeles might get an answer within 3 seconds after making a request to a computer in New York. (See Figure 1-5 for an example of the time-sharing system.) In this example is shown a simple processing unit with a number of users who may all be entering different jobs from their end, and probably are.

Time-sharing has the effect of giving the user a complete computing system at his disposal at all times; but he pays only for the time he actually uses. The cards are read by a remote terminal at the user's location and relayed, usually via telephone lines, to a central processing unit. The central processing unit analyzes the interrupt and the data coming in and eventually gives control to the user, who may then have a program he wants to run or may just want an answer to a particular question. Either way, the computer services the request extremely rapidly and schedules more input/output, such as it might to a tape or printer; only now it is going across telephone lines and back to the original requester. Because the owner of the central processing unit has a large number of users, he can divide up his cost among them, in effect, giving each user his own computer at a very low cost compared with the user having the computer in his own location. As the user has more and more applications for the computer, though, it becomes more profitable for him to have a private computer at his location as he approaches the state where the computer is kept 100% of the time. The RJE, R

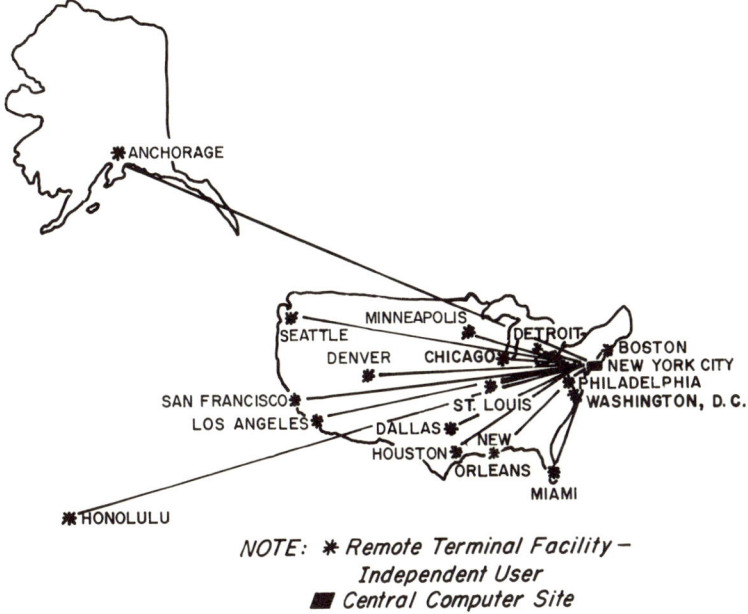

NOTE: * *Remote Terminal Facility —*
Independent User
■ *Central Computer Site*

Figure 1-5. Extensive Time-Sharing Network

batch, and TS features are examples of this type of operation. There are also *entire* operating systems devoted to time sharing: DEC TSS/8, IBM TSS, SDC ADEPT. See the appendices for detailed explanations.

Real Time

Another type of operating system is the real-time system. At first glance, real time seems much like time sharing. We have comparable terminals at remote locations; the user types data in and gets data back out. The difference between the two systems is that since a time-sharing system may run different jobs from user to user, it has, in effect, a hundred different programmers feeding into one processing unit at the same time and getting their programs executed and back out. In a real-time system, however, there is a program running in the CPU which controls remote terminals along with a background* batch partition. The remote user is usually feeding data into this one program. The program will process the data and send data back out to the remote terminal. Since the remote terminal is not entering programs, but rather data, the user of the real-time system is performing more of a clerical function.

Process control is another type of real-time application. In this application the user—such as an oil pipeline—is a process. At regular intervals along the pipeline there are flow-rate sensors which continuously give flow-rate information to the CPU. The CPU then regulates valves along the pipeline to maintain a constant flow. The IBM 1800 MPK is an example of this kind of system. Examples of the two systems are: In a time-sharing system with time slicing the typical user is the service center. This computer utility sells time on the system to many users and allows each user to run his own programs into the system perhaps for eight hours a day. 100 users would each get 100 microseconds of time as it became their turn for control of the CPU. User one would get 100 microseconds, user two would get 100 microseconds, user three would get 100 microseconds, and so on, all the way down through user 100. When user 100 used his 100 microseconds, control would return to user one, who would get his second 100 microseconds. From quick calculation we can see that the entire time for all 100 users would be 10,000 microseconds or 10 milliseconds, which is still a relatively short time, almost negligible to the user.

On the other hand, an example of a real-time system is a parts inventory system where remote stations are located throughout a huge warehouse. A clerk in this warehouse might want to know how many of a certain type of part are on hand. He would typically key in a part number. The program in control of the CPU would take this part number, schedule an input/output operation to secondary storage devices, requesting data about that part number. The program would then find the data after the input/output operation was completed and extract the number of parts on hand, then schedule input/output back to the requester, who would then receive on his display unit or teletype the number of parts available. He would then be in a position to order more parts or notify a customer that he has the parts to fill his order.

Basically since there is little computation involved—but rather mostly input/output—we would typically find many more users, perhaps up to 500 or 1,000 remote terminals in use. These terminals, however, would be doing the same thing: finding the number of parts on hand from all parts of a huge warehouse.

Another example of the real-time system is an airlines reservation system where a ground stewardess keys into the computer, perhaps across the country, a flight number and request to determine the availability of a seat on that flight. The program then searches its secondary storage records concerning that particular flight, finds out whether or not there is a vacancy on the flight, and gives this information back to the ground stewardess at the remote location. You might have 300 different airports doing much the same thing. Again, with computer speeds, the reaction time is comparable to human reaction time, which gives us the name: real time.

In review, the types of operating systems are: the serial batch system, or uni-programming; the multiprogramming system, or concurrent execution of programs; the time-sharing system with a number of users—to each user it seems that he is getting exclusive use of the system; and the real-time system which, basically, is clerical work at computer speeds, basically a means of greatly facilitating data entry and information retrieval.

Parts of an Operating System

Whatever the kind of operating system you might see, a typical operating system has three main parts; job management, or the executive portion of the program; task management, or system resource management; and data management, or input/output management.

Job management, or the executive, basically, handles the total environment of a computing system. That is, it will arrange for the operator to communicate with the system and for the programmer to communicate with the system either through operator commands or control cards presented with the program to be run. The operator must be able to communicate with the operating system so as to tell the operating system what resources must be made available for his program.

Task management, or system resource management, basically, is concerned with allocating system resources to the program once it is executed. Typically, these system resources include main storage, CPU time, input/output operations, and a system clock arranging the programs in main storage in their proper place, taking programs from secondary storage libraries, and bringing them into the computing system to be executed.

Data management, or input/output management, is that portion of the operating system which controls the utilization of space on disks for direct access, controls the allocation of tape drives if it is a tape data set, or controls the reading in of cards and the output of printed matter. In short, all I/O operations must be scheduled and executed by the operating system, not the problem program. The next three chapters will be devoted to a closer, more detailed, study of these three major areas of an operating system.

THE FOURTH GENERATION

The preceding discussion has centered on third-generation operating systems. There is now, however, and there has been in the recent past, talk of the advent of the fourth generation in data processing. In most cases this talk is theoretical and is concerned with ideas on what the fourth generation will be. In examining the past advents of generations relative to software only, the following classifications appear:

First Generation. Single-job operation, operating system functions included within each job, vendor-supplied system consisting usually of a loader and a dump.
Second Generation. An operating system providing basic services to executing jobs while maintaining control of job-to-job transition for a sequential mode of operation.
Third Generation. An operating system that provides all the basic services and control necessary to allow scheduling and execution of jobs in other than a sequential manner; in other words, multiprogramming.

In regard to the possible characteristics exhibited by fourth-generation operating systems, there is no clear-cut picture at the present time. However, it appears that for a truly fourth-generation operating system to emerge, there must be a striking departure point from today's third-generation systems. This could mean that, rather than being an improved version of a third-generation operating system and thereby providing upward compatibility for existing software, the fourth generation will exhibit the best characteristics of the third generation while consisting of a totally new operating system design concept.

QUESTIONS—CHAPTER 1

1. Of the new features in the second and third generations, which was the most beneficial in terms of allowing the development of present operating systems? (Use [a] multiprogramming, [b] ease of I/O programming, and [c] exclusive reservation of certain operations for the control program as criteria, ranking the criteria in order of importance.)

2. A. For a small user with few (but long-running) jobs, who has a computer with limited main storage and no remote facilities, determine the operating system type best suited for him from among the four types discussed in this chapter.
   B. List three reasons for your choice.
   C. From among the specific systems reported on in the latter chapters of this book, choose the one best suited for the user in A.

3. In your own words, explain why the problem of excessive set-up time spurred the development of operating systems as they exist today.

4. Using the functional outline in Chapter 6, list the three main parts of an operating system, with five direct functions of each part. Give a short explanation of the function. Also, show how each of the three parts interrelates with the others.

2
JOB MANAGEMENT—ARRANGING THE ENVIRONMENT

THE JOB

As stated in Chapter 1, operating systems can be divided up into three parts. We should realize that operating systems can be divided up into any number of parts. Throughout the industry, however, for purposes of communication between operating system users, operating systems are usually subdivided into a few components, which is convenient for the people who are doing the communicating.

An operating system must do three primary things: set up the environment; allocate system resources; and supervise data activities. Job management is setting up the environment (arranging the external conditions necessary to run a computing job or jobs). This function is also commonly called the executive, or control, function. We will see later that task management, otherwise called system management or system resource management, does the day-to-day running of the system. That is, task management handles the interrupts, takes action when needed, and allocates some system resources.

To look at it another way, job management is a macroprogramming idea. By macroprogramming we mean having the range of time of seconds, minutes, or hours. Job management includes such things as scheduling jobs that are entering the system, producing system output data, arranging for programs to be called in, and communicating with the operator via the console. At the microsecond level, the task manager, operating at CPU speed, examines various fields to see if something has to be done at the moment. He transfers control of the computer from one task to another. This activity at CPU speed we might regard as a microprogramming or execution-time type of system activity.

Perhaps it would help to define a "job," since we are terming this macroprogramming portion of an operating system as job management. A job is a major unit of work performed by an operating system. It is an entire program or series of programs presented by the programmer to the computer system as an entity. It may consist of one step or a number of steps. It is the smallest complete unit of work that can be presented by the programmer. As we shall see later, jobs are usually accompanied by some sort of control data or command language, usually in the form of cards punched in a special language which varies from manufacturer to manufacturer. In an IBM operating system it is called job control language (JCL) and serves to communicate to the operating system information about the job, dividing it into subunits of work if necessary; input/output requirements and certain commands are given to the system. Other manufacturers have different names for this control language, but basically the language performs the same function: telling the computer what the job needs in order to operate under a particular operating system.

A task, or computing unit of work, is defined as the smallest unit of work which can contend for system resources. This unit of work is in fact a subdivision of a job; it is what task management supervises. When a program is read into the input queue along with appropriate control language, the operating system divides the job into as many units of work as it needs, loads the job into main storage, and finally causes it to start executing. Once this program starts executing, it is then a task.

It is not necessarily true that a task is equal to a job step or an entire program. It is possible for a program, in turn, to invoke other programs. These programs may already be in the computer; if not, they may be called in from secondary storage. In either event, they would then be separate computer units of work. In some schemes a job called in in this manner by another task is called a subtask.

Consider this example: Program A is operating. Perhaps it is concerned with data correction. It determines at some point in time that it needs another programming routine to do some calculation, so it calls in the routine. The routine comes in. The first task may or may not wait for the called in task to complete before he continues. In fact, they may be running concurrently and might each be contending for system resources. This is an example, then, of simple routines, parts, or programs as separate tasks. By system resources we mean such things as main storage, central processing unit time, the computer internal clock, or allocation of priorities, so that perhaps this program would have priority over other programs operating under the operating system. Input/output would be another system resource that would certainly be contended for by the various tasks in the system.

Data management is, of course, involved with input/output requests. It handles such things as getting secondary storage space for the new file or data set that is to be written. It determines what kind of input/output programming is necessary to handle a particular type of data set. It allows for multiple I/O and buffering, as opposed to serial input/output. In the multiple I/O and buffering method the input/output operation is set up in the following manner. We know we want to read a data set, and wish to increase efficiency in the input/output operation. The general scheme for accomplishing this is to have two or more (we will use two as an example) data areas in main storage. These two areas may be called buffers (an operational definition). The buffer is then filled from a read operation. We wish to read from a direct access device. We will read into a buffer, while at the same time the next sequential read from the following record in the data set is scheduled. The buffer is filling while the next read is being organized or set up.

When the second read is ready to be transferred from the input/output device to the main storage area reserved for it, the first buffer read is now empty or, in any event, the data in it can be assimilated by the operating system or the program running under it. At this time the first buffer is used to prepare for the third read from the data set. In effect, we then have an alternation of reads and set-ups for input/output, which allows for much more efficiency in input/output programming. Job management's function is to accomplish this efficiency without bothering the programmer. The operating system tries to handle input/output operations, more or less automatically, depending on the level of control the programmer wishes to retain over his input/output.

Now we have seen the need for three areas, subdividing the computing system into the outer job control programming portion; the inter, or execution time, portion; and the input/output supervision portion. We shall look at the various divisions in more detail. The reader is reminded that various manufacturers of operating systems may divide their systems differently. Generally speaking, the three areas will be comparable among manufacturers. For purposes of this discussion, it is better to divide the conceptual operating system for ease of communication and understanding of the concepts.

Again, job management is preparing the computing system to accept a job. Some of the things it must do to prepare this environment, or to accomplish the macroprogramming, are scheduling jobs, maintaining queues or stacks, handling communications between the operator or programmer and the operating system, starting the job, and finally, making the job ready for converting its various steps into the tasks or computer units of work. At the end of this discussion there will be a short discussion on the implications for users.

THE JOB SCHEDULER I (1.1.1)

There are two basic kinds of job schedulers—the serial scheduler and the priority scheduler. It stands to reason that if more than one job is to be run at a time (for instance, under the multiprogramming environment), we will want to be able to read in a number of jobs so that when the system is ready to accept a job, the job is available for its use instead of having an operator go over to an input/output device and read in the job while the operating system waits. It would be much better if we were to have the jobs lined up or queued on secondary storage and ready to be read in as they are needed, instead of having to tell the operator to read in a job.

Operating systems do maintain these queues. Typically an operator will have 15 or 20 jobs he wishes to run through the operating system. When he is ready to start the operating system, perhaps after a weekend, he will first want to read the jobs into a card reader, or in some larger operations, from magnetic tape. The jobs and their job control blank cards are read, usually onto direct access storage using disks, drums, or data cells. Direct access is sometimes called intermediate storage, as is secondary storage. Once these jobs are on intermediate storage, which is a much faster data transfer medium, they are allowed to *queue* up, hence the name. Now our 15 or 20 jobs have been read onto the intermediate storage device or direct access device, which later reads, in turn, into the operating system as the operating system requires new units of work to work on.

THE QUEUE CONCEPT I (1.1.1)

Our queues, or stacks, can be imagined as decks of punched cards transformed to magnetic data or direct access devices. The data would still be in the same form it was on punched cards or tape. The difference now is that it is more accessible to the system in terms of speed and is already under control of the system, as opposed to the operator having to be told to read a job in; the system already has the jobs at its disposal.

If the jobs are read into the computer sequentially, or as they are placed in the card reader and read onto intermediate storage, the scheduling is called serial scheduling; in other words, jobs will execute as they are encountered. For large installations or for small special usage installations, this is not enough. We find in the typical operating system that these jobs can be arranged with certain priority schemes. The priority may be in terms of numbers; for instance a job may have a priority of one and another job a priority of 15. The job with priority one is read into the system first from intermediate storage after having been placed on the job queue. The job with priority 15 is run after all jobs of higher priority, in this case priority one having been read in.

If we have five jobs with priorities of 1, 3, 5, 3, 1 read into the system in that order, they will be automatically placed on secondary storage or direct access queue in the priority order so that the jobs as they were being read from the reader onto the direct access device will be arranged in priority 1, 1, 3, 3, 5 after the operating system job scheduler manipulates the input queue. As the system is ready for new units of work, it will accept the jobs from the input queue in this order. That is, the number 1 job will go in first. The second number 1 job encountered will be read in second. The first priority 3 job encountered will be read in third. The second priority 3 job encountered will be read in fourth. The last job to be run in our example will be the priority 5 job.

This is an extremely important and useful concept. It allows the data processing installation to be more flexible in its planning. As an example, perhaps the job mix (operating combination of jobs) for a particular operating system is as follows: a payroll job, two inventory reports, an engineering job containing many mathematical calculations, and a job for building a product history file for a data set.

Through proper arrangement of the job classes, some of the jobs which largely include input/output operations such as the inventory and payroll jobs could be placed on a higher priority within the system, so that other jobs in the system would run only while this job does its input/output process. (Remember the disparity between central processing speed and input/output speed on the order of magnitude of 1,000 in terms of time. The input/output speed then takes 1,000 times as much time as the computer speeds within the central processing unit, giving plenty of time for other jobs to execute while it waits.)

Our typical installation wants to ensure that the job that was largely input/output-oriented has a high priority within the computer. Our sample job of the engineering/mathematical variety would, on the other hand, require much computer time. With a mix of input/output and computer time we can in effect run these two jobs almost as fast as we could run either one by itself, because the mathematical job would only be processing while the input/output job was waiting for results from its input/output operations. By proper scheduling of its job classes, the installation can put all mathematical or compute-bound jobs in one class, all high input/output activity or I/O-bound jobs in another class, and achieve a reasonable mix. This mix, in turn, gives us the highest efficiency in terms of job throughput.

Many operating systems use combinations of these two types of priorities, for example, the job class priority and the numeric priority, so that within each job class there is the capability of giving the jobs numbered priorities. This, of course, allows us to accommodate a job of an emergency nature and give it a high priority, put it into its proper job class, and force it to be the next from the class to be read into the computing system. This double priority scheme can be very efficient or it can be very inefficient, depending on the skill of the system programmer at the installation. (See the questions at the end of this chapter.)

Job Management—Arranging the Environment   25

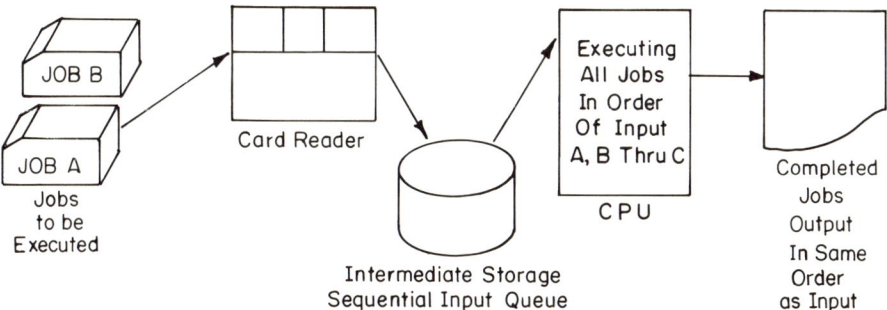

Figure 2-1. Sequential Scheduler—Jobs Execute as They Are Presented to the System

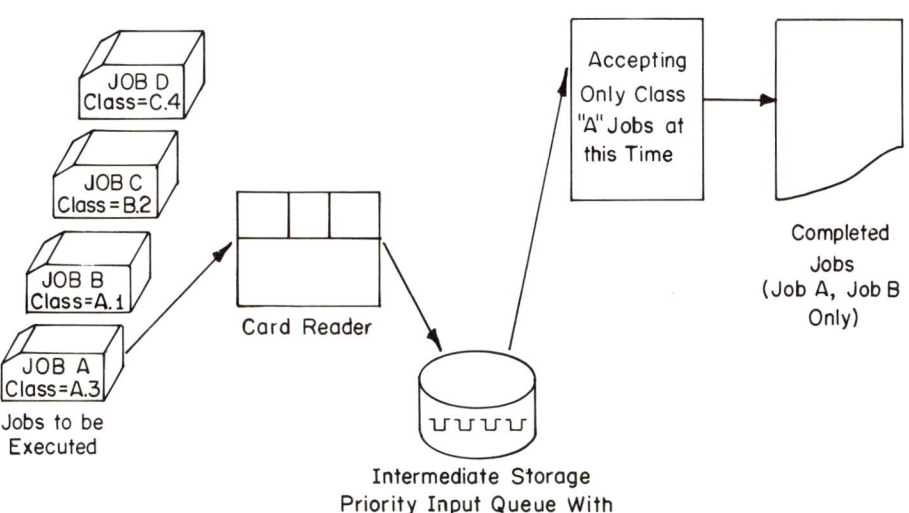

Figure 2-2. Priority Scheduler—Jobs Execute by Class and Priority as Specified by Program

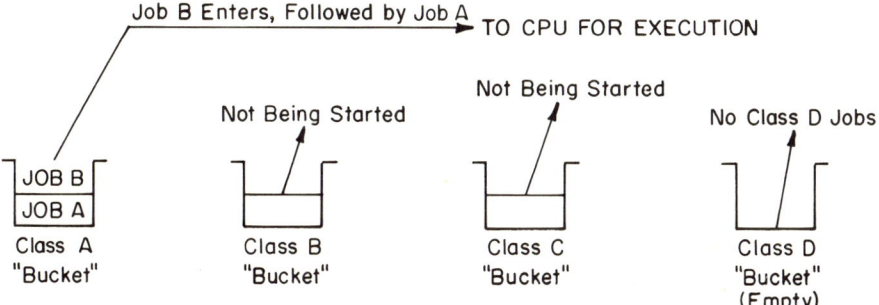

Figure 2-3. Detail of Priority Scheduler Input Queue

The system programmer must take many variables into account in setting up his job classes and schedules. The priority scheduler is concerned with manipulation of jobs in terms of the order of their presentation to the operating system; the serial scheduler, on the other hand, takes jobs as they are read into the computing system and presents them to the computing system or operating system in that order. (See Figures 2-1, 2-2, and 2-3.) The system programmer must consider the type of job and his installation's accounting requirements in arriving at his job scheduler/class configuration.

Another widely used device which uses the queue concept is the output writer. If a programmer wants data printed out and wants to exercise minimum control over his output, most operating systems offer a device known as the output writer. It is much the same as the input job queue, or stack, except in reverse. Output writers can have output classes and priorities within a class, so that if a job is to be read into a particular class with a high priority it also enjoys the same high priority when it gets to the output writer.

The output writer is similar to the input queue, in that it has intermediate storage where the output from various jobs is stacked. The intermediate storage, or direct access device, usually has a backlog of jobs in each of its output classes since the CPU spews out jobs much faster than a printer can operate. One way of alleviating this problem is to have multiple output printers. Another way is to have the output writer not write directly to a printer, but instead write to magnetic tape to be printed out at a more convenient time.

The intermediate storage contains the output classes, which work exactly as the input classes do. If a high priority job is placed in the input queue and, because of its high priority, is executed almost immediately, it takes its place at the front of all output from all jobs of that class in the output queue, and therefore will be the next job to print. Many operating systems have the ability to modify the priorities of these jobs as they are coming in or going out of the computing system, which allows greater flexibility in times of emergency.

COMMUNICATIONS BETWEEN THE OPERATOR/PROGRAMMER AND THE OPERATING SYSTEM I (1.3.2)

Console Communication

Another area which must be handled by the operating system job management portion is communications between the operator and programmer and the operating system. This is done by means of console communication to the operator and input control cards from the programmer, which is the job control language mentioned above.

The console communication task is necessarily one of the highest if not the highest priority class in the system. The operator must have immediate access to the system resources if he needs them; therefore, communication from the operator and his console to the central processing unit must be nearly instantaneous. Some of the commands an operator might be concerned with giving the operating system are the ability to start the output writer so as to get printed output. He might wish to know the status of all tasks within the system; to do this he asks the system to display the active tasks. He may want to know the status of certain I/O operations; he can ask the system to give him the status of these input/output operations. He may want to change the system so that it only starts one task at a time, or he may want to change it so that it starts more than the number of tasks he has available to him at the time. In short, the operator must be able to control the system so as to make changes in the system when necessary. When conditions change, the system must change. This is a most vital function of an operating system; if there were no facility to modify the operating system dynamically, its effectiveness would be reduced.

An operating system must be flexible in order to handle contingencies as they occur. The operating system is informed of the need for a change in the environment by the operator's use of the console. The operator may see a need for more or less internal storage to be allocated to a different job. Although this does not change the operating system, it definitely changes the job environment; with a competent operator this manipulation of the job environment can aid the operational effectiveness of an operating system.

In addition to main storage allocation, there are also such things as input/output scheduling, priority rearranging, and emergency actions entering the operator's functions. If the operator is competent enough to manipulate the environment for a particular job as well as manipulate the operating system as a whole as it is needed, he becomes a very valuable member of the data processing installation. This beneficial operator intervention, although not strictly necessary, is one sort of communication between the operator/programmer and the operating system.

Control Cards

Another type of communication is the control cards already mentioned. The control cards are usually defined as follows: a card to tell the operating system that another job or macrounit of work is entering the system, a card to tell the system that a task is about to be initiated or started, and a card to define data sets to be used or created, depending on the application. There are less important types of control cards, but these three main types are in the province of the programmer and tell the operating system how to set up the environment for the job.

Typically a job card has such information as the name of the job, the programmer's name, and the department number having the job run; the priority and class of the job, if the system has a priority scheduler; the amount of core storage needed for the job to operate in; and the disposition of the operating system's comments about the running of the job—for instance, notification of errors, notification of completion of a job, notification of input/output allocation. The job card usually tells the operating system where this information is to be sent.

Another kind of card is that which prepares a given job step for conversion into a task, which we have defined as the smallest unit of work that can contend for system resources. The job might be divided into three steps—a compile, a link-edit, and a go step. The compile step might be written in the COBOL language; the compiler is going to convert it into machine language. This would be the first step. Then, after using the task card to tell the system that this is the first step, we have a number of other cards: our input source deck.

Another step, or task, might tell by way of another task control card that the compiled or transformed source deck is now ready to be worked on, so that relocatability and readdressing can be effected by the linkage editor, or loader. In this step the output from the first step, the compile step, will be transformed into a load module suitable for execution under the operating system. Following the rest of the control cards connected with this step we might then have a third step (the task card), which informs the system that the result of the execution of the linkage editor and compilation—the load module—is now ready to be executed by the system. This is the original program that the programmer has written, but now it has been transformed from a high level language into operational machine language. The addressing has been resolved and the program is to be executed. This is the third step, which the operating system has to process in this one complete job.

In most operating systems, unless a special type of command is given, each task will *not* be concurrently run. Once a system has recognized a job card, it will locate for the first task card and complete execution of that task before reading the following task card and starting the next task. Obviously this prevents trying to use the result of task 1 in task 2 before task 1 is finished with its execution. Once a job card is recognized, all tasks between it and the next job card must be executed serially, since one task depends on the completion of the previous task.

Along with the job card and the task card we have the data card. This control card describes data sets which we are either going to read or create. Typical information on the data card is data set name; the location of the data set in intermediate or secondary storage, whether the data set is to be disposed of at the end of this job or whether it is to be kept; and various other information that is needed by the operating system before the data set can be used. In the case of output data sets (data to be created), the operating system must be told how much space on the output device is needed to hold the collection of data which it is going to create. This space parameter is also found in the data control card. These three cards, then—the job, the task, and the data cards—are the second step of communications between the operator/programmer and the operating system.

STARTING THE JOB

Allocation of I/O I (1.1.2.2), I (1.1.5.1)

The job management function of an operating system must also prepare the job to start. Having read the job control cards with the job of the programs to be executed, we must now prepare this job to be transformed into a task or computer unit of work, so that it can execute under the operating system. At this moment, we have seen that jobs reside on input and output queues and that there are certain control cards which will inform the operating system of the resources needed to operate the job.

In order to start the job we must have the operating system now prepare the environment for the job which is soon to become subdivided into tasks to execute. One of the things we must do to prepare a job to start is to allocate input/output devices for our data sets. Taking the information from the data control cards, the operating system will determine which devices are to be used for all the data sets connected with the job. It will seek out and allocate space for any new data sets to be written by the job. While allocating I/O the operating system must be conscious of the fact that other jobs may also be requesting the same data sets (or the same space if they are also creating data sets); the operating system must monitor input/output activity for all jobs within the operating system. Allocation of I/O is a very important part of an operating systems function.

Initiating the Job I (1.1.3)

Once the input/output space or data sets have been allocated to our job, we must prepare the job for execution. The individual job step is brought into the system as a program; this program has been specified earlier in our control cards, specifically on the task control card. This task control card specified that we needed a particular program in order to do this task. Job management takes this request for a program and finds the program. It may be in a permanent library or on direct access or it may be the direct result of earlier steps in the same job. If it is a result of earlier steps in the same job, it will be in temporary storage. Whether it has to go to temporary storage or a permanent library, the appropriate job management routine finds the program and brings it into the CPU and begins executing it. If the routine cannot find the job, it notifies the operator and ends the task and therefore the job. This process of bringing in a program and beginning execution is sometimes called initiating a job; some operating systems have routines whose sole purpose is to be ready to initiate any job or mark it for execution and bring in the appropriate program for execution.

Accounting for System Resource Usage II (3.3)

Before the job is started we must accomplish another important function of starting a job: accounting and keeping records of system resource usage. Most installations have accounting routines that are sometimes grouped within the job management function and sometimes within the task management function of an operating system. These routines keep a log of how much control processing unit time is being used by this job; it also might keep a record of how long the job took to execute. There is a difference. A job may run for half an hour on a system, but use only five minutes of central processing unit time because it was an I/O bound job and most of its time was spent in input/output servicing.

Since central processing unit time is more expensive than input/output processing time, there is a definite need to keep the records of both types of time. Typically this information is used for billing a customer for the amount of computer time he needed for his job to run. In fact, more sophisticated kinds of routines will come to a point where they will write out a bill for the time. Within the routine there is a computational routine which takes the amount of computer time or CPU time used, multiply the cost by some factor, and arrive at a charge, so that when the customer gets the results of his computer run for that particular program, he gets his bill at the same time. This greatly simplifies recordkeeping for the data processing installation manager.

IMPLICATIONS FOR THE USER

The implications for the user in the area of job management include linkage-editing or relocatability, default options, and space on input/output devices. The user must be aware that the programs are relocatable and must be link-edited. The result of a linkage edit or loading operation is the placing of the program in the program library, which is data containing executable programs.

Libraries may contain other types of information, but the program library is the concern at this point. The system programmer must know the space available in the various program libraries; he must plan so as to ensure sufficient room for new programs in the program libraries.

The management of libraries is an important function of the system programmer's job. Either he or the system must keep detailed records of space available or remaining in the libraries. He must be aware of the possibility of running out of space in these libraries and losing computer time while he reorganizes the libraries. It is far better to plan well enough so that there will be space for the programs as it is needed.

The job control cards usually have many options. In an effort to make the operating system more flexible, the cards have literally hundreds of parameters which might appear on them. To the programmer used to working without a control program, this is possibly the hardest part of learning to work with an operating system. Although the operating system does many things for him, the programmer must, on his part, learn a whole new set of rules for running jobs under an operating system. He pays for the convenience of an operating system with a need for retraining; he must learn the parameters used on the control cards and how to use them effectively for his particular program.

In many installations, when converting from a nonoperating system environment to an operating system environment, education of programmers in the job control cards area can take months. When first converting, the programmer will doubtless be frustrated by the mistakes he will likely make in using the control cards, because prior to the operating system he merely had to write a program and run it into the computer to get results. Now he must take into account the many variables possible on the control cards, in addition to the programming.

In an effort to simplify this job control area, operating systems provide default options. If a programmer forgets a job control parameter, the operating system attempts to insert it for him, so that the parameter is included. Unfortunately for the programmer, the operating system's choice of parameter options may not be the current choice for him, so care must be taken in the area of default options.

Another important part of the system programmer's job is the management of input/output space. The operating system manages input/output space on a per-job basis. The system programmer must project his use of space on input/output devices, particularly direct access, for a period of weeks and perhaps months so that he will have an operational plan. If he does not, it is entirely likely that he will find himself out of direct access space and waiting for more volumes on which to place his data. He may have to wait one or two weeks to get more disk packs* from a manufacturer. On a day-to-day basis, the operating system may run out of space on the disk packs, which are mounted at a given time; this can place a system in a wait loop.* The system programmer must plan well in advance of his needs or they will not be met on time. This function of the system programmer's job necessitates many hours of planning, educated guesswork, and hard labor in order to come up with an efficient plan for his installation.

The system programmer must set up procedures for proper utilization of job classes so as to achieve a proper and effective job mix between input/output-bound jobs and computer jobs. If he achieves or even approaches this optimum mix, he achieves a great improvement in job throughput. Much of the system programmer's time is spent in an attempt to accomplish this. He will spend long hours studying a month's output from the system to see if he can come up with a more efficient way of organizing his installation.

Typically the system programmer will communicate with the regular programmers, telling them that all high-computational jobs will go in one job class, all jobs which mainly produce written material will go through another job class, and so on, through all his job classes. He must be extremely careful to communicate his rules to the operator, who, in turn, is responsible for the operation of the machine. With an operating system prompt, accurate communication between the system programmer and the operator of the computing system is a necessity.

QUESTIONS—CHAPTER 2

1. A. List the advantages and disadvantages of (a) priority and (b) serial schedulers.
   B. Give an example of the kind(s) or data processing environment(s) best suited for each.
   C. List three applications for using job classes in a data-processing installation.
   D. Referring to the functional outline and to the various studies of special operating systems in this book, list the systems that use the following kinds of schedulers, picking any three:
      (1) Time initiated
      (2) Event initiated
      (3) Conditional
      (4) Program initiated
      (5) Algorithmic

2. Communication between the operator/programmer and the system is usually handled by operating system routines, as opposed to the problem programmer writing a communication routine within his program. Why?

3. Define the functions of each type of control card found in the input stream.

4. Which function of the operating system should handle I/O device allocation? Defend your choice with three reasons.

5. Give a short, conceptual explanation of the job step initiation process.

3
TASK MANAGEMENT

THE INTERRUPT SCHEME I (1.1.4.3)

Role

The hardware device used to achieve multiprogramming is the "interrupt scheme." A computing system operates in two modes, the control and the user program mode. When the operating system has control, the computing system will be executing in supervisor mode; when the operating system has given control to one of the user programs, it is operating in the nonsupervisory, or user program, mode. To keep a user program from gaining complete control of the system until it is done executing, the scheme of interrupts is used. At the time an input/output operation is complete, the input/output device will send a signal to the central processing unit, which, in turn, will signal the operating system that an interrupt has occurred. The operating system will typically stop all new user program operations, go into supervisor mode, and then determine the task that initiated this input/output operation. When it learns which task has submitted the input/output request, control will be passed to that program so that it can utilize the input data or write some output data, depending on whether the request is for input or output activity.

In some operating systems all active tasks are examined to determine which ones are ready to be executed after each interrupt is detected. Perhaps the tasks have been waiting for an input/output event for free main storage to become available. When an interrupt occurs in these kinds of operating systems, the system passes control to the highest priority task waiting with work for the operating system to do. When this highest priority task is done, the computing system will pass it to another task. When the other program is finished, control will pass to yet another program, which is now ready, and so on, starting with the highest priority task and going to the lowest priority task as they are ready to be run. Certain precautions are taken so that the low priority tasks will eventually get an opportunity to gain control of the computing system even though there might be another, higher priority task waiting for the operating system. After a low priority job spends a specified length of time waiting for control of the CPU, the operating system is forced to give control to that job. (Remember that switches between tasks are done when an interrupt occurs.)

Types of Interrupts

One kind of interrupt already mentioned is the input/output interrupt. Another is the program interrupt. The program interrupt occurs when an attempted execution of an instruction results in violating a condition required for the action to be correctly completed. These conditions can be arranged by the control program by turning on special portions of a control word. The special portions (bits) are called "masks,"* which the operating system interrogates during execution of the current task to see if a particular kind of program interrupt is to be given. When a program violates these conditions, hardware usually supplies a program interrupt, which signals the operating system that an unusual, or error, condition has been detected by the hardware. Another kind of interrupt occurs when there is a problem on the input/output device or in the CPU hardware itself. The interrupt is commonly called the machine check interrupt, meaning some of the hardware had problems and the operating system has been informed of it.

Some operating systems also have provisions for the program, whether user or operating system, to *force* a program interrupt, not as a result of a violation of rules but only because an interrupt is desired, perhaps to effect task switching. This is called a program controlled interrupt (PCI interrupt).*

Another type of interrupt occurs when the problem program is operating and requests service from the supervisor. Typically this service is done in the privileged, or supervisor, state; only the control program can perform the service. This type of interrupt is an interrupt which gets the attention of the control program for service. It is called a supervisor call interrupt, a service interrupt, or other names, depending on the operating system.

Interrupt Handling

Resource Queues

Interrupts are usually handled within operating systems by intercepting the interrupt and determining whether another task is to get control. There is an I/O interrupt, for instance, from one program, which tells the operating system that the I/O event has started. The computing system knows it has plenty of time before that program will need the system again. So the operating system looks down through long chains or queues (these are not to be confused with job queues). These resource queues[1] will be searched to determine whether the job needs the resource. There might be a queue or stack of requests from various programs for main storage allocation. If the problem program is not in control, but rather is waiting for the computing system to make some resource available, the computing system will take the request of the program for this resource and place it on a queue.

When the resource becomes available the operating system examines the queues and determines which task gets this resource next. As an example, the computer has 10,000 bytes of main storage available. It searches the requests from the various programs awaiting main storage and determines which one is to get the 10,000 bytes of main storage next. For instance, it will, while searching the queue, determine whether 10,000 bytes is enough for a request by a program. When it finds a request to match the amount of main storage it can give to the program, it will honor the queue request at that time and communicate to the program that it now has the required main storage. The program will execute again when the operating system allows it to do so.

Internal Priorities

Another example of resource allocation or resource queues besides main storage is the input/output request. Perhaps three user programs are vying for the same volume on direct access. The supervisor or the task manager examines the request queues for this direct access device and determines which one he wants to give control of the device to. Some operating systems handle these request queues on a first-in, first-out basis. In other words, they are serially stacked. As it becomes a program's turn to get a resource, the operating system automatically gives it to him because he is at the top of the queue.

There is another type of queue in which a program can be assigned a different priority for the task manager's request. When his request is put into a queue waiting for a system resource, he may be *assigned* the highest priority on the queue even though his is not the first request; he would then get the resource first. This assigned priority type of queue is more flexible than the serial queue. Even more flexible, these resource queues may be handled by a combination of first-in, first-out priority *and* assigned priorities. Basically, then, there are two ways of handling resource queues, plus a combination of the two. These priorities may be established by software or hardware and the interrupts may be handled

---

[1] A resource queue is a line-up of tasks waiting for a particular resource. There is a resource queue for each type of resource in the system. Examples of resources are main storage, control of CPU, system timer, channels, I/O devices, and program library.

by software or hardware, depending on the manufacturer. In more instances, however, it is a software function.

RESOURCE ALLOCATION I (1.1.2)

Types of Resources

Main Storage and Virtual Memory I (1.1.2.1)

While discussing resource allocation it would be well to look at the types of resources that are available and used in user programs executing under, or routines contained in, an operating system. Main storage is an important resource, which is handled by operating systems. There are various schemes of main storage addressing. This resource may be contained within a single physical hardware unit or in several physical hardware units. It may be of various types of storage. The basic type of storage we use is high-speed main storage. This storage can be accessed at ranges of two microseconds or less. (The latest developments in fourth generation computer memories* have effectively brought this figure to 80 nanoseconds or less through the use of special high-speed circuitry in place of magnetic core storage.) A computer may typically have 64,000 through 5 million bytes of main storage and more if it is to be used with an operating system. Smaller computers, of course, have less storage but can use operating systems. Basic operating systems may be used with less storage, but for the most part, if a full-capability operating system is to be used, greater amounts of main storage must be available to it. If there are 512,000 bytes,* they may be contained in one hardware configuration.

Main storage is addressable, going from a range of 0 to 512,000 bytes or more. These addresses are usually expressed, as are all addresses in digital computer usage, in binary or combinations of binary, such as Honeywell with a base of 8 and IBM with a base of 16. The bases of 8 and 16, tho, are merely convenient ways to express binary addresses. Binary is used because it lends itself so well to the basic unit of a computer, the on/off switch. The switch has two states; therefore, the base of 2 is used. Individual programs will vie for portions of this high-speed storage.

Some advanced operating systems operate on the concept of virtual memory,* so that lower utilization of high-speed main storage is practical, thus lowering the cost of CPU hardware significantly. Virtual memory uses a combination of high-speed main storage and secondary storage, usually a device that has a fast data transfer rate. Of the types of input/output equipment now available, either a drum direct access device, auxiliary magnetic core or new high-speed monolithic circuitry are best suited for this purpose.

Virtual memory makes use of the secondary storage by giving it imaginary addresses above the limits of the high-speed core storage. For example, a single track on a drum device may hold 4,000 bytes. Perhaps this high-speed drum device has 200 tracks. This gives us a total of 800,000 bytes of storage. If this were to be combined with 200,000 bytes of high-speed storage, we would have a total 1,000,000 bytes of storage at a greatly reduced cost as compared to 1,000,000 bytes of high-speed storage. The operating system acts as though the secondary storage were an extension of the high-speed main storage by the use of segments and displacement. The segment would correspond to addressable information on the secondary storage device. Assuming increments of 4,000 bytes, the 4,000 bytes would be brought into the high-speed storage and the displacement would tell the control program or operating system how far into this segment of 4,000 bytes the desired data is, once it is in main storage.

Many virtual memory schemes are more complex than this. They may break segments into two units and then use a displacement into the segment. But the basic idea is the same. To use the example above, with 200,000 bytes of main storage and 800,000 bytes of drum storage, we would have 50 segments within main storage which we could address. All segments from 51 through 250 would be automatically fetched by the control program from the drum, so that as far as the programmer and the control program are concerned, there is 1,000,000 bytes of main storage available. At first glance it might seem that this would be much slower, but in practice this is not the case. Many studies have been made—in terms of the probability, given a particular block of core or main storage—of the chances of branching outside the main core. Once we have an area of 8 to 10,000 bytes of core, the probability of branching outside the core, or accessing storage outside the core, is reduced considerably. Given large enough blocks of storage and programmer cooperation, there will be no branching outside the block.

Using this principle, segments are usually made so that either by bringing one track or a number of tracks from the drum into memory there is little probability that information outside this area of memory will be required. Once in memory, the segments are accessable at computer speed, as opposed to drum speed, which is faster than normal input/output speed. As a result of one input/output request, we have put perhaps 10,000 new bytes into main storage. Since the ratio of input/output requests to machine requests is very small, efficiency nearly approaches that of a system with no virtual memory which is relying on expensive high-speed memory.

There is another consideration which must be made in designing virtual memory schemes in terms of segment size. If the segments are too small, there is too much waiting on input/output activity. If the segments are too large, not enough of the (reduced amount of) high-speed main storage is available to a given problem program. Again, many studies have been made of this, and an optimum has been arrived at by each manufacturer which has been incorporated into the manufacturer's virtual memory system. Because of changing conditions, however, the optimum number may not always be right for the individual user's circumstances. Certain circumstances may require much smaller segments because of a program having very large main storage requirements. If the program is extremely large, and does much branching, the system programmer may wish to alter the segment size so that the size of the input/output request most closely (and easily) approximates the amount of main storage needed.

The size of a segment or amount of secondary storage brought in per I/O request may vary dynamically within a system. It proves more effective in programming, however, to have a constant size of secondary storage brought in as virtual memory. To keep this constant size many manufacturers have developed the concept of paging, where, although the size of the segments may differ, a standard sized subdivision called a page will be extracted from the segment. The segment is the optimal I/O request size, and the page is the most efficient in terms of branching probability. There may be two pages in a segment and there may be three segments in a page depending on the installation. To bring in a page with three segments would require three I/O requests. To bring in a page with ½ segment would still require 1-1/10 request, meaning input/output request, for this particular virtual memory address. It is worth it to the programmer, however, to take the three I/O requests in order to have the uniformity of core storage blocks coming in. This is why many manufacturers use pages as well as segments in displacements.

Leaving the virtual memory concept, we will now examine the allocation of main storage, whether simple or virtual memory, to the problem program. One such scheme for dividing main storage is the partition concept. A partition is an initially fixed amount of main storage. A partition is given to a program when the program is preparing to execute. As an example, say the operating system under consideration allows 10 partitions in addition to the amount of core needed for the operating system nucleus. The operating system takes up 200,000 bytes of core, leaving 312,000 bytes of core in a 512,000-byte machine. With 10 partitions, we arrive at a figure of 312 thousand bytes for each problem program.

In practice the initially allocated sizes of the various partitions in main storage varies. Some jobs with high input/output activity may require only 15,000 bytes in a partition, whereas a compile job such as a COBOL compilation may require maybe 95,000 bytes. The system programmer generates the system in the process known as system generation, so that certain partitions may become 10,000 bytes and others 100,000 bytes. Using the concept of job classes, many operating systems assign job classes by partition. As a result, if all compilations were class C jobs, the system programmer would be sure to assign the 100,000-byte partition to class C jobs. Operating systems that use the partition concept typically include a scheme for the operator to change the size of partition while operating the system, so that if a special job comes in for a computer run, the operator is told of the special main storage requirements for the job. He modifies his partition sizes accordingly for execution of the job.

Basically, then, the idea behind the partitioned main storage scheme is to give each job its own computer with a predesignated main storage size. This program would enjoy exclusive control of the partition while it is in the computing system. Through the device of storage protection or programming checks, no other program—with the exception of the operating system—is allowed to read from or write into this part of main storage.

Another kind of main storage scheme use of job control cards or input stream control cards tell the operating system how much main storage is required for a given job. As the job is transformed into a task and vies for system resources, the operating system assigns that amount of core to the job. If the requested amount of core is not available, the job is not transformed into a task at that time, but, instead, is put on a queue or stack awaiting the resource.

An example is the IBM OS/MVT system. Although the system is more difficult to maintain, it can be more efficient if there are a large number of jobs. Because its handling of main storage is more complicated, due to dynamic storage allocation, the system typically takes more core storage as overhead, which is another parameter a system programmer has to take into consideration when deciding what operating system to use at his installation.

Input/Output Operations I (1.1.2.2)

Another type of system resource an operating system must handle is input/output operations. The way in which most operating systems handle input/output is predicated on the concept of the channel. We have seen that the channel is a miniature computer which will supervise input/output. The channel will operate at the same time main storage is operating as a more or less separate entity. A CPU does not concern itself with input/output. It merely passes input/output requests to another part of the computer—the channel. The channel, via hardware, schedules the various input/output devices and determines whether the device is ready. If the device is ready, the channel determines whether it is used by another program. If the channel is not in use, it can then allocate that device to the request.

If the channel is in use, it passes a signal back to the control program (via hardware) that the channel is busy or is not ready. If the channel is unavailable, the operating system places the request on one of the input/output resource queues. If the channel is not busy, the request is honored at that time and the channel searches to see if the device is still available. If the device is available, the input/output operation is done. If the device is not available, the channel again passes information back to the operating system via hardware and the request is again placed on an I/O resource queue. (Note: Some manufacturers handle both the channel and the device at the same time, while others use two stages. The first stage is to get the channel allocated; the second stage gets the individual device on a channel allocated.)

A channel, to further define it, is also a logical data path. An operating system will take this logical path in combination with other logical paths, determine what is the best available path to a given device, and assign the path to the operation. The hardware channel and the logical channel are separate entities, although the logical channel must use the physical hardware channel to transfer data. Another way of approaching the definition is to say that the physical channel provides for the data transfer, while the logical channel provides for the logical connection between the device and the control program, so that the control program knows which device is assigned to its request. The physical channel can operate independently of the central processing unit once the request is started, so that the central processing unit can go on to something else while the physical channel is handling the rest of the request.

The channel concept produced a tremendous increase in computing capability between the second and the first generations. Today the central processing unit is not forced to wait for completion of input/output, since it no longer has to control the input/output, other than simply requesting it.

The System Timer or Clock I (3.0)

Another system resource is the system timer or clock. Most operating systems in use have a facility which a programmer can have his program "time out," or terminate, at the end of a day or any specified period of time. This prevents a program from getting into an instruction loop and remain running inside the computer indefinitely. In some computing systems there are two kinds of clocks. One, which is used by the system mainly to regulate its functions, measures elapsed time or intervals. The other keeps track of time in terms of days, hours, minutes, and seconds and is available to the user programmer for his programs; it is especially useful for real-time applications.

The programmer may also want to utilize the clock which is synchronized with the time of day established at system initialization time for purposes of maintaining the accounting information already discussed. Accounting routine can interrogate the system clock for the exact time and enter the time in a data field, so that the exact time of day a program is run is known. (Many installations will charge more for first shift, or daylight, operation and nighttime operation.)

CPU Time I (1.1.4.1)

Another important system resource is the time allotted to a job or program by the CPU. CPU time allocated to a job is the time when that task has control of the system resources when it is actually executing. First we will examine the time-slicing concept. Time slicing and time sharing are very similar in operation. The operating system using the system timer or clock allocates equal portions of time to each program in the system, so that although each program is not getting exclusive usage of the computer it will get fast enough response from the computer so that to the user it seems as though he is getting exclusive use of the computer.

Usually with time slicing each partition or region (or whatever term is used for the main storage allocated to a program) will be allotted a finite amount of CPU time. At the end of this time the next program will be given CPU time. For example, one program may operate for 500 milliseconds and stop. The next program immediately starts to execute from where it was interrupted, executes for 500 milliseconds, and stops. A third program commences using its CPU time, executes 500 milliseconds, stops, and so on, until the last program using the system uses its 500 milliseconds, at which time the first program again uses another 500-millisecond portion of time on the central processing unit.

The central processing unit, however, would still utilize the interrupt scheme. That is, if the first program were to be given the 500 milliseconds and during that time request input/output operation, the operating system takes his request, presents it to the channel and, if the channel is available, gives the input/output to the program. Since the program has to wait for the completion of the input/output operation, the operating system starts searching through the CPU time resource queue and takes the next program that had a request in on that queue and allocates the remainder of the 500 milliseconds to the program. If that program were to request a resource, the operating system would pass control of the CPU to a third program for the remainder of the 500 milliseconds. At the end of the 500 milliseconds, control would be passed to the second program as if the first program had made no I/O request and had only executed main-line machine instructions. Many systems have both normal partitions and a number of partitions in a time-slicing group.

Time-sharing and time-slicing systems are most useful when many different users want to enter tasks or jobs from remote locations but do not have enough work for an entire computer in their own installation. For example, a user may only have to pay CPU time per day or less, instead of the full monthly rent or purchase price they would have to pay if they had the computer in their own installation.

Central processing unit time is a very important, in fact possibly the most important, system resource available to a program. There are various ways of allocating CPU time, but multiprogramming, in whatever form it takes, depends on multiple-user programs individually being given control of the central processing unit. Although multiprogramming may seem to be simultaneous execution of more than one program, it is still a fact that only one machine language instruction can be performed at a time. This machine instruction logically can be in only one program at a time. We take the central processing unit time and allocate it to a program until that program makes a request for a resource and then pass control to another program, which will then begin to execute while the first program is waiting for his request to be honored. In effect, the executing of the other program is transparent to the program that made the request because it has to await completion of whatever event it requested, whether in a multiprogramming environment or not. Since it has to wait, there is no reason why another program cannot be using the CPU.

Program Libraries II (2.0)

Another type of system resource is the program library, which is a special data set. The computer user will have one or a number of these data sets, which consist of different programs and subprograms and are frequently referred to as "members." The programs can be requested as an I/O operation and read into the central processing unit. At the time they are given control, the job step requesting one of them has been turned into a task and is waiting to execute. These programs are typically used one at a time. In other words, two job steps probably would not be able to use the same member because the jobs would probably be contending for the same resources. If it is a library member that is strictly used for calculation, provisions are made so that more than one program can use this library member.

The library may also be used as a normal input data set. If so, it is not a program library but rather a collection of data. It stands to reason that we want only one program using this data set at a time, unless both programs are merely going to read the data. It would not do to have one program revising data while another program is reading the data, assuming it has not been revised yet. This is one type of control that must be exercised by an operating system. It is usually done through examination of the data control cards in the input stream. If more than one job requires a given data set for its own exclusive use (so it can write on it, for example), one job will be made to wait and not broken down into its component tasks until the other job completes its execution.

These are the main types of resource an operating system must be responsible for allocating to the various programs. There are other, lesser, resources related to operating systems. They will be left for the reader to examine at his leisure, and may be found in the appendix dealing with the operating system the reader is interested in.

TASK SUPERVISION I (1.1.4.1)

Serial Tasking

After resource allocation is initially done and a program starts executing, the execution of the task must then be supervised. *Task supervision* can be defined as the monitoring of all tasks within the system and the distribution of system resources to these tasks as the resources become available. One type of task supervision is serial task. Serial tasking is the type of task supervision used in less sophisticated programming systems, which do not allow for multiprogramming. The sophistication referred to is in terms of multiprogramming. However, some serial task systems, particularly real-time systems with telecommunications, are in themselves very sophisticated in another way: their controls on input/output operations and protection of data. In terms of task supervision, however, they are limited to a task at a time. No multiprogramming is possible because the system can handle only one task at a time.

These systems can still be extremely useful to the small user because they can exercise control of input/output that will release the installation programmer from consideration of input/output space, disposition of data sets, and so forth. The serial tasking system is frequently used when converting from a nonprogramming system environment to a multiprogramming system environment. Many multiprogramming operating systems offer a serial task programming system that utilizes many concepts of the more complex operating system. As the user builds his data banks and formulates his installation's operating procedures, the time comes when he wishes to convert to multiprogramming. Then he only has to consider the multiprogramming aspects of the conversion (as opposed to the total conversion, which would be necessary in switching from a nonprogramming system environment to a multiprogramming system environment).

Multiprogramming

Multiprogramming operating systems rely heavily on the resource allocation routines, particularly the queuing of resources, discussed previously. The task supervisor utilizes these resource queues in determining whether to give a task control at a particular time. It can check the resource request queues and determine whether the resource requested is available at that time. If the resource is not available, the task supervisor ignores the request of the task asking for control until such time as it can allocate the resource that the task will need. Instead, the task supervisor gives control to a task which can use an *available* resource.

This ensures that no task will be prevented from executing within a reasonable period of time. The task supervisor uses the queues by placing the contending tasks within these queues. When it searches a queue, the last task on a queue will typically have a pointer to the first task on the queue, thereby effecting a "circular" request queue for the task supervisor. The programming within the task supervisor is so arranged that once started in determining which task will next get control, we must make a complete circuit of the queue and return to the beginning, so that the task will not be forced to wait for an unreasonable period of time for system resources. Naturally, the amount of time a task has to wait for control of the CPU will depend on the number of tasks currently residing in the operating system. This multiprogramming, then, is a sophisticated resource queue. In fact, some operating systems treat the task supervisor as another form of resource allocation, combining the activities of the task supervisor and the CPU resource queue.

Multitasking Within a Program

The more sophisticated multiprogramming task supervisors allow for multitasking within a program. This would in effect provide "sub-resource-queues" which would in turn be circular queues that would be entered at some time during the execution of a given task (see Figure 3-1). The multitasking within a program or task could not be allocated system resources unless the originating task, which we will call the mother task, were first given control as a functional unit of the main task supervisor queue. Once the mother task has assumed control, the daughter tasks, with their small sub-resource-queues could then, in turn, share her resources.

Queue Priority Schemes

There are numerous ways to establish priority on the resource or task supervisor queues. Two common ways are storage address priority and internally calculated priority. In address priority, the priority of tasks on the queue—in other words, their position on the task supervisor queue—depends on their address in main storage. As an example, we will assume that our operating system places the highest priority task at the highest address in storage. In this case, the operator, when feeding jobs into the computer, has to consider whether he wanted this job to have a high or low priority when he prepares to run the job into the computer.

    This type of priority is found primarily in partitioned, or "fixed space," main storage operating systems. The operator arranges the partitions as the main storage requirements of his various jobs require. Taking the size of the partitions, he then arranges the job class of the job so as to match the correct job with the correct partition. Next, using the storage address priority scheme of task supervision, he knows the dispatching priority of the job from the address of the partition the job was placed into. If the job is in the high end of the main storage in our sample system, it has the highest priority in the queue and as such is the first task to be considered for system resources as they become available. Once having started on the queue, the task supervisor is usually required to make a complete circle through the task supervisor queue. Multitasking within a program operates similarly, except that if this partition had a job in it or a task in it, and the task

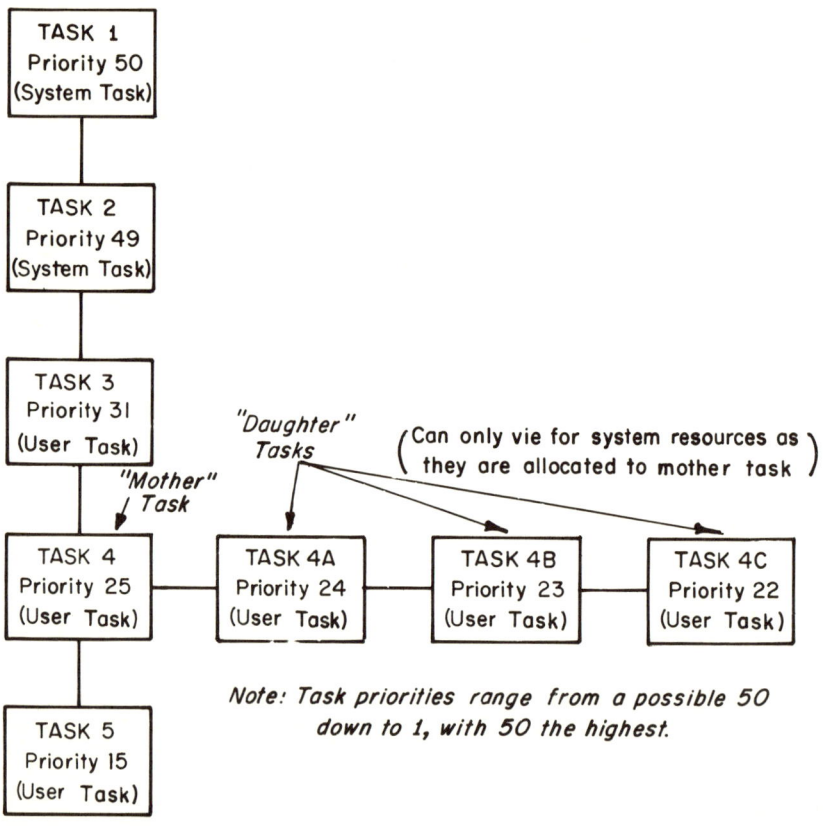

Figure 3-1. Task Priorities within a Multiprogramming System, Showing a Subtask Queue

wishes to set up subtasks, these tasks would also be located in that partition so that they could get a chance at system resources when their mother task is given control.

Another type of priority is internally calculated priority. In a nonpartitioned operating system—one that depends, instead, on priorities being entered via the job stream or by operator commands—it is usually an internal priority assigned to the task when it is created. This internal priority is ordinarily computed by taking the priority entered by the operator or job control card, multiplying by an algorithm, which would take into consideration the importance of the particular kind of request and certain overriding system priorities, and finally arrive at an internal priority, which would then determine the position of the task in the task supervisor queue. The task supervisor queue is probably the most important single facet of an operating system. It must take all operations of the operating system into consideration when determining which task it is to pass control to.

Multiprocessing

Having discussed the queue concept and the task supervisor, we can now consider the multiprocessing concept. Multiprocessing is the combination of the operating system (usually the multiprogramming type) and multiple CPUs. It will be widely used in future computer generations.

With the multiple CPUs, we also find shared main storage. All of the CPUs have access to the same main storage as it becomes available. Multiple CPUs also maintain communication with each other to prevent two or more CPUs trying to execute the same program or gain exclusive use of system resources, particularly I/O devices and data sets.

All CPUs operate under one operating system, sharing the same resource queues. The main difference between multiprocessing systems and others is that there is more than one CPU to be allocated to a task, allowing doubled or trebled job throughput. Multiprogramming is a powerful version of the operating system. It offers a potential of vastly increased throughput, as compared to a normal multiprogramming system.

Although the hardware is fairly esoteric, the operating system requires few basic changes. Allowing for the multiple CPU's to be used by the same resource queues and task queues is the main change. It is required in the multiprogramming operating system. Another important change required is the additional few machine instructions which allow the multiple CPU's to communicate.

Because of the inherent superiority of multiprocessing systems over uniprocessing systems, it is probable that future operating systems will rely more heavily on multiprocessing concepts as an integral part of their design. The problem facing the manufacturers is that of bringing the cost of the hardware down to the point where it is competitive with uniprocessing systems, particularly for the smaller users.

SYSTEM ERROR RECOVERY I (1.4), I (2.0)

In a discussion of system error recovery we should first consider the types of errors an operating system is likely to encounter. These types of errors have been arbitrarily classified into three types—user programming errors, machine or hardware errors, and operating system programming errors.

There are several types of user program errors. One is the violation of system architecture and/or programming design. The computer manufacturer, when designing a computing system, must take into consideration certain parameters. An example of these parameters is the design of an instruction set, which is that set of machine instructions that the hardware will recognize. Timing considerations—the interaction of machine speed and storage retrieval speed (and interrupt speed)—are another design parameter. After examining these parameters and others of a similar nature, the manufacturer builds the hardware.

In order to use the hardware a programmer must follow the limitations imposed by the manufacturer on the computer when it was designed. As a consequence, it may be forbidden to the programmer to branch to a point in main storage outside of his assigned storage protect area, or it may be illegal to advance to an address in low core storage such as zero, which may be reserved for the operating system's use. Perhaps the manufacturer has set up certain addressing specifications. As an example, a programmer may not be allowed to refer to an odd main storage address, only to an even address. In another example, if he is trying to read or write into main storage he may be forbidden to read or write to an even address.

Since the basic concept behind the digital computer is the binary numbering system, then by restricting an instruction storage or a storage fetch instruction so that it can only access even numbered storage addresses, the manufacturer may be able to reduce the required circuitry to a considerable degree. This set of restrictions on the programmer generally is termed as programming rules or rules based on the "architecture" of the computer. Any violations of these architectural rules, depending on the manufacturer, may or may not be recoverable. If the violation of a rule is of a nonrecoverable type, the task may be terminated by the operating system or by the hardware. A programming violation of architecture or rules is one type of user programming error.

Another major type of user programming error is the data programming error, which can be subdivided into two different classes: format of data and handling of input/output resources. In the data-formatting type, the programmer may issue a read or a write to input/output, receive the data, or transmit it in such a way that is not compatible with a later set of instructions in his program. As an example, he may read a data set, obtain a record, access the record in buffer in core storage, and then handle it improperly. If the record had a specific length, he might, for instance, try to tell the operating system to handle data, assuming the wrong length of a record. This would be a type of programming exception or violation. In another type, he might not be aware of the type of data that is coming in from input/output request. Again taking our read for an example, he might read a data set, obtain a record, and, once the record is in core in a certain format, assume the data is in a different format and try to operate on the data under the wrong assumption. This action alone will also typically cause a programming violation to be signaled to the operating system.

Wrong handling of input/output resources is a slightly different situation. This type of programming error is a type in which the programmer tells the system that the data is contained in a certain data set on a pack or is in a certain format. However, the data management portion of the operating system, in performing the input/output request, might find that the data set is not available, or if it is available, that the data is different than the programmer thought it was. Therefore, the operating system signals a programming violation while still in the data management routine and typically passes to the main supervisor of the operating system an indication that the task is in trouble. The main task may or may not at this time bring the task to an abnormal end.

Another prevalent type of programming violation is the programmer's assumption that he has more main storage allocated to him than is actually the case. The program may require more main storage than the programmer realizes or the programmer may inadvertently tell the operator or through job control cards tell the system that he needs less main storage than he really needs. Consequently, when he arrives at the limit of the main storage allocated to him by the operating system and attempts to go beyond it, the operating system terminates the task abnormally. Typically this occurs because the program is attempting to violate storage protection rules.

Another type of error is the problem of machine or hardware malfunction. Types of hardware malfunctions might be central processing unit errors when a circuit goes awry. It is entirely possible that this circuit could modify the operating system or modify the user's program if it were allowed to do so by the operating system or by the hardware, depending on which had control of the particular area. CPU errors will ordinarily cause abnormal termination of a task, regardless of whether a user or the system is in control. Recent developments in hardware have reduced the severity of the impact of these CPU errors.

Input/output device failures can also be classified as machine errors. If an input/output device such as direct access were to fail, either in the track accessing portion or in the data transfer portion of its data gathering effort, it could affect a program. Consequently, manufacturers insert checking circuits into the hardware. If the checking circuit determines that an error has been encountered, it will signal the channel hardware, which in turn will signal the CPU hardware that an error has occurred and the type of error encountered. The operating system will determine whether or not it is correctable. If it is, perhaps the program would be allowed to restart the operation some specified number of times in an attempt to recover the data, or it might require that the task be abnormally terminated.

Between the input/output and the CPU hardware lies the channel hardware. In its monitoring of input/output activities, it can also encounter errors in its own hardware, perhaps during data transfer or perhaps while it is in control of various input/output requests. These, too, would be signaled to the central processing unit as errors and the system will take action similar to the action taken with input/output device errors.

The system action in error recovery is dependent on the type of error. We have seen that users can make programming errors and the hardware can cause a programming error by falsely modifying instructions. One more type of error should be taken into consideration, and that is the system programming error. These programming errors can be caused by two eventualities. First, the control program or the operating system might have been badly programmed initially; second, some CPU or I/O error separate from the software modifies that software. Most examples of system programming errors are due to faulty programming. In turn, most faulty programming is committed by the system designer (the programmer who wrote the system) and his failure to take all eventualities into consideration when doing his programming. A seldom encountered situation, which might occur when three or four minor eventualities are all interacting, may cause the system program to take an erroneous branch or store data at a storage protected location, thereby violating some rule and bringing the system error recovery into play. Indeed, some of these eventualities which are seldom encountered are in fact unforeseeable by the programmer when he is writing an operating system.

Manufacturers attempt to get some source of feedback from users on these infrequent situations, so that an attempt can be made to repair the program, of which the users of the operating system would be informed. Some manufacturers engage staffs of programmers whose sole function is to intercept these reports for programming errors, fix them, and disseminate the fix to the users. The system action taken in the event of system errors is an attempt to, *first*, minimize the effect of the error, and *second*, protect other tasks within the system from the error. If a system error causes a programming malfunction or is a programming malfunction, the manufacturer of the operating system will try to prevent the malfunction from affecting another task, which, of course, would not be possible in an ordinary or a nonerror environment.

The system basically breaks errors into two types, correctable and not correctable. It may have hardware circuits to do the correction, or it may have fields in main storage which it maintains and examines as the need arises. These fields typically contain flags which are indicative bits (on-off switches) which the system will examine. If a flag is on, it might indicate that an error of a certain type has occurred. If the error has occurred, and it can affect other portions of the operating system, the operating system might be informed that it can go no further without possibly endangering other tasks. If so, it might take two actions.

One is a wait state, and the other is a wait state with an attempt to first clean up and quiesce the system. If it is a simple wait state, the system places some sort of indicator on the console or sends a message to the operator and stops. If the system determines that the operator can take certain actions without endangering other system or user tasks, the operator may attempt to terminate I/O activity on some data sets or place information in system control blocks, which would make the problem more easily definable by a programmer when he analyzes a storage print. Many systems always give a storage print if they encounter an error of high enough severity. The system may attempt to put input/output devices in such a state that they can be restarted or retrieved later.

The same principle applies to the contents of main storage. The system may attempt to conserve the data in main storage. If the damage is correctable, the system will attempt to repair the damage. If the error is of a machine error type, the operator may attempt to recover whatever data was lost and then switch the base device—if it is an I/O error, or portion of main memory if it is a main storage error—to a duplicate device or part of main storage, and inform the operating system that the hardware in error is no longer available to it. After this, the system may run at a reduced efficiency rate, but at least still operate until service help is available (as opposed to the alternative of shutting down the entire system and waiting for service personnel to come, which might be several hours).

Another device is the principle of duplicate (redundant) circuitry. The duplicate circuits typically have more than one of the important circuits being utilized for the same function. In other words, instead of having a single series of switches in a portion of the hardware that is employed in accessing main storage, that circuit and two duplicate circuits are all performing the function simultaneously. Should one of the three circuits malfunction, the hardware takes the result of the two circuits of the three that have agreed, discards the other, and makes a note of the difference of opinion in the system log, which will usually be maintained on auxiliary storage or in certain main storage areas reserved exclusively for the hardware.

Service personnel at regularly scheduled preventive maintenance periods examine these system log records, which are on I/O or in main storage, and replace any component that had been consistently disagreeing with the companion components. If it is a program malfunction rather than a machine malfunction, perhaps due to electrical noise or a temporary input/output error when reading in the particular operating system component from secondary storage, the operating system may attempt to address the program by issuing another input/output request to secondary storage for the same component. This program module is then brought into main storage in place of the one in error. After it is in main storage, the operating system can examine it to determine whether or not the same error occurs. If it does not, it restarts operating from the last checkpoint before the error, and continues. Recent developments in hardware and software technology have resulted in error recovery circuits so fast as to be transparent to the user in many cases.

The scheme used to restart at a recoverable point is that of storing certain essential information in registers or main storage or both and placing this information back into appropriate storage areas in the program module which encountered the error so that the operator can restart from a point where the information was originally stored in this module. After the correction of the error, the operator is usually informed of the error action—if the error was severe. If the error is not severe enough to be recorded, then the error recovery is obvious to the user.

IMPLICATIONS FOR THE USER

The implications for the user are basically those of education of a system programmer so that he is aware of the error recovery options at his disposal, and also education to ensure his using the system error recoveries to the most efficient degree. This efficiency is another important part of a system programmer's job: awareness of system error recovery facilities and the proper use of them. This will often necessitate that the system programmer include these system error recoveries in the system at system generation time.

Many manufacturers offer a choice of system error recovery packages ranging from a simple wait state package, which, if used, places the system in a wait state after encountering any error, to a very sophisticated error recovery procedure, which allows a high percentage of error recovery. Usually the problem the system programmer encounters is making the choice of which error recovery package to use in the problem of core storage. The more sophisticated and all-encompassing the system error recovery package is, the more core storage it will require. Since errors can occur at any time, the system error recovery package must always be available to the system. The package usually resides in core storage, at least in part. Some system error recovery programs will have portions of them in main storage at all times and portions of them residing on or in auxiliary storage. But whether the modules reside in auxiliary or main storage, the system programmer must balance the cost of the storage against the benefits of the various system recovery modules. The option that probably makes the best balance for his needs is the least sophisticated error recovery package which uses less core. He will depend on the manufacturer and the manufacturer's quality control to hold the errors down to a minimum.

Another user may have a larger amount of main storage available and at the same time have a system such as an on-line real-time system which cannot afford any system wait states or malfunctions. He would be well advised to take the most sophisticated error recovery package and use it. In short, the system programmer must first make an accounting of his needs before determining the type of system error recovery package to use.

QUESTIONS—CHAPTER 3

1. Describe the general resource handling schemes used by any three of the operating systems specifically studied in the latter portion of this book.
2. List three advantages offered by the program library.
3. A. Give a short explanation of the following types of main storage allocation:
    1. Dynamic
    2. Partitioned
    3. Virtual

    B. Which of the above schemes is best suited for a user with many short jobs with no remote facilities?
    C. List two operating systems using each type of allocation, referring to the specific operating systems studied in this book.
    D. What kind of I/O devices are necessary for a virtual memory system?
4. Describe the handling of interrupts and the relationship of the handling to task dispatching.
5. Give a detailed explanation of each of the four kinds of task supervisors, citing one operating system that uses each kind. Refer to the systems studied in this book.

4

DATA MANAGEMENT

DATA SETS AND RECORDS

Terms

An operating system supplier typically offers a series of data management programs to take some of the load of input/output data management from the shoulders of the main operating system supervisor. Instead, the system will treat the data management function as another task. Although data management might enjoy a high internal system priority, it must still contend for system resources.

The tasks the system uses are variously called access methods, I/O supervisors, or input/output programs. Before examining them, however, it would be well if we examined the types of data sets and input/output devices used.

Types of Data Sets III (1.2.1)

Data sets are part of a general scheme of data classifying. An input/output storage device will usually be arranged in a large package sometimes called a "volume." In most auxiliary storage devices, such as magnetic tape or direct access devices, data is contained on physically replaceable devices called packs, in the case of magnetic disks, or tapes in the case of magnetic tape devices (packs and tapes are both called volumes). Packs are stacks of pancake-shaped disks which can be "written" on. They will usually have magnetic coverings, as magnetic tape does, and an arm that can go anywhere on the disk surface, so that information retrieval can be made randomly. In other words, an arm will search* and seek[1] to a concentric circle, or track, on the surface of the pack and read the data that

---

[1] A seek is the act of the disk arm, which contains the magnetic head, moving to a specified track. A search is the act of finding a specified record on the track, which has been accessed by the seek.

55

has been placed around that circle. This track may have from 2 to 19 or more disks above or below it. The disk pack is constructed of 200 concentric circles, called tracks, on *each* disk, which are paralleled on the disks above and below the track in question. The set of vertical parallel circles, or tracks, is called a cylinder. The data will be transferred to the channel and then to the operating system by a magnetic head, which will sense the changing magnetic field passing under it as the disk rotates.

The disk typically rotates at a high speed. As a means of data transfer, magnetic disk packs are as fast or faster than magnetic tapes. Also, by virtue of the fact that the seek can be to a given concentric circle on the disk, data can be accessed in a nonsequential manner. A magnetic tape must be read sequentially. That is, we must start at the beginning of the tape and read it as it passes by a magnetic head until the designated portion (the data set) of the data on the tape has been found. This data set is then deblocked into records. Therefore, the scheme for organizing data on magnetic tape is: volume subdivided into data sets, or files, and further subdivided into records. The records, of course, are made of bytes or words of data.

On the other hand, the direct access device, since it can access data at any point on its surface, lends itself to nonsequential operations. At the same time, it can also be read sequentially merely by starting the arm containing the read/ write head on the outside of the disk and moving one concentric circle or track at a time toward the center. These magnetic devices of the direct access type will usually have a finite number of possible areas on the surface of the disk it can go to. For instance, an IBM 2314 direct access device will allow accessing to any one of 200 tracks on the surface of each disk. Each pack has 20 usable disk surfaces, so a full pack has 4,000 tracks. Track 0 is the track on the outside, track 200 is the innermost track, and the seek arm containing the magnetic head can be directed to find any one of the imaginary tracks from 0 to 200 inclusive. The arm does not have to start from the beginning and go one track at a time. It may have been told to go directly to track 100, for example.

Because of this added random access capability on direct access, various data set types have been created to take advantage of it. The first type of data set type is a sequential data set. This is the only possible data set allowed on tape by most manufacturers, since tape can usually only be read serially from the beginning to the end. Because it is relatively inexpensive, tape is the most prevalent type of auxiliary storage used on computers. Direct access devices, on the other hand, permit the utilization of other types of data sets. These types of data sets attempt to utilize the track-seeking capability of the direct access device.

The next type we will consider is a partitioned data set. The partitioned data set is, in reality, nothing more than a sequential data set with the addition of certain dividing points that can be seeked to, so that it is not necessary to read the entire data set to get the desired information. For example, a partitioned data set can be divided into 10 sections, each section starting a different track on the surface of the disk. Any one of the 10 parts can be requested in an input/output request for the data set. These points are known to the operating system and their addresses on the disk surface are stored by the operating system in an area of the data set called a directory, so that when a certain portion of a partitioned data set is needed by the operating system, the operating system already knows on which track on the direct access device this portion was to begin, and a request sends the arm directly to that track. When the track is found, this portion of the data set is then read sequentially as in sequential operation.

In summary, then, a partitioned data set is similar to a sequential data set, except that it consists of a number of individually accessable sections which may or may not contain related information and which are called members. This accessing of the individual members allow for certain parts of a data set to be read without the necessity of reading the whole data set before obtaining the data.

A good analogy to illustrate the difference between a sequential data set and a partitioned data set is found in many homes. Consider the difference between two types of music reproduction media, a reel of tape used on a tape deck and a phonograph record. The music on the reel of tape is analogous to a sequential data set, in that we thread the tape onto the tape deck and play the whole tape until we hear the music we want to hear (assuming that our tape deck does not have a footage counter). It holds a large amount of music economically, but it is difficult to find a specific selection on the tape.

On the other hand, there is the phonograph record which is analogous to the partitioned data set. There is a *directory* (the label in the center of the record), telling us which band (analogous to the partition or member) the selection we want to hear is on. We can place the tone arm on any band (analogous to a track) and listen only to the music we wish to hear. Alternatively, we can start at the beginning and listen to the entire side of the record.

Here the analogy stops. The phonograph record usually has similar music on all bands, while the partitioned data set may have unrelated data in the separate partitions, and, as a matter of fact, the data may not be in sequential order. This would be like taking a band on the record and placing each measure of music in random order on the band instead of having the measures in the order in which the selection is written.

A sequential data set is read sequentially, so is a partitioned data set, either from the beginning of the data set or from the beginning of the partition or member if so desired. For this reason, a partitioned data set is perfectly suited for the storage of program modules, which are essentially sequential pieces of data. Each member usually contains one program. When the user or the operating system calls for a program to be brought into main storage and executed, the operating system searches the directory of the partitioned data set, which in this case would be used as the on-line library discussed before, for a member with the same name as the desired program. The data in the member is actually the program to be executed and is brought into main storage for execution. Because of this use of a data set, the terms "partitioned data set" and "library" are often used synonomously.

Another type of a data set is an indexed sequential data set. In this case there is probably a desire to have the data in approximately sequential order, but the data can be a vast number of individual fields. There is an elaborate set of indices which inform the operating system as to the exact track location of the data through the use of keys. As an example, this type of data set may be used in inventories where perhaps a million different part numbers are being utilized by a company's warehouse. The operating system would then have a list of the part numbers, which would then be used as keys by the operating system. In a table, either in main storage or in another place on secondary storage, the various part numbers are kept along with the exact track address of the pertinent information about the part number, such as the number of parts on hand, the price, the amount on order, and so forth.

The table of addresses is called an index. There may be more than one level of index. In this case the first address is called the *master index*, which in turn points to a track *index* on an individual track, which will, in turn, point to an individual record on that track. Some indexing schemes also have intermediate levels of index between the master and track indices, such as a cylinder index, for example.

If information is requested about this particular part number, the part number is fed into the operating system. The operating system then goes to the master index, searches the master index until it finds the address of the track index for that part number. The track index is then interrogated by the operating system to find the specific track, and the information in the index or table is passed to the operating system, which issues an I/O request to the direct access device for the specific record on that track, which might contain a number of different part numbers. A track is read until the beginning point of the record is found. Then the fields with the part numbers in them (some of which could be duplicates of the part numbers in the index) are read until a correct part number field is encountered. When the desired part number is encountered the operating system is signaled. Since the computer is so much faster than the input/output speed, the computer has time to direct the I/O device to transfer the data that follows the part number.

The last kind of data set organization to be discussed is the direct, or random data set, organization. This data set makes use of a special part of each record, which is called the *key* and is associated with that record logically. Instead of using a field in the user's record to find the record, the operating system uses the separate, but logically associated, *key* for that record to locate the record.

There are two kinds of direct files: directly addressed and indirectly addressed, which are very different in concept. The directly addressed direct file uses the key *directly* as the address. The user will write a direct access address into the key portion of each record as it is created, which the direct access channel program will later use as a search address when retrieval of the record is desired. An example is the application of writing inventory records on a direct file. The part number is entered in the key field, for example, part number 080104. At retrieval time the channel program searches for a record as follows: key equals 080104, so the search will be for cylinder 08, track 01, record 04.

In order to use this direct method all records must be sorted to appear in sequential order within the data set. If a key is out of sequence, the I/O operation will fail. Also, if there are numbers missing in the sequence of keys, space must be reserved for them in many systems; they must be numeric keys. If there are too many missing key numbers, there will be too much wasted direct access space, and the *indirect* addressing method should be used.

The *indirectly* addressed file does not use the key directly for the search address. If there is a range of 0 to 999 possible key values, but only 200 are used, there will be much wasted space. We must go through an intermediate step called randomizing. Randomizing takes the original keys and converts them into a smaller range which will be nearly entirely used as key numbers. This is normally done by various computational means called algorithms. One such algorithm is called "hashing," which is particularly suited to alphabetic keys. The alphabetic name is run through the algorithm routine, which assigns the alphabetic name to an entry in a "hash" table, which in turn contains the actual keys to be used. Once a record name is assigned to a hash table, the record being created is written at the address given to it by the numeric key in the hash table, which fits into the smaller range of keys. If a record key name also hashes to this entry in the hash table (and one or more normally will), a pointer to another record location is provided in the hash table.

Besides hashing, there are other kinds of key-randomizing techniques, many of which actually use random numbers within the new key range to assign to the records as they are created.

This data set organization is the most efficient if care is taken when the keying system is established by the system programmer.

Relationship Between Data Sets and Records III (1.2.2)*

Data sets are further divided into records which are the smallest portion of data that can be requested by the operating system. A data set might be composed of from one record to thousands of records, depending on the type of application. Operating systems ordinarily make provision for retrieval of data at the record level (as opposed to the entire data set), so as to save time wasted in gathering the data from the storage medium, which is not really needed by the program requesting this data.

TYPES OF I/O DEVICES III (1.3.4), III (2.2.2.4)

Magnetic Tape and Direct Access

Magnetic tape and direct access devices have already been discussed. To review, magnetic tape only lends itself easily to sequential data sets. Direct access lends itself to all four types of data sets (or more types, depending on the manufacturer).

Unit Record

A third type of input/output device is a unit record device, sometimes called a data entry device. Whereas magnetic tape and direct access are essentially storage mediums, input unit record devices are used for entering data into the system, to be stored on auxiliary storage later or to be utilized in main storage during the life of the program and dropped from the system; output unit record either print, display, or punch output data from the program.

Unit record devices or data entry devices can be subclassified into *local* and *remote entry*. Local unit record devices are devices such as card readers, card punchers, and printers which have a specified record length and are limited to that size (remote entry devices are discussed in the next chapter). As an example, many card readers will read only 80 bytes or word cards. A computer card has a certain number of columns in it. As an example take the 80-column card. The 80-column card contains 80 columns of punched holes. These 80 columns may be subdivided

---

* The basic unit of data is the logical record. Simple logical records are units of data separated by blank spaces called inter record gaps (or some equipment term), and pieces of information about the record. In the case of short records, we can waste much space with inter record gaps (IRG's). If we combine a number of records into large pieces of data, we will not use so many IRG's. These combined logical records are called blocked records, blocks, or physical records. When a blocked record is brought into main storage, the blocks must be broken down into logical records. This is called deblocking.

into fields for use within a program. Typically, each time a card is read into a card reader, that card is one record. The program within the operating system requesting the cards then subdivides the data on the cards into fields or subfields. The same principle applies to the card punch, which punches holes in a computer card that later will be read into main storage or put into a data set as required.

A printer puts information onto paper which is called *forms*. The printer may have 120 or 132 print positions. The operating system either has to have data in each position or in blanks. The basic unit of a printer is the print line. The output to the printer is again a complete record of 120- or 132-byte length. The programmer adds or subtracts spaces as desired, to make up the printed output. If he adds a space, the space shows up as a blank portion of a line when the printing was requested from the operating system.

Remote Entry

The simple unit record devices all have one thing in common—finite record length. At data transfer time the remote entry or complex unit record devices are typically used in telecommunications (remote entry) applications where variable length records will be inserted into the system with a keyboard. The user of the remote entry unit record device may enter as much data as he needs through the keyboard. The system will process the record, then act on it or place the data on a storage I/O device. The data from these remote unit record devices can be processed by the system as a request for information, raw data input or a command, particularly if the remote unit record device is a console and is being used by the system operator. The operating system must recognize the various types of input/output devices and data sets and provide various program modules to handle them. We will examine them next.

ACCESS METHODS

Categories

Access methods have been arbitrarily categorized into three types. There will be an access method for each type of data set and possibly specialized access methods for specialized input/output devices. These access methods, whether for differentiation between data sets types or for differentiation between specific input/output devices, can be at three levels: the queued level, the basic level, and the channel program level. The reason for the three separate levels of access methods is to give the programmer various options between ease of programming and the amount of control over the desired input/output operation. The programmer may wish to use the easiest type of programming, as he would, for example, if the program being written were only to be used occasionally. Or, he may use the level of control over which he would have the most control for two reasons—either to conserve main storage, since the more automatic access method requires more of it, or to achieve more efficiency in programming. (Note: the access methods supplied by a computer manufacturer must be flexible in order to accommodate the majority of users.) As an individual, a user can install the access method that allows the most control in his particular installation and leave out the programming necessary to accommodate all of the contingencies the general access method would use. At the level where the programmer has the most control, however, he must also have the most knowledge about programming, and he must also create a much more complex program to compensate for the system's smaller degree of control.

Queued Level

The queued level is the highest level in terms of the language used to communicate to the computer. The highest level language is that which most closely approaches the English language. The system will handle most input/output contingencies automatically in the queued level. The programmer need not worry about the problems that might occur. The queued level is used for sequential and indexed sequential data sets. It is also used in telecommunications. The queued level provides many automatic features, and has some limitations. It will only read whole data sets; the starting address of the data set is determined, and the entire data set is brought into main storage block by block, in the case of blocked records, or logical record by logical record in the case of unblocked records. These records, of whatever kind, are brought into sections of main storage called buffers, so named because they act as a buffer between main storage speed and I/O speed. Although all of the access methods can use buffers, the queued access method will usually build and use them automatically. A buffer is used because of the length of time required for I/O operations. As long as the program has to wait for I/O, why not use that time? With buffering we do use it. After filling one buffer, let us issue an I/O request to fill another while we process the data brought into the *first* buffer. In this way, we are not sitting idly while we wait.

The queued access method level uses as many buffers as it needs for maximum efficiency. It will also deblock records automatically, passing the executing program one *logical* record at a time if the programmer desires.

The programmer does not have to concern himself with deblocking, buffering, channel programs, and so forth. The queued level does these for him. The queued level will also supply standard error routines, which is a significant concern to a programmer working at the other levels.

Basic Level

The basic level is an intermediate level which allows the programmer to enjoy some control over the input/output programming, but which also allows the operating system to exercise some control. The basic level can be used with sequential and indexed sequential data sets, and usually *must* be used with partitioned and direct access sets. The basic method is also available for remote processing.

In the interest of flexibility, this access method requires a knowledgeable programmer, because the functions which it provides are not automatic. The programmer must deblock his records if necessary, supply the buffer area in many cases, and provide standard error routines. Among the error conditions usually encountered are: (1) record not found; (2) invalid key (direct files); (3) end of file; (4) member not found (partitioned files); (5) actual I/O equipment failures; and (6) other conditions. The programmer must supply routines to correct the condition or else ignore that record and process a new record.

Channel Program Level

In the channel program[1] level the programmer must build and maintain most control blocks and/or storage areas used by the operating system in supervising input/output operations. He must also take into account more of the contingencies and possible error conditions in the input/output programming. The programmer must also build the input/output command words that are ordinarily done for him by the operating system. Although this is a difficult level to program, it can save a great percentage of the main storage utilized by the queued access methods.

The control blocks the channel program level programmer must build are blocks of main storage. These storage blocks are called control blocks because they contain information the system requires to perform its functions. The channel programmer only has to supply a few of these blocks. One of the functions of an operating system is to schedule input/output requests from a user program. The control blocks required by the operating system in order for it to perform this I/O scheduling are the responsibility of the channel program level

---

[1] A channel program is a series of one or more channel control words (CCW). These CCW contain command codes, data addresses, and so forth. They are used only in I/O programming and are limited to commands for the channel and I/O devices. They are not executable in the CPU, since the CPU does not direct I/O operations. Examples of CCW commands are: Read, Write, Transfer in Channel, Search, Seek.

programmer. One of the control blocks will contain control information about the data set and its attributes, while another might contain information about the channel program, and still another might contain information regarding the secondary storage space. At this level of I/O programming the operating system supplies very little of the control information, so the programmer *must* supply it. This is the price he pays for the extreme flexibility and degree of control he enjoys.

The channel program level programmer makes up his own string of channel control words (CCW), which are supplied by the system in the queued and basic levels. In order to do this programming he must have intimate knowledge of the I/O devices that he is using.

Since the programmer is taking responsibility for writing CCW, he must also supply nearly all of the I/O error routines his program will use, because the system does not form error routines when it does not know which CCW will be executed during the operation of the channel program; it does not know which errors to provide routines for.

Again, this level of I/O programming is more difficult for a programmer to use, but the flexibility and degree of control which is given to the programmer may very well be more than justification for the use of this level, as well as the lessening requirement for main storage.

FEATURES

Catalog III (1.1.1)

Operating systems have various features for the user to use in his programming. These many features are often unique, depending on the particular operating system being considered. In the second half of this book we will see that many data management features on one operating system are considered part of the supervisor, monitor, or executor in others. The following discussion concerns features that have been arbitrarily categorized here as data management functions. These features are logically part of data management as much as access methods and the others that have been discussed. One such feature is the automatic data set retrieval feature. In order to relieve the user of maintaining a large listing of the various pack locations of data sets at the console, operating systems have incorporated an automatic data set retrieval feature (also called a catalog).

A list of data sets the user wishes to be retrieved or which the operating system must know the location of, is kept in an area known as the catalog. This data set retrieval list, or catalog, may contain such information as the data set name

The disk pack, being a volume, contains one or more data sets. These data sets are listed in an area somewhere on the pack, which is called the volume and location of the data set—in other words, which disk pack it is on or possibly which magnetic tape volume it is on, so that in the job control cards the user need only specify the data set name and use the operating system to automatically retrieve the data set, having previously stored in the data set retrieval list or catalog the whereabouts of the data set. In a larger installation, which perhaps might use 200 or 300 data sets, this is a significant time-saving device, because the programmer does not have to refer to some master list to look up the location of a data set before he can use it. He can merely name the data set; the operating system finds the data set for him and allows him to use it.

Direct Access Space Management III (1.3.2.2)

Another feature which many operating systems provide is the automatic accounting of direct access or external storage space. Some operating systems maintain a list of all the available space on each secondary storage volume or tape volume. In other cases, the operating system maintains on each volume certain areas or tables showing where all unused portions of the volume are available. To use our example of a 200-track disk pack again, assume that one data set takes up the first 30 tracks. Then there might be free spaces for 30 30 tracks, and then, finally, a third data set of 70 tracks to make up the total 200. tracks; then another data set might take up 40 tracks, then another free space of table of contents (VTOC). A data set entry in the VTOC will contain the data set name, its length, its starting and ending addresses (in cylinder, track, and record units), and other information about the data set.

In order to find a data set—or a record within the data set, if the data set has been accessed and is now in the process of having its records read—the system will issue channel commands to seek or search to the cylinder, track, and record desired. If he does not have space management facilities provided by the operating system, the system programmer is forced to maintain elaborate listings showing the location of the data located on each track. When the disk pack is to be used to create a new data set, the programmer or operator, depending on the installation, has to study the listings until he finds enough free space to hold the data set he was attempting to create. This is an obvious bottleneck in a computer installation.

Through this direct access space management feature, the operating system keeps continual records of all free space and can allocate it as required. Not only does it know the whereabouts of all free space, in the more sophisticated operating systems it also knows the *amount* of free space in each free area. The space may then be allocated by the operator or by job control cards, usually in the data control card that is describing the new data set. The operating system takes the request for space, searches through its tables, and if it finally locates enough free space, allocates this free space to the new data set. If it finds on the other hand, that it does not have enough free space, it may very possibly terminate the program, informing the operator and programmer that not enough space was available. The programmer and operator, of course, would then be forced to supply a new path or in some other way provide the space required for the program to be run.

Other Features

Another feature of data management is the automatic insertion of the access methods into assembler programs, during assembly, compilation, leading, or execution time. After the programmer decides to utilize the queued, basic, or channel program level, data management (in many operating systems) supplies the necessary modules to accomplish the input/output operation through the input/output supervisor (IOS) function of data management.*

Another data management feature is to provide for the security of proprietary data sets. Data sets can be protected in various ways from other users of the system gaining unwanted entry to data set. This is accomplished by bits, by using passwords or other inquiry-controlling methods that the user might want to use; it also depends on the operating system involved. The data management function could arbitrarily and automatically prevent the I/O operations of a certain program by simply refusing to perform I/O operations when one of these security bits is encountered on a volume or if the password is not given correctly.

I/O ERROR RECOVERY I (2.0)

Any operating system must provide recovery for I/O errors. I/O error recovery, particularly with direct access devices, is a very complicated process since there are so many possible conditions under which input/output errors may be noted. To flow chart an error recovery module for input/output is a major undertaking.

There are ways for the user to help error recovery routines do their job more efficiently with less impact on his operation. For instance, if the operating system resides on direct access, as many do, the input/output error recovery module for direct access devices should be resident in core storage with the operating system. If it is not, and an error is encountered on the direct access device upon which the system resides, the operating system will not be able to call in

* See glossary.

its own error recovery modules. Unit record and magnetic tape error recovery modules may or may not be resident in main storage, depending on the amount of storage available.

Error recovery procedures have another more or less standard option. These error recovery routines usually involve retrying the I/O operation a specified number of times when an I/O error is encountered. Should the error be corrected before completing the specified number of retries, the error may or may not be noted in some operating system table or data set, and system operation will continue.

I/O error recovery procedures, then, are predicated on retrying unsuccessful operations a number of times. If after retrying, a successful completion of the operation is not effected, the error is classified as permanent and the system or the task involved stops. These error modules are often made optional to the user. He may not wish to have them taking up space on his storage paths or in internal storage. The user, particularly with more complex systems, must make a determination as to what *kind* of error recovery procedures he wishes in the system.

There are both sophisticated and primitive error recovery systems available. The simplest one merely puts the system in a wait state. The most complicated writes detailed records concerning the error, attempts recovery of all system functions, switches to another channel, or retries the operation, utilizing all conceivable alternate devices. Unfortunately, for some users this results in a rather high amount of overhead in core storage, or at best uses much direct access space. The more functions a program allows, the more programming that is required to do it, and therefore the more space that will be taken up by the program. The user must take the needs of his installation into account before determining which error device to use.

The most complex, most automatic, error recovery package is not necessarily the best for a given installation. If the installation has medium to small internal storage capabilities or small external storage capabilities, or both, *and* has experienced relatively little hardware malfunction down time on his system, it may be well advised to ask for the less extensive error recovery procedures, thereby conserving storage and making it available for more production programs. While there are no magic formulas for determining this, there are some calculations that can help. In the end, though, it is the "educated guess" of the system programmer that will probably determine which input/output recovery procedure to use.

Checkpoint-Restart

Another type of I/O error recovery sometimes included in operating systems is the feature called checkpoint-restart. Checkpoint-restart is simply the stopping of a task program or series of tasks at intervals, saving current system and program data in main storage and on direct access data sets in safe intermediate areas, then continuing processing so that in the event of a failure or an unforeseen contingency the task is capable of being restarted at the point where the data was stored in a safe place.

The action of storing the data in a safe place is called taking a checkpoint, and the action of going back to the place that can use the data is called restart. The two are commonly referred to together as checkpoint-restart. Checkpoint-restart is a very significant feature, because the user may have a long program. For example, assume that the program has 10 steps and takes 20 hours to run. It is a huge inventory program which is run once a year. The installation can ill afford to waste a significant amount of this 20 hours in starting over. For example, if the program were to fail somewhere in the 10th hour, without checkpoint-restart it would have to be restarted from the beginning, at the expense of 9 hours. With checkpoint-restart, the user might be taking checkpoints at half-hour intervals so that the most time he could lose in restarting would be a half-hour. The advantage of this facility is obvious. However, it also has a major drawback: much valuable secondary storage space is used in storing the data for safekeeping. Again, the system programmer must take the needs of his installation into account in determining whether the facility justifies the space used.

USER IMPLICATIONS

Two of the user implications involving data management have already been discussed—I/O error recovery routines and checkpoint-restart. There are other implications. In a large installation, if the operating system has used data management facilities extensively and the programmers are allowing the operating system to handle allocation of all the auxiliary storage areas, it may very well be that two or three programmers will be required full time merely to maintain the direct access facilities of the operating system or installation.

Even though the operating system will handle much of the record-keeping in terms of device addresses, how much space is available, and so forth, the system programmer must still make careful plans. He must anticipate the needs of his installation in the future. He must try to prevent the operating system from arriving at the point where it has no direct access space available for a new data set, a situation that is avoidable by judicious planning which allows for contingencies. If the system programmer, in projecting his installation needs for a 6-month period, determines that he will need three full direct-access volumes for the new data set which he anticipates the creation of, he must check the operating system tables when doing the planning to see if the space is available. If not, he should order additional new volumes for his installation, or else he could reposition the data sets on the existing packs so as to obtain more usable room.

Another responsibility of the systems programmer in the data management area is supervising the deletion of old data sets from direct access. Many current programs use intermediate data sets while doing their functions or performing their functions. These intermediate data sets may not be deleted automatically by the system, which causes a gradual depletion of usable space.

Operating systems are usually equipped with various utility programs to handle data management. One program, for instance, might scratch the data sets that are no longer of use to the installation. The system programmer would probably use this program to delete the excess data sets. Another utility may serve to check on the physical well-being of the direct access packs, looking for damaged tracks and assigning alternate tracks when necessary. Other utilities are used to automatically retrieve and print data from data sets.

In short, the operating system provides the system programmer with a number of programs he can use as tools. He must, however, be knowledgeable in the areas of data management. The operating system can only tell the user when something is wrong. Predicting things going wrong, particularly in the data management area, is an art that is not yet well advanced.

QUESTIONS—CHAPTER 4

1. Give an explanation of each of the four data set organizations, with a hypothetical application of each.

2. A. Give the advantages and disadvantages of each of the three levels of I/O programming.
   B. What is an access method?
   C. Why is buffering used in I/O operations?

3. A. Describe the direct access space management scheme used in any three of the operating systems studied in this book.
   B. In your opinion, which is the best scheme? Use three criteria to justify your position.

4. What responsibilities is the I/O programmer relieved of by data management? List five and explain the benefit (to the I/O programmer) of being relieved of each.

5. Give the data set organization which best meets each of the following criteria, explaining why:

    1. Economy
    2. Speed of retrieval
    3. Efficiency of external program storage
    4. Suitability for easy retrieval of a large number of records

5

TELECOMMUNICATIONS— THE WORLD OF NOW

REMOTE—ENTRY CONCEPTS III (1.2.1.4)

Remote entry and processing is another facet of the use of computers. There are four basic concepts that are used in remote processing. One is real time and another is time sharing. A third takes in the majority of remote processing and entry applications: Data Entry/Inquiry/Update programs. A fast-growing fourth is message switching.

First, we will examine the application most often used: data entry/inquiry/update, which is essentially a clerical function. A typical application is a terminal removed from the central computer, whereupon a user enters a request for information or enters new data. The user may be doing a remote inquiry, remote data entry, or data update. These are three facets of the same process. A person at the remote terminal is in effect telling the computer to perform a clerical function for him. There will be a program in the central computer devoted entirely to this service. As an example of inquiry, a user of a terminal may want to know the balance in his bank account. (Note: nearly all remote terminals have something in common—a keyboard for manual data entry or for requesting data.) The user typically will type in a code word, which in our example, would be his account number. After the user types in his account number, the inquiry program in the computer takes the request, converts it into a keyword, and uses his input/output routines to access information on secondary storage, usually direct access.

This secondary storage will have thousands, perhaps millions, of small records. Each record will have a unique number, which in our application, is an account number. The data management facility of the operating system will search through all of the data banks the data set encompasses. Once the operating system finds a record with an identifier key matching this account number, it will read the account into the buffer area in the inquiry processing program, which in turn, will cause this record to be written across telephone lines or some other means of data transfer and eventually appear back at the remote terminal where the request came from.

In effect, then, the computer has performed a clerical inquiry function instead of having a clerk look in a file drawer. Before the advent of the computer, there may have been 10 clerks whose job it was to take requests for information about account numbers, look in a filing cabinet in a room full of filing cabinets, look in a given drawer in that cabinet, look for a folder in the drawer, get the information from the folder, and give the information back to the requester. This might take 10 to 15 minutes while the requester waited. At computer speeds, however, clerks are relieved of handling tremendous amounts of paperwork and consequently generating new paperwork as information changes about the subject (in our example, as the bank account had changes in the balance through deposits or withdrawals). Instead, the amount can be keyed in on a remote device and gotten back at human speeds, usually in 2 to 5 seconds. The results—much timelier bookkeeping and inventory keeping, much less storage space needed to hold the files, and nearly total elimination of human error—are a good sales point.

REMOTE DATA ENTRY

Hardware and Software

The types of remote data entry input/output devices are generally divided into two basic classes. One is a cathode ray tube (CRT), a television-like screen, attached to a keyboard. The keyboard sends the information into the computer, which then transfers the information to a data bank in secondary storage. A CRT screen will display the reply, if requested, at a much faster rate than printing out a page, because the reply is displayed on a screen in its entirety, rather than being displayed a line of data at a time. The other type of remote data entry device is a keyboard combined with a printer instead of a CRT.

The CRT is useful when immediate information only is desired. Occasionally, these video devices have no keyboards; they are for information display only. An example is the CRT seen at airline counters in airports. The computer periodically updates the display after computing the latest flight departure/arrival information. Although an installation may be predominantly video screen device-oriented, it will usually have at least one hard copy device (page printer) in case a permanent record is needed.

This CRT type of application is concerned primarily with retrieving quick answers to questions for immediate use and then dropping that particular piece of information and retrieving some more. Again, an installation like this will still normally have a device capable of receiving printed matter of a hard copy for purposes of record-keeping at the remote terminal. On the other hand, there are systems weighted heavily in the opposite direction: many hard copy devices and only a few CRT devices. A user's place in this continuum depends on whether he primarily wants hard copy for permanent records or an information-only type system (which would give essentially temporary CRT displays).

Besides the keyboard/printer and keyboard/video display device, there are specialized remote devices in use. One such device, found in many modern industrial plants, is a badge reader that will accept a particular type of data input: an employee's badge roughly the size of a credit card and made of plastic with holes punched in it. These holes, of course, are read by the central computer as this particular employee's man number. His man number, along with the time, is transmitted to the central computer, which, in turn, enters the information on the employee's payroll record. This device has neither keyboard nor receiving device and is strictly a remote data entry device. It is a rather specialized type of device.

Another device which is fairly widely used is the card reader/page printer terminal. This is essentially similar to a normal card reader and printer, but is set up for remote use.

New devices appear in the marketplace regularly as a new application is found for remote data entry or remote information retrieval. If a customer has an application and has a use for enough machines to justify developmental costs, the chances are good that one of the manufacturers will agree to make the machine for him, because the manufacturer can then sell that machine to other customers who have use for the same type of device.

The software used in remote processing has at least two aspects in common: (1) it is complex, usually using a fairly large amount of main storage, and (2) it is in many cases taking over many of the management functions of the operating system under which it is running. Remote processing applications are usually the foreground job in a multiprocessing system, while the rest of the jobs are background jobs.[1] The remote processing job needs high priority because the I/O requests must be honored as fast as possible, due to their being on line.*

The reason for the great complexity of remote processing systems is twofold: first, the system usually is capable of utilizing many different kinds of remote processing devices and must therefore be able to handle the peculiarities of each device; second, it handles many normally unlikely combinations of I/O events due to the asynchronous** nature of remote processing.

The remote processing system takes over some of the operating system man-

---

[1] "Foreground" is a term meaning the highest priority job in a multiprogramming system, while the remaining, lower priority job(s) will be called "background."

agement functions for remote I/O activity because it has proved more efficient in terms of speed of turnaround (answering a request) to have it do so.

The interrupts we have studied so far are predictable. For instance, if a program gives an input/output request, the computer programming is predicted on the fact that there will be a response of some sort in the input/output device in a certain amount of time. The hardware can handle the interrupts, because the computer, knowing when to expect a return interrupt, can have timing circuits built into it which will be expecting the interrupt. In remote data processing, however, the interrupt cannot be predicted because of transmission line delays or remote operator unpredictability. We never know when the remote end will want to enter data; it could happen at any time. Another term for this type of interrupt is asynchronous interrupt, as opposed to the synchronous or predictable interrupts, which we previously have studied.

Since the central, or control, program must handle asynchronous interrupts, special programming has been developed to handle it. The system control program must be set up, in effect, as though it has already issued an input/output request and is awaiting a return interrupt. Computers do this through an action called polling. The central computer program, or control program, will have one program within the problem program or user program area of main storage which handles remote data processing. All of the lines, whether switched or leased, are known to this program.

The program sends out periodic signals to all devices. If the user at the remote end wishes to enter data, for instance, he types the data he wishes entered on the keyboard and hits a key when he is done, which will try to send a signal back to the central computer. The computer can accept the signal even though it does not know when it will be coming because the computer is sending out the signals at all times in a sort of a ring, called a polling list, starting with the first remote entry data device on his list of remote devices and working down to the last in order, and then starting over.

These polling signals will have to be sensed at the remote location before the data just entered can be transmitted back to the central processing unit. The central processing unit, in effect, has initiated an input/output operation by sending these special polling characters to the device for which the control program expects a return interrupt. It might seem, then, that the computer cannot predict when an inquiry will come from a remote station. But in fact, the operation is much the same as any input/output device. Of course, if the remote station has no data to send back to the central computer, the polling signal is switched to the next device in the list of devices to see if it has data to send back to the central computer, and so on, in a never-ending cycle.

As in the three levels of I/O programming studied in Chapter 4, there are various levels in remote data processing also. There is the queued method, with which the programmer can write, in language approaching the English language, that he wants to initiate an input/output operation and the message-switching program will recognize these pseudo-English commands and build large amounts of machine code to accomplish them. This is a fairly easy way to program remote applications, but again we run into the main storage problem: it will probably require much more core storage than the basic remote data processing access method, where the programmer must write much closer to the machine-language level. Depending on the central program, or operating, system to translate his commands and convert them into machine language, he writes near the machine-language level. More efficient programs can be compiled and executed in this manner using the basic method, but at the cost of significantly more programming time.

Another factor, which may weigh against using the basic method, is the relative lack of programmers skilled enough to program the basic method. Many programmers can code the queued message-switching program because of its similarity to the English language. However, it is probably to the system programmer's advantage to code the main data collection program, whether queued or basic, so as to conserve the main storage; the program will probably be running from 8 to 24 hours a day. If a savings of 500 bytes of main storage can be achieved in this program, then over the course of a year this 500-byte addition to available main storage will allow many programs to execute that would have had to wait for main storage to become available, assuming a multiprogramming environment.

The data inquiry/entry/update remote processing systems, although comprising the majority of telecommunications applications, are not the only kinds of remote processing programs. We have divided remote processing into two main categories: remote data entry and remote program entry. We will examine remote data entry in this section. Remote data entry is further divided into three parts, all of which are characterized by the common fact that their main function is to take remote input data and store, modify or retransmit it (or a combination of the three) and/or write data to a remote terminal. The emphasis is on *data* manipulation within and by a perpetually executing program in the central computer.

The three subdivisions of remote entry are (1) the previously discussed data entry/inquiry/update applications, (2) true real-time systems, and (3) message-switching systems. Having already examined the first type, we will proceed to the second, real time. Real-time systems have a unique characteristic—the remote input data continuously *modifies* the program that is accepting data. That is, the program *depends* on the remote data input to tell it (the real time executing program) what to do next. The input data will change a process or executing program dynamically while that process is actually operating. Another way to think of a real-time system is that it is essentially an electronic servo-mechanism, with the exception that the remote input data can be, and usually is, digital data, as opposed to the analog data normally found in servomechanisms.[2]

There are many examples of real-time systems. One is the program used in the moon shots in the early 1970s. After the rocket takes off, the central computer receives continual pieces of digital data from the on-board measurement instruments which give the velocity of the rocket and other information.[3] The computer's real-time program, then, analyzes this data and sends back in-flight corrections to the rocket which will cause it to stay on a predetermined course. This is an example of remote data altering the results of a process or program (our previous definition of real time). Other examples of real-time programs are aircraft landing approach, or process-control, programs.

The final category of remote data entry programs to be discussed is the message-switching program. Message switching is basically the act of a computer accepting an input message, scanning the message contents, and automatically routing the same message to the appropriate locations based on the contents of the message. As in all applications or remote processing, the control program typically is the foreground job in a multiprogramming environment.

An example of message switching is the application used by a corporation that has grown into a conglomerate and consists of many separate, seemingly unrelated, divisions. Let us assume that a vendor's bill has to come to the main corporate offices and will ultimately be routed to the department that bought the service or product from the vendor. We will also assume that the vendor is required to supply the number of the department he dealt with when he presents his bill. The information from the bill is key-punched and fed into the program. The program outputs the information from the punched card input on the company's standard internal billing form at the appropriate terminals, which is in the offices of the department concerned, the head office of the division that the department is in, the corporate controller's office, and so on. Most message-switching systems operate in this kind of application.

[2] To understand the difference between digital and analog data, we can compare examples of each. A counter and an odometer are digital, at least as the data is presented to the user. The counter window presents the units counted, one at a time; the odometer window presents the miles counted, one at a time. In other words, the term *digital* data implies *discrete* amounts of data.

On the other hand, analog data is not discrete. Examples of analog data are the indications presented by a thermometer and a speedometer. There is always heat presented, and a thermometer indicates the variations in the amount of heat present. While the vehicle is in motion, the speedometer indicates variations in the speed of the vehicle and never shows an absence of motion. *Analog data,* then, is *continuous* and shows variations in the level or intensity of some measured phenomenon.

[3] This form of remote digital data, because it is the transmission of measurement, is often called telemetry.

Transmission Media

The sine qua non for remote data entry is the medium of transmission. Most typically, this medium is the telephone line. The customer leases long distance telephone lines from a telephone company for an extended period, places the central computer at one end and the remote terminal at the other. Usually this user establishes a net of long distance remote terminals at strategic locations within a geographic area.

There is another type of arrangement, in which, instead of leasing the lines, the user has the capability of using the special telephone to access the regular dial network in order to dial the remote terminal. Some manufacturers provide equipment for the computer so that this dialing is automatically done by the computer. In this way the company pays only for time it actually uses the telephone lines, as opposed to a permanent lease situation, where a flat monthly charge is paid regardless of the amount of usage.

The choice of type or arrangement used for renting telephone lines will depend on the application at the system programmer's installation. If the system is one that requires a great many entries for extended periods of time—as, for example, a computer in a state police headquarters which has remote terminals at various key police stations in the area—then the lines probably remain in use 24 hours a day. It would probably be more economical for this installation to permanently lease the lines. On the other hand, where a user only needs access to the computer for a short period of time, perhaps half an hour, to enter data and knows that he will enter data for only half an hour a day, it is to his advantage to use the switched line or dial-up line system, because the rate of charge by the telephone company is cheaper.

Of course, there can be combinations of the two types of rental arrangements; some large organizations may have a central computer and probably 5 or 10 key subwarehouses around the state. These subwarehouses are on-line to the central computer for perhaps 10 or 15 hours a day. This portion of the network is likely a leased line. However, from the subwarehouses to numerous remote locations, perhaps a small dealer, the dealer might not use the utility for more than an hour total during a given day, so that these small substations would in all probability be linked to the subwarehouses via dial-up lines.

It is also possible to use microwaves as well as telephone wires. This is usually done through the telephone company which installs microwave relay stations instead of long overland trunk lines.

Another type of telecommunication system is the situation called process control, where there is a central computer and slave computer connected by telephone lines. As an example, say we have a process control type of application with a central computer which is handling the real-time monitor program, a small computer at the remote end of the line, which is operating an assembly line through sensors at various points along the line. The process control computer is installed mainly to monitor the progress of items as they are being assembled on an assembly line. As conditions change, the computer adjusts control variables which can speed up or slow down the assembly line. These conditions may or may not be determined at the remote computer. It is possible that the remote computer will merely take the sensory information from the various points on the assembly line; pass the information from the remote computer to a central computer, which analyzes the information; determine what, if anything, needs to be changed; and transmits commands back to the remote computer, telling it to alter the speed of the assembly line. Or the remote computer may do the entire job itself.

So we have video tubes, hard copy, specialized devices such as badge readers, and even remote computers themselves, all used in remote data processing.

Types of Applications

Some types of applications, which may be encountered in remote data processing were cited in the above examples, which are parts inventory and bank account maintenance. Another application is nationwide or worldwide reservations systems such as airlines, motel, and car rental systems. For example, General Motors uses remote processing to obtain current reports on the parts inventory status at various manufacturing plants around the country. In some states the police keep records of all license plates, so that any police station in that state has access to the central computer. The station feeds a license plate number in and receives the name of the owner back in seconds, instead of waiting an hour or more for an answer, as used to be the case.

Another application of real time is a traffic count operating a city's traffic lights. As traffic flow increases, the duration of red and green lights at a given traffic light at a major intersection may need to be changed. This could be done with remote specialized terminals, which may be electric eyes counting the number of cars passing a point within a given time. The central computer takes samples, and as the number of cars exceeds a certain limit, it sends a signal to another specialized remote device which changes the timing of the traffic light. Basically, then, anything a clerk can do a computer can do better and faster with less chance of error.

REMOTE PROGRAM ENTRY I (1.2.4), I (1.3.2.2.)

The remote program entry (job processing from remote terminals), as previously noted, is more a time sharing than a remote data entry application. The rationale of time sharing is to utilize the time the central computer spends waiting for an interrupt from a remote device, thus allowing other users to process their programs in main storage while the original program is waiting for the results of an input/output operation. This is particularly effective in remote data processing because the machines at the remote end, such as the hard copy machines, are often quite slow, thereby causing a longer wait for completion of an I/O operation. It is often a great convenience to have remote locations with remote program entry allowed at them.

Time sharing, in effect, is the process of dividing a large main computer into a number of small computers, with each user using a partition, or region, of core storage. A typical system may have 15 or 20 jobs executing concurrently under multiprogramming, with each job having a relatively small amount of main storage. The user pays only for time on the computer while his program is executing and his data is being transmitted back from the computer when the program has finished executing. *True* time sharing would be a situation in which each terminal user has his own main storage area, which is large enough to contain his entire program. However, due to present limitations on the amount of main storage allowed in a given computing system, we find that the virtual memory facility, discussed above, is utilized in the larger time-sharing systems. We refer to all such systems, whether virtual or real, as time-sharing systems. All have this in common: programs are initiated from remote locations, usually with multiprogramming.

There are various schemes to effect this remote initiation of jobs. We will examine five—remote batch entry (RBE); conversational remote batch entry (CRBE); remote job entry (RJE); conversational remote job entry (CRJE); and full time shared. (Note: these names do *not* refer to a particular manufacturer's programming product, but are rather intended to be generic names for remote program entry schemes.) We will now examine each of these schemes in order.

Remote batch entry is the simplest scheme. A remote card reader device transmits a stack of data cards to the central computer. The RBE control program examines a control field on each card as it is received. Depending on the contents of this control field, the RBE control program selects and starts the appropriate program to process this particular kind of data, which processes all like cards until all cards are transmitted. Some sort of output may be sent back to the remote location, or perhaps data sets at the central location are updated. For efficient operation, it is usually advisable to sort the input data cards into like batches before transmitting the entire data deck. This saves CPU time and main storage.

Conversational remote batch entry is much like RBE, except that the user also has a terminal device with a keyboard at the remote location. This user may wish to key in the program he wants the CRBE control program to start.

In this way, he saves the space taken up on each card by the RBE control field. The user tells the CRBE control program to start the desired program by using the keyboard, then he enters the processing data through the card reader. Some CRBE systems also allow the processing data to be entered with the keyboard, and most allow some interactivity. Interactivity means that the user of the system can send messages to the CRBE control program and receive the same from it. These messages are normally of the control variety, telling the program to do something or informing the remote user of actions taken or needed. (This interactivity is a form of *conversation* between the user and the CRBE control program, thus the word "conversational" in CRBE and CRJE.)

Remote job entry is a slightly different concept. Instead of having a control program which will start or attach* a specific, preordained task when it receives a control word, as in RBE and CRBE, RJE instead extends the regular system reader task, in effect, to the remote terminal. This terminal does not have a keyboard. As in RBE, it is probably a card reader and page printer. The user punches a program as he would in a nonremote environment. This program has normal operating system job control language (JCL) with it. In order to submit his job the user also places special RJE control cards in front of his program and starts his RJE card reader. The RJE control program recognizes its special control cards, sees the normal operating system JCL, and gives the entered program and its JCL to job management. The program then executes as a normal job would in a multiprogramming system. The output from the job is passed to the RJE control program which then transmits it to the remote location.

Conversational remote job entry is similar to RJE, except, as in CRBE, that there is a remote keyboard terminal. The remote terminal is interactive with the CRJE control program. The user can type his JCL input data from JCL input data entry. The CRJE control program gathers the JCL and data and submits it to job management, as in RJE. After the program completes execution, output may go directly to the terminal or it may be relayed by the CRJE control program.

Full time sharing, depending on the manufacturer, is one of various combinations of the preceding four schemes. In addition, the control program usually is geared to the speed of the remote keyboard terminal operator instead of to the speed of the card reader. There are usually more features with full time sharing, such as the ability to enter source statements to a compiler built to accept conversational input, so that the user can key in his source programs instead of being required to first key-punch them. These extra features in a time-sharing system are designed to increase the interaction between man and computer. (Note: Some CRBE and CRJE systems also allow the interactive languages, such as ITF, to be used.)

USER IMPLICATIONS

Interface with Multiprogramming

As far as remote processing with multiprogramming is concerned, the internal priorities are important. That is, with multiprogramming the system programmer must be aware that remote data entry (sometimes called telecommunication) is slow. Many remote input/output devices take a relatively long time for operations. Since the remote data processing applications take so long in waiting for input/output, it is to the advantage of the installation for the system programmer to place the remote control program or remote data processing control program in the region or partition having top priority.

This means that when the input/output interrupt is finally received, the remote processing program receives control first. The most likely occurence is an immediate request for more input/output. This means that the remote processing program may be the first program to gain control of the CPU in any given interrupt, but because of the length of response time, the rest of the programs will have ample time to utilize the computer while the computer waits for the results of the remote input/output request. By the same token, a job which mainly executes in core storage and does not perform input/output operations, such as a scientific calculation program, would need to be in the lowest priority region or partition so that it could be interrupted by the operating system and the remote processing program would gain control as it needed control.

This arrangement of priorities prevents the job with a large amount of CPU usage from gaining control of the computer and making all other jobs wait until it receives interrupt. The system programmer must weigh input/output-bound jobs against computer-bound jobs. Telecommunications, or remote data processing, jobs will be the most input/output-bound. In other words, they will have the largest percentage of their execution time taken up by waiting for input/output results.

Most of the remote on-line systems, whether remote program entry or remote data entry, are executing concurrently with other batch programs in the same computer. Of course, the system programmer must do much more planning for remote data processing applications then he must for regular programs. He must plan all possible telephone line combinations and he must be sure to include them in the operating system at system generation time so that the operating system has knowledge of all the devices at its disposal.

The system programmer must be proficient in the art of determining the location of problems—are they in the hardware, the system software, the user software, or is this a problem for the telephone company? He now has two, three, or more different service organizations he must consult. He must determine where the problem is, since it would not do for him to make the mistake of calling the hardware service organization when the problem is a software problem. In fact, many large installations have a full-time system programmer who devotes his time entirely to remote data processing applications.

Protecting the Data

As far as data protection is concerned, the remote processing systems will utilize many of the same techniques as data management. The user can be required to type in an entire password or possibly only a prefix, along with the number he wishes to use as a key. For instance, he may have to give his location using an abbreviation such as NYC for New York City, then perhaps some key word, and then start his data request or entry. The program recognizes the password and allows processing to continue from this input/output device. If the program does not recognize the password, he may send an error message back to the remote entry point, telling him that the wrong word was used.

There can be serious consequences if this data is not protected. Again, the example of the bank's account numbers: if there is not some sort of data security scheme employed, it is possible for anyone to call up a bank if he finds the input telephone number and ask the computer information pertaining to a bank account that is not his. The computer would recognize the telephone call through another specialized type of remote entry input device (also connected directly to the main computer in certain applications), called a voice receiver, audio response unit, or the equivalent. This unit recognizes key words over the telephone and may even have a vocabulary of its own of a limited nature which the central computer can use to answer the person making the request. The person making the request is then told by the computer by voice that he has not given the correct key word.

Another type of security application concerns payroll records. When a person wishes to make changes to his payroll, perhaps allowing for more deductions or less, this data has to be protected so that no one else has access to the person's payroll records. The basic device used in protecting the data is key words and pass words.

Protecting data becomes more and more important as computer banks contain more personal information about people. The moral question of the right of organizations (banks, government, credit unions, etc.) to have access to people's private business enters heavily into the data processing sphere. The problem is particularly significant in remote data processing, especially real-time applications, because it is through remote data processing that a person not needing the information is the most likely to have access to it. It is possible for a person with a certain type of telephone in his home to obtain a bank's data inquiry telephone number. If this person were to key in or state the correct sequence of numbers after having reached the central computer in the bank he could easily get information on any depositor's bank account, which, of course, he has no right to. The same type of problem arises regarding such things as credit records on individuals and the government information bank on individuals. Security of data is rapidly becoming an important aspect of the system programmer's job, particularly when he is involved in remote data processing.

Programming Considerations

Programming considerations have already been discussed. To reiterate, the system programmer should be aware of the cost in core storage of the queued higher level machine language. The queued level is easier, hence faster to program, and is useful for programs that will have a low usage level. The basic level is harder and slower to program, using less core. It may be more efficient for a particular installation, especially if the program has a high level of usage. Again, the manufacturer of the operating system can design a very flexible, high level program that will accommodate many or all users. Since the particular installation in question is only one user, it may not need many of the facilities in the program. If the user does not use the entirety of the high level program, he wastes core storage which could be put to better use in other programming.

Another problem facing a telecommunications programmer is in the field of new applications for new I/O devices. The trouble is that the operating system is not equipped to process the peculiarities of the new device. The programmer must often write his own access methods if he wishes to use the device. When a device is not handled by an operating system, it is said to be *unsupported* by that system. Although included with remote processing implications, there are occasional nonremote devices that are unsupported. This question of support for a device should be weighed when considering the purchase or rental of a new I/O device.

The basic question facing the remote processing system programmer is that of programming cost versus programming efficiency. His basic job is to strike a balance that will give him the optimum combination of both for his particular installation, which is also his job in all other operating system computer programming.

QUESTIONS—CHAPTER 5

1. A. What is real time?
   B. Give two applications of a real time system.
   C. Give two examples of real time operating systems from the systems studied in this book.
2. Give a hypothetical example of a complete application of remote data entry, inquiry, and updating, showing all three functions in a unified flowchart of your application, along with an explanation of the flowchart.
3. A. What is the difference between remote job entry and remote batch entry?
   B. What does "conversational" mean and what added functions does it imply in RJE and RBE?
   C. Name an operating system from among the systems studied in this book which has each of: RBE, CRBE, RJE, CRJE.
4. A. What is time sharing?
   B. What is time slicing?
   C. Name two operating systems from among the systems studied in this book that have a time sharing feature, and one that has time slicing.
   D. Set up a hypothetical time-sharing system, describing the facilities offered to each user.

6
AN OVERVIEW OF CONTEMPORARY OPERATING SYSTEMS

OPERATING SYSTEM FEATURES

Evolution

The job management, task management, data management, and telecommunications features described earlier in this book evolved gradually. Only as hardware capabilities made it possible and user convenience made it worthwhile did programmers add new features to the operating systems they were using. The result was an evolution culminating in the existence of the five major types of operating systems we know today. The role of some of these features is worth noting.

First-generation "operating systems," though they were not so designated at the time, consisted of a minimal number of manufacturer-supplied routines of general enough utility to merit distribution to most computer customers. Initially, these routines performed such functions as loading programs and displaying and dumping computer main storage. Many of these computer systems did not have hardware instructions for certain arithmetic operations such as multiplication and division, and as a result, subroutines to perform the operations were also distributed. Frequently, computer users replaced or rewrote the programs to meet their own needs. Eventually, as mnemonic and problem-oriented programming languages were developed, the manufacturers distributed assemblers and compilers as part of their basic system support packages.

A distinguishing characteristic of the early programming support packages was the absence of any integration of individual support modules. Each module was a stand-alone entity which operated independently and did not interface with any of the other modules. Even though a few manufacturers provided minimal capabilities to perform serial job-to-job transition, control languages were merely a series of delimiter statements separating each job from the next and each program from its data.

The significant feature of second-generation systems was the development of an integrated system concept that provided basic services to executing programs while maintaining control of job-to-job transition. This, in turn, introduced the concept of a main storage resident system that monitored system activity. Further, the support programs were no longer independent entities, but became integrated modules which could be called and executed as required. Consequently, the term "operating system" was formally introduced at this time to distinguish the software that provided support functions from an installation's application-oriented software.

Input and output device control was the most commonly implemented support feature of the systems. This service eliminated much of the programming previously required for I/O error conditions and provided additional facilities such as record blocking/deblocking and label checking. Other services included capabilities to request full and partial core dumps, load subroutines dynamically, and maintain inter-job communication regions. Also, the concept of on-line libraries for executable programs and subroutines was introduced and much greater flexibility was developed in the area of job-to-job transition. For example, the libraries gave rise to the multistep job, whereby programs residing in an on-line library could be interspersed and/or combined with programs in the input stream to accomplish a series of given tasks.

Finally, the controlling system language ceased to be a composite of delimiter and sentinel cards and became, in effect, a control language. The concept of an input job deck was developed, whereby both job and user were identified, I/O device assignments enumerated, and program-execution sequence specified. In the job deck could be interspersed the input data required for each job step, along with sentinels to prevent application programs from reading subsequent control cards. These operating systems, nevertheless, retained the serial processing orientation of first-generation systems.

Current third-generation operating systems, while retaining most of the features of earlier systems, have expanded total system control so that serial job-to-job transition represents only one of many possible operating system functions. The most significant advance made by third-generation systems has been the development of a capability to schedule and execute jobs in other than a sequential or serial manner. This capability, called multiprogramming, not only allows the concurrent execution of two or more programs, but permits execution scheduling to be based on such factors as resource availability and job priority rather than strictly on job input sequence.

In order to provide these and other capabilities, third-generation systems have assumed complete control of the computer system and inhibit executing application programs from performing any action that could degrade system performance or interfere with system monitoring. Unlike second-generation systems, which relied on programming conventions to maintain system integrity, third-generation systems make use of hardware features which physically prevent application programs from executing certain types of instructions or from utilizing the core areas assigned to other executing programs or to the resident supervisor. Thus while earlier operating systems could be circumvented intentionally by the knowledgeable programmer (or perhaps inadvertently by the novice), third-generation system hardware makes this much more difficult, if not impossible.

However, the most distinguishing characteristics in the development of third-generation systems has been the emergence of the operating system as a necessity rather than as an aid. The typical third-generation system not only controls the scheduling and execution of application programs, but also performs all I/O operations, fields, and processes all machine and program error conditions, and supervises or invokes recovery and restart capabilities when needed. Consequently, the scope of control has expanded well beyond the initial job management facilities originally associated with operating system technology and incorporates almost total control of both the hardware and software environment.

Since third-generation operating systems characteristically support a number of different system applications, the type of application supported would at first appear to be useful in discussing system characteristics. For example, the following major applications are supported by contemporary systems: batch processing; real-time processing; communications-oriented processing; and interactive terminal usage.

Unfortunately there is enough diversity among contemporary commercial operating systems in the amount of support provided to each area to make such a categorization awkward. Many systems fail to make any provision within the supervisor for one or more of these applications. Others provide only minimal support for some applications while providing extensive support for other applications. Consequently, if this were the classification scheme, a system might be described as full batch processing, extensive real-time processing, partial communications support, with no interactive capability. While this description provides an excellent picture of the particular system, it also creates a potentially large number of different system categories. Furthermore, the terms—full, extensive, partial, and minimal—are too likely to reflect the cataloger's biases.

On the other hand, most systems employ one of three basic design approaches: serial processing, multiprogramming, or time-sharing. Although these categories are somewhat too broad (and to a degree, overlapping), they do provide a basis for ascribing certain characteristics to various types of operating systems.

These design approaches may be illustrated by the manner in which a primary system resource, main storage, is allocated to application programs. When this resource is totally allocated to one application at a time, the system is called a serial processing system. When main storage may be shared by two or more application programs at one time, the system is a multiprogramming system. A time-sharing system is identified by the fact that several programs may be allocated the same area of main storage for interleaved program execution.

Types of Operating Systems

With these storage allocation modes in mind, five systems types can be selected to categorize operating systems. Since the preponderance of the systems observed provide multiprogramming facilities, a further distinction can be made concerning the degree of multiprogramming support available and the type of time-sharing service offered. This distinction permits the isolation of several attributes which, while not common to every multiprogrammed system, created major subsets in the area of system design. The five systems types are:

1. serial processing systems,
2. basic multiprogramming systems,
3. extended multiprogramming systems,
4. serial time-sharing systems,
5. multiprogramming time-sharing systems.

The simplest type is the serial processing system. This system is designed predominantly for batch processing applications and provides simple job-to-job transition for consecutive programs in the input stream. This type of system does not permit any concurrency of operation either from a multiprogramming or a time-sharing standpoint.

The multiprogramming systems cover a wide range of sophistication, from rather small real-time-oriented processors to large batch and interactive multiprocessor systems. The definitive characteristic of the multiprogramming system is the concurrent core residence and interleaved execution of two or more programs. Many multiprogramming systems are designed only for single processors. However, some systems are designed to permit multiple processors, thereby achieving simultaneous as well as interleaved program execution.

A basic distinction can be made in the way storage is allocated to problem programs in a multiprogramming environment. If main storage is divided into fixed partitions or areas, and each area is allocated only to jobs from a separate input stream or device, the system is a basic multiprogramming system (e.g., IBM's DOS/360, RCA's TDOS, and XDS's Batch Processing Monitor). In contrast, if separate input streams are merged on secondary storage prior to scheduling a job, and main storage is allocated to the first program capable of using the area, then the system is an extended multiprogramming system (IBM's OS/360, GE's GECOS III, and UNIVAC's EXEC-8).

This distinction can be further illustrated by the scheduling process. In a basic multiprogramming system the scheduling process is external to the system. The area of main storage assigned to the program for execution is determined when the input device is selected to load the program. In an extended multiprogramming system, on the other hand, scheduling is internal. Although every program may not be able to execute in every partition (due to partition size, priority, or other scheduling restrictions), the determination of the storage partition to be used is conceptually independent of the input device from which the program was entered. Thus successive programs loaded from the same input device may execute concurrently in an extended system, but can only execute serially in a basic system. In many cases, a basic multiprogramming system may be thought of as a collection of several serial processing systems where each serial system operates in a uniquely assigned storage partition.

The time-sharing systems also permit several programs to execute concurrently. A varying time slice, or time quantum, is assigned to each program and the program is allocated the CPU and main storage for that period of time. At the end of the quantum, if another time-sharing program is waiting, the storage area and CPU may be reassigned to the next program. This usually involves removing the first program (and data) from main storage and storing it on an intermediate storage device. After all programs in the system have received separate execution time quantums, control is returned to the first program for another time quantum.

Serial time-sharing systems operate in much the same sequential way as a serial processing system. All of the programs in execution are placed into a cyclic scheduling table and each program is activated in a fixed sequence. Some serial processing systems buffer the loading and unloading of the time-shared programs by using two or more main storage partitions. However, even though the system thus permits concurrent core residence of more than one program, if the actual execution sequence relies on cyclic rather than interleaved execution of these areas, the system still has a serial orientation.

Multiprogramming time-sharing systems are those systems which provide the same time-sharing services mentioned above, but, which, in addition, interleave these services with the execution of other programs. In some extended multiprogramming systems one partition or storage area is devoted to time sharing while the remaining areas process nontime-sharing applications. Consequently, systems with this orientation (GECOS III, EXEC-8) appear in both the multiprogramming time sharing and the extended multiprogramming categories. Other systems are basic multiprogramming systems that have been extended to provide time-sharing services. Also, there are a few time-sharing systems that provide interleaved execution of core resident time-sharing programs in addition to the normal cyclic execution sequence. Many of these systems do not support the batch processing capabilities normally associated with a multiprogramming system (RCA/TSS, IBM/TSS). Thus this category not only has a large degree of overlap with other categories, it also has a wide variety of different design approaches employed to provide time-sharing services in a multiprogramming environment.

OS TYPE	DEFINITION
Serial Processing System	Provides core residence for a single application program. Program flow through the system occurs in a sequential manner.
Basic Multiprogramming System	Provides for concurrent core residence and processing of multiple programs. Execution occurs either simultaneously (multiprocessing) or by means of an interweaving process. Each partition or program area is independent of the others, is assigned its own unique input and output devices, and is scheduled by external control.
Extended Multiprogramming System	A multiprogramming system (as defined above) that has the additional capability of internal program scheduling. Input streams are queued on direct access devices so that the input readers serve all partitions. Programs are not necessarily confined to execution in any particular partition.
Serial Time-Sharing System	A system which provides for concurrent serial processing of multiple programs by allocating the system resources (including core) on a round robin basis. A program resides on secondary storage, is brought into main storage to execute for a fixed time period (quantum) and then returned to secondary storage.
Multiprogramming Time-Sharing System	A multiprogramming system where one or more of the partitions are assigned to process time-sharing programs.

Figure 6-1. Definition of Operating System Types

Operating System Levels

The degree of sophistication of an operating system generally corresponds to the amount of main storage required for its effective operation. System levels, therefore, have been established for all of the systems analyzed, based on computer main storage size. The minimum storage requirements for each system have been largely ignored since they generally apply to a primitive version of the system which offers relatively few options and usually does not reflect the full capabilities of the system. Similarly, maximum sizes are not considered. While most operating systems will operate on the largest storage size available with the computer, they will not normally make effective use of the resources of the larger machine. Therefore, an attempt has been made to determine the size of main storage required to support the operating system and user programs in a normal operational environment. In general, three broad computer levels have been selected:

Level A: large-scale computers with main storage in excess of 132K bytes (where a byte consists of 8 bits);
Level B: medium-scale computers with main storage ranging from 32K bytes to 132K bytes; and
Level C: small-scale computers with main storage generally less than 32K bytes.

It should be noted that many computers are not byte-oriented. However, due to the lack of common word size (in bits) among the computers analyzed, the 8-bit byte was arbitrarily chosen as the standard. The storage requirements for all operating systems were then stated in terms of the 8-bit byte. In this way the main storage requirements of each system, regardless of the storage organization, could be compared roughly with others.

Figure 6-2 classifies the operating systems of 13 vendors in terms of the system types and levels described above. It must be noted that the classification has been made on the basis of documentation supplied by the respective vendors. No attempt has been made to determine the effectiveness of each operating system in terms of performance or the degree to which each of the functions is actually implemented.

Operating System Functions

The analysis of contemporary operating systems was directed toward developing a functional classification structure to identify common operating system functions. Because of the wide variety of systems observed, a hierarchical classification scheme was selected as being the most convenient means of presenting both the general and the common capabilities, along with specific implementation techniques used in various system designs. The following guidelines were developed to aid in determining the structure of the classification scheme:

- The structure must be oriented in such a way that it accurately describes the attributes of the wide variety of operating systems surveyed;

BURROUGHS CORPORATION

B2500/B3500	C	Basic Control Program	Serial Processing
B2500/B3500	B	Master Control Program	Extended Multiprogramming
B5500	B	Master Control Program	Extended Multiprogramming
B5500	B	Master Control Program/ Time-Sharing System	Multiprogramming Time-Sharing
B6500	A	Master Control Program	Extended Multiprogramming and Time-Sharing

CONTROL DATA CORPORATION

31/32/33/3500	B	Mass Storage Operating System	Basic Multiprogramming
31/32/33/3500	B	Real-Time Scope	Basic Multiprogramming
3600	A	Scope Operating System	Serial Processing
3600	A	Drum Scope System	Basic Multiprogramming
3300/3500	A	Master Operating System	Extended Multiprogramming
6400/6500/6600	A	Scope 3	Extended Multiprogramming

DIGITAL EQUIPMENT CORPORATION

PDP-8	C	Disk Monitor System	Serial Processing
PDP-8	C	Time-Sharing System	Serial Time-Sharing
PDP-15	C	Advanced Monitor System	Serial Processing
PDP-10	B	Single User Monitor	Basic Multiprocessing
PDP-10	B	Background/Foreground Monitor	Basic Multiprogramming
PDP-10	B	Multiprogramming Monitor	Multiprogramming Time-Sharing
PDP-10	B	Swapping Monitor	Multiprogramming Time-Sharing

GENERAL ELECTRIC CORPORATION

600 Series	A	GECOS III	Extended Multiprogramming/ Multiprogramming Time-Sharing

HEWLETT-PACKARD COMPANY

2000A	C	2000A System	Serial Time-Sharing

HONEYWELL, INC.

Series 200	C	MOD 1 Operating System	Basic Multiprogramming
Series 200	B	MOD 2 Operating System	Extended Multiprogramming
Series 200	A	MOD 4 Operating System	Extended Multiprogramming
Model 8200	A	MOD 8 Operating System	Extended Multiprogramming

- The structure must account for varying sizes or scales of operating system support capability;
- The structure must be amenable to operating system validation in that the functions identified could become the items to be validated;
- The scheme must be flexible enough to accommodate new techniques and facilities as operating system technology advances;
- The scheme must be sufficiently broad to account for the variety of operational modes such as real time, time sharing, and batch job processing.

The resulting structure relied on external or user-oriented functions at the up-

INTERNATIONAL BUSINESS MACHINES CORPORATION

1800	B	Multiprogramming Executive	Basic Multiprogramming
System 360	C	Basic Operating System	Basic Multiprogramming
System 360	B	Disk and Tape Operating System	Basic Multiprogramming
System 360	B	Operating System—PCP	Serial Processing
System 360	A	Operating System—MFT/MVT	Extended Multiprogramming
System 360 (Model 67)	A	Time-Sharing System	Multiprogramming Time-Sharing

NATIONAL CASH REGISTER COMPANY

Century Series	C	B1 Operating System	Serial Processing
Century Series	C	B2 Operating System	Basic Multiprogramming
Century Series	B	B3 Operating System	Basic Multiprogramming

RCA CORPORATION

SPECTRA 70	C	Primary Operating System	Serial Processing
SPECTRA 70	C	Tape Operating System	Basic Multiprogramming
SPECTRA 70	B	Disk Operating System	Basic Multiprogramming
SPECTRA 70	B	Tape-Disk Operating System	Basic Multiprogramming
SPECTRA 70 (Model 46)	A	Time-Sharing System	Multiprogramming Time-Sharing

SYSTEMS ENGINEERING LABORATORIES, INC.

810A/810B	C	Operating System	Serial Processing
810B	B	Real-Time Executive	Basic Multiprogramming

UNIVAC DIVISION, SPERRY RAND CORPORATION

9300	C	Operating System	Basic Multiprogramming
9400	B	Operating System	Extended Multiprogramming
418-111	B	Real-Time Operating System	Extended Multiprogramming
494	A	Executive Omega System	Extended Multiprogramming
1108	A	EXEC-8	Extended Multiprogramming Multiprogramming Time-Sharing

XEROX DATA SYSTEMS, INC.

SIGMA 2	C	Basic Control Monitor	Basic Multiprogramming
SIGMA 2	C	Real-Time Batch Monitor	Basic Multiprogramming
SIGMA 5/7	B	Batch Processing Monitor	Basic Multiprogramming
SIGMA 5/7	A	Batch Time-Sharing Monitor	Multiprogramming Time-Sharing

C = Small scale (less than 32K)
B = Medium scale (32K to 132K)
A = Large scale (greater than 132K)

Figure 6-2. Examples of Levels and Types of Operating Systems

per levels of the hierarchy and internal or implementation-oriented functions at the more detailed lower levels of the hierarchy. To retain sufficient generality certain functions that were actually system-dependent techniques were not listed as subfunctions, nor were they assigned a hierarchical level number within the structure. Instead, they were identified under the function to which they applied, but were preceded by a bullet character (•) indicating that they were attributes, techniques, or examples.

The following overview of the functional structure illustrates the categorization method employed (the detailed structure is given in Appendix A):

Part I: *Executive/Control Functions:* The components of the operating system that maintain real-time execution control of the system environment.
    1.0 *Job Management:* The real-time initiation, scheduling, monitoring, and control of normal system operations, together with the necessary allocation of resources.
    2.0 *Diagnostic Error Processing:* The recognition of the occurrence of error conditions within the system, along with the corresponding corrective actions.
    3.0 *Processing Support:* The routines within the supervisor which accomplish a variety of miscellaneous real-time services for an application program.

Part II: *System Management Functions:* The nonreal-time components of the operating system which support and maintain both system and application programs.
    1.0 *Operating System Management:* The generation and maintenance of the computer operating system.
    2.0 *Program Maintenance:* The support functions provided to the user for the maintenance and modification of application programs.
    3.0 *Compiler Interfaces:* Operating system functions that provide supporting services to the system language compilers.
    4.0 *Management Support Utilities:* Utility programs provided for the use of the system manager. These programs perform a wide variety of functions in support of initializing, testing, and monitoring the system.

Part III: *Data Manipulation Functions:* The components of the operating system that permit the user to access and process data. These functions may either be independent utility programs or subroutines incorporated within a user program.
    1.0 *Data Management:* Comprehensive facilities which provide support for programmed access to the data files within the system. These facilities may take two forms: routines supporting application program access to the data base and an independent data management system supporting user access to the data base.
    2.0 *Data-Handling Utilities:* Utility programs which provide a variety of independent services to manipulate and/or display various groupings of data elements.
    3.0 *Sorting and Merging:* Those routines that sequence strings of records according to keys within each record.

In the structure, upper hierarchical levels are common to most operating systems. Lower hierarchical levels, as mentioned above, are not universally implemented. For example, one of the functions under *job management* is the function *scheduling*. All operating systems have a scheduling function, though in some it is implemented simply on a first come, first served basis. The next functional level under scheduling considers the types of scheduling functions available—algorithmic, time initiated, event initiated, and program initiated. Each is a separate form of scheduling, of which one or more may be available in any given system. However, since all forms are not equally available on all systems, that functional level marks the division between common functions and implementation-oriented functions.

It should also be recognized that while some system operations are germane to a unique functional category, many operations can be attributed to a number of different functional areas. The greater the level of detail within the hierarchy, the greater the possibility of overlap among functional categories. In an effort to minimize this overlap while retaining a valid classification structure, decisions were made to allocate subfunctions to only one category where feasible even though the subfunction could legitimately be included elsewhere. *Input/output error correction,* for example, is categorized as a part of *hardware error control* rather than as a part of *I/O control.*

In some cases overlap cannot be avoided. In these areas an attempt has been made to identify the function at one point and identify it as an attribute or example elsewhere. The roll-out, roll-in feature, whereby a program of low priority is removed from core to provide additional working space for a higher priority program, is an example of this type of problem. *Roll-out, roll-in control* is defined as a subfunction of *program loading*. On the other hand, *roll-out, roll-in* is one of the possible attributes or methods of the function *system initiated restarting.*

The functional classification scheme is presented in Appendix A in a hierarchical format. Each level is a detailed functional breakdown of more general functions of a preceding higher level. Consequently, each lower level is identified by a more detailed hierarchical level number (e.g., 1.4.1.2 is a lower level within the hierarchy than 1.4.1).

I. EXECUTIVE AND CONTROL FUNCTIONS

1.0 JOB MANAGEMENT

The job management function is responsible for the initiation, scheduling, monitoring, and control of system operations for all jobs submitted to the system. In this context a job encompasses all of the programs required for the execution of a given application. The job management subfunctions consist of: job control, input/output control, system communication, and recovery processing.

1.1 Job Control

In processing a job the supervisor is actually concerned with independent job elements called tasks. The task (or, as it is sometimes called, the process, or activity) is the basic unit of work within the operating environment. The operating system job control functions are those functions that regulate the use of the system resources by the various tasks comprising each separate job.

1.1.1 Scheduling

The purpose of the scheduling function is to select a job which is available for processing and prepare it for execution. The function may be extremely complex, as in an extended multi-programming system where several jobs may be simultaneously available for execution, or quite simply, as in serial processing systems where the order of programs in the input stream may dictate the execution sequence.

Each mode of system operation (batch, real-time, or time-sharing) requires a distinct scheduling philosophy. The most straightforward method, assigning priorities to each type of event that may produce an external signal to the computer, is generally found in a real-time environment. When any event occurs, if a higher priority event is currently being processed, this event remains pending until that processing terminates. On the other hand, if a lower priority event is being processed, this processing is suspended and the system resources are made available to the interrupting event. The programs which process the real-time events may be permanently resident in core or may be loaded dynamically. In several systems designed primarily for real-time processing (e.g., the XDS Sigma 2/5/7, IBM 1800), this scheduling function is performed by the system hardware. Other systems require a software scheduling routine to provide this function in lieu of the hardware capability.

Scheduling for time-sharing systems is also relatively straightforward. When a time-sharing user logs-in on his console, the scheduling routine determines whether the system is currently saturated. If it is saturated, the user is not allowed to proceed; if not, he is immediately placed in an execution mode. Some systems require that the user identify his resource requirements at log-on time and will not schedule the user until all these resources are available. Other systems do not include this feature within the scheduling routine. Instead, if the user attempts to use a committed resource, he is suspended until that resource becomes free.

The greatest variation in the implementation of the scheduling facility exists in the handling of batch processing. The most elementary approach is to schedule each job for execution in its sequence in the input stream. When a system has separate input streams for several processing areas, as in serial processing or basic multiprogramming systems, each input stream serves as a scheduling queue which is external to the system.

Further sophistication of the sequential approach is achieved by prereading the entire input stream and storing it on a secondary storage device such as a disk. By so doing, jobs may be executed in an order other than input stream sequence. In this type of system scheduling parameters are introduced to control the execution sequence. Normally these parameters are priorities, where a higher priority job is executed before a lower priority job. Alternatively, the parameters may be clock times, where a job is initiated at a selected time or is initiated to be completed by a certain time. Clock-time scheduling may also be used to initiate selected real-time jobs.

The batch scheduling philosophy of an extended multiprogramming system allows jobs submitted from more than one input stream to complete for execution assignment. Under this philosophy a scheduling queue on an intermediate storage device is mandatory. Jobs are placed on this queue whenever they are entered from either a local or remote input terminal. In this type of system an input stream symbiont is used to read the input stream and store it on the scheduling queue. The symbiont is itself scheduled by an external event such as an operator or user command to initiate input stream processing.

Other scheduling capabilities available in various systems permit algorithmic, program-initiated, and conditional scheduling. Conditional scheduling permits the user to specify scheduling criteria which must be satisfied before the program can be scheduled. Criteria may be the presence or absence of certain errors in a previous job step or the setting of internal switches by another task. Program-initiated scheduling permits an executing program task to request that another program task be scheduled for either asynchronous or subsequent execution. Algorithmic scheduling is an extension of the priority scheduling concept where many factors will influence the selection of the next program chosen for execution. The relationship of these factors to one another is known as the scheduling algorithm. Some commonly used factors are: estimated run time, resource availability, job priority, CPU-I/O relationship, and the length of time an element has been in the queue. A few of the more sophisticated systems permit the operator to modify the scheduling algorithm during system operation.

Since most systems handle more than one type of processing mode, different scheduling philosophies are used for the real-time, time-sharing, and batch processing applications. Frequently, the lack of a processing workload in one of these modes will permit the scheduling mechanism of another mode to utilize normally reserved facilities. For example, the lack of current real-time or time-sharing processing may be recognized by the batch processing scheduler, which would then initiate more batch processing jobs than under normal conditions. Similarly, a heavy real-time workload may force the suspension of some or all batch processing jobs so that core may be assigned to the more critical routines.

1.1.2 Resource Allocation

The resource allocation function is responsible for assigning resources to each executing job in such a way that conflicting resource assignments are avoided. In general, system resources may be discussed in terms of CPU time, internal storage, I/O devices, and information files. The allocation of CPU time to a program is called *dispatching* and is covered separately under Part I, Section 1.1.4. The other three areas are discussed below.

In a serial processing system resource allocation routines do not exist to any significant extent, since all of the system resources are normally made available to the executing program. In a multiprogramming or time-sharing environment, however, two or more programs may be executing concurrently and can produce conflicts if common resources are not controlled. Because of this problem, many scheduling algorithms require that all needed resources be assigned prior to scheduling the program. When this requirement is levied, each job must provide information to the scheduler describing the resources it will need during execution. These are usually stated as job control language parameters in the input stream or are contained in generated data blocks produced by the program binding process.

Some systems permit dynamic resource allocation. This allocation method allows an executing program to request the use of a resource only when it is needed. If the resource is uncommitted it will be assigned to the program. Otherwise, the program will be suspended until the resource becomes available. Dynamic resource assignment is usually found only in extended multiprogramming systems and is primarily advantageous where a large number of programs are executing concurrently. Since resources are only committed when they are being used rather than for the duration of an entire job, the technique may significantly reduce the total number of resources required for operating efficiency when compared to an environment using static allocation.

Internal storage. There are four basic methods for allocating internal storage in a multiprogramming environment. The first method involves the static assignment of fixed foreground and background processing areas. The foreground processing areas are generally allocated to real-time or time-sharing processing, while the background area is generally allocated to batch processing. This form of storage organization is characterized by the fact that program priority is determined by the storage assignment: foreground areas always have execution priority over background areas.

The second method of storage allocation involves a series of fixed independent partitions of varying sizes. Each partition may have a separate input stream, or programs may be assigned to the smallest available partition that will contain them. In the latter case, the system may also provide parameters that prevent some programs from being assigned to certain partitions. A distinction between real-time, time-sharing, or batch processing is not provided in terms of partition definition.

The third method involves maintaining all free internal storage as a large pool of storage. Each program is assigned the exact amount of storage that it requires from the pool and, upon terminating, returns the used storage to the pool. If time-sharing operations are undertaken in this environment, a block of storage is normally removed from the pool to handle all of the time-shared applications.

In the fourth method internal storage is segmented into a series of fixed pages of relatively small size which are maintained in a pool. Likewise, program instructions and data are segmented into pages. A program may then be assigned the number of pages it requires. The assigned pages need not be located contiguously in main storage. Many advanced systems keep unused pages of programs on a fast-access drum. During program execution they are shuffled in and out of internal storage as needed by a process called paging (described in Part I, Section 1.1.3).

Once internal storage has been allocated to a program, additional storage may be required for buffers, program expansion, and so forth. For these requirements, most systems utilize special purpose storage pools which are independent of normal allocatable storage. When an executing program requires storage in excess of its original allocation, it can request an additional allocation from the supervisor. The pools are scanned for an area of the proper size and when found, the area is assigned to the program. The area is returned to the pool either explicitly by the executing program when it has finished using it or implicitly when the program terminates.

Normally, storage protection mechanisms are also provided to prevent a program from modifying or accessing main storage areas outside its allocated regions. Conversely, many systems also provide common areas of main storage which may be shared by several executing programs.

I/O devices. In the background/foreground mode of storage assignment, I/O devices tend to be permanently allocated to one of the background or foreground partitions such that the allocation may be altered only by the console operator. Some systems in this class, predominantly real-time process control systems, do not control I/O device assignments at all and rely on programming conventions to avoid conflicting utilization.

In partitioned and paged processing environments, I/O devices may be allocated statically at job initiation time or dynamically during job execution. In general, systems oriented to the use of unit record or serial devices rely on static assignment. On the other hand, systems oriented to the use of random access and teleprocessing devices are most likely to use dynamic assignment techniques since several programs may access a common device concurrently.

Information files. The information files available to a system consist of files or data and libraries of programs or subroutines. The allocation of each of these facilities is handled somewhat differently.

Data files may be statically assigned to a program during the scheduling process and treated in much the same way as an I/O device assignment. In such systems the data files may not be assigned to a second program until the first program has terminated. Other operating systems are designed to permit access to the same data file by a number of concurrently executing programs. In this type of system the file is dynamically allocated based on the type of access the program requests. Read-only access requests are normally granted unless the data file is being modified. Write access requests are usually held in a pending state until all current read across requests have been satisfied. In a great many systems only one program is allowed write access, whereas any number of programs may be allocated concurrent read access. Operating systems of this type usually feature some form of security control that must be satisfied before file access is permitted. This aspect is described in greater detail in Part III, Section 1.1.2.

Programs or subroutines that can be used by more than one program are frequently designed to be loaded and executed when needed, rather than incorporated as a part of the executing program during the binding process. These routines may be loaded into a specially designated transient execution area, into any available area of core the executing program can find, or, if used frequently enough, made a part of the resident system. Allocation of these routines to requests is almost always dynamic rather than static.

There are three types of subroutine organization that require different allocation procedures. Nonreusable subroutines are subroutines that must be loaded "fresh" each time a request is made for the routine. Serially reusable routines need not be reloaded. However, the routine, because of possible modification of constants or instructions, can only be used by one program at a time. Reentrant routines may be used by any number of executing programs simultaneously. Thus allocation of reentrant routines is straightforward, whereas serially reusable routines must have a lock/unlock facility which limits their assignment to a single program at a time.

1.1.3 Program Loading

Loading Control. Once a job has been scheduled for execution and the request resources have been assigned, the operating system loads the initial task of the job into the core area assigned for job execution. The system obtains the required load modules (see Part II, Section 2.2) either from a system library, a user library, or a temporary load module file.

Some systems only provide facilities for absolute loading. In this design a program is loaded into a single, fixed main storage location which may have been determined when the load module was generated. However, most systems permit relocatable loading, which allows a program to be loaded into any given storage location. Address resolution is usually accomplished by setting a base address register to the initial address of the loaded area. In a few systems the program may be further relocated during execution by moving it to another area changing the contents of the base address register.

Structure control. Operating systems may support several different kinds of program loading structures. The more common structures are categorized as simple, overlay, paged, and dynamic.

A simple program structure consists of a single module occupying a fixed amount of main storage. An overlay program allows for repeated use of the same blocks of core storage during different stages of program execution. Thus the overlay program is segmented and each segment is loaded as it is required.

Paged and dynamic structures are considerably more sophisticated in scope and, consequently, are common only in the larger multiprogrammed and time-sharing environments. Dynamic loading allows a relocatable module to be loaded into main storage upon a request for that module by an executing program. It differs from an overlay structure in that the area of main storage need not be prespecified, nor does the module necessarily replace or overlay an existing program segment. One of the major problems with dynamically loaded programs is that the process creates unused core fragments. The unused core fragments result when all dynamically loaded programs do not terminate concurrently. Consequently, some systems will relocate all active program segments to a contiguous core storage area prior to dynamically loading another module. Other systems only compact storage when core becomes exhausted or when certain high priority programs require loading.

When storage is divided into pages (as described in Part I, Section 1.1.2), the program loading function may consist of simply loading all of the required main storage pages, or it may entail preparing the system for a process called paging. Paging requires a fast access secondary storage device (usually a magnetic drum) as a supplement to main storage. Both the secondary storage device and main storage are configured to the same fixed page size. A program resides on both devices; the page of the program containing the instruction sequence currently executing is in main storage, most of the other pages are in secondary storage. Whenever another page is referenced for data or to transfer control, a page area is made ready in main storage—perhaps by moving an in-core page to secondary storage—and the required page is read in. A page map is maintained, indicating the physical page assignments (main storage or secondary storage) and the actual storage address (core locations or track). This map is consulted to resolve addresses when accessing the data or instructions within the page. In many systems this address resolution is accomplished through hardware circuitry. In others, it must be accomplished via software.

Implementation of the paging concept provides for programs of seemingly unlimited size, since a program need no longer be restricted by the actual main storage memory of the computer. On the other hand, paging involves considerable overhead in shuffling pages between main and secondary storage so that the increased capability is not without cost. Because of this cost, several interesting techniques have been developed to minimize the amount of page transfer between secondary and main storage. A common technique is to attempt to determine the page least likely to be referenced in the future and remove this one from main storage whenever a new page area is required. Another technique is to remove only pages that have not been modified in the time since they have been read in. The latter method avoids the requirement for writing the page contents onto secondary storage since the previous version of the page on secondary storage can still be used.

Swapping control. Swapping is a technique of sharing main storage among several jobs by maintaining each job and its status on secondary storage and loading each one into main storage as needed. Though primarily the basis for time-sharing systems, it is also found in nontime-sharing applications under the names roll-out, roll-in and paging.

In a time-sharing system the swapping mechanism is usually activated each time a program's allocated time quantum expires. The time quantum is the maximum amount of time that a program can control the CPU during each execution cycle. In some systems the time is fixed either by the system, the operator, or the user. However, many systems also permit the quantum to vary during execution as the relationship of compute time to I/O processing time or as the relative program activity in relation to other time-shared programs varies. Consequently, time quantum determination is one of the major differences among time-sharing operating systems.

1.1.4 Event Monitoring

Event monitoring refers to the control the operating system maintains over executing programs. The function includes dispatching control, interrupt processing control, event synchronization, and program limit monitoring.

Dispatching Control. The function at the heart of a multi-programming or time-sharing system is the dispatching function. Responsible for allocating processor time to each contending task, this is perhaps the simplest of all operating system functional areas in implementation. Simplicity is mandatory because it is one of the most frequently used supervisor routines. If the system is to operate with any degree of efficiency, the dispatching overhead must be held to an absolute minimum. The following description applies primarily to extended multiprogramming systems. However, it illustrates the simplicity of the dispatching function within the most complex type of system.

An extended multiprogramming system must maintain some form of dispatching queue. This queue contains only those tasks capable of using the processing unit. Thus, for example, when a job is scheduled, the program is loaded into main storage, assigned resources, and the program designator is entered onto the dispatching queue. The queue is normally maintained in priority sequence, so that the first entry on the queue is the highest priority program available for execution. Consequently, the dispatching routine merely locates the first queue entry, removes it from the queue, and assigns the processor to it. The program is allowed to execute until it is interrupted (in which case the interrupt routine places the program designator back onto the dispatching queue) or until it must suspend itself due to required supervisor service such as I/O processing. When the required service has been performed, the supervisor again enters the program designator onto the dispatching queue. All interrupt processing routines and all supervisor service routines return control upon completion to the dispatching routine to select the highest priority program that can execute next.

In a time-sharing system the scheduling queue corresponds to the cyclic or round robin scheduling list and the implementation philosophy is similar. In a basic multiprogramming system or a real-time-oriented system, the dispatching queue may in fact be implemented via hardware circuitry rather than software. Nevertheless, the basic concept, as illustrated above, remains the same.

Interrupt Processing. An interrupt, as the name indicates, is a break in the normal flow of program execution. An interrupt is usually caused by a hardware-generated signal such as an I/O event, a program error, a machine error, or an operator-initiated signal.

In a real-time system the interrupt levels of the various events to be monitored are usually specified when the system is generated. In general purpose systems they are usually intrinsic to the system and may not be specified. Normally, processing on a given level will be interrupted whenever higher level interrupts occur. Interrupts of a lower level than the processing program will be held pending. If several interrupts occur simultaneously they are stacked and honored according to their priority. Unfortunately, in some systems inadequate stack lengths can cause multiple interrupt signals to be lost. Interrupt acknowledgement can be altered by disabling interrupts to prevent their recognition or by masking them to defer their recognition.

When an unmasked interrupt occurs the current instruction is usually allowed to complete execution. Then the program and the contents of the machine registers are saved in main storage and control is transferred to a program, which will service the interrupt. This program may complete execution, or in turn may be interrupted by a still higher priority interrupt. When an interrupt processing program does complete execution, control is returned to the highest pending interrupt processing routine or to the supervisor dispatching routine if no interrupts are pending.

Event Synchronization. Event synchronization is the process of delaying task execution until some specified event occurs or the process of triggering a task upon the occurrence of a specified event. The most common types of events, which may delay or initiate task execution, are I/O completions, selected time intervals, subtask completions, and unsolicited key-ins.

Event synchronization may also be effected between several tasks of a job. One task may initiate any number of subordinate tasks and may execute concurrently with them. This main task may, at any time, issue wait requests which will suspend main task processing until one or more of the subordinate tasks have been completed.

Program Limit Monitoring. Many systems monitor various resources during job execution to ensure that certain specified limits are not exceeded. Limits are usually established for such elements as central processor time used, output records produced, and the amount of main and secondary storage space allocated. While installation maximums for each resource are normally established at system generation time, they can usually be overridden by job control cards. Some systems automatically cause abnormal job termination when any of the system limits for a particular job are exceeded. Other systems permit the user to specify other actions to be exercised, such as operator or program notification, whenever the various limits are exceeded.

In some smaller real-time systems, execution time limits are not explicitly set. However, the supervisor maintains a countdown loop which will time out unless it is periodically reset by the executing program. If the countdown loop times out, an interrupt is generated and program execution terminates.

1.1.5 Program Termination Processing

A program terminates normally when it has completed all of its processing and returns control to the supervisor. A program may also be abnormally terminated by the operating system under a number of different circumstances. This is frequently caused by a programmed request for abnormal termination of the job, a system determination to abort due to lack of corrective actions for certain error conditions, or a console command to terminate issued by the computer operator. The standard abnormal termination procedure is to discontinue execution of the executing task, or possibly of the entire job, depending on how critical the task is with respect to the job.

When a job is terminated (either normally or abnormally), the supervisor deallocates and returns to the system all areas of core and all devices assigned to the job, and performs whatever operator or program notification is necessary. A summary showing CPU time utilization and overhead, local and remote device utilization, file access, error statistics, and so forth, may also be recorded. Additionally, when a job is abnormally terminated, some of the following may be recorded: the condition causing termination, a dump of all or selected portions of core, the results of special program-defined abort procedures, and the contents of registers and status indicators.

1.2 I/O Control

System control over the activity of input and output devices is a fundamental feature of third-generation operating systems. This control is maintained for two separate reasons. First, it simplifies the work of the application programmer, since he need not be concerned with the intricate details of programming for a variety of channel and device characteristics. This upgrades the overall effectiveness of the programming staff because a standard and well-defined approach, rather than a number of widely varying approaches, is always used to interface with I/O devices. Secondly, since the system is in control of I/O activity, the application program need not be alerted to process I/O interrupts. Consequently, in multiprogramming and time-sharing environments, the job management function is considerably simplified by maintaining a single system I/O interrupt processing routine. Thus the queuing, dispatching, and timing requirements that would arise if multiple I/O handlers were competing for CPU use simply do not exist.

The I/O control function usually supports all devices the hardware vendor supplies with the computer system. These normally include direct access storage devices, magnetic tape drives, paper tape drives, unit record devices, typewriters, remote terminal display devices, and plotters. Additional devices which are uniquely attached to a computer system are not normally supported and require special augmentation programs to bring these devices under supervisor control.

1.2.1 I/O Scheduling

I/O scheduling is the process of acknowledging a request for I/O services and initiating the physical input or output operations to satisfy the request. Requests for service may be processed immediately or they may be serviced according to a queuing scheme. In the latter case, queues are provided to hold requests for channel or device services.

Typically, when an I/O request is issued, both the channel and the device are checked for availability. If both are free, the operation is initiated. If either is busy, the request is placed on a channel or device queue. Whenever the channel becomes free, the channel queue is checked for pending operations. A pending operation will be scheduled if the referenced device is free. Otherwise, the queue will be checked for other pending operations on available devices. Some systems will allow a device to be attached to more than one channel. Then if one channel is unavailable for the I/O operation against the device, the channel scheduler will attempt to use the second channel before entering the request on the channel queue.

Queues are usually maintained in a priority order. This order may be device priority, job priority, or simply first-in, first-out. In any case, an I/O operation will ordinarily be dispatched according to its position within the queue. However, in some cases the supervisor may consider hardware optimization over priority when selecting an entry from the queue. For example, requests for access to a disk device are frequently serviced in a manner that minimizes disk arm movement, rather than queue priority.

1.2.2 Data Transfer

Data transfer controls the movement of input or output data between main storage and secondary storage, or between main storage and input/output devices. Prior to initiating the data transfer operation, an area of main storage (called a buffer) must be set aside. The buffer will either contain the output data to be transmitted or will receive the input data as it is being transmitted. Techniques for allocating buffer areas vary greatly among the various operating systems.

Many systems, particularly smaller systems, require that the application programmer suballocate parts of his allocated main storage as buffer areas for his files. There are three basic methods he may use to provide these areas—single buffering, double buffering, and buffer pooling. Single or double buffering techniques allocate either one or two fixed main storage areas as buffers for each designated file. The areas are allocated in advance and remain allocated whether or not the file is being processed. A buffer pool, on the other hand, is a large core storage area containing several buffer areas. Each of these areas can be made available as an input or output buffer for any file. Whenever an I/O operation is required for a file, the user removes a buffer from the pool and assigns it to the file. When the data transfer and subsequent processing are complete, the buffer is returned to the pool. As a consequence, buffer pooling can reduce the total area required for user buffers if all files are not concurrently active.

More sophisticated operating systems provide system-controlled exchange or dynamic buffering facilities. Dynamic buffering is a technique which provides buffers to an executing task in response to an actual demand for a buffer area. Dynamic buffering is similar to buffer pooling, except that the system controls buffer allocation rather than the user. Dynamic buffering is an example of the dynamic main allocation function discussed in Part I, Section 1.1.2.

Exchange buffering is a technique that eliminates the need for moving data between a system buffer and user storage. In this type of processing, a system buffer is filled by an input action on a file. Rather than moving this data to a user-processing area, the system simply exchanges buffer areas with the application program. Similarly, on output, when a user buffer is full, the system exchanges it for an empty buffer and user-processing continues. Exchange buffering allows complete system control of buffer activity while minimizing system overhead.

As data transfer operations occur, the system may have to initiate routines to translate data codes. This occurs frequently in telecommunications, where the input or output line data coding structures differ from the internal computer data codes. When code translation is required, it occurs as a part of the system interface to the I/O device. Thus differences in coding structures are generally transparent to an applications programmer. Many smaller systems, however, do not provide this feature and the function must be performed by the application program.

1.2.3 Device Manipulation

Device manipulation is a control function which allows a physical I/O device to be positioned without actually requiring data transfer. Device manipulation facilities normally permit volume positioning (rewinding, forward spacing, back-spacing, disk-arm positioning, etc.), printer spacing and forms control, and card stacker selection. These features are generally available on every type of operating system for the devices associated with the system.

1.2.4 Remote Terminal Support

Control over remote terminal operations is found in all time-sharing systems and in batch processing systems that provide remote job entry. While it may be possible to attach a remote terminal to practically any computer system, many operating systems are not designed to specifically support remote terminals and special terminal support routines must be designed to augment the normal supervisor facilities.

Operating systems that do support remote terminals as independent input or output devices generally provide a line-service software package to supplement the normal data transfer routines. There is a great variation in the support provided by these packages. Some systems only provide for a standard terminal processing speed and format, while others offer a mix of line speeds in addition to such features as CRT paging and data compression.

In a time-sharing or remote job entry environment, the remote terminal is the main input and output device of the system. Consequently, the system customarily provides all the services of input and output stream control, as described in Part I, Section 1.3.3, to the terminal. In these environments a capability is usually also provided for the remote terminal user to communicate directly with the computer operator via the terminal keyboard.

Many systems-supporting terminals also provide a capability for the various terminal users to send messages to one another. Thus a user in one location can use the terminal to communicate with users in other localities. Messages can be sent to a particular user or broadcast to all or to a selected list of users. When this feature is available, terminal users may inhibit message receipt by requesting the system not to forward messages from other users. Consequently, this system function may be looked upon as a telephone switchboard controlling a series of separate conversations.

1.3 System Communication

System communication incorporates all of the functions involved in the exchange of information between the user or the computer operator and the operating system. The communication may be oriented either to controlling the execution of scheduled jobs within the system or to configuring system components and monitoring system status.

1.3.1 System Startup

System startup is performed by the computer operator to initialize the operating system for normal processing. In batch processing environments this is the normal beginning-of-the-day procedure once computer power has been turned on. In real-time environments operating around the clock, however, startup is only performed when the system has been shut down for some reason.

System initialization is usually achieved by loading a system-tailoring routine. The tailoring routine reads and processes specific system configuration information from the operator's console or the system card reader. The amount and type of configuration information supplied is dependent on the capabilities of the total system and the versatility of the operating system. Options provided by various systems include patching the supervisor, specifying partition sizes, specifying system resource availability, and setting the system clock. A few systems (for example, General Electric's GECOS III) allow a complete form of system tailoring tantamount to system generation (see Part II, Section I.0) during each initialization.

When telecommunication capabilities are present, the supervisor may incorporate a special startup routine to initialize the system for communications processing. This is frequently required to build communication buffers on secondary storage, open the on-line processing files, and establish the telecommunication line connections.

When all of the startup functions have been performed, the system is ready to initiate processing. In some systems control is passed directly to input symbionts which will read the input job control streams and develop the scheduling queues. In others, the system enters an idle state and remains there until an interrupt signals the initiation of a real-time or time-sharing processing requirement. In this case, the operator may also issue an interrupt to initiate batch job processing.

System restarting is required when a failure occurs that affects the total system, rather than a specific job. Restarting functions are oriented to restoring as much as possible of the system environment that was valid at the time of the error. In critical real-time environments, for example, system checkpoints are frequently taken at regular intervals. These checkpoints can be used to reload a previously valid version of the operating environment when no other immediate method of repair is possible.

Recovery from certain hardware malfunctions may indicate a need to replace certain supervisor routines that have been damaged. The use of refreshable modules greatly facilitates this procedure. A refreshing module is one that is not modified by itself or by any other program during execution. If there are indications that program damage has occurred and if the damaged module is a refreshable module, the system merely replaces it with a new copy.

Other restarting elements may also be provided to dynamically reconfigure the system by eliminating failing components such as I/O devices or storage elements. In general, the more critical the environment, the greater the capability for system-controlled restarting. Real-time systems, for example, are frequently designed primarily around the restart capability.

In batch processing environments, restarting may be designed to provide recovery for incomplete jobs, reinitiation of interrupted system output, and preservation of in-core accounting information. Extended multiprogrammed systems generally retain the scheduling queues of all jobs not executing at the time of system failure, though they may or may not be able to recover jobs in execution. When no total system restart facilities exist, a system restart is identical to an initial startup.

1.3.2 Job Control Communication

Job control communication refers to communication between the operating system supervisor and either the user or the computer operator relating to the initiation, running, or termination of individual jobs within the system. In batch processing systems, user/system communication is generally noninteractive, whereas in time-sharing systems it is almost always interactive. Operator/system communication is predominantly interactive.

Noninteractive user communication frequently takes the form of system control cards imbedded within the input job stream indicating the hardware requirements for a job (I/O devices, files, main storage, time, etc.), the sequence of task execution, and pertinent error procedures. These specifications frequently can be stored within the system as a cataloged procedure and invoked by the user on a single control card. Interactive user communication consists of single commands issued to the system from an on-line terminal as the job is executing. Interactive commands may also invoke predefined sequences of commands.

Operator communication is usually conducted via the operator's on-line console. Generally, the operator can control the actual execution of a job by raising or lowering its priority, by assigning or removing I/O devices, and by suspending or cancelling a job when necessary.

1.3.3 Input/Output Stream Control

The input job stream is the sequence of system control statements and program data submitted to the operating system on an input device specified for this purpose. In serial processing and basic multiprogramming systems the device tends to be the system card reader, though, in fact, any input device can be used. In these two system types jobs are read, processed, and output in the order in which they occur in the input stream.

Input stream control consists not only of reading the input stream, but of recognizing the presence of system job control cards within the input stream and transferring control to the proper supervisor routine for interpretation and processing. Program data that appears in the input stream must be distinguishable from system control cards. Special system control card identifiers may be used or delimeter cards may be inserted to precede and follow the data cards. In either case, the input stream control function must not permit an application program to read beyond the program data included within the job stream.

The output stream consists of diagnostic messages and other data issued by the operating system or the processing program to the output device specifically designated for user communication. In practice, the output device is normally the system printer, though, again, any device could be chosen.

In larger systems, particularly extended multiprogramming systems, the input and output streams are maintained as separate files in direct access storage. Programs called symbionts are used to read and transfer the system control and data cards from input devices to the input stream files. Other symbionts transfer output data from output stream files to the actual output devices.

The advantage of intermediate input and output stream files can be best illustrated with an example. Consider the concurrent (either multiprogrammed or time-shared) execution of two independent application programs in a system that has a single system printer. If both programs require the use of the printer, only one can physically be assigned the device. If the device were assigned to both programs, output data from both jobs would appear intermixed in the listing. However, if one program is assigned the device, the other must be suspended until the device again becomes available. On the other hand, if both programs create separate output stream files on a direct access device, both programs can execute concurrently. When each program closes its output stream file, the file can be transferred to the printer by an output symbiont when the printer is available. Thus the single system printer does not inhibit concurrent processing. A further benefit is that the system printer is not reserved during the entire execution period of either application program. Rather, it is reserved only for the length of time it takes to transfer the output data from secondary storage.

Thus symbiont processing enables input/output devices to be utilized at physical data transfer rates, while permitting programs to process input and output stream data at storage file transfer speeds rather than at the lower peripheral device speeds. The overall effect on the system is a considerable increase in throughput without requiring additional peripheral devices.

Since, in time-sharing applications, the terminal is usually dedicated to a particular time-sharing job, and since both the input and output stream are usually located at the same terminal, no significant equipment or time-saving is afforded time-sharing programs by using symbiont processing techniques. On the other hand, when the terminal is used for remote batch processing, symbiont processing can offer both time and equipment savings, particularly when multiple jobs are submitted.

1.3.4 Resource Status Modification

In most computer operating environments it is desirable to alter the computer configuration without physically terminating all system operations. For example, a tape drive may require cleaning, a disk file may require maintenance, or an off-line operation may have concluded and additional peripheral devices may have become available for system use. As a result, most systems allow the computer operator to alter the status of resources available to the system during system operation. Generally, this is accomplished via direct operator console commands to the operating system supervisor.

The resources affected may vary from peripheral device utilization to main storage and CPU allocation. The following list is indicative of the types of modification provided in several systems: addition, deletion, and replacement of input and output devices; modification of partition sizes and/or their relative priority within the multiprogramming scheme; initiation or termination of activity in any or all partitions; and alteration of the amount of CPU time allocated to various processing types supported by the system.

1.3.5 System Status Interrogation

The computer operator is usually given the capability of displaying the status of various system elements. This may range from the status of specific jobs to the status of I/O devices and main and secondary storage. Systems vary considerably in the capabilities provided. Where some may provide only status information on particular items, others will produce extensive visual displays showing the current status, relative usage, and accumulated error statistics for any system element.

In time-sharing systems each terminal user can usually query the system on the current status of his job, the current state of his and other terminals, and the current status of system I/O devices.

1.4 Recovery Processing

Recovery processing is invoked whenever an external error (as opposed to a programming error) occurs, which prevents a particular job from continuing normal processing. The recovery routines attempt to avoid abnormal job termination by restarting the executing job from an earlier point in the processing cycle. Although recovery processing may also be required for the entire system, a discussion of this situation was presented earlier, in Section 1.3.1. The following discussion, therefore, is concerned only with job, not system, recovery.

1.4.1 Checkpointing

Checkpointing is the recording of information about a program and its environment on secondary storage, so that at any future time the program may be reinitiated from that point. Small operating systems, particularly serial processing systems, checkpoint all of core while most multiprogrammed systems checkpoint only individual storage partitions. The checkpoint record is maintained on an on-line (usually tape or direct access) checkpoint file and usually contains main core storage contents. In addition, checkpoints may also contain selected register settings, I/O device-repositioning requirements, and the contents of critical permanent and temporary data files.

A checkpoint record is created whenever a request for a checkpoint is issued. The request may be initiated by the operating system, by a problem program, or by a computer operator command. In general, the operating system initiates checkpoints to accomplish roll-out, roll-in processing or for automatic restarts in real-time environments. User programs usually initiate checkpoints only when system-directed checkpointing is not provided. The computer operator normally initiates a checkpoint only when he must temporarily terminate system operations for some reason.

Some systems only support checkpointing for certain types of jobs. For example, the IBM 360 DOS permits background but not foreground checkpoints. Many time-sharing systems do not even provide a specific checkpoint capability. However, some of these systems do allow the user to save the current status of his program for subsequent reloading. This could be considered a de facto checkpoint, since the program can be re-initiated from that point.

1.4.2 Restarting

Restarting is the process of restoring the status of a job to some previous point in time. The three basic types of restart capabilities used within all operating systems are checkpoint, task, and job. A restart taken from a checkpoint reestablishes the program and its data in the operating environment as they existed when the checkpoint was taken and resumes execution at the restart address included in the checkpoint. A task restart reinitiates processing from the beginning of the identified task. A job restart reinitiates processing from the beginning of the entire job.

Except in some cases where the supervisor checkpoints a program to provide roll-out, roll-in services, restarts normally require device repositioning. The extent to which devices may be repositioned varies, although most systems will, as a minimum, reposition sequential devices. Some systems also reposition direct access device arms and reestablish broken teleprocessing line communications. Repositioning not performed by the system must be provided by the application program or the computer operator.

2.0 DIAGNOSTIC ERROR PROCESSING

The diagnostic error-processing function is responsible for recognizing hardware, program, and interface errors. Recognition is usually based on hardware interrupts or program testable switches. The function also supports the diagnosis and resolution of error conditions.

2.1 Hardware Error Control

Hardware error control encompasses the recognition of hardware errors and the corresponding support provided for error recovery. Error control routines are generally available for core storage parity errors, processor errors, I/O control memory parity errors, I/O data parity errors, and power failures. Although recovery routines are usually provided with the system, they may be augmented by the installation during system generation. As previously mentioned, real-time processing environments are particularly concerned with error recovery procedures and often the entire vendor-supplied error recovery system is redesigned for these environments.

When an error occurs, control is transferred to an appropriate diagnostic routine to determine the cause of the error and possibly the extent of the damage. If the error is minor, as in an I/O data check, the operation is reattempted to determine whether or not the error is permanent or merely transient. Permanent errors usually require some form of operator-controlled action, such as replacing the failing element. If the error is transient, a tally may be updated to indicate which system elements are producing a relatively high level of transient errors.

Major errors on nonreal-time systems normally require termination of system operations and some form of corrective maintenance. If the system has extensive job recovery routines as described earlier, operational processing of the jobs may be resumed once the maintenance has been completed. If not, a system initialization and startup will most likely be required.

In order to minimize the likelihood of error occurrence, some systems provide on-line diagnostic testing of system hardware components. The testing routines are comparable to the off-line tests run during scheduled system preventative maintenance, except that they are executed within a normal operating environment and do not disrupt other concurrent system processing. These routines may be scheduled to execute on a periodic basis by using the system's time-initiated scheduling capability or they may be explicitly invoked by the computer operator or hardware engineer.

Some systems, particularly real-time systems, also provide dynamic reconfiguration capabilities for hardware errors that affect overall system performance. These capabilities remove failing hardware components and replace them with alternate or backup devices. If a backup device is not available the system can "fail soft," which means that it will continue to perform with less than the normal number of hardware components. Generally, when a system fails soft, the execution workload is reduced, as necessary, by not processing lower priority programs.

2.2 Program Error Control

Almost all systems recognize program errors occurring in user programs and assume control to prevent the system from being adversely affected. The user is frequently allowed to supply his own error-handling routines for certain types of errors such as arithmetic and data errors. More serious errors, from a system integrity standpoint, are core storage violations, invalid addresses, and improper use of privileged instructions. The occurrence of these errors will usually result in abnormal termination of the offending program.

A different approach to program error processing is taken by most time-sharing systems. Since the terminal user is interacting with the system, an elaborate error-processing sequence is not generally required. Instead, the system can simply notify the terminal user of the program error and allow him to determine what corrective action, if any, should be taken.

2.3 Interface Error Control

Most systems edit interface message formats with the operating system prior to acting on a communicated request for system service. For example, input stream control commands, operator key-ins, remote terminal communications, and program linkages to the supervisor are invariably edited in great detail for accurate formats, calling sequences, and valid codes and parameters. Errors will normally result in job termination, task termination, command rejection, or a request for operator or user clarification.

3.0 PROCESSING SUPPORT

The processing support function consists of supervisor routines which may be called upon to accomplish a variety of miscellaneous services for an application program. In general, the services are utilitarian in nature and provide convenient, rather than necessary, functional support. The services are described below in terms of timing, testing and debugging, logging and accounting, and system description maintenance facilities.

3.1 Time Service

Most systems have an internal timing device which provides timing services to application programs. A few systems, to reduce the size of the resident supervisor, only include these services as an option during system generation.

Timing services tend to be of two types: interval timing and real-time clock services. Interval timing services are used to suspend processing for specified times or to alert the program when a specified time interval has passed. Interval timing services may thus be used to schedule intermittent checks for specified conditions or to serve as watchdog timers to prevent unending program loops.

Real-time clock services are most frequently used to provide the date and time of day to executing programs. However, they may also be used to schedule interrupts at specific times (rather than intervals) so that events can be scheduled or terminated on a time-of-day basis.

3.2 Testing and Debugging Service

The facilities available for testing and debugging application programs vary considerably among operating systems. Some systems, such as IBM's System 360/OS, provide an independent program testing and debugging package that operates in conjunction with the resident operating system. Other systems, such as Honeywell's Mod 4 OS, incorporate testing and debugging support as a part of the resident system service package. Thus, not only do the services offered vary, but the method of implementation may also vary from system to system.

Many systems maintain two distinct user operational modes, a normal mode and a testing mode. Usually when errors occur under a normal mode of program operation, the program is subject to abnormal termination. However, under a testing mode, the occurrence of errors usually triggers a series of prescribed debugging routines which gather extensive information about the error condition. For example, storage dumps and selected data file dumps are frequently requested for programs abnormally terminating in a test mode. The advantage of a test mode is that the routines are not invoked until errors occur, whereas in a normal operating mode, or in a system where no distinction is made, their invocation is usually unconditional.

Storage dumps generally allow the user to display all of core or only specified portions. They are frequently initiated during the execution of a program (snapshot dumps) as well as upon termination of the program (postmortem dumps). Generally, these dumps are highly formatted and are oriented to providing as much information about program status as can be presented.

Tracing facilities provide a sequential history of program execution. In general, the history records each particular instruction being executed, its address, the data fields affected, and their contents before and after the operation. Though there are many different types of traces, they all generally display the same types of information and are only distinguished by the occurrences that cause the information to be displayed. For example, several common types of traces are: full instruction tracing, instruction tracing within specified address limits, traces of interrupt occurrences, supervisor entry and exit sequences, and traces of instructions which modify selected words in main storage.

In an interactive time-sharing environment, testing and debugging facilities are usually quite extensive. In this environment the terminal user can normally examine, and modify task elements such as instructions, numeric values and coded information, insert breakpoints into a task, and control execution by directing or redefining the instruction executing sequence.

3.3 Logging and Accounting

Operating systems normally provide accounting and statistical information on job execution and resource utilization. In most systems this function simply records the following information at the termination of each job: job identification and termination status, number of records added to or deleted from each permanent file, CPU time utilized, time used by each channel and each device, number of lines printed, number of cards punched, and number of records written on system output units.

While most systems record this information, it is often left to the installation to write the accounting and analysis routines required to process the statistical summaries, although a few systems do provide system programs that can process this type of information.

Many systems also provide error statistic accumulation to identify hardware devices or programmers that have a greater than normal occurrence of error conditions. It is assumed that some form of repair or replacement would be undertaken in either circumstance.

Some systems also provide logout facilities which record the environment of the system during a system failure (CPU malfunction, power outage, etc.), so that a postmortem analysis may be conducted by software and hardware engineers.

3.4 Program Accessible System Description Maintenance

Almost all systems maintain a certain amount of descriptive information in a supervisor communication region, which may be interrogated by an application program. Three types of information are likely to be maintained: system defining, current system status, and individual job information.

Hardware configuration, operating system description, and values of system limits are examples of the types of system defining the information that may be maintained. System status information may include current device status and allocations; a list of currently executing jobs, interactive users, and active terminals; and the limits of allocated core storage. While the information provided in both categories is fairly sketchy in most systems, a general purpose application program or compiler can modify itself to conform to the implemented hardware and software characteristics of the particular installation by interrogating this information.

Individual job information generally includes the name, account number, core limits, and elapsed time and processing time used by each active job. Though it is perhaps questionable how the application program can utilize this information, very little overhead is involved in making the information available, since it must be maintained for normal system accounting purposes.

II. SYSTEM MANAGEMENT FUNCTIONS

1.0 OPERATING SYSTEM MANAGEMENT

Operating system management routines are provided by all systems to enable each installation to generate and maintain a version of the computer operating system.

1.1 System Generation

System generation is the process of tailoring and adapting a generalized operating system to the specific machine configuration and operational requirements of an installation. The generalized master operating system normally is provided every installation by the vendor. The master system contains all the operating system routines required for any allowable system configuration, as well as the vendor-developed optional routines that might be desired by a particular installation.

The master system also contains a series of executable programs which will initialize the system components for the system generation process and create the specific installation version of the operating system. In the larger systems this initialization package is transcribed to a mass storage medium. In the smaller systems it may be bootstrapped directly into core. The initialization package usually contains a basic executive program, an assembler, a loader, a linkage editor, and special routines necessary for implementing the system.

The actual system generation process consists of generating an operating system supervisor based on specifications supplied externally—usually through card or console control statements. This may be viewed as a multistep process. First, the installation's operating configuration is determined by interpreting specifications for the size of main memory, the number and address limits of each partition, the number of CPUs, the number of I/O controllers or processors, the number of communication controllers or processors, the type and designation of each I/O device, and the type and designation of each local and remote terminal. Additionally, this step usually includes differentiation of device roles such as distinguishing between user and operator terminal devices.

Next, installation tailoring criteria for system software features are interpreted and the features are incorporated into the generated system. For example, the establishment of memory protection limits, error recovery options, and accounting options would occur within this step. Many of the tailoring capabilities are highly dependent upon the type of operating system orientation the generalized system can support. For operating system supporting real-time processing, specifications for the number and type of interrupt levels, their respective priorities, and processing assignments are normally specifiable. Batch processing systems generally allow scheduling and dispatching priorities to be defined, while time-sharing systems permit authorized user declarations, passwords, accounting controls, resource limitations, and priorities to be enumerated.

Several systems also permit specifications of those operating systems supervisory modules that are to be core resident and those that are to be transient. The use of this feature is extremely desirable in those situations where the usage of system modules may vary greatly from installation to installation. By including frequently used routines as a part of the resident system, operating overhead can be reduced significantly.

The last step involves selecting from the wide range of operating system support programs, those that will be included in the system to satisfy the specific application requirements of the installation. By including only the appropriate compilers, data management systems, and utility programs needed by the installation, the overall size of the operating system file may be kept to a manageable level. Most systems also provide facilities for incorporating user-developed routines during this final step to augment the operating system support programs.

The resulting generated system is capable of supporting normal installation processing. In most cases the system file is maintained on an on-line immediate access device. When immediate access devices are not available, however, the file is normally maintained on magnetic tape. Unfortunately, tape systems, due to their serial orientation, tend to have a much higher overhead rate than the other systems.

1.2 System Maintenance

System maintenance allows an installation to update the operating system in response to changes in the operating environment or to changes of the programs within the operating system itself. The latter category is generally related to vendor-supplied updates which are distributed periodically. Consequently, this type of maintenance tends to be performed fairly regularly, and generally necessitates suspension of all other processing activity until the update is complete. Extensive updates to the system may involve a total regeneration of the system. Minor changes, however, may frequently be effected by simply replacing selected system modules.

Dynamic maintenance is a capability whereby a system can alter its physical configuration tables on-line to adjust to additional or deleted processing elements. This capability is particularly important for critical real-time systems. As described in Part I, Section 2.1, some systems also have the capability to fall back into a degraded state of operation (fail soft) upon the failure of some processing elements that cannot be replaced by others.

Some systems such as IBM's TSS/360 also allow the individual terminal user a limited system tailoring facility. These systems allow the programmer to adapt certain features of the system to his particular requirements without disrupting the utilization of the same features by other users. The terminal user thus creates his own system profile, which is activated only when he properly identifies himself. Therefore, each user may maintain an entirely distinct profile without affecting other users.

A few systems provide an on-line testing capability for updates or modifications to the operating system. If an error occurs within the system module being tested, the system will restore the unmodified version of the module. Consequently, modifications can be tested without requiring regeneration of the entire system. Further, the testing can be conducted in a live environment rather than in a special off-line mode. This approach to system checkout is most valuable in two environments: first, where there is such a diversity of system use (e.g., a time-sharing interactive and remote batch environment) that off-line tests could not exhaustively test the modified module; and second, where continuity of operations is critical (e.g., in some real-time environments).

2.0 PROGRAM MAINTENANCE

Program maintenance facilities support the maintenance and modification of application programs within the framework of the system. These facilities are distinct from the support features an application program can call on when executing; rather, the facilities treat the application program as a product by itself.

2.1 Library and Directory Maintenance

Many systems provide capabilities for maintaining one or more program types in indexed libraries. In general, a program library is a collection of routines or instruction sets which are all represented at the same code level. The code levels generally found in contemporary operating system libraries are: macro code, source program code, relocatable program code, executable code, and job control procedures. Macro libraries are composed of unique source code instruction sets which perform relatively small and distinct functions. When writing a program, a programmer may invoke a reference to this library by inserting a macro library call statement within the program source code statements. The language translator will recognize the call statement and replace it with the appropriate instruction sequence from the macro library during compilation.

Source program libraries contain routines or programs in the original programming language used by the programmer, such as COBOL and FORTRAN. Source programs may be combined with other routines for compilation or input directly to an assembler or compiler.

Relocatable program libraries contain the relocatable programs produced by the system compilers and assemblers. Generally speaking, a relocatable program is not directly executable and must be converted into a load module prior to being loaded and executed. Libraries of common relocatable programs are useful when a single routine such as an input/output routine for a transmission line is used by several programs. Retrieving it from the relocatable library saves recompiling the routine for each separate program requiring it.

Load module libraries consist of programs in executable form, which may be directly loaded into main storage and executed. Several systems make a distinction between user and system load module libraries. The former consist of various application programs, whereas the latter consist of the executable programs comprising the operating system proper. The advantage of maintaining separate libraries is that a user library may be taken off-line when it is not required.

Systems which require a great number of system control cards for the execution of a job will frequently provide a procedure library to contain defined system job control card sets. A single control card in input stream may then be used to reference such a procedure in the library. The system will, in turn, process the job control card set from the procedure library as if it had been in the input stream. This relieves the programmer of the responsibility of preparing an elaborate set of job control cards each time a job is submitted.

Various utility functions are provided for the maintenance and modification of these libraries. The primary facility is the cataloging function, which enters new elements into the appropriate library and updates the library directory. A system may provide both static and dynamic cataloging capabilities. Static cataloging requires the explicit execution of a library maintenance program to perform the cataloging function. Dynamic cataloging permits the user to add an element to a library without explicity invoking a librarian program. For example, a user may request the system to catalog a job or procedure upon successful execution.

Other library and directory maintenance facilities include copying, renaming, punching, listing, and displaying library elements as well as allocating or deallocating library space on secondary storage devices.

2.2 Load Module Generation

A load module is an instruction set that may be directly loaded into the main storage of the computer and executed. An absolute load module can only be loaded into one specific main storage location for execution, whereas a relocatable load module may be loaded into any main storage location. Most contemporary systems do not directly produce executable load module code from either the system compilers or assemblers. Rather, they produce what is termed relocatable code (which should not be confused with relocatable load modules). Relocatable code is an instruction set coded in machine language, but which for one reason or another is not directly executable. For example, it may not have been assigned physical main storage locations from which to execute, or it may have unresolved linkage sequences to the supervisor or to other instruction sets. The process of converting these programs to a format capable of being loaded and executed is called load module generation.

The element of the system that performs this function occurs in two different forms, depending on the system. In some systems it is an independent job step that must be scheduled explicitly; in others, it is a supervisor service that may be dynamically invoked by an executing task. Also, the resulting load module may in some systems be immediately executed, while in others it may require subsequent loading as part of a separate job step.

In many systems capabilities exist to combine the relocatable code modules produced by various language compilers with subroutines and other relocatable code modules to provide a single load module. When these modules are combined they are normally assigned to contiguous storage locations and the internal storage references within each module are appropriately modified. Next, the intermodule linkages (whereby one object module transfers control and data to another) are resolved by determining the newly assigned storage locations of the respective modules and inserting these addresses into the linkage sequence. This process is known by a number of different names, but the more frequently used terms are binding, linkage editing, and collecting.

Many systems also offer an additional capability that provides for the implicit inclusion of relocatable elements. If any intermodule linkages are unresolved at the end of the linkage editing process, the system assumes that the unresolved entries are implicit calls for relocatable subroutines and initiates a search of the system library for subroutines of the same name. This feature is particularly handy for program code generating routines (such as compilers, data management systems, and report generators), since an explicit list of supporting subroutines need not be specified during code generation.

3.0 COMPILER INTERFACES

Those operating system functions that provide supporting services to the system language compilers are the least standard of all operating system functional categories. Furthermore, differences can not be directly attributed to the size, orientation, or sophistication of the operating system. As a result, only a very few systems provide all of the functions noted below and several do not provide any. Because of this wide diversity, the functions are only described in general terms.

3.1 Executive Routine Support

Many operating systems grant the system compilers selected privileges which are not available to other nonsupervisory programs. For example, several systems allow the compiler to use communication tables within the resident executive for passing parameters and storing specifications about the compilation. Many systems also provide special job control cards for compilers; these include compilation parameters along with normal operating system parameters. In some cases the executive system may actually decode these parameters and place them in an appropriate compiler communication table.

Other types of executive routine support that are found in those systems recognize uniquely formatted compiler input/output files and provide nonstandard input and output symbionts for processing them. Finally, some systems also provide a series of compilation error codes which can be used as conditional scheduling parameters by subsequent tasks and steps within the job.

3.2 Library Support

A few systems provide and maintain unique libraries for the exclusive use of the system compilers. These libraries may take the form of compiler source program libraries, macro statement libraries, or compiler subroutine libraries. In general, the same maintenance facilities that are available for other system libraries are available for compiler-oriented libraries.

3.3 System Utility Program Support

Some compilers have the capability of generating linkage sequences to selected system utility programs in order that these facilities can become available to the compiler language programmer. For example, COBOL compilers commonly allow references to the system sort and merge functions. Other utility functions that can be invoked in some systems are the data management and data handling support functions described below in Part III.

4.0 MANAGEMENT SUPPORT UTILITIES

The management support utilities are primarily for the use of the system manager rather than the average user. Utility functions provided for normal users are described in Part III, Section 2.0. The functions described there enable the system manager to add and maintain sequential and direct access volumes, simulate certain system facilities for testing purposes, obtain statistics of system and device performance, and initiate recovery from total system failures. In many cases these routines may not directly interface with the system supervisor and may be executed independently.

4.1 Peripheral Device Support

The function of peripheral device support is normally invoked when a new volume such as a system component is to be added. The volume preparation function writes a standard system label on the volume, formats the records and/or tracks where track formatting is required (such as for disk files), creates any necessary volume directory entries, allocates space for additional directories, communication buffers, and so on. Only upon completion of this function is a volume available for normal system use.

Volume maintenance functions may also provide diagnostic routines to verify the correctness of all volumes in the system. Normally, these routines perform a surface analysis of the volume to detect failing surface areas and identify or replace any defective areas. Certain file-purging functions may also be invoked to erase selected areas on a volume or to clear main or secondary storage.

4.2 System Simulation Routines

The capability of simulating certain system functions is very important during the development of many real-time and telecommunication-oriented programs. For example, if certain real-time programs can only be invoked by the occurrence of specific interrupts, these programs must be tested by providing the actual interrupt. This may be difficult to effect or may disrupt the operational system. Consequently, a capability to simulate the occurrence of the interrupts and to thereby invoke the program permits much greater flexibility in program testing.

Similarly, an exhaustive test of communication and line support programs might require a scenario so complex that it could not be performed from available support terminals. Again, the capability of simulating the arrival of a series of communication messages provides a needed testing capability. Many of these routines might also be used by the system manager to test and validate the operating system itself. Unfortunately, few systems provide extensive capabilities in this area. Those that do are primarily small systems for real-time applications rather than large, general purpose systems.

4.3 System Measurement Routines

Systems measurement routines enable the system manager to obtain various statistics about the operational use of the system. Typical statistics include job throughput times, file or device utilization figures, and the identification of bottleneck conditions. In addition, there are a few systems that provide visual displays of current and past system utilization reflecting error statistics on all configured devices, channel usage, memory allocation, programs in core, programs swapped out of core, and processor time consumed by each program at that point in time.

The proper interpretation of these statistics enables the system manager to better "tune" the operating configuration to the actual processing environment by adding new files or devices, redistributing files between devices, modifying the scheduling and/or dispatching algorithms, and by changing the degree of multiprogramming.

Unfortunately, too few systems provide the necessary statistics to adequately measure system performance. For this reason several independent software vendors provide supplementary programs to support the operating system in the performance of this function.

4.4 Stand-Alone Utilities

These routines are primarily used when the system has failed and normal diagnostic routines are incapable of restarting the system. Two types of routines are provided. The first type includes the status display routines that produce core dumps, file dumps, and dumps of selected diagnostic logout areas. These dumps are presented for interpretation by a hardware or software engineer to determine the cause of the failure.

The second type consists of recovery support routines which enable the system to reconstruct much of its pre-failure environment and to reinitiate processing by rebuilding selected queues, reloading various programs, and restarting checkpointed programs. The recovery support functions are most often found in systems oriented to supporting real-time-or communication-based processing.

III. DATA MANIPULATION FUNCTIONS

1.0 DATA MANAGEMENT

Data management functions consist of file management facilities, I/O support facilities, and data management system facilities. File management facilities provide file support for the system files as entities rather than for the individual data records within the files. Support for the latter is provided by the other two data management categories.

I/O support facilities enable a program to access and process individual data records within the file. These facilities are normally invoked by using macro instructions within the problem program and eliminate the need for programmers to be concerned with many of the problems of reading and writing data records.

Data management systems allow a user with limited programming interests to perform on a data file functions such as retrieving and displaying selected portions of the file. Generally, data management systems are adjuncts to an operating system and are more or less self-contained, depending on the architecture of the particular system. Consequently, a data management system will make use of many of the features provided by other operating system functions in its own internal design.

1.1 File Management Facilities

As indicated above, file management facilities are oriented toward controlling the various data files within the system. File management functions are invoked to locate on-line and off-line files, permit or restrict user access to files, and to provide backup and restoration services in case of file damage.

1.1.1 File Location Recognition

In most systems permanent data files are identified by labels assigned by the user or the system. File labels may be composed of such items as the file identifier, the file edition number, the owner's name and account number, and perhaps a file utilization privacy code. Several systems permit file names to be a composite of several names in order to provide hierarchical levels of file indexing.

In larger batch processing and time-sharing systems the location of all permanent data files known to the system is usually maintained in a master directory or catalog. A file can then be located for processing by searching the master directory of on-line and off-line files. However, if the system does not maintain a directory, a sequential label comparison must be performed physically against each on-line file until the desired file is located. In this environment, there is also usually no capability to locate off-line files; instead they must be presented to the system by the operator.

Whenever master directories or catalogs are maintained, various cataloging controls are available to the user. In general, he may add new file descriptions to the catalog and modify or delete existing descriptions. He may also be allowed to extend or contract the amount of space made available to an existing file or to alter the list of authorized file users. Additionally, all of the features available for maintaining system library directories (as described in Part II, Section 2.1) are usually available for file directories as well.

1.1.2 File Access Control

The designation and restriction of file access may be a function under control of the operating system or it may merely be established by a set of installation programming conventions. When controlled by the system, the owner of a file can usually designate that the file is to be maintained for his use only, for the use of a designated group only, or for general use. Frequently, the owner may also specify the level of access afforded each designated user. For example, access may be restricted to a read-only level for some users while others are allowed full read and write capabilities.

Concurrent access control is required to maintain the scheduling and handling of concurrent or simultaneous requests for a data file from separate programs or users in a multiprogramming or time-sharing environment. Basically, the control function must determine if multiple user access can be permitted or whether the file must be restricted to single user access. In situations where multiple users may access a single file simultaneously, it is usually desirable to grant any number of them read-only access, but to restrict write access to a single user at a time.

1.1.3 Backup and Restoration Facilities

Most file-oriented systems require a capability to recover from inadvertent damage to the file system. Consequently, some operating systems provide facilities for maintaining various types of backup files—checkpoint files, transaction data files, and previous versions of the data file (grandfather files). These files may be available to the system on either an on-line or off-line basis. Restoration functions may be initiated automatically by the system (particularly in real-time systems) or may require operator intercession.

1.2 I/O Support Facilities

An important distinction is made in describing the levels of I/O support provided by a system. The basic level of support, physical input/output, is provided by routines that initiate the actual data transmission process and provide program access to the data in the format of transmission. This function includes most of the features discussed in Part I, Section 1.2.

The extended level of support, logical input/output, allows manipulation of data without regard to the physical structure of the data. It thus serves as an intermediary between user data-handling operations and the physical input/output services of the system. All systems provide physical input/output support and all but the smallest systems provide logical input/output support.

1.2.1 Data Access Control

The most common file access methods supported by contemporary operating systems are the sequential, indexed, keyed, random, and telecommunications organizations. Each method can provide for data storage and retrieval on a physical or logical record level.

Sequential access methods process records serially and read or write them consecutively on a storage volume. Sequential access may be provided for data stored on any secondary storage medium, although certain storage media such as magnetic tape obviously dictate a file organization of this type.

Indexed access methods create and maintain files which, in addition to the data records, have directories of selected record field values and their corresponding record addresses. Records may then be located by searching the directory rather than the file. Some form of immediate access storage, such as disk, is necessary for indexed access methods to have value.

Keyed access methods rely on a selected data field within each record to uniquely identify the record. This data field, called the record key, frequently corresponds to the record identification code, though it need not do so. Keyed access is useful for secondary storage devices which have a physical design that features hardware-implemented search instructions. In such systems a record request will cause the read/write mechanism of the storage medium to scan the entire file in search of a selected record key. The technique is advantageous, since processor time need not be spent in scanning secondary storage and may thus be employed with other execution functions. The technique is also frequently augmented by software that isolates a portion of the file prior to issuing the keyed search in order to avoid a scan of the entire file.

Random access methods read and write records without regard to the physical sequence in which they are stored. Consequently, records stored in this type of organization must have some type of identification code that will enable the record location to be determined. Usually, an algorithm is used to convert a unique record identification into a unique storage address on an immediate access storage device.

Telecommunication data is usually composed of character strings of varying lengths. While not a file in a classical sense, most systems provide assistance in accessing and processing the relatively unformatted messages that accumulate in the system communication buffers. This assistance normally handles all communication between the computing system and remotely located terminals. The functions performed include allocation of storage for message buffering, polling terminals to determine if any have messages to send, recognizing message priorities, analyzing message headers to determine where input and output messages are to be routed, checking the sequence numbers of incoming messages, checking transmission errors, and maintaining input and output message queues.

1.2.2 Data Blocking/Deblocking Control

Blocking combines two or more individual records into one physical data block. Deblocking isolates the individual records within a physical data block. Record lengths may be fixed, variable, or undefined, and all of the types may be blocked or unblocked.

Operating systems that provide only physical input/output support require the user to perform his own record blocking and deblocking functions. Operating systems which provide logical input/output support allow the user to operate on all data at the individual record level without regard to the structure of the physical block. Blocking and deblocking are usually accomplished by moving data between the input/output buffers and a user processing area or by using special location pointers to isolate and process information within the buffer.

1.2.3 Label Processing

Most systems provide facilities for writing and checking file labels when a data file is opened or closed. Many systems also permit the user to specify his own labels and to supply special routines for processing them. A few of the smaller systems provide no label generation and checking facilities, and all label processing functions must be performed by the user.

1.3 Data Management System Facilities

A data management system is a group of integrated routines developed to create and maintain an organized collection of related data, known as the data base, and to interrogate the data base and produce various types of formatted reports. A data management system will create files from various input sources; maintain these files by additions, deletions, and alterations; create new files and reorganize and merge existing files; select data via user-prepared queries; make computations on this data; and produce reports in system-defined or user-specified formats. A data management system may be designed to operate in either a batch or interactive mode.

1.3.1 Control Specification

A data management system must be provided with a set of specifications or commands delineating the jobs it is to perform. The system interprets these specifications, and generates functional modules to perform the selected jobs. These modules may take the form of interpretive tables or executable programs or subroutines. Generally, the system will maintain an extensive library of functional subroutines, which may be incorporated as needed into the final support modules. These subroutines range from arithmetic and data conversion routines to file searching and positioning capabilities. The generation of the resulting support modules is analogous to the process used by a compiler to convert user code into machine executable code.

1.3.2 Data File Generation and Maintenance

Data file generation and maintenance is concerned with defining the internal structure of a file, allocating space for the file on a storage device, processing input transactions against the file, performing logical and interactive maintenance on the file, and reorganizing the file when the structure must be modified.

Internal Structure Definition. The most common file structures are sequential, hierarchical, indexed, list, and ring. A sequential structure is one in which the data elements are all of equal rank and are maintained in a serial order. In a hierarchical structure the data elements are classified and stored according to a ranking scheme. An indexed structure is one in which portions of the file are reserved as keys to locate information in other parts of the file. A list structure is one wherein each data element contains the address of, and thereby points to, a successor element. A ring structure is a circular list structure in which the last data element points back to the first.

These file structures should not be confused with the access methods discussed earlier. The access methods relate to the set of routines a programmer may use to store and retrieve data records from secondary storage devices. The data management file structures refer to a type of file organization that permits a user to classify and store data. The data management routines will utilize whatever access methods are available to implement the various file-structuring forms.

Secondary Storage Allocation. Techniques for allocating storage to data files vary widely from system to system. While the more sophisticated systems dynamically allocate and reallocate storage as required, many systems leave this function almost entirely to the user. In the latter case, associated functions such as protection from inadvertent destruction may also be under user control. At either end of the spectrum, however, the function generally includes production of requested or periodic reports describing the status of allocated and unallocated secondary storage.

Input Transaction Processing. Input transaction processing provides for defining input data element formats, validating the data elements as they are entered, converting them into internal formats, and storing them in the data file. Input format definitions may be established prior to the entry of the data into the system or the data entry may be self-defining.

Prior to acceptance, the data elements may be subjected to one or more validation tests. Range verification may be used to ensure that a data element is between a minimum and a maximum value or to determine if an element is less than or greater than a specific value. An internal comparison test may be used to compare data elements to those already accepted by the system and stored within the data base. A masked comparison may be used to examine one or more specific characters within the data element. Sequence checking may be used to locate data elements which are not entering the system in accordance with an established ordering. The system may be designed so that an element which does not satisfy its validation criteria is rejected or is conditionally accepted and flagged in a description of the transaction processing. Additionally, some systems provide for operator intervention to accept, reject, or correct data that does not satisfy the criteria.

Logical and Interactive Maintenance. Logical file maintenance permits conditional or programmed updating of a data file. Logical maintenance may or may not be transaction-oriented. If it is, the transaction updates the object file only when specified criteria are satisfied. Nontransaction-oriented maintenance is usually accomplished via internal actions generated by a computer pseudo-language program. For example, a logical maintenance job might specify the deletion of every record written after a given calendar date, or conversely, the retention of only those records written between two given calendar dates.

Interactive maintenance, as its name implies, is the updating of a data file from an on-line terminal. Almost all interactive maintenance applications utilize logical file maintenance features. Prior to initiating the actual transaction the terminal user must usually establish logical parameters to isolate records of interest.

File Reorganization. This function provides for reorganization of one or more existing data files into a new composite output file. Data fields may be added, deleted, or changed in size or type under the restructuring process. For example, a single fixed-length field might be respecified as a repeating variable length field. When the reorganization involves more than one input file, the resultant output file is composed of several merged, and possible restructured, data fields from each of the input files. This file maintenance function, unlike the others, is usually invoked on a rather limited basis. Consequently, the function is often performed by a self-contained adjunct to the system, and often uses its own control specifications.

1.3.3 Data Qualification and Retrieval

Almost all data management systems are designed so that data qualification and retrieval may be accomplished in either a batch or interactive mode. In the batch mode, the data base may be interrogated by individually prepared logical queries or by prestored logical queries in which specific operands can be altered. In the interactive mode interrogation may be by a cue-response form of query, by a prompting query which "guides" the user through the interrogation, or by a user-programmed query. Each record satisfying the parameter of the query may be directly displayed, retained on an intermediate file for subsequent processing, or passed on to another portion of the data management system, such as data output or file maintenance. Thus a single data qualification scheme generally serves the entire data management system.

The basic format of a qualification statement takes the form of a data base field, a logical operator, and an operand. For example, AGE EQUALS 14, where AGE is a field in the data base, EQUALS is the Boolean operator signifying equality, and 14, a numeric operand for comparison. While almost every system permits the full range of Boolean operators (equal, greater than, less than, not equal, etc.), some systems provide additional types such as quantitative or occurrence operators, arithmetic or statisical operators, and application-dependent operators. Complex statements may frequently be formed by joining simple qualification expressions with the logical connectors AND, OR, NOT and by nesting simple qualifications at several levels. The operand of a qualification statement may be a constant, another data field, the result of another qualification statement in the same retrieval, or an arithmetic expression.

Some data management systems limit qualifications and retrieval statements to a single file search. Others permit several files to be searched as the result of a single request. The more sophisticated systems also provide interfile searching whereby a second file is searched for qualifying information based on the results of the primary file search.

1.3.4 Data Output

Almost all data management systems produce certain standard reports such as a listing of directories or a listing of input transactions processed against a file. Additionally, data management systems often provide one or more methods of report definition. In some systems this may take the form of report program generators or the capability to include user programs developed by programming technicians. Additionally, many systems include schemes whereby an interactive or batch user with limited programming interests can influence the form of output data. In either case, the data output function of a data management system normally operates either on the results of a user's retrieval or on an entire system file. Reports may normally be produced on printed listings, punched cards, tape, or on-line display devices.

Controls of data output include labeling, data formatting, and pagination control. Labeling consists of specifying page headers, trailers and data labels. Data formatting includes character insertion or deletion, affixing mathematical or commercial symbols, punctuation, and element decoding prior to output. Pagination provides top-of-form control for printed output and forward/backward spacing frame control for CRT devices.

Both the capability to control these items and the extent of intrinsic support vary widely among systems. For example, some systems will include support facilities to develop horizontal and vertical displays appropriate to the indicated output device, while others leave such processes entirely to the user, and simply truncate if the output exceeds device capacity.

2.0 DATA-HANDLING UTILITIES

The data-handling utility programs are generally fairly uncomplicated routines of general usefulness to the installation. Classically, these routines were independent programs which were loaded and executed when required. However, in contemporary systems they have been incorporated into the operating system and are activated by a program call, a system control card or an operator key-in. These utilities rarely interface directly with an executing program, though they are frequently included as a separate job step in a multistep job.

2.1 Display Facilities

The utility routines that produce visual output as final products are termed display facilities. While the printer is the most common output medium, CRTs, console typewriters, and similar devices may also be utilized by various display routines.

The most common display facilities provided are for main storage (by "dumps"), system catalogs, tables, and directories. Other display facilities are generally provided for data stored on any secondary storage media supported by the system. Typically, these include tape to printer and disk to printer. Since these media conversions are normally performed expressly for visual display to human consumers, they often incorporate special formats and visual aids in addition to simple data translation (e.g., octal to decimal). Generally, the formats and visual aids are predetermined, although some systems allow the user to influence the output by exercising certain options.

2.2 Peripheral Device Support

The utility routines that provide peripheral device support perform such functions as volume positioning, media conversion, data editing, and test file support. Volume positioning may be used to backspace, forward space, or rewind a magnetic tape, or to locate a file on a tape or direct access volume, or to locate a specific record within a file.

The media conversion facilities simply permit data to be copied from one secondary storage medium to another. Generally, these facilities are provided for all combinations of peripheral devices supported by the system. Typical examples are: card to tape, tape to card, and tape to disk. Of course, these transfers between media may be accompanied by additional formatting or data translation. Unlike the display facilities discussed above, however, these transfers are not performed expressly for human consumption. As a consequence, media conversion tends to be straightforward and occurs within the limits of the media involved. Thus a card to tape conversion may be expected to duplicate the data from each card in sequential 80 character tape records.

An extension of the media conversion facilities discussed above provides facilities for dumping and reloading secondary storage. These facilities are generally employed for backup file creation and for storage compaction.

Additional data-handling features available in many systems support file- rather than device-oriented processing. These features are included here, however, due to their basic similarity to the media conversion facilities. For example, data editing facilities permit the user to scan a data file to detect logical data errors (e.g., out-of-sequence conditions) and to compare files residing on separate media. Furthermore, several systems provide test file support utilities which can be used to develop device-oriented data files for use in application program testing.

3.0 SORTING AND MERGING

Programs that sort or merge sets of data records normally comprise a part of the operating system. The sorting function takes strings of unordered records and sequences them according to a given key or set of keys within each record. The merging function, on the other hand, takes separate strings of records which have already been ordered by keys and produces a composite ordered output string. The design of most sort programs is such that the unordered records are placed into ordered strings and then merged. Consequently, a single program usually suffices to perform both functions.

3.1 Sort Module Development

The first phase of the sorting or merging process is to develop the programming module that will actually perform the sorting or merging function. Two basic approaches are used. The first provides a general set of tables which enable a general purpose sort program to tailor itself to the specific sorting requirements. The other actually generates a special purpose sort program specifically designed for the application.

In both cases control parameters are interpreted that describe the characteristics of the available hardware: available core space and the amount and type of intermediate storage available (e.g., tape and disk). Additional control parameters describe the characteristics of the data: record size, number and relative location of control fields, number of records, and so forth. Finally, still other control parameters are introduced, which permit special options: ascending or descending sequences, user-specified collating sequences, special data conversion requirements. The control parameters are normally edited, and if no errors are found, are used as the basis for developing the executable sort module.

3.2 Sort Module Execution

The sort module execution phase normally consists of three separate steps—input reading and string creation, intermediate string sequencing, and final string merging.

The first step reads the input data from wherever it is located, isolates the sort key, and modifies the input record by any user-written routines that have been specified. The purpose of the first step is to create a series of sequenced strings from the unsequenced input. Consequently, as input records are read, they are sorted internally and written onto an intermediate device as a sequenced string. Three types of sorting are possible: a record sort where the full record is written out; a field select sort, where certain fields are deleted from the record prior to writing it out; and a tag sort, where the record is stored on an intermediate device and only its sort key and address are used. Several internal sorting techniques are used to create the sequenced strings. Among the more popular are tournament, exchange, radix, and sieve sorts.

The second step merges the strings produced in the first step until there are as many strings as the order of merge. Thus if the order of merge is four, then the strings would be merged until four sequenced strings or less remained. The types of merging techniques used in this phase vary with the characteristics of the intermediate devices available. For example, if magnetic tapes are used as the intermediate storage device and if the tape drive has a read backward feature, a polyphase merge is the most economical. Other techniques used are: balanced merges, cascade sorts, and oscillating sorts. Each technique has advantages and disadvantages, based on the hardware capabilities and the number of the intermediate storage devices.

The final step is the merge proper operation, whereby the strings are merged one more time to create a single sequenced string. If a merge function was initially specified, the first two steps are bypassed and only this step is executed. In either case, the records are reformatted to their final output appearance and written on the output device. Provision is usually made for user-written routines to modify each record prior to placing it on the output device. When a tag sort is used, the user may also be given the option of accepting the sorted record address list rather than producing the actual output string.

7
OPERATING SYSTEMS FOR SMALL COMPUTERS

OVERVIEW

This and the next two chapters summarize the characteristics of some of the many operating systems available. In preparing these summaries, a major question has been what to leave undescribed. To summarize each in terms of the full outline given in Appendix A would make a very expensive book.

The solution to this problem, selected for use here, is to condense the full outline, concentrating on the executive and control functions. This condensation can serve as a useful base of knowledge for anyone who wants to explore further any of the operating systems summarized. This does not downplay the importance of the system management and data manipulation aspects of operating systems, but rather does focus attention on the popular executive and control aspects.

The condensation of the full outline is concentrated on four topics: job management (1.1 from Part I of the full outline), I/O control (1.2 from Part I), diagnostic error processing (2.0 from Part I), and processing support (3.0 from Part I). Each of these in the summaries is assigned its own new number, 1 through 4 inclusive. Subtopics within each go in a hierarchial form, as before. But the numbering assigned differs from that used in the Appendix A outline, and is summarized below, with the Appendix A number shown in parentheses.

1.0 Job Management (1.0)
    1.1 Job control (1.1)
        1.1.1 Scheduling (1.1.1)
        1.1.2 Resource allocation (1.1.2)
        1.1.3 Program loading (1.1.3)
        1.1.4 Event monitoring (1.1.4)
        1.1.5 Program termination processing (1.1.5)

      1.2 System communication (1.3)
           1.2.1 System start up (1.3.1)
           1.2.2 Job control communication (1.3.2)
           1.2.3 I/O stream control (1.3.3)
           1.2.4 Resource status modification (1.3.4)
           1.2.5 System status interrogation (1.3.5)
      1.3 Recovery processing (1.4)
           1.3.1 Checkpointing (1.4.1)
           1.3.2 Restarting (1.4.2)
2.0 I/O control (1.2)
      2.1 I/O scheduling (1.2.1)
      2.2 Data transfer (1.2.2)
      2.3 Remote terminal support (1.2.4)
      2.4 File handling (1.1 from Part III)
3.0 Diagnostic error processing (2.0)
      3.1 Hardware error control (2.1)
      3.2 Program error control (2.2)
      3.3 Interface error control (2.3)
4.0 Processing support (3.0)
      4.1 Timing service (3.1)
      4.2 Testing and debugging service (3.2)
      4.3 Logging and accounting (3.3)
      4.4 System description maintenance (3.4)

Using this condensed outline, this chapter presents summaries of operating systems for the following computers: SEL 810A/810B, DEC PDP-8, XDS Sigma 2, and IBM 1800. These are all small computers (the first two are minicomputers), without the internal or external storage, or the peripheral equipment to support a large complex operating system.

Each of these operating systems, therefore, is relatively simple. Yet each provides different ways of meeting the user needs discussed in Chapter 1, partly in reflection of the different classes of common uses for the respective computers, and partly in reflection of the configuration of hardware features. Specific hardware features combined with the vendors' desire to win customers in certain application areas (such as process control) motivate the vendors to offer differing operating systems.

The operating system for the SEL 810A/810B is the simplest one summarized in this book—and is appropriate, therefore, as the first one summarized. It provides for executing single-task jobs sequentially one after the other.

The operating system for the DEC PDP-8 is a time-sharing operating system. It supports concurrent use of the computer from simple terminals. The TSS/8 is the simplest of the time-sharing operating systems summarized in this book.

The Real Time Batch Monitor for the XDS Sigma 2 computer is designed to handle real-time operations in a well-defined environment (in terms of priorities). It is the simplest of the operating systems for real-time operations summarized in this book, and is a simple multiprograming operating system.

The MPX (Multiprograming Executive) operating system for the IBM 1800 is more complex. It, too, is designed for real-time applications but offers different options in the handling of priorities among the application (user or problem) programs.

SEL 810A/810B OPERATING SYSTEM

The SEL 810A/810B Operating System is a modular serial processing system designed to facilitate job-to-job transition. The SEL 810B computer is a fairly small computer ranging in memory size from 8K to 32K words (equivalent to 16K to 64K bytes). The operating system under discussion is the most basic system offered by SEL for this computer. It has been selected to illustrate the functional requirements of a very fundamental serial processing system. The system is simple and does not support the many functions found in a more complex system.

1.0 JOB MANAGEMENT

The SEL 810A/810B operating system is a modular software system. The maximum memory required by the OS for controlling the operation of a particular function, at any one time, will be 2K words (equivalent to 4K bytes) of main storage. Contained within the reserved storage, the OS consists of resident and nonresident components. The resident portion of the OS is called the "control system." The remainder of the system's reserved memory is used for processing modules and system service routines which are brought into memory from the system residence (which may be tape or disk), as needed. All memory other than the system area is allocated to the user, and contains user file tables, user programs, assemblers, compilers, and so forth.

1.1 Job Control

The control system consists of an executive control routine, absolute loader, I/O handlers, conversion routines, and a control command interpreter. This control system remains resident in memory once it has been loaded. The only exception to this is the I/O handlers; whenever a new device assignment is made, the appropriate handler is overlayed. The executive routine controls the initiation, execution and termination of all programming operations for the single user partition.

1.1.1 Scheduling

Programs are scheduled serially as specified by control commands or by dynamic load requests from an executing program.

1.1.2 Resource Allocation

A fixed portion of main storage is allocated to the resident control system; the remainder of main storage is allocated to the currently executing user or utility program.

Storage access protection is an optional hardware feature and is not mentioned in the OS documentation.

All I/O devices are allocated to the currently executing program. I/O units are referenced and device assignments are determined by control commands or by dynamic requests from the executing program.

1.1.3 Program Loading

Programs are loaded by a relocatable loader which resolves external references (references to locations outside a program or subroutine) at load time. Program (or subroutine) loading may be initiated by control commands or by supervisor requests from the executing program. A program may thus dynamically load overlay subroutines.

1.1.4 Event Monitoring

A program, once loaded, is given control of the CPU and continues to execute until it returns control to the system.

Two interrupt levels are standard on the 810B; additional interrupts are an optional hardware feature.

The system does not provide facilities for placing prespecified limits on program output or execution time.

1.1.5 Program Termination Processing

Normal termination occurs once a program has completed its processing and has returned control to the supervisor. The supervisor places the system in a ready state and waits for the next job assignment. All system resources are then available to the succeeding job.

Job summary statistics are not maintained by the OS, nor are any special abnormal termination procedures provided.

1.2 System Communication

1.2.1 System Startup

The operator must perform a series of manual operations to bootstrap the system from tape or disk and place it in a ready state. When the system is in a ready state (which also occurs after program termination), the operator enters job control commands to initiate processing.

1.2.2 Job Control Communication

Almost all job control commands can be entered either through a control input device or issued as supervisor requests by executing programs. Functions controlled by these commands include I/O device assignment, program loading, and file directory maintenance.

1.2.3 Input/Output Stream Control

A control command interpreter is loaded by the executive when a control command is recognized. The interpreter decodes the command and then returns control to the executive, supplying the information needed by the executive to perform the assigned task.

System messages are output to the I/O unit assigned as the "control output" device. Messages are output to indicate errors or the completion of program loading or processing.

1.2.4 Resource Status Modification

I/O device assignments may be changed at any time by external control commands or internal supervisor requests.

1.2.5 System Status Interrogation

No system status interrogation facilities are provided by the system.

1.3 Recovery Processing

Neither checkpoints nor restarting facilities are provided by the OS.

2.0 I/O CONTROL

2.1 I/O Scheduling

The system provides six core resident I/O handlers to control the transfer of data to and from memory and to perform requested peripheral functions. Each serves to control one of the following six functions: symbolic input and output, binary input and output, and control input and output. There are several versions of each handler; the device assigned to a specific I/O function is determined by which version of that I/O handler is core resident when it is called. External control commands or internal supervisor requests are used to assign specific I/O devices (and hence specific handlers) to each of the six functions.

Alternate routing control is not automatically provided by OS, but the operator or user can easily reassign I/O devices, as described above.

2.2 Data Transfer

Data transfer takes place to and from user specified buffers. Data code translation is performed automatically, as part of the I/O operation. The specific type of code conversion performed is dependent upon the I/O function being performed and the type of I/O device assigned to that function. No blocking/deblocking control is supported by the OS. All the I/O handlers are oriented strictly toward sequential access methods.

2.3 Remote Terminal Support

Remote terminal support is not provided by the system.

2.4 File Handling

Programs stored on disk may be given one to six character names. The OS maintains a directory to the file of named programs. Neither symbolic data file reference nor access limitation control is provided by the system. All label handling must be performed by the user.

3.0 DIAGNOSTIC ERROR PROCESSING

Error control is mentioned only briefly in the information received. Evidently, when an error occurs, the system notifies the operator and halts. When the operator presses the console "Start" button, after (presumably) correcting the error, the system resumes operations.

4.0 PROCESSING SUPPORT

4.1 Timing Service

A real time clock is available as an optional hardware feature on the SEL 810B, but specific timer services are not provided by the system.

4.2 Testing and Debugging Service

A debug utility program is provided to assist in debugging a program while it is in memory. The debug program permits a user to modify specified memory locations, dump and reload memory areas, enter breakpoints, search for specified address references, and initiate execution at a specified address.

4.3 Logging and Accounting

No job charge summaries or error statistics are maintained by the OS.

4.4 System Description Maintenance

No system status or definition information is maintained by the system for user interrogation.

DEC PDP-8 TIME-SHARING SYSTEM (TSS/8)

The Time-Sharing System (TSS/8) for the PDP-8 family of computers is a general purpose, stand-alone system offering each user a library of system, service, and utility programs. The programs provide for compiling, assembling, editing, loading, saving, calling, and debugging user programs on-line. From one to a maximum of 32 users are permitted in the largest configuration.

1.0 JOB MANAGEMENT
1.1 Job Control
1.1.1 Scheduling

The Time-Sharing System for the PDP-8 provides for a maximum of four concurrent users in the smallest machine, up to a maximum of 32 concurrent users on the largest machine. Several programs are run concurrently by employing the technique of bringing a program into core from the disk, allowing it to execute for a short time, marking the state in which its execution is stopped, returning it to the disk, and picking up the next user program.

User programs are serviced regularly on a round-robin (time-slice) basis. After a user program has been executed, it is placed last in the queue of user programs waiting to run. Each program is allowed to run a fixed interval of time and then it is exchanged for the next user program. If only one program is in a condition to run, it is allowed to run without interruption.

To schedule a program for initiation, the user logs-in on his console. If the console from which he logged-in is free, and there is an available disk track, and the user has provided a valid account number/password, the user is logged into the system. If any of the above conditions fail to be satisfied, the user is not permitted to log into the system. Once logged in, the user's account number and password are associated with a job number and that job number are associated with a specific disk-swapping track and the user console. The account number also establishes ownership of the input buffer attached to the user program and the output buffer attached to the printer on the user console. Once logged into the system, the user receives fixed time quantums for program execution up until the time he removes himself from the system by logging out.

The user is in continual control of the execution of his program and any succeeding programs via the on-line console.

Thus, forms of conditional scheduling can be exercised via appropriate on-line user commands.

1.1.2 Resource Allocation

Each user is assigned 4K words of core memory for program execution and a corresponding 4K words of disk for temporary storage of his core image when it is swapped out by the monitor. There is no provision for expanding beyond the 4K core space; this area must provide sufficient core for buffer and I/O areas. The input and output stream buffer areas, however, are allocated independently of the program area.

Input/output devices may be allocated either by user requests from the console or by supervisor requests from the problem program. The device remains assigned to the user program until it is either released by a user or program command or the user logs out from his console. Devices are allocated by the specific device identification.

The user may also request that additional consoles be slaved to his console. By slaving other consoles, he makes them available as additional input/output devices and removes their ability to submit and control programs. They regain the ability to submit and control programs only when they have been released by this user.

Since each user, in effect, has complete control of the system during his time quantum, the only subroutines that can be allocated to the user are the various monitor routines. There is no problem of reentrancy or reusability, since only one user is in core at any one time and all monitor functions are completed prior to swapping the user out of core.

1.1.3 Program Loading

Program loading consists of placing a user program onto the user disk track. There are three methods in which a user can perform this function: (1) he may prepare an octal program at a console, using a degugging technique such as the system supplied DDT-8 and save the image core on disk, (2) he may load a previously saved core image, or (3) he may load the binary output file of a previous assembly or compilation. Once loaded, the program is executed via the swapping mechanism. The mechanism is the heart of the Time-Sharing System. In TSS/8 the entire 4K core memory is written onto disk each time the user's quantum expires, and the entire memory is read back into core each time the user receives control of the system.

A program may be swapped out of core memory for a number of different reasons. Some of these are: (1) the quantum of time has expired; (2) the program has requested that the quantum of time be terminated; (3) the program has filled an output buffer or has requested input but the bufler is empty; and (4) the program has tried to execute an illegal instruction.

In the smaller versions of TSS/8, core is written onto the user disk track prior to loading the subsequent program. However, under versions of TSS/8 with additional core memory, overlapping the running time of one user program with the swapping time of another, is permitted.

1.1.4 Event Monitoring

Dispatching is handled by a round-robin scheduling algorithm with the exception that programs having disk requests pending are run out of turn to optimize disk usage. The scheduling routine decides whether to remove the current program from core and if so, which program is to be run next.

Each user program that is considered ready to run is activated by the following conditions: (1) when an output buffer is almost empty, thus assuring continuous output of information to the user console; (2) when an input buffer is almost full, thus assuring continuous input of information from the user console; (3) when input requested by a user has arrived; (4) when a user determined activation condition has been satisfied; and (5) when the user specifically commands the system to begin execution.

The user program can specify conditions which will cause the program to be activated. These conditions are called delimiters. A delimiter may be some specific type of character appearing in the console input stream or it may be a change in the source of characters. The input buffer becoming full is always a delimiter. The general input routine places all incoming characters in the user's input buffer until a delimiter is encountered. When a delimiter appears, the user program is alerted and activated to receive all the characters in the input buffer.

On an interrupt basis, the device service routines receive information from all input devices, distribute that information out to the appropriate buffers, and inform the activation routine when a user program must be activated to receive its information. The device service routines also accept output from user programs, buffer it, and send it to output devices whenever the devices are able to receive it.

One important instruction available to the user program is

called *quantum synchronization*. This instruction is used to ensure a full-time quantum to perform some critical operation. When issued, the user program is dismissed so that a full-time quantum will be available to perform the following operations. during the next cycle of the round robin.

1.1.5 Program Termination Processing

A program may terminate processing by issuing a halt request to the system monitor. The system monitor will then request additional input control statements from the user console.

The user releases control of the system via a log-out command. This command disconnects all consoles and temporary disk tracks that the user owns, places the programs in a free state, and resets all devices and consoles that were owned by that user. The routine also writes an account record on the disk showing how much computing time and how much console time were used by the user's program.

1.2 System Communication

1.2.1 System Startup

There are two types of system startups that must be considered for TSS/8. The first type is the startup of a user console. This startup is accomplished when a user logs into the system. At this time, the user establishes ownership of the input buffer. An output buffer is attached to his console and the disk area reserved for swapping his program into and out of core.

The second form of system startup refers to the initialization of the TSS/8 monitor. No information was provided on this form of startup.

1.2.2 Job Control Communication

All job control statements are submitted from the user's console and each statement is preceded by a specific character that alerts the monitor that a job control statement follows. Many of these statements may also be issued from a problem program via specific monitor requests.

Whenever the job control call character is encountered, the monitor routes all subsequent characters up to and including the first carriage return to the system interpreter's input buffer. The system interpreter then reads and deciphers the specific command issued. The system interpreter may be receiving messages from many keyboards and user programs; therefore, it must be run often. Consequently, it occupies a private position in the round robin, being activated whenever there are characters in its input buffer.

1.2.3 Input/Output Stream Control

As noted earlier, the input and output streams are the means of communicating with the user console. Each stream is oriented toward character transmission. Each console has both an input and an output buffer assigned by the system. Since programs vary in how promptly they must pay attention to incoming characters, two options are provided for the using program. One method activates the user program whenever the input buffer is full. The other method alerts the program every time a character is typed.

Output routed to the console is placed into the output buffer and when the output buffer is full, the program is suspended while a console routine prints the buffer on the required user's console.

1.2.4 Resource Status Modification

Consoles may be slaved either by a user at another console or by a problem program. No information was provided on the ability to add or delete peripheral devices from the system.

1.2.5 System Status Interrogation

Each user can from his console cause the monitor to type out information on the current state of his programs or on the numbers of the devices he owns. He may also request information on the devices owned by other users of the system, or that are currently unassigned. The user may also, at any time, request the monitor to type out the processing time used by his program since he last logged-in.

1.3 Recovery Processing

1.3.1 Checkpointing

While a checkpoint capability is not specifically provided by the system, the user may at any time save the current status of the program for subsequent reloading. By issuing a "save" command, the system writes portions or all of the user's core image onto a previously created output file.

1.3.2 Restarting

The user may load the save file at any time and restart execution at the point where processing terminated.

The user also interrupts program processing when he issues various monitor commands from his console. He may restart program execution by issuing a "start" instruction. When the command is issued, the program state is restored and the program continues execution at the point where it left off.

2.0 I/O CONTROL

2.1 I/O Scheduling

Specific I/O devices are assigned to each user via device assignment instructions. In servicing paper tape readers/punches, the line printer, the incremental plotter, and the card reader, the requested operation is either performed or the program is suspended until the operation can be performed. In servicing magnetic tape, on the other hand, the requested operation is queued on a device queue and control immediately returns to the user without waiting for the request to be completed. Only one request can be queued for each tape unit. Therefore, up to four different tape requests may be overlapped if they refer to different units. An attempt to overlap a tape request on the same unit will result in the user program being suspended until the first request has been completed.

Each user may refer to four disk files simultaneously. An internal file number is associated with each of the user's active files. All references to file storage are by internal file number. The act of associating the internal file number with the file referenced by an account number and name is called "opening" the file. All input or output directed against a disk file is placed in a disk file request queue, and the processing is identical to that of magnetic tape.

2.2. Data Transfer

On an interrupt basis, the device service routines receive information from all input devices, parcel that information out to the appropriate buffers, and inform the activation routine when a user program must be activated to receive its information. The device service routines accept output from user programs, buffer it, and send it to output devices whenever they are able to receive it.

Only sequential access routines are provided by TSS/8. All named data files are located on disk and are composed of sequential segments of file storage. The size of a file segment is an integer multiple of disk records specified at system initialization time. A record consists of 128 machine words.

A telecommunications access method is also provided in the handling of the input and output streams, as discussed in Section 1.2.3. In addition, the system will support a local connection to a data communication system where user output containing certain control characters will be diverted to the data communication system instead of the user's output device. Characters received from the data communication system are directed to the user's input buffer.

2.3 Remote Terminal Support

The remote terminal is the system input and output device for the TSS/8. Consequently, extensive remote terminal support is provided. In addition to the facilities necessary for controlling the user and providing system input and output stream control, the monitor also has a provision to permit various console users to communicate with each other or with each other's programs. Information typed at one user terminal may be printed out at another or many other terminals. User programs can communicate with each other and with the system interpreter; thus, several user programs may run as one system coordinating their separate tasks. Users at consoles can set up general links for conferences, monitoring or chatting and user programs may receive from and send to more than one terminal. This, in effect, can allow a user program to act as a time-sharing system controlling its own set of terminals.

2.4 File Handling

Disk storage is divided into logical areas called files. Facilities are available for creating new files and extending, contracting, and destroying old files. A user file directory is assigned to each user by the person responsible for the system before the user first logs into the system. The user file directory is associated with the job number assigned to the user by the monitor each time the user logs in. Each user may have access to up to four active files at any time. An internal file number is associated with each of the user's active files and all I/O commands operate in terms of the internal file numbers.

The user can protect his files against unauthorized access. He can also specify the extent of access certain other users may have to his files. For example, a user's associates may be permitted to look at the data of certain files but not permitted to alter that data. Files may be both read- and/or write-protected.

3.0 DIAGNOSTIC ERROR PROCESSING

3.1 Hardware Error Control

Errors occurring in I/O operations result in the user being notified of the erroneous condition. Error recovery or retransmission is the responsibility of the user. No information was provided on the extent of hardware error control facilities for non-I/O units.

3.2 Program Error Control

Whenever an error condition occurs in the user's program, a system error routine will determine whether or not error interrupts have been enabled by the user program. If error interrupts have been enabled, control will pass to a specific user routine. If they have not been enabled, an error message is typed on the user console. Follow-on action is at the discretion of the console user.

3.3 Interface Error Control

The system interpreter reads and decodes all job control statements in the input stream, checks each statement for legality, and prints error messages on the remote console for any illegal conditions.

4.0 PROCESSING SUPPORT
4.1 Timing Service

A real-time clock service is provided that will allow the program to interrogate time of day and date. An interval timer facility is also available that permits the user program to suspend itself for a specified time interval or to schedule intermittent checks for specified conditions on a timed basis.

4.2 Testing and Debugging Service

Two commands are available to the console user which enable him to patch and/or look at specific core locations in the program area during program execution. In addition, an extensive debugging program (appropriately named DDT) is available to operate with the system. DDT provides storage dumps and tracing control.

4.3 Logging and Accounting

The TSS/8 accounting package keeps track of system and peripheral usage. When a user logs-out, his system usage is printed out and recorded on a disk file. Terminal time, processor time, and allocatable device time are all recorded for reference by the system controller.

4.4 System Description Maintenance

The user program may interrogate the system to determine the account number of the current job, the console number assigned to the current job, the total run time used for this execution, and the type of system that is currently being executed. This latter feature is available to determine whether TSS/8 or some other monitor is supervising the PDP-8 system. Thus programs may be written to run under both TSS/8 and conventional PDP-8 software, and instructions unique to each system can be controlled.

XDS SIGMA 2 REAL-TIME BATCH MONITOR (RBM)

XDS RBM is a small system which will multiprogram several resident foreground programs, one nonresident foreground program, and one background program.

1.0 JOB MANAGEMENT
1.1 Job Control
1.1.1 Scheduling

Under the RBM system, main memory is partitioned into a protected foreground area and an unprotected background area. The size of these two partitions is fixed at system generation time.

The foreground area is reserved for resident user foreground programs, a single nonresident user foreground program, Monitor tasks which must respond to high priority interrupts, Monitor service routines and, optionally, a library of user and system subroutines used by both foreground and background programs.

The background area is used by language processors, batch users' programs and, occasionally, by foreground programs requiring temporary use of additional memory.

Resident foreground programs are defined at system generation time and are loaded at system startup time. Nonresident foreground programs may be loaded (only one at any given time) at the request of the operator or another foreground program (including the previous nonresident foreground program). Background programs are loaded sequentially, as they occur in the job stream.

Dispatching is largely controlled by hardware. The interrupt priority sequence is the basis for the priority level of tasks in the RBM system. That is, the priority level of a program is dependent on the position of the associated hardware interrupt in the interrupt priority chain. Thus, no two programs in the system have the same priority level. Up to 134 user foreground programs can be connected to interrupts. The background is not connected to any interrupt level in the system, that is, its priority is below all hardware levels.

An executing program retains control of the system until processing is completed or until it is interrupted by a higher level program. Upon termination of a foreground program, control will be given (or returned) to the highest level pending program or if no interrupt levels are pending, to the background. Upon completion of the background program, RBM will load and execute the next program in the job stream (if any).

1.1.2 Resource Allocation

Core storage is partitioned at system generation time into fixed areas. Associated with each program is what is termed a "temporary stack," a block of core storage associated with a particular task and used by monitor service routines for temporary storage to achieve reentrancy. (All monitor service routines function in a reentrant manner.) These temporary stacks are allocated as needed and released when they are no longer necessary.

Common storage may be allocated within an area for communication between overlays of a program. Foreground areas and monitor tasks are storage protected against modifications by the background area.

I/O devices are referred to by logical *device unit numbers* which are assigned at system generation time and which may be changed at any time through use of control cards or monitor service routines. Each device unit number is equated by the system to a specific I/O unit; several logical device unit numbers may point to the same physical I/O device.

An additional level of device reference may be achieved by using a *device name* which is equated to a specific I/O unit (which may also be changed by control cards or service routines) or by using a file name (for files on random access devices only) which is equated, through use of a directory, to a specific area on a specific random access device.

Thus I/O device allocation is maintained by the system, but is controlled by the user.

Common subroutines may be placed in a library in the foreground area for use by foreground or background programs.

1.1.3 Program Loading

Resident foreground programs are loaded with the system supervisor during system startup. Nonresident foreground programs may be loaded by calling a system service subroutine through an operator key-in or through use of a control card in the batch job stream. Background programs are loaded serially as they occur in the job stream. Programs are loaded into preassigned areas and, therefore, are not relocated within core storage.

Both simple and overlay program structures are supported by RBM. Overlay programs consist of a root segment and two or more overlays organized in a tree structure, which permits overlay segments to serve as root segments to succeeding overlay segments. Segments are not loaded automatically, but must be requested through a monitor service routine. A common area may be defined for use by the root and overlay segments.

Foreground programs may use the background area as a temporary expansion area by utilizing the checkpoint/restart feature. The checkpointing feature permits a partially processed background job to be saved in secondary storage along with all registers and other environment. The vacated background space is set to protected status and is then available to the interrupting foreground program for either instructions or temporary data storage. When the foreground program calls the monitor restart routine, the previously checkpointed background program is reloaded and continues execution.

1.1.4 Event Monitoring

Dispatching is based on interrupt priorities. When no interrupts are active, background processing will take place. When any interrupt occurs, a related foreground program starts executing and continues to execute until it completes its processing or until a higher level interrupt occurs.

User subroutines may be specified to handle I/O device completion operations.

Interrupts can be controlled by calling system subroutines which mask/unmask or disable/enable interrupts. Masked interrupts will not be recognized by the system, but will be held pending until unmasked. Disabled interrupts are totally ignored by the system. A monitor service routine is also provided to simulate the occurrence of any interrupt. The system does not provide execution time or output line limitation facilities.

1.1.5 Program Termination Processing

A program may terminate normally or through a call to a system abort routine. The operator may also abort any program. In the event of a program abort, an error code is printed on the operator console specifying the reason the program was aborted.

1.2 System Communication

1.2.1 System Startup

At system initialization time the bootstrap program reads in the resident foreground programs one by one and executes any required initialization routines. The system then sets protection registers, outputs some messages, and enters a wait state until an interrupt or operator key-in initiates processing.

1.2.2 Job Control Communication

Job control is performed through input steam control cards and operator console commands. The commands from the operator console may or may not be interactive.

1.2.3 Input/Output Stream Control

Input/output is performed directly by the various foreground and background programs, through use of device-dependent or device-independent system subroutines.

1.2.4 Resource Status Modification

Subroutines may be used to request loading of overlays and allocation of temporary stacks. The operator may use the console to terminate program execution or to allow modification of system files on the random access device.

1.2.5 System Status Interrogation

The console operator can key-in a request for file control tables and information. This information includes the channel registers, the channel status table, and status response information from Test I/O and Test Device operations.

1.3 Recovery Processing

1.3.1 Checkpointing

Programs in the background area may be checkpointed by foreground programs to allow temporary use of the background area by the foreground program. No facilities exist to allow checkpoints to be taken for use during error recovery.

1.3.2 Restarting

When a foreground program no longer requires the use of the background area it can reload and restart the background area through use of a restart monitor service routine.

2.0 I/O CONTROL

2.1 I/O Scheduling

I/O is performed through use of system subroutines which may be either device-dependent or device-independent. File or device names or device unit numbers are equated to specific physical I/O devices at execution time. I/O requests are queued by the system, but no details are provided as to queue organization or control.

2.2 Data Transfer

Both sequential and random file structure are supported by RBM. The device-dependent and device-independent routines provide buffering control. Buffers are assigned in buffer pools through use of open and close subroutines.

Data code translation takes place in several instances. Random access files may be automatically compressed on output and decompressed on input. Cards with certain punches in them are automatically read as binary cards by the system. Additionally, cards may be read in BCD or EBCDIC codes.

2.3 Remote Terminal Support

Although RBM is real-time-oriented, it provides no direct support for remote terminals.

2.4 File Handling

RBM maintains directories to disk files which may be referenced by names. No support is provided for directories of the contents of a file. File labels, if used, must be generated and checked by the user.

3.0 DIAGNOSTIC ERROR PROCESSING

3.1 Hardware Error Control

If a memory parity error occurs in a background program, the background program is aborted without disturbing the real-time foreground. Parity errors in the foreground are ignored until the total number of parity errors equals a limit specified during system generation. At that time RBM will halt and indicate the bad address.

3.2 Program Error Control

An attempt by a background program to modify the contents of protected memory or to execute a privileged instruction will cause the background program to be aborted. A multiply-divide interrupt is provided on Sigma 2 computers which do not have the multiply-divide hardware; the system software, on receiving this interrupt, will simulate the multiply or divide instruction.

3.3 Interface Error Control

No mention is made in the reference manual as to what interface error checking is performed.

4.0 PROCESSING SUPPORT

4.1 Timing Service

No timing services are mentioned in the RBM Manual.

4.2 Testing and Debugging Service

The operator may request a memory dump specifying all of RBM, all of the background, or all of the foreground. Additionally, specific addresses may be entered as dump limits. The random access device(s) may be dumped via an operator key-in which specifies the lowest and highest track and sector numbers to be dumped. File control tables may also be dumped. These dumps indicate the channel status for a specific device on the channel.

A call to an abort subroutine will clear the background program from core and terminate all I/O requests from the background program. All I/O in progress is allowed to complete and if a postmortem dump is requested, it will be performed at this time.

4.3 Logging and Accounting

No user utilization or error statistics are maintained by this system.

4.4 System Description Maintenance

A fixed system area contains many entries which may be of interest to a user's program; however, no system subroutines are provided to facilitate status interrogation.

The IBM 1800 Multiprogramming Executive (MPX) Operating System is a real-time multiprogramming system with fixed partitions, including one background area and up to 24 foreground areas.

IBM 1800 MULTIPROGRAMMING EXECUTIVE (MPX) OPERATING SYSTEM

1.0 JOB MANAGEMENT

1.1 Job Control

1.1.1 Scheduling

The MPX system is designed to multiprogram several foreground programs concurrently with a background program. Program execution priority is closely aligned with hardware interrupt priorities. In general, a program will continue to execute until it completes operation or until a higher level interrupt occurs. Program execution will be suspended for the duration of a higher level interrupt or an I/O operation. During suspension for I/O, lower level interrupts may be processed.

Batch jobs are executed serially as they are encountered in the job stream; real-time jobs are queued for execution in the background area or in one of the up to 24 foreground areas. Each area has its own queue, and programs are placed in each queue by priority. Up to 24 priority levels may be specified at system generation time. A job is placed in a queue by being named in a control card in the job stream, by the occurrence of an interrupt, or by a programmed call to the supervisor.

A call to the supervisor may cause a specified program to be queued immediately, after a specified time interval, or on a cyclical basis at a specified time.

1.1.2 Resource Allocation

Internal storage is allocated in fixed partitions; a background area, not less than 5K words (equivalent to 10K bytes), and up to 24 foreground areas may be specified at system generation time. These partitions can be changed only by regeneration of the system. Common areas may be defined within an area for communication between subroutines or overlays.

A special system area is available for commonly used reentrant subroutines. Most system subroutines are provided in both reentrant and nonreentrant forms. The shorter, nonreentrant, form is used when the subroutine is included as part of the application program. The longer, reentrant, form is used when the subroutine occupies the special system area and is available for use by all programs.

Storage protection is used to prevent inadvertent modification of system tables and to prevent modification of a user's I/O control lists for the duration of the I/O operations.

I/O devices are not allocated by the system, but are directly addressed by problem programs. The problem programmer, rather than the system, must prevent attempts by two programs to simultaneously use the same I/O device.

1.1.3 Program Loading

The loadable unit under MPX is a "core load," a block of object code, on disk, with all relocation and linkages resolved, ready for execution immediately after being read into core. A core load may contain a complete program or it may have one or more related overlays, each containing one or more subroutines.

Only one level of overlays is supported; that is, the overlays may not themselves have suboverlays. The programmer selects the subroutines to be grouped into overlays at core load build time and the core load builder automatically resolves linkages between the main core load and the overlays. Overlays, once loaded into internal storage will not be reloaded unless they in turn have been overlaid.

Programs may be dynamically loaded by program requests to the system during execution. These requests may specify immediate queueing of a job, queueing after a specified time interval, or periodic queueing at specified time intervals. A special request from the batch area will cause the current program to be rolled-out and saved on disk while a specified core load is executed in the batch area. Another special request will cause the last rolled-out program to be rolled back into internal storage. Batch jobs will be rolled-out of the background area to permit a process job to execute, and then rolled back in.

Core loads are loaded from permanent or temporary disk areas. They are not relocatable and must be executed in the area specified at core load build time.

1.1.4 Event Monitoring

Dispatching is dependent primarily upon the 1800 hardware interrupt structure. Up to 24 interrupt levels are supported by the 1800 MPX System (12 standard, 6 to 12 additional levels optional). The user, when ordering his hardware, specifies which events are to be assigned to which interrupt levels. In general, processing on a given level will be interrupted by higher level interrupts and lower level interrupts will be held pending; however, higher level interrupts can be masked.

For interrupt control the system maintains a "pseudo interrupt status word" (PISW) for each interrupt level. Each type of interrupt on a given interrupt level will cause a specific bit in the corresponding PISW to be set. A subroutine is provided to set any bit in any PISW, including both of those bits that correspond to hardware interrupts and those that do not. Programs may be linked to a specific level and bit and thus be queued in response to either hardware events (real or simulated) or software events. Additional interrupt control is provided by subroutines which mask or unmask interrupts. Program execution will also be suspended for the duration of I/O operations and this time will be allocated to programs on lower interrupt levels or to batch programs.

Upon I/O device completion, control is returned to the task that initiated the I/O operation, unless a higher level task has subsequently been started. Upon task completion, the highest priority job queued for the released area is loaded and control is given to the highest level task in a ready state.

When a timer interrupt occurs, control is passed to an "interval timer control" (ITC) module. ITC services the three hardware interval timers and 10 programmed timers, plus a programmed real-time clock. ITC also resets the "Operations Monitor" during batch processing.

No execution time limit can be set; however, an Operations Monitor will time out after a set time interval unless it is periodically reset by the program being executed. The timer may be set for an interval of 5 to 30 seconds and will, if it times out, turn on a console light and a customer-supplied alarm. Thus a job which goes into an uncontrolled loop will be detected and can be cancelled by the operator even though overall execution time cannot be limited.

1.1.5 Program Termination Processing

Upon program termination, the system will load the next program in the queue for the freed area. No summary information is provided by the system.

Abnormal termination is normally preceded by a message including the reason for the termination and various status indicators at the time of the error.

1.2 System Communication
1.2.1 System Startup

System startup consists of loading a two-card loader program followed by a data card specifying initial start and reload core loads. Logical/physical disk drive assignments are also indicated on this card. The current time must be entered through data switches on the console. The system executive is loaded and processing begins with execution of the user written initial start core load.

System restarting consists of reinitializing the system executive and calling a user written reload core load. A restart may be initiated by the system (as a means of error recovery) or by the operator.

1.2.2 Job Control Communication

Job control is exercised through control cards in the job stream or calls to the executive from problem programs. Operator control is restricted to manual procedures to initiate batch processing or restart the system.

1.2.3 Input/Output Stream Control

Batch input is read through a card reader and processed in the sequence it occurs; no I/O symbionts are provided. System output is directed to the printer or, if there is no printer, to the console. Crucial messages are directed to both the printer and the console. I/O queues are maintained for each device.

1.2.4 Resource Status Modification

Partition sizes are fixed and can be modified only by system regeneration. Console failure will result in automatic redirection of its output to an alternate unit, specified at system generation time.

I/O devices may be placed in on-line, off-line, or C.E. mode. All mode settings are effected through calls to the system executive. On or off-line software settings permit or disallow, respectively, accessing an I/O device. The hardware C.E. mode disables a device except when the CPU is operating on the C.E. interrupt level.

1.2.5 System Status Interrogation

The only system supported status inquiry is a dump of the disk directories which may be requested via a control card in the job stream.

1.3 Recovery Processing

1.3.1 Checkpointing

No system support is provided for checkpointing.

1.3.2 Restarting

The MPX system provides facilities for restarting programs as part of error recovery in the event a serious error is detected. A reload core load may be specified, for any program, which will be called in the event the program causes or encounters a serious error.

2.0 I/O CONTROL

2.1 I/O Scheduling

System I/O subroutines are provided to handle the intricacies of I/O device manipulation and to maintain I/O request queues. Since I/O devices are specifically referenced by the user, the system performs no device resolution functions.

An I/O queue is maintained for each I/O device. Up to 16 priorities may be specified to control the sequence in which the queued I/O requests are handled. When an operation complete interrupt occurs, I/O is started for the next item in the queue.

When more than one console device is included in the system, a system generation option specifies a backup for each unit. In the event a console fails, output directed to it is automatically rerouted to its backup.

2.2 Data Transfer

Buffering support is not provided except for console messages; console messages may be buffered in core or on disk, as specified at system generation time. The amount of core or disk reserved for this buffering is also specified during system generation. All output to the console is automatically buffered.

Data is input to the 1800 in several codes. Although no automatic code conversation is performed, system subroutines are provided to perform conversion from one code to another.

I/O blocking/deblocking must be performed by the user; no system facilities are provided for this function.

Since the user determines each specific I/O and control operation for each specific I/O device, no particular access methods can be said to be supported; however, messages, like any other I/O will be queued by the system.

2.3 Remote Terminal Support

System facilities do not directly support remote terminals; however, system interrupt handling and I/O request queueing facilities provide a good base for the development of user-written remote terminal support routines.

2.4 File Handling

MPX maintains a table of program and file disk addresses. The user can, in a source program, refer to file names, but these references are made address-specific in load modules.

Write protection is available, but applies to disk cylinders rather than files. A program which overrides this protection can modify all data files. No read protection is supported.

Any file labels desired must be written and checked by the user.

3.0 DIAGNOSTIC ERROR PROCESSING
3.1 Hardware Error Control

MPX is designed to maintain itself in an on-line, responsive state. Therefore, the basic system philosophy, with respect to errors which may affect system operation, is to abort the offending program and restart its area or to abort the entire system and reload it, even at the expense of current operations. More importance is placed on preserving the system's integrity and keeping the system operating than on preserving any particular program or operation.

An "internal" interrupt will occur if an invalid op code or a parity error is detected. This is the highest level of interrupt and cannot be masked. An error message will be printed indicating the nature of the error. The system will be reloaded after a parity error; after an op-code error, it may be reloaded or the core load area may be restarted depending on the location of the error.

An internal interrupt will also occur if an attempt is made to write to a protected core storage word. Words are individually protected by setting a protect bit associated with each word. The MPX system protects various areas in the system executive and also uses the protection feature to protect I/O call control lists (in the users' programs) from modification while the I/O request is queued for execution.

Errors detected in I/O operations cause the operation to be retried. If the error condition still exists when return is made to the calling program, an error parameter in the user's control list is set to indicate the nature of the error and an error message is output to the console typewriter. It is the user's responsibility to check the error parameter and take appropriate action if a successful call completion is not indicated.

Since I/O devices are directly addressed, elimination or reassignment of devices must be accomplished by coding in user programs, with the exception of I/O from or to the console typewriter-printers. A backup unit is specified, at system generation time, for each typewriter-printer and will automatically be used by the system if the primary unit fails.

On-line checkout of I/O devices can be accomplished through use of the 1800's C.E. mode. I/O devices which are set to the C.E. mode can be accessed only when the CPU is operating on the C.E. interrupt level. Devices may be set to the C.E. mode by programming. A C.E. interrupt is caused by pushing a button on the console.

3.2 Program Error Control

In general, program errors will result in termination of the program in error. If a program detects an error, it may cancel subsequent tasks through use of a clear queue subroutine.

3.3 Interface Error Control

System control card errors will cause the job stream to be flushed until another control card is encountered. Errors in system program linkage may be detected if core or disk tables are found to contain erroneous data.

4.0 PROCESSING SUPPORT

4.1 Timing Service

MPX maintains the three hardware interval timers and 10 software interval timers, plus a software real-time clock.

Subroutines are provided to set the real-time clock and to read it in hours and thousandths of an hour or in hours, minutes, and seconds.

The interval timers may be used to suspend execution of a program or to queue a program for execution either after a specified time interval or at regular intervals.

4.2 Testing and Debugging Service

Core may be dumped by calling a system core dump subroutine which will print all core between two specified addresses in either hexadecimal or decimal format. A dump analysis program will print a memory map directly from core.

A "trap" facility is provided, which will cause a specified portion of core storage to be saved (in an in-core buffer) for later dumping if an error occurs within a specified area. The number of words saved is fixed at system generation time.

A disk dump routine will dump sectors to the printers, starting from an address specified on the console data switches and ending when a consile sense switch is turned off.

Program tracing is provided in three forms: (1) full tracing within specified addresses, (2) a program halt at a specified address and a trace of the previous 10 instructions, and (3) a trace of the instruction executed before and after each change to a specified word in core. Program or subroutine call tracing is not provided.

4.3 Logging and Accounting

Control cards and messages are recorded on the typewriter-printer. The time (in hours and thousandths) is printed with job identification and with all error messages. No facilities for accounting are provided.

4.4 System Description Maintenance

The system does not provide dynamic status information.

8
OPERATING SYSTEMS FOR LARGE COMPUTERS

OVERVIEW

This chapter uses the condensed outline format presented in Chapter 7 to summarize a selection of multiprograming operating systems for large size computers and for medium size computers capable of running a large number of peripheral equipments. All of these operating systems are more complex than those summarized in Chapter 7, and none offer time-sharing capabilities.

The Tape-Disk Operating Systems (TDOS) for the RCA Spectra 70 computer closely parallels and serves as a base for the operating system for RCA-2, RCA-3, RCA-6, and RCA-7. This operating system places a heavy emphasis on input-output functions.

The Disk Operating System (DOS) for the IBM System/360 and System/370 computers is a smaller operating system with less extensive facilities than the other IBM operating system summarized in this chapter. Like the RCA TDOS, the IBM DOS places considerable emphasis on input-output functions.

The MASTER operating system for the CDC 3300/3500 differs from that available for other Control Data Corporation computers. Perhaps as a reflection of the fast internal speeds of the CDC 3300/3500, MASTER gives relatively more attention to CPU functions than the two operating systems just summarized.

The Mod 4 Operating System for the Honeywell Series 200 computers is available for use on the larger computer models in the series. It provides for remote job entry and interactive terminal communication, but not a full time-sharing capability.

The OS (operating system) for the IBM System/360 and System/370 family of computers is normally used on only the larger members of the family because of the relatively large minimum internal storage requirement. OS offers a wide range of facilities to the computer user.

The SCOPE 3 operating system for the CDC 6400/6500/6600 is the only operating system summarized in this book that offers multiprocessing as well as multiprogramming capabilities. Partly because of this additional complexity of the hardware, the SCOPE 3 operating system displays a greater complexity of job management than any other operating system summarized in this chapter.

RCA SPECTRA 70 TAPE-DISK OPERATING SYSTEM (TDOS)

The SPECTRA Tape-Disk Operating System (TDOS) is a disk-resident multi-programming system having multichannel communications capabilities.

1.0 JOB MANAGEMENT
1.1 Job Control
1.1.1 Scheduling

The multiprogramming capability of the Tape-Disk operating system (TDOS) provides for the current execution of up to six programs in variable sized portions.

Programs may be scheduled for the execution either by the TDOS Monitor, which may only control the programs scheduled into one partition, or by the operator, who controls the programs scheduled into all partitions.

The TDOS Monitor is a nonresident component of the system that controls the sequential execution of programs from a job input stream. The Monitor is scheduled by an operator console command and remains resident until it terminates itself at the completion of the total job stream. When one program completes execution, the Monitor schedules the initiation of the next program from the job stream. Only one program may execute under control of the TDOS Monitor at a time.

The operator controls the initialization of programs not supervised by the Monitor by means of console load commands.

Any program may be executed as part of a chain of programs which are executed sequentially. This mode of operation is accomplished either by having a program call another program internally after having completed execution, or through control statements entered on the job stream. The successor program is loaded into the same main storage area as the previous program. In order to provide sufficient core, the initial program in the chain must reserve memory for the largest program called. Any devices that are assigned and not de-allocated by a previous program remain assigned to the successor program.

1.1.2 Resource Allocation

Main storage is assigned to each job, based on the requirements of the job and the available memory at initiation time. Allocation is controlled by a free memory table. This table defines the areas in memory that are currently not assigned. The supervisor determines, by examining the free memory table, if the amount of memory required by the program is available. If memory is not available, the operator is notified and the program is not loaded.

A storage protect feature is optionally available. If the memory protect feature is included within the supervisor, memory is always assigned in multiples of 2,048 bytes. If the storage protect feature is not present, memory is assigned in multiples of 8 bytes.

Actual I/O devices may be assigned by means of control statements entered through the job stream initiation or by operator commands from the console. A program may also dynamically assign a device during execution. A program may be suspended to wait for a device previously assigned to another program. Only one program is allowed to wait for a given device. All I/O devices may be passed on from one program to the successor in a program chain.

A device may be de-allocated in three different ways. The user may at any time issue a macro to de-allocate the device. All devices that are still allocated at program termination will be de-allocated unless they are passed on to a successor program. Finally, any device may be de-allocated by the operator via a console command.

Programs may share random access under TDOS. However, the system does not provide protection for areas on the random access device assigned to one program, from being erroneously overwritten by another program.

1.1.3 Program Loading

Both simple and overlay structures are supported. Programs are relocated at the time they are loaded. Memory is assigned by the system according to the requirements of the program and the available memory initiation time. No storage compaction features are available.

1.1.4 Event Monitoring

Each program that has been initiated shares central processor time with other programs that are executing. Each executing program is assigned a priority number ranging from one to six.

The highest priority program is serviced first and control is not given to the next lower priority program until the higher priority program temporarily relinquishes central processor time. Programs gain control only if they are ready to utilize the CPU immediately. The operator may enter a command to change any program priority during execution.

When an interrupt condition occurs, the program currently executing is interrupted and control to the interrupt control routine of the supervisor which decodes the interrupt and transfers control to the appropriate routine for servicing.

For telecommunications processing, the Communication Interrupt Analysis program, a resident extension of TDOS, acts upon communications interrupts. This system component is executed only during periods of communication activity. Only one communications program is permitted, and it must receive the highest priority when active.

1.1.5 Program Termination Processing

A program may terminate itself or be terminated by a console command issued by the operator. The system will also automatically terminate a program when it is determined that the program can no longer continue. The following functions are performed by the supervisor for program termination: all devices assigned to the program are de-allocated and returned to the system; entries in the executive tables for the program are deleted; and a message is typed to the operator informing him of the termination.

When a program is terminated, the memory that is used is de-allocated and returned to the system. The free memory table is then updated to include the additional available memory.

A program is abnormally terminated when an unrecoverable error condition occurs.

1.2 System Communication

1.2.1 System Startup

During initialization the system is provided with the current date and time. Information about I/O devices available is entered at the time of system generation and is not modifiable during system initialization.

1.2.2 Job Control Communication

Control statements entered through the input stream at program initiation assign peripheral devices and chain nonmonitor-directed programs.

A monitor control language is used to direct the sequential processing of jobs. This control language consists of a series of parameter statements, each indicating a particular function to be performed.

The operator communicates with the system by means of console commands. The first character of an operator entry identifies it as a command to the supervisor, a command to the TDOS Monitor, a reply to a system message, or a reply to a user program. From the console, the operator may initiate procedures that are not included as part of the normal job stream.

1.2.3 Input/Output Stream Control

For programs running under Monitor control, the Monitor handles all input from the job stream and all output to the system output devices.

The system input device, from which the job stream is read, may be a card reader, tape, paper tape reader, drum, or disk. This device is assigned at Monitor initiation and is only de-allocated upon Monitor termination.

A printer, tape, disk, or drum may be the system output device on which listings, error notations and messages are recorded. An optional system output device (card punch, tape, disk, or drum) handles the output from system programs such as compilers.

1.2.4 Resource Status Modification

The operator may modify the status of resources assigned to any program. He may increase or decrease the amount of core assigned to the program, allocate and de-allocate devices to the program, and change the level of priority of the program.

1.2.5 System Status Interrogation

The operator may request displays of the core boundaries of a specific program and of all devices assigned to it. He may also request a display of the names of the programs currently running, their priorities, and an indication of the program (if any) running under Monitor control. A display of current boundaries of unassigned memory can also be obtained. The operator may additionally request the status of a specific device and information on all unassigned devices in the system.

1.3 Recovery Processing

1.3.1 Checkpoint

The purpose of a checkpoint is to save a program and its environment on secondary storage so that at any future time the program can be reinitiated from that point. Program checkpoints are taken whenever the program issues a checkpoint macro instruction.

1.3.2 Restarting

A restart routine reestablishes a program and its data in the operating system environment and resumes execution at the restart address saved at checkpoint time. The restart routine is initiated by a console request which indicates the program to be restarted, the program priority number, and the device containing the program checkpoint. Device reassignment, label checking, and file positioning may be performed by the system or the user, depending on the type of I/O method being used. Device assignment following restart must be made from the console. Only those programs not running under Monitor control can be restarted. Since restart programs are not relocatable, programs restarted must occupy the same area of memory that they occupied at the time the checkpoint was taken.

2.0 I/O CONTROL

2.1 I/O Scheduling

Input/output routines initiate all I/O operations on all devices except the console typewriter. The TDOS system maintains a channel queue for each selector channel that contains more than one device. When an I/O request is encountered for a device whose channel is busy, the request is placed in the channel queue. Queueing and subsequent initiation are accomplished on a first-in, first-out basis provided that communication devices are not being supported. If telecommunications is being supported, these requests receive priority. Up to six channels can be handled. When dual channel tape stations are available, an attempt will be made to reach the device via the alternate channel before entering the request on a channel queue. If both channels are busy, the request is entered on both queues.

2.2 Data Transfer

The file control processor (FCP) is a generalized input/output system that functions in conjunction with the supervisor to control all I/O processing for all programs that are executed under TDOS. The FCP may be used on two different levels.

Logical FCP allows the user to work at a logical record level and not be concerned with physical record-reading or writing. Logical FCP provides buffering services, makes logical records available for processing (blocking and deblocking), and makes files available for processing.

If the programmer desires to write his own logical data handling routines, physical FCP provides the necessary supervisor routines to control I/O.

The FCP provides for processing files recorded serially on devices such as magnetic tape. It also provides for processing sequential or random files recorded on direct access devices.

The communications interrupt analysis (CIA) program, an option extension of the system, provides for the execution of one user communication program concurrently with five other noncommunication programs. The CIA program monitors all telecommunication activities. The system also provides a multichannel communications program to interface between the user communication program and the CIA program.

The system hardware also allows one processor to communicate directly with up to five other processors over an interface independent of the I/O channels. Only one byte of information may be transferred between processors using this feature. The TDOS supervisor responds to all external signal interrupts either by interpreting the control byte or by passing the transmitted byte to the user program when it is a user communication.

2.3 Remote Terminal Support

The information available does not indicate that any remote terminal support is provided by the supervisor.

2.4 File Handling

The system does not provide a catalog of data files, nor does it provide any file access security controls.

Routines for checking and/or writing standard labels on a tape file are provided within FCP.

3.0 DIAGNOSTIC ERROR PROCESSING

3.1 Hardware Error Control

Standard error recovery routines have been provided to handle most error conditions that can occur on all peripheral devices supported by the system. The error recovery segments reside as overlay segments on the system resident device along with the resident supervisor.

When a device error occurs, the appropriate error recovery segment is loaded. An attempt is made to recover from the error by retrying the failed operation. The number of times recovery is attempted is variable, depending on the device type. If the error persists after error recovery has been attempted, a message is typed to the operator indicating the device in error and the error condition. The operator may attempt recovery again or may specify that the error is unrecoverable. If the user program has provided an unrecoverable error routine, control is transferred to the program. If not, the job is terminated.

When either a power failure or a machine check occurs, the processor is set to idle. In the case of a machine check, an informative message is typed before idling.

3.2 Program Error Control

Whenever program error conditions such as privileged operation, address error, exponent underflow, or overflow cause an interrupt, a test is made for a user error procedure. If no such procedure is available, an indication of the error is typed and the operator is given the option of dumping before the program is terminated. If the procedure is available, control is passed to the user routine for corrective action.

3.3 Interface Error Control

Control statements are checked by a system routine as they are read. If shuffled or invalid device assignment parameters are found, the system de-allocates the affected device and the operator is notified.

Erroneous conditions detected in a Monitor control statement are printed or typed and appropriate action is taken by the Monitor.

Messages entered by the operator are checked for validity. Commands are rejected when certain error conditions are encountered; for example: if the operator were to enter a command to load a communications user program without having previously loaded the multichannel communication program, the operator's command would be rejected.

4.0 PROCESSING SUPPORT

4.1 Timing Services

If the elapsed time clock feature has been specified at system generation, user programs may obtain the time of day request elapsed time interrupts.

4.2 Testing and Debugging Service

TDOS provides an automatic integrated debugging system (AIDS) to facilitate preparation and testing of programs. AIDS provides the ability to automatically perform the testing of one or more programs without requiring a programmer to be present. AIDS also provides facilities to perform the console control testing of any program.

TDOS provides a complete package of diagnostic routines. Facilities are provided for dumps of memory and devices in case of machine or program errors.

4.3 Logging and Accounting

TDOS provides accounting functions for all user programs. The desired information to perform job accounting is provided to the system and/or the user program via macro instructions and to the operator via console typeouts.

4.4 System Description Maintenance

User programs may interrogate the system to obtain the elapsed program execution time.

A macro instruction provides user programs with the address of a supervisor communication region, where information on memory size, options present in the system, and the processor type (70/35, 70/45, or 70/55) is available. This region also contains the addresses of the device list, the program table (with entries for each program executing), and other tables and system parameters.

IBM SYSTEM/360 AND IBM SYSTEM/370 DISK OPERATING SYSTEM (DOS)

The Disk Operating System (DOS) is a medium-scale general purpose multiprogramming operating system. DOS is designed to provide background batch processing facilities in conjunction with up to two active foreground tasks.

1.0 JOB MANAGEMENT
1.1 Job Control
1.1.1 Scheduling

The Disk Operating System permits concurrent execution of one background and up to two foreground programs. The background programs are initiated in the sequence in which they appear in the batched job input stream. Foreground programs are initiated by direct operator commands from either the console keyboard or an assigned card reader.

The batch job stream is executed serially, one job step at a time. The initiation of each job step is contingent upon the successful completion of the previous job step.

One of the foreground partitions may also be used to process a separate batch job input stream. The I/O facilities used by the batch job executing in a foreground partition are physically distinct from the I/O facilities used by batch job programs executing in the background partition.

1.1.2 Resource Allocation

The size of the background and foreground partitions is specified at system generation, but may be modified by the operator at any time. Core storage allocation is fixed, in that the program receives all of the core allocation to the partition in which it is executing. The storage protect feature prevents programs in any one of the three partitions from writing into or directing an I/O operation into any of the other partitions or into the supervisor area.

A new facility has recently been added to the DOS to permit multiprogramming in any one of the three partitions. The facility permits the main task to initiate execution of up to nine subtasks within its partition. Consequently, the core required by these attached subtasks is allocated dynamically from the core available within the fixed partition size.

With the exception of the ability to multiprogram within partitions, there is no dynamic resource allocation facility available within the DOS.

Input/Output devices are allocated either permanently to the partition or temporarily to the job. In either case, they are allocated by physical device identification via assignment cards in the job control stream (for background tasks) and via operator console commands for foreground tasks. Device sharing is permitted for subtasks within any of the given partitions, and in certain selected cases between background and foreground tasks.

The input/output control system consists of a number of reentrant routines imbedded within the supervisor and serially reusable routines loaded into a transient area. The routines may be accessed by either foreground or background programs.

1.1.3 Program Loading

The DOS supports simple, overlay, and dynamic program structures. Programs are normally loaded from the system execution library, though they may also be loaded from a temporary execution library. Though programs are maintained in a relocatable format in a relocatable library, these programs must be processed by a linking loader before they can be executed. Once processed, they are stored on the execution library. Normally, background load modules are not relocatable, though foreground programs must be self-relocating. Since the three partitions are fixed, there is no provision for storage compaction routines.

1.1.4 Event Monitoring

All programs operate with interruptions enabled. When an interruption occurs, the supervisor gains control, processes the interruption, and gives control to the highest priority program that is in a ready state. By definition, foreground one contains the highest priority program. Foreground two contains the next highest priority program, and the background area contains the lowest priority program. Control is taken away from a high priority program when that program encounters a condition that prevents continuation of processing until a specified event has occurred. Control is taken away from a lower priority program when an event for which a higher priority program was waiting has been completed. When utilizing the facility of multiprogramming within a partition, the order of priority of the subtasks within a partition is dictated by the order in which the subtasks were initiated. The first subtasks initiated have the highest priority. As each subsequent subtask is attached, it has a lower priority. The lowest priority is reserved for the main task in the partition.

The DOS recognizes five separate interrupts. Each of these occurs within an interrupt hierarchy so that simultaneous interrupt occurrences will always cause the highest priority interrupt to be taken. Normally, upon the occurrence of an interrupt, I/O and external interrupts are masked off to prevent additional interruptions during the interrupt handling routine. Upon the completion of interrupt processing, the interrupts are unmasked and any that are pending are recognized.

The supervisor offers facilities to transfer control to selected routines, upon the occurrence of certain interrupt conditions. These conditions are: an interval timer runout, an external interrupt, or a program check interrupt. Communications programs, normally residing in a foreground partition, may be initiated directly by telecommunication control routines upon the arrival of unsolicited input or through periodic timer interrupts.

1.1.5 Program Termination Processing

The job termination routine de-allocates all I/O devices that were assigned to the job (as opposed to the partition). A message on the operator's log is typed indicating either job completion or abnormal termination and the elapsed clock time used by the job. In addition, for jobs abnormally terminated, a core dump will be automatically produced if this option was selected by the user. If a program terminates abnormally, all subsequent tasks within that job are disregarded.

1.2 System Communication

1.2.1 System Startup

The system is initialized and loaded from the operator's control console. Prior to initiating processing, the operator is permitted to modify the availability of system resources. He may also modify the size of the foreground partitions. To complete the initialization routine, the operator is required to enter the current data and time. No total system restart facilities exist, so a system restart is identical to an initial startup.

1.2.2 Job Control Communication

Background programs are controlled from the system input device (normally the card reader or the console typewriter) via a job control language. Foreground programs are normally controlled by special commands from the operator console or a separate card reader. If the batched job foreground mode is selected, the job control language is also used for this partition. There is no provision for remote terminal job processing or for maintaining cataloged job control procedures in a system library.

All system produced messages are identified by a message code. This code allows reference to the system operator's guide for more detailed information. The date and time parameter formats are standardized at system generation, and this standard format is used throughout the system. There is no provision for standard formats for messages either to or from problem programs. The job control language is free format, though control cards are identified by fixed punches in the first two columns of the job control card. The job control cards utilize both positional and key word parameters, and default options are assumed for most parameters.

1.2.3 Input/Output Stream Control

The system input device is normally the card reader, though it may be a tape drive or direct access device. Input is read on-line with no prior symbiont processing. Similarly, the system output device is written on-line with no automatic symbiont processing.

1.2.4 Resource Status Modification

As a part of system initialization, the operator is allowed to add and delete peripheral devices from the system-generated tables. During processing, he may also change the availability of peripherals as well as modify the core size allocated to the two foreground partitions.

1.2.5 System Status Interrogation

The operator may request at any time the status of resources assigned to the system. He may initiate these requests either from the operator console or by imbedding the requests in the input stream.

1.3 Recovery Processing

1.3.1 Checkpointing

Checkpoints may be initiated by any batch processing job, but are not available for nonbatch programs. The checkpoint routine is loaded into the supervisor transient area and checkpoints the full partition. The checkpoint file may be on either tape or disk. I/O device repositioning information is included in the checkpoint record. The operator is notified of the checkpoint via the operator console.

1.3.2 Restarting

Restart from a checkpoint is initiated via a card in the input batch job stream. The restart card is substituted for the normal program execution card in the job stream control deck used to initiate the job. All sequential tape devices as well as direct access devices, are repositioned. Neither the input stream, the output stream, nor any unit record devices are repositioned. Positioning of these devices must be handled by the application program.

2.0 I/O CONTROL

2.1 I/O Scheduling

The I/O Scheduling routines determine the channel and advice address of the logical file when an I/O operation is scheduled. Both the channel and device are checked for availability and, if both are free, the I/O operation is initiated. If the channel is busy, the request is placed on an I/O request queue; if the device is busy, the program is suspended until the device becomes free. Whenever the channel becomes free, the channel request queue is checked for a pending operation. The operation is scheduled if the referenced device is free; otherwise, the queue is checked for other pending operations on nonbusy devices.

A magnetic tape device may be attached to two channels. In this case the tape drive is called "switchable." If one channel is unavailable for the I/O operation against the device, the channel scheduler will attempt to use the second channel if it is available, instead of entering the request on the channel queue.

2.2 Data Transfer

The DOS provides two types of routines for controlling input/output activity. Physical IOCS supervises the execution of channel programs without regard to the logical content, format or organization of the data being read or written. Physical IOCS includes facilities for scheduling and queueing I/O operations, checking for and handling error conditions, and handling I/O activity to maintain maximum I/O speeds without burdening the problem program. Logical IOCS provides the interface between the user's file processing routines and physical IOCS. Logical IOCS routines are normally assembled as a part of the problem program. The user is required to provide routines to process nonstandard I/O devices.

The system supports sequential, indexed sequential, direct, and telecommunication files. Both simple and queued handling techniques for these files are available. The system also provides for fixed and variable length record formats and handles both blocked and unblocked records. In handling blocked records, the user may process blocked records either through location pointers or by physically moving the data between the input/output buffers and his program area. Only simple buffering techniques are provided by the system. Automatic code translation is provided primarily for paper tape and telecommunication devices.

The DOS provides two telecommunication access methods, basic and queued, to handle the user's telecommunication requirements. These access methods permit a number of different telecommunication devices to be attached to the system, and provide for the recognition of priorities, routing information, and polling specifications. In addition, the queued telecommunication access method provides for input and output message queue maintenance.

Device manipulation facilities are also available and may be requested in two manners. For most devices, manipulation commands are issued as a direct I/O command. Some devices, though, such as printers and card punches, may also be controlled by control characters imbedded within each data record.

2.3 Remote Terminal Support

The DOS does not provide remote terminal support.

2.4 File Handling

The system does not provide a catalog of file and volume indexes. Data file access is not restricted beyond the requirement to properly specify the file label.

Label handling services within the DOS are quite extensive, and permit both system labels and user labels. The user may also include coding to supplement processing of system labels, as well as for processing his own labels.

3.0 DIAGNOSTIC ERROR PROCESSING

3.1 Hardware Error Control

Non-I/O hardware malfunctions are recognized via a machine check interrupt in the supervisor. A diagnostic message is typed on the system operator's console and, depending on the seriousness of the error, the condition will either be retried or the system will terminate processing.

The physical IOCS routine for each peripheral device contains the necessary coding to sense error conditions and attempt correction of these conditions. Device error statistics are maintained within the system and are printed out on the operator's console at the completion of each job. These statistics are also maintained within the supervisor and may be interrogated by maintenance personnel. Problem programs may also supply error processing routines that will be executed whenever an error condition arises.

3.2 Program Error Control

Program errors may be processed by the user via the inclusion of special user-coded routines. In addition, the user may specify on a control card whether or not automatic core dumps are to be taken upon the occurrence of an abnormal termination.

3.3 Interface Error Control

Operator responses are generally limited to single-word responses such as "retry," "ignore," or "cancel." If the correct response is not presented, a default option is normally assumed. System control cards are edited and any recognized errors are typed on the operator's console for correction from that device. Errors in linkage between problem and system programs normally result in problem program termination.

4.0 PROCESSING SUPPORT

4.1 Timing Services

If the timing feature is included at system generation, a real-time clock is maintained and may be interrogated by the user program. The user may suspend task processing for a specified interval and may also request to be alerted at various time intervals.

4.2 Testing and Debugging Service

Facilities exist within the supervisor to provide intermediate as well as terminal core dumps. Intermediate core dumps may be for the total user partition or for selected areas. No tracing facilities exist within the supervisor. Abnormal end of job conditions always result in the termination of all subsequent steps within that job. Consequently, file dumps that are desired for abnormal terminations must be scheduled as a separate job.

4.3 Logging and Accounting

Each job is identified on the operator's console when it initiates and terminates processing. If timer facilities are included within the supervisor, the total time used by the job is also included. The user may include routines to supplement this facility and maintain accounting information. The system also maintains stored summaries of error statistics for each peripheral device. These summaries may be interrogated by maintenance personnel.

4.4 System Description Maintenance

A certain amount of descriptive information is maintained within the supervisor communication region and may be interrogated by a problem program. This information includes such items as the job identification, the beginning and ending core locations of the background partition and the last byte of the current problem program itself. In addition, an area is provided for interprogram communication between various steps within a given job. System descriptive information defining the system components, number of users, and so on are not directly obtainable from the supervisor, but may be obtained by users having a detailed knowledge of the supervisor layout itself.

CDC 3300/3500 MASTER OPERATING SYSTEM

MASTER is a multiprogramming executive operating system for the Control Data Corporation 3300/3500 computers. The design of the system permits expansion to multiple central processing units for multiprocessing applications.

1.0 JOB MANAGEMENT

1.1 Job Control

MASTER deals with basic program entities known as tasks, of which there are two types: program tasks and I/O tasks. Tasks are executed on two types of processors: central processing units (CPU's) for program tasks and data channels for I/O tasks.

1.1.1 Scheduling

The basic multiprogramming scheduling philosophy of MASTER is that a new job will be initiated whenever possible.

MASTER considers variables such as job class, equipment requirements, core requirements, and accumulated wait time in the input queue as scheduling parameters. All required mass storage and I/O devices must be available before a job can be initiated. In addition, except for highest priority (emergency) jobs, sufficient core for the job must also be available. MASTER will initiate emergency jobs even if all of the required internal storage is not available and will suspend tasks of lower priority whenever the emergency job reaches a point where it requires more core than is currently assigned.

Each submitted job is assigned to one of five job classes either by the user via a control card or by the job scheduler by default. MASTER attempts to keep active at least one job from each of the four nonemergency job classes: buffering, special, input/output, and compute. Multiple jobs from the same class are initiated only when scheduled jobs from other classes are not capable of being initiated. Within a class, jobs are initiated primarily on a first-in, first-out basis. However, the first job in the list might not always be the first initiated. For example, if storage or I/O requirements could not be satisfied, another job from the class would be selected. A job cannot be refused initiation because of lack of equipment more than a certain number of times as determined by an installation parameter. When the limit is reached, all nonemergency jobs are inhibited until the equipment required by the waiting job is released. Once the equipment (or core) becomes available, the waiting job is initiated and normal job scheduling resumes.

MASTER includes a facility which permits several user-supplied real-time routines to be linked into the system executive. A real-time interrupt is recognized by the supervisor which routes control to the user-supplied routine.

Executing tasks can also request the execution of other tasks by issuing a call for the task. The calling task remains suspended until the call is connected. Then, according to a parameter of the call, the calling task may be multiprogrammed with the called task or it may wait for the task to complete before resuming execution.

1.1.2 Resource Allocation

Internal storage is divided into addressable blocks containing 2,048 memory locations. Each of these blocks is called a page. Individual pages may be divided into four 1/4 pages of 512 memory locations each. Programs may have full, 3/4, 1/2, or 1/4 pages of memory allocated to them. Internal storage is assigned to each program as it is loaded by either the relocatable or absolute loader. Though actual storage allocation is performed dynamically during loading, a parameter on the job control card estimates the maximum amount of storage used by all tasks that will reside in internal storage simultaneously. A job is not permitted an internal storage allocation in excess of its estimate; if a storage request occurs that exceeds the estimate, the job is terminated abnormally.

The system provides facilities for internal storage to be shared by two or more tasks of the same job. Storage allocated in this manner is called "common storage" and may not be preloaded with data. Common core is not assigned physical memory until the task is actually established. During task execution, provision is made for any task to expand its common area or release common storage that is no longer needed.

MASTER allocates three different types of I/O facilities: input/output stream devices, unit record devices (including magnetic tape), and mass storage files. Each job is allocated an input stream and two output stream files upon initiation. All other peripheral equipment except displays and teletypes required by a job must be scheduled prior to job initiation. Unit record devices are assigned from a pool maintained for each device type by the system.

Mass storage may be either permanent files or scratch files. The number of segments required for a scratch file is specified on an input control card. Space on the scratch file is allocated dynamically during task execution and may not exceed the amount specified by this parameter.

Permanent data files are allocated on a dynamic basis and need not be scheduled via an input control card. Permanent files may be shared among any number of tasks. Should a task attempt to access a file that is being used by another task, the access request will be queued and the task will be temporarily suspended until the using task completes its I/O activities. When the access request has been dequeued and initiated, the suspended task will be resumed.

A task may also dynamically inhibit any other task from performing I/O on a file until it issues a specific file release. If a task attempts to perform I/O on a file reserved by another task, the call is queued until the reserved file is released.

When a program task in execution requests execution of another task or I/O task, it calls the supervisor which routes control to the called task. When a program task has completed operation, it relinquishes control by issuing a return to the supervisor which notifies the calling task of the completion.

MASTER service routines are treated as independent tasks when requested by a user program. If the service task is in use, the calling task will be suspended until the service task is released and available for use. Copies of some service tasks are made available to each job (for example, I/O blocking/deblocking routines), while other service tasks exist in a single copy for the entire system. Each service task is serially reusable and need not be reloaded for each call. Facilities for reentrant routines are not available.

1.1.3 Program Loading

The basic element of execution is the program task and each task is loaded and executed dynamically. When a system or a job calls for loading of a program task, one of the two MASTER loaders (relocatable or absolute) loads the task into available pages of physical memory, where it resides until its memory is released by the job or by MASTER. A program task can be loaded from the system library or from any file open to the job. Active jobs can continue to call for tasks as long as they do not exceed their core scheduling requirements. When a task completes its work, its core can be released and assigned to another task.

The memory allocator makes physical memory available to the loaders on a page basis as a task is being loaded. Each time a task is placed into execution, its page map is written into one of the eight areas of the page index file so that the physical page assignments are available to the hardware.

Memory for "common core" is assigned on a ¼-page basis after the entire task has been loaded and the memory assigned to the loader has been released. Thus this portion of memory is frequently used for the common area.

When a memory request from a high priority (emergency class) program cannot be filled by the physical memory available, the memory allocator initiates task suspension. This operation selects a task for suspension, preserves the suspended task on mass storage, and makes the released memory available to the memory allocator. A task is recalled from suspension if it is in a ready condition (not waiting for the completion of another task or for access to a reserved file) when sufficient core becomes available.

1.1.4 Event Monitoring

All program and I/O tasks are contained in task lists and have priorities assigned to them. MASTER assigns I/O tasks to data channels and program tasks to the CPU on a priority basis in such a manner as to maximize the work load on the computing system. In general, when an interrupt occurs, the supervisor processes the interrupt, updates accounting information, initiates as many I/O tasks as possible, and transfers control to the highest priority program task ready to execute.

When a task is placed in execution, a timer is set to cause an interrupt. The time limit is the minimum of: the allocated time remaining for the job, the time specified in a limit request, or the time for an execution cycle (the maximum time a task is allowed to be executed without interruption). When a time interrupt occurs, it is processed to determine which time expired. If it is the job or limit time, the job is terminated. If it is the execution cycle time, the system places the next highest priority task in execution. Execution cycle time is an installation parameter that prevents any one task from occupying the CPU indefinitely.

Event synchronization may be maintained between several tasks of a job. One task may initiate any number of subordinate tasks and may execute concurrently with them. It may, at any time, issue deferred wait requests which will suspend its processing until one or more of the subordinate tasks have been completed. The subordinate tasks may either be program or I/O tasks.

All interrupts cause the computer to enter the monitor state and transfer control to the system executive. The system recognizes eight types of interrupts: internal fault interrupts, trapped instructions, request interrupts (halts), clock (timer) interrupts, I/O interrupts, real-time-dedicated channel interrupts, manual interrupts, and other interrupts.

Monitoring limits are established for CPU time, and the two system output streams. If any one of these limits is exceeded during processing, MASTER will terminate the job abnormally.

1.1.5 Program Termination Processing

When a task and all the subtasks it may have called are completed, it returns to its calling task. If the task was specified on an execution control card, the calling task is the job monitor. Processing of a job ends when the job monitor, seeking more work form the job input stream, detects an end of file condition. Task processing can also be terminated by the operator or when a returning task notifies the job monitor of an abnormal condition.

At job end, any open files are closed. All scratch files, the input stream file, core, and any scheduled devices are released. The output post-processor is initiated to process the output stream files if any were produced.

Upon abnormal termination, if the user requested a core dump, the dump will be written as part of the system output stream. Otherwise, the user will receive only a dump of the console registers and certain basic locations in internal storage.

1.2 System Communication

1.2.1 System Startup

The operator begins a MASTER run by auto-loading a version of the MASTER system from the library. The portions that are loaded include the system initialization routine, permanently resident portions of the supervisor, tables, and the I/O control routines. MASTER automatically begins executing the initialization routine. At this time the operator enters time and date and may optionally enter commands to modify system installation parameters. These commands may be entered from either the console typewriter or the card reader. When all modification commands have been entered, the system establishes the system files and transfers control to the input symbiont (an operating system task which prepares job files for the system).

1.2.2 Job Control Communication

A user submits a job to the system as a set of control cards which may be accompanied by source language decks, binary object decks, and data. Through control cards, the user provides information the system needs to: allocate storage and equipment, schedule a job and initiate its tasks, assign priorities, and perform other job monitoring functions. If a control card is out of sequence or contains an error, the job is terminated and a message is written on the job's output stream.

1.2.3 Input/Output Stream Control

All user job decks are presented serially to the system through the input card reader. The input symbiont loads the card images onto a job input stream file located on mass storage. Jobs can be transferred continuously to input stream files by the input symbiont until there are no more jobs in the input card reader.

Symbiont pre-processing may be bypassed by specifying a direct input/output requirement for the job. In this case, input is read directly from the input card reader as required. Output stream files are processed similarly by output symbionts after the job has terminated. Output symbiont specifications may also be overridden and the output produced directly by the program on a line printer or card punch.

1.2.4 Resource Status Modification
No information was available for this functional area.

1.2.5 System Status Interrogation
No information was available for this functional area.

1.3 Recover Processing
The system does not appear to directly support checkpoint and restart facilities for user programs.

2.0 I/O CONTROL
2.1 I/O Scheduling
The MASTER I/O control system (MIOCS) makes available a comprehensive I/O facility for all equipment. The user calls the *open* routine to prepare existing file definitions for data transmission. The *open* routine sets up internal tables and, when necessary, requests the operator to prepare mass storage devices associated with the file definitions.

MIOCS processes I/O calls from program tasks as well as from the resident supervisor. For each I/O call it assigns equipment and a channel to the I/O task and adds the request to a work queue for the respective channel. As each channel becomes idle, the task with the highest priority in the work queue is initiated. In addition, MIOCS processes all nonreal time I/O interrupts.

2.2 Data Transfer
MASTER provides both logical and physical input/output facilities for data transfer. The two logical I/O routines (blocker and deblocker) perform input/output with logical blocked records and thus reduce the number of actual data transfers. Facilities are available for the user to directly control his own I/O via read and write macro commands. Although the operating system always uses blocker and deblocker for its job files, the user may elect either logical or physical I/O for processing.

Logical I/O routines use a buffer for each I/O operation. Each system file, including the input and output streams, has a permanently assigned buffer within the protected supervisor core area. The user is required to establish buffers for nonsystem files within his own program area.

The MASTER system operates in an environment in which all files have an identical basic structure. All files are subdivided into groups having identical logical block sizes. The logical block size is the number of 6-bit characters in each block. Logical block sizes may vary among files, but no files may exceed system specified limits. Only sequential access control techniques are provided within the MIOCS structure. A separate file management system (linked indexed sequential access) provides support for indexed sequential files.

2.3 Remote Terminal Support

Remote terminal support is not included as an integral part of MIOCS. It may, however, be provided by user written routines.

2.4 File Handling

Permanent files may be allocated as Class A storage (nonremovable) or Class B storage (removable). Mass storage file labels contain identification information consisting of the owner name, file name, and edition number. Part of the label includes an access privacy code and a modification privacy code. Use of the file requires the access code; modification of the file size or label requires both codes. The system will reject any I/O command when a mismatch occurs.

A catalog of file labels for all mass storage devices is maintained as a system file. The user must provide information (file identification) that uniquely identifies and describes each file he creates. MASTER provides the user with a broad range of functions for manipulating the permanent file definitions. The user may call functions to create a file, to build entries in system files, to reserve additional mass storage for the file, to remove a file from the system, or to change parts of the file definition itself.

3.0 DIAGNOSTIC ERROR PROCESSING

3.1 Hardware Error Control

Hardware errors on mass storage devices and unit record devices permit either automatic system recovery or user specified recovery. If user specified recovery is desired, control is given to a user routine to provide the necessary recovery procedure that is compatible with the system. If automatic recovery procedures are requested, control is transferred to an executive routine which determines the exact nature of the error and types a diagnostic message.

Error recovery techniques vary and are based on the characteristics of the particular device. The applicable error recovery procedure is executed and, if successful, returns control to the user. If a recovery procedure is not successful, another diagnostic message is typed, the error is declared irrecoverable, and control is returned to the user.

3.2 Program Error Control

Program errors occuring during requested I/O operations return control to the user with an appropriate program error code in the I/O status word. Program checks (internal faults) are interpreted by a portion of the resident supervisor, which immediately passes control to a user interrupt control routine. A user interrupt control routine is required for each task and it is the responsibility of this control routine to take whatever corrective action is necessary.

3.3 Interface Error Control

When interface errors occur in requests for system services, the system response depends on the source of the request. If the service was requested by an executing program via a macro call, the error is treated exactly like an I/O program check, and an error code is set in the I/O status word. The user program is allowed to take whatever corrective action is necessary. If the service was requested via an external control card (e.g., storage allocation) the job is terminated abnormally.

4.0 PROCESSING SUPPORT

4.1 Timing Service

A task may request the time and data via a supervisor request. It may also request that a time limit for the execution of a task or a portion of a task be set. Only one time limit per job can be in effect at any one time; a later request will take precedence over an earlier request. Another supervisor request may be used to remove the time limit restriction.

4.2 Testing and Debugging Service

The user may request snapshot core dumps through an internal request to the system supervisor or through use of a snapshot control card submitted with his job deck. In either case, coding is inserted into his program, which will transfer control to the snapshot routine. The snapshot routine will provide a partial core dump in octal, character, decimal, or floating point format. A core dump is provided upon abnormal termination only if it has been specifically requested by the user via a system control card.

Another testing service facility permits the user to direct MIOCS to ignore all I/O operations for a specific file requested by any task of a job. Whenever a reference to the bypassed file is specified, the request is ignored and treated as if it had been completed successfully.

4.3 Logging and Accounting

The system maintains accounting information for each job processed and, as each job terminates, writes this information on the job's output stream and onto an optional system accounting file.

The system accounting file is a mass storage file allocated at the option of the installation. Accounting information is stored in 30-word binary records. When the information stored nears the capacity of the file, a diagnostic message requests the operator to take specific action. Normally, the operator will direct the system to write the mass storage file onto either magnetic tape, another mass storage file, or punched cards.

No mention is made in the documentation provided of the maintenance of any error statistics for hardware or software.

4.4 System Description Maintenance

A program may ascertain the type of I/O device that is currently assigned to a permanent file. No other information was provided regarding the capability of the system to provide executing tasks with information regarding current system status.

HONEYWELL SERIES 200 MOD 4 OPERATING SYSTEM

The Mod 4 operating system is a multiprogramming system capable of executing up to 20 independent programs concurrently. The communication facilities of Mod 4 allow both remote job entry and interactive terminal communication.

1.0 JOB MANAGEMENT
1.1 Job Control
1.1.1 Scheduling

The Mod 4 operating system allows the definition of up to 20 partitions, each of which may process as many as three different job classes. Separate input queues are maintained for each job class. Each queue collects control information for jobs of that class as they are read into the system. Entries may be entered on each input queue from the local job stream, a remote terminal, or the operator's console. There are four levels of job onto each class queue in that priority. There are two levels of priority in the Mod 4 Operating System, and jobs are entered first-in, first-out priority—an urgent level that supersedes all lower priority jobs, and a "hold" level where the job is entered into the system but cannot be run until its priority is raised.

When one of the partitions is ready to accommodate a new job, the monitor loads the scheduler into that partition. The scheduler then proceeds to search the class queues of that partition for the next eligible job. The scheduler will schedule only those jobs with class designations that correspond to the class designations of the partition.

After selecting a job from the input queue, the scheduler determines if the resources needed for the job are available. If they are not, the scheduler proceeds to examine the next job in the partition's queue. If the available resources are not adequate for any of the jobs queued for that partition, the monitor suspends the scheduler until additional resources become available. When the requirements of a job can be satisfied, the scheduler proceeds to allocate memory, make the physical device assignments, and type the mounting instructions to the machine operator.

The scheduler then loads a transitional monitor into the partition. This monitor reads, analyzes, and processes the monitor control cards for the job. Upon its completion, the transitional monitor is overlaid in the partition by the first job step. The transitional monitor reenters the partition at the conclusion of each job step to read and process the monitor control cards for the next job step. The transitional monitor recognizes "conditional" control cards which allow job steps to be bypassed based upon condition codes and/or sense switch settings.

1.1.2 Resource Allocation

There are two types of partitions within the Mod 4 operating system. The first is of fixed length, the other of variable length. Internal storage allocation for fixed length partitions consists merely of scheduling the program into that partition. No further internal storage allocation is required. Programs in variable length partitions, on the other hand, may expand or contract as the job proceeds from step to step. In scheduling these jobs, the user specifies the maximum size required to accommodate the largest job step in the job. The job is not scheduled until the space is available. The user may reduce the size of the variable partition during job execution, but may not increase it.

The system has a memory protection feature that prevents one program from writing into the core area allocated to another program. A memory protect violation results in an internal interrupt. Though no provision is made for passing information between jobs in different partitions, the system also allows a five-character common communication region for passing information between job steps.

I/O devices are allocated either by specific physical device identification or from system provided device pools. A device pool is a group of interchangeable physical units (tape drives, disk pack drives, etc.) defined at system generation time. In allocating I/O devices, the user specifies from which device pool the unit is to be selected. Devices may be returned to the device pool at any time through appropriate job control cards. Device sharing is permitted on direct access devices unless specifically prohibited by the user.

Core and I/O devices are allocated on a job basis. Consequently, there is no dynamic allocation of these facilities available to the problem program. The problem program can, however, dynamically load and execute programs within its partition during program execution.

The resident monitor also permits serially reusable subroutines and provides the associated lock routines that are required for this type of processing.

1.1.3 Program Loading

The Mod 4 system loader is used to load all system and user programs. It is capable of loading programs from resident disk files, temporary disk files, and temporary tape files, and supports simple, overlay, and dynamic structures. Any program is capable of executing a calling sequence for the loading and execution of another program within its partition. All program load modules are in absolute format; however, the hardware of the Series 200 provides a base relocation register which permits programs to be executed in any partition.

1.1.4 Event Monitoring

Time is allocated to the partitions on either a linear basis, round-robin basis, or a combination of the two. The method selected is generated with the system during initial system generation. The linear distribution system guarantees that the partition with the highest processing priority will receive central processor cycles as long as it can use them. The partition with the next highest processing priority can receive only those CPU cycles that the highest priority partition is unable to use. This continues down to the partition of lowest priority, which receives only those CPU cycles that cannot be used by any other partition in the system. When processing priorities of several systems are equal, associated partitions receive equal chances for obtaining CPU cycles, resulting in what is commonly termed "round-robin task switching." A combination of the linear and equal priority schemes is normally desirable in a combined real-time and nonreal-time environment. The real-time partitions receive higher processing priorities than the nonreal-time partitions.

The Mod 4 operating system recognizes and handles two levels of interrupts, internal and external. A protection violation, illegal operation code, floating-point error, or instruction time-out can cause an internal interrupt. An external interrupt can be caused by a monitor call (from a problem program), a peripheral interrupt, or a control panel interrupt. Control is passed to the routine designated by one of the two interrupt registers when the given type of interrupt occurs. A high level interrupt gains control if the machine is in a low level interrupt mode.

The user may employ a limit control card which will specify the maximum number of pages to be printed or cards to be punched. If either of these limits is reached during the execution of a job, the job will be terminated abnormally.

1.1.5 Program Termination Processing

At the completion of a job, the transitional monitor performs job accounting, releases the jobs resources to the central resource pool, and prepares the job's output file for disposition by the system output writer. It then exits to the resident monitor which loads the scheduler back into the partition to schedule the next eligible job.

1.2 System Communication
1.2.1 System Startup

The system initialization program consists of a bootstrap routine and a routine to set up the machine configuration, read the daily information, and initialize the partitions. The system-generated partition sizes may be adjusted by the operator during initialization. Control is then passed to the communications startup routine to initialize the communications supervisor if real-time operations are required.

In case of a total system restart, a restart capability permits all the queued jobs to remain enqueued within the system for subsequent processing. Only those jobs that were in process at the time of shutdown must be rescheduled.

1.2.2 Job Control Communication

The input reader (see 1.2.3) processes the job control cards and loads them onto an input queue. The user may have as many input readers active as he needs and has memory to accommodate. Once initiated, the input reader is capable of accepting job control language (JCL) commands from the operator console, the local job stream, an on-line remote terminal, or from the system library (in the case of cataloged procedures).

The job control language is of fixed format using positional parameters. Each job control card is identified by the characters MON$$ in columns 6 through 10. The control function is specified in columns 16 through 20 and the operands are specified starting in column 21. All parameters are separated by commas, and a missing parameter is indicated by consecutive commas.

Communication between the operator and monitor, or user program, is handled by the console inquiry routine. Each message that is typed out on the console is preceded by two characters that identify the source of the message. Key-ins by the operator must be preceded by a similar prefix to identify the partition or portion of the system that is being addressed.

The communications supervisor also controls the execution of various job steps. Unlike batch jobs, the execution of a communications job step is directed not through JCL statements but dynamically through data input from a remote terminal or by means of a request from another communications program being executed.

1.2.3 Input/Output Stream Control

The system input device, called the input reader, preprocesses the input job stream and places it onto the input job queue. It also validates the job control cards and determines the device and file requirements for the particular job. These requirements are supplied to the Scheduler during the scheduling process. The system input device is capable of processing input from the card reader, magnetic tape, paper tape, remote console, opertor's console, and sequential disk files.

The output data is normally written onto a job output file on disk. The system provides a symbiont called the output writer which transcribes the contents of the job output files onto the devices specified by the user. The output writer is loaded into an area of memory either by a console key-in or through job control language statements. It may be removed only through a console key-in by the operator. Although it is resident until removed, the output writer is active only when there are output files eligible for transcription. The output writer suspends itself whenever there are no output files available. It is reactivated by the system monitor whenever a new output file becomes available.

A user may create his own system output writer to satisfy special output writing or formatting requirements. User written output writers are scheduled and executed just as the standard system output writers are.

1.2.4 Resource Status Modification

The operator may alter the status of system resources at any time from the operator console. He may initiate or terminate activity in any or all partitions. He may add or delete peripheral devices from the system. He may also modify the sizes of partitions and/or their relative priority within the multiprogramming scheme.

1.2.5 System Status Interrogation

The operator may initiate inquiries from his console at any time. He may display a list of active jobs and their respective partitions, all the job queues, all jobs in any class queue, and the status of any job (by name). He may also, any time, display the error counts accumulated for each physical unit.

1.3 Recovery Processing

1.3.1 Checkpointing

A problem program may checkpoint its partition at any time during processing. As with most checkpoint systems, I/O device positioning information is recorded.

1.3.2 Restarting

There are four primary types of restart capabilities available within the Mod 4 operating system: checkpoint, job step, job and system. Restarts may be taken from a checkpoint within a job step or the job may be reinitiated at the beginning of the previous job step or at the beginning of the job. A restart is initiated by a phase of the resident monitor which is optionally scheduled whenever an abnormal termination occurs. Scheduling of this phase is specified by the user job control card. The phase, when called, determines if the current job is a communications job and if so, loads the communications recovery routine. If not, it exits to the transitional monitor to interrogate the operator for restart information. The operator may optionally select job restart, step restart, checkpoint restart, or no restart. An additional capability allows the system to be shut down while needed information still exists in the job queues. The system restart permits all queued jobs to remain in the system for subsequent execution. However, jobs that were being processed at the time of shutdown must be rescheduled.

Recovery capabilities for communications jobs are handled through the communications supervisor. Whenever any of the queues used by the supervisor is changed, it can be recorded on either disk or drum. If a system restart point is required, the information can be retrieved for a smooth recovery of the system. The supervisor also provides a history tape routine for the recovery of data files used by a communications job program. This capability can be used to write "before" and "after" images of each disk/drum record updated by communication programs. This allows a broad range of recovery procedures for each data file used in a communications job.

2.0 I/O CONTROL

2.1 I/O Scheduling

When a logical file is opened by a problem program, the open routine determines the physical device address for the file and inserts this address in the logical file control table. Since this address will be static until the file is closed (or an end of reel condition occurs), device resolution is required only at this processing point.

The I/O Control system maintains one read/write list for each peripheral control unit available to using programs. The elements on read/write lists represent requests for input/output operations and are normally processed in the order received.

2.2 Data Transfer

The Mod 4 input/output file control system (IOFCS) consists of program modules which supervise all input/output processing in the system and provide the overlapping of I/O operations necessary in a multiprogramming environment. The data access function is performed by two groups of modules: logical I/O, which is charged with file control, and physical I/O, which controls the physical input/output units. Logical I/O serves as the interface between the user program and physical I/O. It blocks and unblocks records received or transmitted, control file access, resolves contradictions in I/O requests, directs physical I/O to execute specific input/output operations, and receives a termination signal from physical I/O when the operations are complete. Physical I/O performs input/output processing for physical units. It schedules read/write channels, performs necessary I/O housekeeping functions, and interfaces logical I/O with the various device service routines.

A device service routine is constructed for each physical unit type. These routines match the particular characteristics of the peripheral device to the uniform interface of physical I/O. The routines check the status of peripheral control units and issue the physical peripheral data transfer instructions. Device manipulation routines are also executed by the device service routines.

The Mod 4 operating system supports three types of file organization: sequential, indexed sequential, and direct access. Services are provided for both blocked and unblocked, fixed and variable length records on tape, and for blocked fixed length records on direct access devices. The system provides deblocking facilities for blocked records and automatic buffering facilities.

A resident communications supervisor that handles the communication lines and the many special actions required for the control of a communication network, couples the remote terminals to inquiry/response programs in user partitions. The communications control program formats messages, performs error and sequence checks, polls terminals, and handles the numerous other housekeeping tasks which communications processing entails. The supervisor decodes input messages, schedules the appropriate program to process each message, and performs code translation and message-editing functions. The communications supervisor also allocates storage for message buffering.

2.3 Remote Terminal Support

The communications supervisor couples the remote terminals to the input reader and output writer programs as if they were local peripheral devices. A batch job may be entered from a remote terminal exactly as it is entered from the local card reader. All of the options and capabilities offered to the job entered locally are also offered to the job entered from a remote terminal. The communications supervisor also couples the remote terminals to inquiry/response programs that occupy user partitions. Interactive I/O support is handled via this supervisor.

2.4 File Handling

All files are assigned symbolic names, and the operating system maintains a symbolic file catalog. The catalog is constructed with several qualifying levels so that each file is categorized by a symbolic description of its functions. Files may be requested by means of these symbolic descriptions and the catalog provides the unique location from which the operating system retrieves each file. An additional capability is available to the disk user, which enables him to specify exclusive control for a record or a file. This capability assures the user that the file or record will not be disturbed as long as it is so designated. Data file security may also be preserved by limiting file access to those programs supplying a correct password. Programs that do not supply the correct password are denied access.

All system files are labeled and the system provides label checking facilities. The user may include his own label handling routines to supplement the system routines. He may also provide his own labels that are not system labels and must, of course, supply the routines to process them.

3.0 DIAGNOSTIC ERROR PROCESSING

3.1 Hardware Error Control

An error routine is provided for each type of input/output device. Each error routine attempts to correct the error conditions directed to it for correction by reexecuting the relevant I/O operation or by other means peculiar to the affected I/O device. If the error recurs, the operation is continually repeated until a specified error threshold is reached. When this maximum value is reached, the error is considered uncorrectable and the system determines if a user error routine has been provided. If so, control is passed to the user's error routine. If not, the program is terminated abnormally. All other hardware malfunctions result in abnormal program termination.

The communications supervisor requests retransmittal of input messages containing errors. It may also initiate corrective action whenever such an error is detected. If a failure in a remote terminal or a communications line is indicated, the communications supervisor will reroute output messages.

3.2 Program Error Control

A program error automatically causes the system to terminate the program abnormally. Considerable flexibility is available for this type of processing. The programmer may specify that a core dump or partial dump is to be taken. He may specify file dumps for tape, disk, or drum files. He may also specify that the operator be notified of the condition and given the option to provide additional dumps. If the job is a communications program, recovery procedures are automatically initiated, while if it is a noncommunications program, the operator may initiate restart either of the job, job step, or last checkpoint.

3.3 Interface Error Control

The system input reader edits and validates all job control cards prior to placing the job in the input queue. If a fatal error—one that would prevent successful execution—is found, the job is rejected by the input reader and the operator is so notified.

A fixed calling sequence is used to request the services of the resident monitor by the problem program. When a monitor call occurs, control is passed to the monitor call interface routine which checks the validity of the call and passes control to the proper routine. Checks are performed to see that the calling parameter linkage is correct. Errors in format cause the job to be aborted.

4.0 PROCESSING SUPPORT

4.1 Timing Services

Three timing service routines are provided which use the time-of-day clock and the interval timer. One routine provides the user with the actual time of day. A second routine allows a task to suspend itself for a specified interval or to generate a branch to another routine after a specified time interval. A third routine allows the user to request the amount of time remaining in the time interval set by the previous routine.

4.2 Testing and Debugging Service

An abnormal program termination routine is provided which permits the programmer to specify the options to be taken under this condition. Included among these options are core dumps, file dumps, and optional operator notification. A utility program called the Program Test System is also provided that permits intermediate core dumps as well as address stop and program-patching facilities.

4.3 Logging and Accounting

Job accounting is available in the Mod 4 operating system as an optional feature. The accounting options supply the following information for each job processed: date, job identification, elapsed time, core memory, and job termination status. A system log file is available to contain all the accounting information on every job processed by the system. In addition, a user exit is provided which enables the user to edit his own accounting records and write his own log file.

4.4 System Description Maintenance

Each problem program has a communication region it may interrogate for such information as the size of the partition, the current program size and name, the number of lines per page allocated to the printer, and the last loaded phase number in the partition.

IBM SYSTEM/360 OPERATING SYSTEM (OS)—MFT/MVT

The IBM SYSTEM/360 Operating System is a general purpose operating system with options for serial processing (PCP); multiprogramming with a fixed number of tasks (MFT) and multiprogramming with a variable number of tasks (MVT). A multiprocessing version of MVT is available for the Model 65 Computer.

1.0 JOB MANAGEMENT
1.1 Job Control
1.1.1 Scheduling

Within MFT and MVT the area of storage not utilized by the system is available to the users. In MFT this area is divided into a number of partitions; each partition may contain one task. In MVT storage is allocated to each job according to its requirements; jobs are not directed to specific partitions.

Scheduling Under MFT

There may be up to 52 partitions under MFT. Of the 52 possible tasks, as many as 15 separate jobs, 3 readers, and 36 output writers may be executing.

Incoming jobs are enqueued on one of 15 available queues, corresponding to a job class parameter specified by a job control statement. Position on a queue is determined by priority within class. Jobs of equal priority are enqueued on a first-in, first-out basis. Each partition can service up to three job queues. Priority among queues for each partition is based on the order on which they were originally defined. That is, if a partition is to serve class A and B, all A jobs will be scheduled before any B jobs. It is also possible to assign several partitions to serve the same job class.

Scheduling Under MVT

As in MFT, jobs are placed on a separate input queue for each job class and the position of a job on a queue is determined by the job priority. A maximum number of 15 jobs can run concurrently. A given job is initiated by an initiator routine assigned to handle a specific job class. Each initiator will handle only one class, though any number of initiators may be started for a given class. The initiator selects a job from the job class and schedules it for execution. It does not schedule another job until the first job has terminated. Thus the number of jobs multiprogrammed is equal to the number of initiators in the system.

In both MFT and MVT, jobs are selected and initiated only if all data sets, sufficient core, and all required I/O devices are available.

Program-initiated scheduling is available under MVT. A program executes a request to the supervisor to attach another task. The supervisor then creates a new task and schedules its execution. The new task is a subtask of the originating task. A different priority may be specified for the subtask than that of the originating task. All tasks within a job step can execute asynchronously.

Job steps within a single job are performed in sequential order.

The system provides for conditional execution of subsequent job steps, depending on the successful or unsuccessful completion of the previous one. The conditional logic is provided via job control cards.

1.1.2 Resource Allocation

Certain system resources such as internal storage and CPU control are assigned only to tasks. This assignment takes place on a priority basis. The system supervises allocation, keeps track of all assignments, and frees resources upon task completion.

In a multitasking environment more than one task may be contending for the same resource at the same time. Requests are queued, and when the resource becomes available, it is given to the ranking member of the queue. To keep track of assignments, the supervisor maintains queues that represent unsatisfied requests for resources and tables that identify available resources.

The amount of internal storage required for a job may be specified for each step or for the job as a whole. Although a fixed amount of storage is allocated to a job or job step, under MVT additional storage can also be allocated through the roll-out, roll-in feature. This feature allows a job to temporarily expand dynamically beyond the amount of internal storage originally allocated. If no unassigned storage is available, another job is rolled-out onto disk and its core area is used by the first job for as long as is necessary.

The system provides three types of buffer allocation. The area to be used as a buffer may be defined at assembly time, acquired during execution by a macro instruction, or acquired by default when opening a file. When the latter method is used, a buffer is not assigned to each input request prior to execution. Instead, a buffer is taken from a pool and assigned immediately before data transfer begins. The buffer remains in use until it is returned to the pool. It can then be dynamically assigned to another active request. Relatively few buffers are needed with this technique.

The supervisor controls and allocates storage space dynamically, and permits problem program requests for dynamic allocation. Under MVT areas of storage can be passed or shared between tasks. The system provides for the creation of subpools (2K blocks of main storage allocated for a particular task under one label). Subpools are made available to a task when it is attached. The subpools may be released at the termination of the task or they may be retained by the attaching task. Core cannot be shared by succeeding steps of the same job.

Main internal storage is protected in blocks of 2,048 bytes. The supervisor area is assigned a special protection key and distinct keys are assigned to each scheduled task. All tasks created from the same job step have the same key.

I/O devices are allocated at the beginning of the job. Jobs are not scheduled until all devices are available. Devices may be allocated by physical device ID, by device type (e.g., card reader or tape) or by device category (e.g., sequential or direct access).

The system provides access control facilities for three types of routines: nonreusable, serially reusable, and reentrant. The reentrant routines may be used by more than one task simultaneously. Serially reusable routines may not be used simultaneously; however, the requests are placed in a queue until the routine becomes available, at which time the first request receives control of the routine. Nonresuable routines are loaded from disk for each access request.

Selected system reentrant routines are loaded at system initalization time in an area of storage called the link pack area and are available to all tasks in the system simultaneously.

1.1.3 Program Loading

Simple, overlay, and dynamic program structures are supported by the system. Since a dynamic structure requires more than one load module during execution, each module required can operate as a simple, overlay, or dynamic structure itself. All core load modules are relocatable under both MFT and MVT.

When a job terminates, an initiator/terminator routine overlays the program to perform the termination sequence. Upon completion of termination, the initiator/terminator determines if some space is available between it and the next lower program in core. If so, the next scheduled job is loaded to eliminate this gap, thus effecting a form of storage compaction.

A roll-out, roll-in feature is available under MVT. It allows allocation of core beyond the amount originally allocated. If not enough assigned storage is available, another job is rolled-out onto disk, so that its core area may be used by the first job. When the core is released by the first job, the rolled-out job is loaded back (rolled-in) into main storage.

1.1.4 Event Monitoring

Time is allocated on a contention basis, with the highest priority program in a ready state receiving use of the CPU. A program releases control of the CPU when it must wait for the completion of some event, such as an I/O operation. At this point a lower priority task is granted use of the CPU. When a higher priority task is ready to resume processing, a lower priority task is suspended and the CPU is given to the higher priority task.

Dispatching priority (CPU access priority) is established as follows:

a. In MVT, when a job is initiated, the job priority is used to establish a dispatching priority and a limit priority. When a task attaches a subtask, the dispatching priority of the new task may be the same as that of the originating task, or it may be set higher or lower as long, as it is within the bounds set by the limit priority.

b. In MFT, the highest partition storage has the highest dispatching priority. The next highest partition has the next highest dispatching priority, and so forth. The priority of each task is determined by the partition in which it resides.

A time-slicing capability is also available. All tasks with a certain priority (MVT), or all tasks within a group of consecutive partitions (MFT), may be allocated CPU time for an equal, predetermined interval. The time-slice group competes for CPU time on a contention basis and the tasks within the group are time sliced only as long as the group has control of the CPU.

Under MFT, when the time-slicing facility is selected, the time-slice group is composed of a group of contiguous partitions. This group is time-sliced only when the first partition in the group is the highest priority ready task.

Under MVT all tasks in the time-slice group have the same priority, and they are time sliced only when the priority level of the group is the highest priority level that has a task in ready state. Time slicing continues within the group until all tasks are in a nonready state or a task with higher priority becomes ready.

Task execution may be suspended until some specified event or events occur. The supervisor will notify the program that the event has occurred and schedule the program for execution. Events recognized are: specified I/O conditions, timer interrupts, and external interrupts. A task may also be suspended until an attached subtask reaches a certain stage of execution.

Five classes of interruption conditions are possible: I/O, program, supervisor call, external, and machine check. Machine check, program check, and I/O interrupts may be masked. Masked interrupts are deferred until they are unmasked. During execution of an instruction, several interruption-causing events may occur simultaneously. In this case, the interruptions are stacked and honored in a predetermined order.

Maximum execution time of a job step may be specified through a job control statement; the program will be terminated if this limit is exceeded.

1.1.5 Program Termination Processing

The system is notified when a task has completed execution. The supervisor then frees resources and disposes of data files. A symbiont is scheduled to transcribe output data to a system output device (see 1.2.3).

The system provides automatic core dumps when an abnormal termination has occurred. The error that caused the termination is indicated. Abnormal termination of a task will always cause abnormal termination of all the attached subtasks. However, a subtask may terminate abnormally without causing termination of the attaching task.

1.2 System Communication
1.2.1 System Startup

A nucleus initialization program is loaded to initialize the system. This program permits last-minute changes to certain options specified during system generation. For example, under MFT the number of partitions and the classes assigned to each partition may be modified. If the time-slicing option is selected, the group of tasks or partitions to be time sliced, the length of the time slice, and (in MVT only) the priority of the time-sliced tasks, can also be modified.

The operator is required to supply the date and time of day. He also gives initialization instructions to necessary system readers and initiators at this time.

A system-supported restart is available, which will use suspended system job and data queues that have been preserved by system restart facilities.

1.2.2 Job Control Communication

The main technique utilized for job control is the job control language. Through the JCL, the user regulates the execution of job steps, specifies data characteristics and device requirements, determines disposition of data, and allows jobs to share data files in a multiprogramming environment. Job control statements are usually entered in the local input stream. However, job control information may also be submitted to the system from remote on-line terminals.

Applications requiring heavy use of control statements and which are used on a regular basis can be simplified through the use of cataloged procedures. These are sets of job control statements that are placed in a system library and are retrieved by a single control statement. Temporary changes can also be made to cataloged procedures by statements in the job stream.

1.2.3 Input/Output Stream Control

Multiple reader symbionts, each responsible for reading one input job stream, may function concurrently. Each symbiont reads job control statements, analyzes their contents, transcribes data from the input device to a direct access device, and places the job control information on an input queue in priority sequence. The reader also builds the necessary control tables that describe the job to the system.

During task execution output data directed to the system output devices is stored on a direct access storage device. A reference to the data is placed on an output job queue. After the termination of the job, an output writer transcribes the data to a system output device, normally a printer or a punch. Each system output device is controlled by an output writer. The output writer selects jobs from the output queue on a priority basis.

Reader and writer symbionts overlap with the execution of other jobs. The executing program thereby receives its input and disposes of its output at disk speed.

1.2.4 Resource Status Modification

The operator may place I/O devices on-line and off-line by means of system action commands. These commands are normally entered from the console typewriter, but may also be placed as statements in the job stream.

Under MFT the operator may also redefine the size and number of partitions and the classes assigned to them at any time.

1.2.5 System Status Interrogation

The operator can request certain types of status information from the console typewriter. He may obtain a display of active jobs, core allocation, jobs in the input job queue, and jobs in the output job queue.

The operator may also request specific information about the status of a given job, such as assigned class, assigned priority, and current status (executing, waiting, etc.).

1.3 Recovery Processing
1.3.1 Checkpointing

A checkpoint may be initiated by any problem program. The program's partition storage area and control registers are written onto the checkpoint file. Device repositioning information is also retained.

A system initiated checkpoint will occur when it becomes necessary to roll-out a job.

1.3.2 Restarting

Checkpoint restarts may be automatic (with the operator's consent) or deferred for later submission. In either case, the supervisor retrieves the checkpoint control information, ensures that volumes are correctly mounted, and repositions tapes. Programs and data are restored to the locations occupied at checkpoint time; control is returned to the problem program, and processing is resumed.

The capability of restarting from the beginning of a job step is also available. It is similar to a checkpoint restart, except that the entire step is initiated. A job step restart is requested through job control statements.

The system provides facilities for recovery from hardware malfunctions. To ensure efficient use of these facilities, refreshable program modules are required. A refreshable module is one that cannot be modified by itself or by any other program during execution. If there are indications that program damage has occurred, and if the damaged module is a refreshable module, the system replaces it with a new copy before attempting normal restart procedures.

2.0 I/O CONTROL
2.1 I/O Scheduling

I/O device resolution occurs during the execution of the OPEN macro instruction. The symbolic file referenced by the problem program is equated to a physical device and the physical device address is saved for future I/O operations against the file.

Two or more simultaneous requests for use of a channel or control unit cause one of the requests to be entered on an I/O queue. I/O queues are normally serviced according to the dispatching priority of the task requesting the service, but in some cases the supervisor considers hardware optimization over priority when selecting an entry from the queue. For example, requests for access to a disk may be serviced in a fashion that minimizes disk seek time.

2.2 Data Transfer

The following file organizations are supported: sequential, indexed sequential, partitioned, direct access, and teleprocessing.

Two general techniques are provided for handling data, the queued technique and the basic technique. The queued technique deals with individual records and may only be used to retrieve records in sequential order. Records are brought into main storage before they are actually requested, thus eliminating unnecessary waiting for programmed I/O operations. The basic technique deals with blocks. A block is brought into core at the time of the request, not in advance of it.

Simple, exchange, and chained segment buffering techniques are available. In addition, a dynamic buffering technique (used only for the queued access technique) takes a buffer from a system buffer pool and assigns it to an input record. The buffer is automatically returned to the pool once the input record has been processed.

The supervisor provides automatic blocking and deblocking facilities as part of its buffering activity.

The data may be accessed in a work area independent of the input or output buffer or via a pointer to a specific record location within one of the buffer areas.

Teleprocessing access routines provide the following functions: polling terminals sharing the same line, analyzing message headers to determine where input and output messages are to be routed, queueing and checking the sequence numbers of incoming messages, translating between external transmission code and internal processing code, and checking for transmission errors.

2.3 Remote Terminal Support

Remote terminal support is limited to remote batch job initiation. This facility allows job control information to be submitted to a system input reader from a remote on-line terminal.

2.4 File Handling

The system provides for data file cataloging. The catalog permits storage and retrieval of a file based on name alone. File name, volume serial number, device type, and the file sequence number are stored in the system catalog. File names can be composed of several words separated by periods for multiple levels of indexing.

The system allows data files to be flagged as protected. This protection flag is tested by the control program. If protected, a correct password must be entered from the console before the file can be accessed.

System routines automatically check and write system standard labels when a file is opened or closed. Facilities for nonstandard label processing are also provided.

3.0 DIAGNOSTIC ERROR PROCESSING

3.1 Hardware Error Control

Different types of recovery management facilities are available under System/360 OS, depending on the model and storage size. System environment recording (with two options) and the machine-check handler are facilities designated to receive control when a machine check is detected. A channel-check handler program receives control when a channel check occurs. If the channel-check handler is not present in an installation, one of the other recovery facilities is selected to log error data for channel failures.

When a hardware malfunction occurs, a machine check interruption is generated and control is passed to the recovery facilities. These programs record the system environment and generate an error record containing the data associated with the malfunction. The error records facilitate the diagnosis and repair of unrecoverable machine malfunctions.

System environment recording, option 0, is the least complex of the recovery facilities. It determines the type of malfunction, writes an error record, and issues instructions to the operator to reload the operating system. If the error record cannot be generated, a message is issued to the operator requesting the use of a diagnostic program.

System environment recording, option 1, performs a selective termination analysis that attempts to associate the error with a particular task. If the routines are successful in establishing this relationship, the affected task is terminated, an error record is written out, and system operation continues. If the error cannot be associated with a specific task or if the error record cannot be written out, a message is issued to the operator requesting him to reload the operating system.

The machine-check handler analyzes the malfunction to determine the level at which recovery is feasible. If recovery is not possible at the functional level (by repairing the failure and/or retrying the interrupted instruction), it then attempts, at the system level, to associate the failure with a specific task in order to allow the selective termination of the affected job.

Recovery may also be attempted at the system-supported restart level by reinitializing the system, using system, job, and data queues that have been preserved by system restart facilities.

The channel-check handler receives control when a channel failure is detected. The analysis performed by this routine aids error recovery routines in setting up for a retry of the failing operation. The channel-check handler also generates an error record containing the environment of the channel failure.

3.2 Program Error Control

The user may provide his own routines to process program check errors. He may specify the types of program interruptions his routines will handle and the types the supervisor is to handle. The supervisor normally acts on uncorrectable program errors such as execution of privileged instructions, violation of storage protection, and so forth.

For abnormal conditions that are possible to correct, control is returned to the processing program with an indication of the probable source of the error. If conditions indicate that further processing would result in destruction of data or possible degradation of the system, an abnormal termination routine receives control.

3.3 Interface Error Control

The system checks messages entered by the operator to ensure that valid response formats have been used. Job control cards are edited by the input reader and any detected errors prevent the job from being scheduled for execution.

4.0 PROCESSING SUPPORT

4.1 Timing Services

A real-time clock is maintained by the supervisor. The system will provide the problem program with both the time of the day and calendar date when requested. The problem program may request that the supervisor communicate with the program after a stated period of time. Intervals may be requested in real-time (actual time elapsed) or task time (the time the task is actually using the CPU). The program may also request suspension until a real-time interval is completed.

4.2 Testing and Debugging Service

Storage dumps can be obtained as part of the abnormal termination procedures. A snapshot dump is also available to the executing program. A separate utility program called TESTRAN, for program testing and debugging, is available with the system, but is not a part of the supervisor proper. This program allows a wide range of debugging capabilities.

4.3 Logging and Accounting

A job account log is provided. For each job, the log shows job name, assigned account number, and the time used for execution of each job step. Information can be placed on the log by an installation-written accounting routine, operator commands, or by user programs. The log data can be printed at specified times or upon operator command. Installation-written accounting routines utilize information provided through job control statements and also receive information from the supervisor on the time spent in execution by each job step.

Recovery management facilities record the environment of the system at the time of a macine malfunction. System environment recording routines record machine malfunctions in the CPU, main storage and channels, determine the type of malfunction, and write out error records (see 3.1).

4.4 System Description Maintenance

Through use of the interval timer facility, the program may request the actual elapse time or the amount of processing time used up to the point of the request.

CDC 6400/6500/6600 SCOPE 3 OPERATING SYSTEM

SCOPE 3 is a large scale, disk-oriented multiprogramming operating system for the Control Data Corporation 6400/6500/6600 computers. The system supports local and remote terminal batch processing operations and interactive time-sharing facilities. Multiprocessing capabilities are provided by the 6500 dual processor system.

1.0 JOB MANAGEMENT

The 6400/6500/6600 computers are highly sophisticated systems composed of several major components, namely, the peripheral processors and their memories, central memory, and the central processor(s). Each component has a prescribed function that is necessary in the operation of the entire system. The role of each component is described in the following paragraphs.

The peripheral processors can operate independently of each other and can communicate with each other. Peripheral processor memory units hold the system components that direct I/O operations, and they serve as buffers for data transmission to and from central memory. Peripheral processor number 0 (actually the memory contained by peripheral processor zero) contains the system monitor routine and is in permanent, supreme control of the system. The system display program is assigned to a second peripheral processor. The remaining eight peripheral processors, which have no fixed assignment, form a common pool available for assignment as needed. These processors cannot perform any function not approved in advance by the controlling peripheral processor. A communication area in the central memory is assigned to each peripheral processor. The first word of each communication area is the input register of the associated peripheral processor, the second word is the output register, and the remainder is the message buffer. The monitor accepts messages from processors and routes them to processors for action. It communicates with the resident programs in the other nine peripheral processors and with programs active in the central processor through the communication locations and the control point areas established within control memory.

The 6400/6500/6600 computers are composed of one, or in the case of the 6500, two high-speed central processors. A central processor, though a main component from the user's viewpoint, is completely in the power of every peripheral processor at all times. Any peripheral processor, by executing one of its own instructions, can alter all of the registers of a central processor, write new information into central memory, or read information out of central memory. A central processor, on the other hand, cannot directly affect a peripheral processor in any way.

The central memory can serve simultaneously as the central processor's private memory, as the buffer between the peripheral processors and the central processor, and as storage for job stacking from the optional extended core storage unit. The low-core portion of central memory is referred to as "central memory resident." This area is reserved for various system tables and is never accessible to a user's central processor job. Eight areas, numbered 0 to 7, are designated within central memory resident as control points. Control point 0 is used for system functions; one central processor job is assigned to each of the other control points. Thus a maximum of seven user control processor jobs can execute concurrently under SCOPE 3.

Blocks of central memory storage are assigned to each control point. These blocks occupy positions in the central memory relative to the control point number to which they are assigned. That is, they are relocated up or down as storage is released or required. Such relocation is possible because all references to central memory are made relative to the reference address assigned by the monitor routine.

The system's multiprogramming capabilities can be augmented by an optional auxiliary mass storage unit known as "extended core storage." This unit holds a large number of scheduled programs and data in readiness for immediate transfer to central memory for use by the central processor.

Currently executing programs and data blocks in central memory can be simultaneously accessed by the central processor, by all of the peripheral processors, and by the extended core storage unit if it is included in the system.

1.1 Job Control

The file concept is the basis for the design of SCOPE 3; all information contained within the system is considered to be either a file or part of a file. A job consists of one file of punched cards or card images of one or more programs. The first logical record of a job file consists of the control cards which identify the programs and data files and control the sequence of the program execution (runs). Control cards specify how the job is to be processed; they determine all operations performed on subsequent logical records of the job file.

1.1.1 Scheduling

The order in which SCOPE 3 assigns equipment to the jobs in central memory and initiates their execution is determined by an extensive priority system. Priorities can be assigned by the system, the system operator, or the user. Also, different priorities can be assigned to a job's main processing and its I/O operations. No other information was provided concerning the scheduling algorithm.

1.1.2 Resource Allocation

Central memory is composed of 32 logically independent banks of 4,096 words (60-bit). Several banks may be in operation simultaneously, thereby minimizing execution time. The estimated central memory requirement for a job, known as its field length, is specified by the user on a job control card. When a control point is available for the job and the required amount of memory and sufficient peripheral equipment are free, the job is brought to that control point. The lower and upper bounds of the contiguous memory area for the job are determined from its field length. Storage is assigned to each program within the job as it is loaded in either relocatable or absolute form. If the job attempts to reference any memory location outside of its allocated area, an interrupt is generated which halts the central processor and notifies the system operator. SCOPE 3 provides no dynamic core allocation capability.

The following types of I/O devices are allocatable by SCOPE 3: disk, disk pave drive, line printer, card reader/punch, and keyboard/display console. Codes also exist for allocating data cells, paper tape reader/punch, and graphic and plotting devices; however, software supporting these devices is not provided by the system.

A user can instruct the operator to assign a peripheral unit to a file and can declare the properties of that file and its assigned unit, via a *request* card. With the *request* function, equipment can be assigned dynamically by a user program operating in the central processor. A *request* card or function must be given to assign a file directly to a private device. The device assigned to the requesting control point becomes the private source of destination of files for that job. As job control cards are processed in order, required private equipment assignments must precede any reference to the corresponding private file.

If a file is not specifically assigned by a request card or request function, the system assigns that file to a disk storage. A job need not assign the card reader, printer, or punch for normal input/output for compilations, assemblies, and so forth, as this is done automatically by the system.

A communications area known as the file environment table must be declared for each file. The user must initiate this area; it is interrogated and updated by the system and the user during file processing. This area contains a device type field which may be used in one of two ways:

1. The file may be assigned to a specific type of allocatable device when an *open* function is given. Such an assignment is effective only if no prior reference to the file has been made.

2. The hardware type portion of the field will be set by SCOPE 3 upon return from any other file action request, if the file environment table is more than five words long.

The device type field contains two 6-bit fields; the left 6 bits specify a hardware device and the right 6 bits declare a type within the device. When the code is 00, SCOPE 3 selects the most easily accessible allocatable device.

Disk pack files must be contained on a single pack; file overflow to a second pack is not possible. A private pack cannot be removed while its file is active to the system. A private pack is associated with a single job. Access is not shared with jobs active at control points other than the assigned control point.

Mass storage random access files which are to endure between runs in a job or between jobs should be declared as common files. At the end of a run which creates such a file, the user should close the file with an unload option.

1.1.3 Program Loading

Three types of loading are performed; normal, segment, and overlay. Segments and overlays allow programs that exceed storage to be organized so that portions or groups of programs may be called, executed, and unloaded as needed.

The documentation supplied for this study described two loaders, the peripheral processor loader and the central processor loader. Their names are derived from the processing area in which they perform their primary operations—text relocation and loader table building. The user may indicate the loader he prefers by specifying its name on the loader control card. When this control card is omitted from a job, or if no name is given, the system selects a loader by default. The default option is defined by a system installation parameter. An unrecognized name produces a message in the system log and the job is terminated. Both loaders function as described below.

Programs are assembled or compiled independently, in absolute or relocatable binary. A number of programs may be grouped together as a segment to be loaded, linked, and, on request, later delinked and removed as a unit by the loader. The user defines the programs to be included in a segment either with control cards or with parameters included in the object program loader call. To facilitate reference to groups of programs, a segment definition may contain both program names and section names. A section is a convenience in the loader scheme to reduce the number of program names appearing in segment calls.

Segments are loaded at levels ranging from 0 to 63_{10}. Level zero is reserved for the initial, or main, segment. Segment zero must be the first segment defined; thereafter segments may be defined and loaded at any level. When a segment is loaded, external references within the segment are linked to entry points in segments previously loaded at a lower level. Unsatisfied external references may be linked to entry points in segments loaded subsequently. Optionally, the user may specify that unsatisfied external references be satisfied, if possible, from the system library, thereby nominally including certain library programs within a given segment. If the level requested for loading a segment is less than or equal to the level of the last loaded segment, the loader performs a delinking operation. All segments previously loaded at a level equal to or greater than the presently requested level are removed, and all linking of external references to entry points within these segments is eliminated, causing the external references involved to become unsatisfied again. Once delinking is complete, the segment is loaded at the requested level.

The loader can also generate overlays which are written out to a specified file in absolute format. The resident loader for overlays is smaller and faster and may be easily retained with the job for subsequent loading of the overlays. Overlays are generated through control cards processed directly by this loader (loader directives). The relocatable binary decks immediately following the overlay control card, up to the next overlay control card or an end-of-file, comprise the overlay deck. When the overlay deck has been loaded, loading is completed by satisfying undefined external references from the system library. The overlay and its identification are written as the next logical record in the file. Writing to the overlay file takes place when a directive is encountered which specifies an overlay level that would overlay a level currently residing in memory. Writing also takes place when the last overlay has been created. Each overlay has a unique entry which is the last transfer address encountered in the overlay programs during preparation. External references that cannot be satisfied, even by the system library, result in job termination after loading is completed and maps are produced for all overlays.

The 6000 series implements its time-sharing system by swapping programs between extended core storage and central memory. The roll-out, roll-in method is employed to provide the central processor with almost instantaneous access to any job and to minimize delay time when switching between users.

The loader includes the central program control subroutine within the field length of each job. This subroutine provides the linkage between user programs and the SCOPE 3 system. All file action requests and system action requests are processed by the central program control library subroutine. The user's programs communicate with the central program control through macro requests and the file environment table.

Errors encountered in assembly and compilation do not automatically cause the system to terminate a job. Rather, the job is terminated when the user attempts to load the assembled program. The loader recognizes the error directive produced by the compiler or assembler which is written in the first record on the binary output file.

1.1.4 Event Monitoring

Input files are executed according to the priority designed on the job card. Jobs assigned to control points and waiting for execution after interruption are stacked by priority. The job using the central processor is at the top of the stack. When it is interrupted (for example, to await completion of a peripheral processor function), the next job in the stack becomes the top, and the first job is temporarily removed from the stack. When it reenters the stack the job using the central processor, along with all jobs beneath it, are pushed down.

The operator may request that a job in control of the central processor at a specified control point be rolled-out so that all memory assigned to the job, except its control point area, is released. Neither the control point files nor the equipment assigned to the job will be relinquished. The operator later can request that the rolled-out job be restored and its execution resumed.

A peripheral processor must request permission from the monitor before using an I/O channel. Since every peripheral processor is capable of connecting itself to any channel, it is essential in preserving order that only one peripheral processor at a time try to use any one channel. To avoid an attempt by two peripheral processors to use the same channel (which would disrupt the peripheral processors and the channel), the monitor maintains a list of channels and their status. Before a peripheral processor can use a channel, it must request the monitor to assign that channel for its exclusive use. When finished with the channel, the peripheral processor requests the monitor to note that the channel is free.

A central processor time limit is specified for each job. Only one time limit can be placed on a job, and this limit must suffice for the entire job, including compilation and execution. If a job exceeds its limit, SCOPE 3 terminates it abnormally.

1.1.5 Program Termination Processing

When a job is assigned to a control point, the first record (or part thereof) of the job deck (control card record) is copied into the control statement buffer of the control point and a pointer is initialized to indicate the first control card. All data following the control card record in the job deck is made available to the control point as a file called INPUT. The first control statement in the buffer is executed and the pointer moves to the next control statement. This begins the first run within the job. This process is iterated until all of the control statements are depleted. Then the job is terminated normally. Any file that is to be printed, punched, or punched binary will automatically be processed by the system.

When a error such as an out-of-bounds memory reference occurs, the job is terminated abnormally and an interrupt is generated, which halts operations in the central processor and alerts the operator. The monitor will also terminate the job in this manner when the *abort* macro is used. If the control card section of the job deck contains an *exit* card (a control card used to separate the control cards for normal execution from a group to be executed in the event of an error exit), then the system continues processing the job with the next control card after the *exit* card.

A summary of all error diagnostics generated during a job and the amount of time used by the central and peripheral processors are always written at the end of a job printout. Dump capabilities, described more fully under Testing/Debugging Service, are also available upon either normal or abnormal termination. No other information concerning the actual termination procedures was provided.

1.2 System Communication

1.2.1 System Startup

System startup operations for the 6000 series are known as deadstart procedures. Deadstart procedures do not require deadstart cards. The system may be deadstart from magnetic tape to any one of the allocatable devices. A single system tape will deadstart on all allocatable devices. Upon request, the operator types characters indicating the type of deadstart.

To define the installation options and configuration, central memory resident tables and system must be preassembled. The allocatable devices onto which the system is loaded are defined by this data. When loading is completed, the deadstart process continues to the extended core storage partition table definition phase if installation parameters have been preset to define extended core storage as an allocatable device. Otherwise, the current data is input and the system is ready to process.

Additional startup operations include a "special preload" procedure: deadstarting is the same as normal preload and load procedure, but the allocatable devices used as systems storage must be specified by display output and operator input. When the "normal load from devices" procedure is employed, the preloading process is bypassed and the system is loaded directly from the device specified in the equipment status table as the system device. After deadstart loading is completed, no activity will be displayed at control points 1 to 7. A keyboard message at the console is needed to initiate the mode of job processing: automatic and manual.

The keyboard entry AUTO selects the mode for automatic processing. Under this mode input from the card reader is assumed. The reader package is assigned to the first available peripheral processor (assigned to control point 1), and then assigns output to the next available peripheral processor (assigned to control point 2). The read package reads, converts the information to display code, and forms input files on the disk until cards are depleted.

Manual operation is similar to automatic, except that each operation must be requested by the operator.

1.2.2 Job Control Communication

A user submits a job to the system as a set of control cards (the first must be a job card and the last a file separator card) which may be accompanied by source language decks, binary object decks, and data. Through control cards the user specifies the job name, priority, memory and equipment requirements, central processor time limit, operator instructions, and other job monitoring control information. If a control card is out of sequence or contains an error, the job is terminated and a message is written on the job's output stream.

The system operator may participate extensively in job control. The operator and the system communicate through console keyboard entries and two or more display scopes. Keyboard type-in commands may be verified prior to initiating their execution.

Specifically, (1) the operator may alter the priority or change the time limit of a job at a designated control point, (2) initiate a job at a designated control point and enter a particular control card in the control card buffer, (3) continue the job at a particular control point if it has paused under program instruction or after unsuccessful tape rereading, and (4) roll-out, roll-in, or terminate a job at a particular control point.

When the operator is operating in the time-sharing mode, SCOPE 3 control cards may be entered directly as commands from the remote terminal, or a control card file can be entered and saved for later reference.

1.2.3 Input/Output Stream Control

Input/output stream control is maintained by symbiont processing. Input files are executed and output is disposed of upon job termination according to the priority designated on each job card.

For an individual job the procedure may be described as follows: When a job file is read from the card reader, it is copied onto disk storage and becomes an input file; it is not assigned to any control point. The file name is that name given on the job control card. The file name/status contains a priority (from the control card) for the file, which becomes the priority for the job.

When the job is assigned to a control point, the input file becomes a local file and its name is changed to INPUT. The original name of the input file is saved in a word of the control point as the name of the job. New local files named OUTPUT, PUNCH, and PUNCHB are established, and if referenced, given disposition codes of print, punch coded and punch binary, respectively.

INPUT, OUTPUT, PUNCH, and PUNCHB are all local files in disk storage. They are the immediate source of card input and the immediate destination of printer output and coded and binary card output. Since several jobs may run concurrently at different control points, several local files called INPUT, several called OUTPUT, and several called PUNCHB are in the file name/status table simultaneously. When a local file is sought in the table, both the name and the control point number are used to identify it.

When a job terminates, the local file called INPUT for the assigned control point is released. Entries in the file name/status table for the local files called OUTPUT, PUNCH, and PUNCHB, for that control point, are altered so that their names are changed to the name of the job itself, which is found in the control point area. The control point is then released.

1.2.4 Resource Status Modification

In addition to the control the operator has over the job stream (see 1.3.2), he may also alter the status of the central processors and various peripheral devices and files.

Specifically, the operator may delegate a particular central processor to a designated control point. Only the job operating at that control point will use the delegated central processor, and it will use only that central processor. Similarly, the operator may release a delegated central processor to the system, making it available to all control points.

The operator may also: activate or disconnect a particular channel; assign a mass storage device of a specific type in response to a directive from a job *request* card; assign a specific piece of equipment to a designated control point; return equipment to the equipment pool; change the priority of a file in the I/O queue; and, remove a file from the I/O queue.

1.2.5 System Status Interrogation

SCOPE 3 allows the operator to examine selected portions of memory and keeps a permanent job history record which can be called at any time. The operator may also request that all portions of job or system status be displayed. A permanent record of system/console communication is retained in the system log and ultimately printed at operator request.

1.3 Recovery Processing

1.3.1 Checkpointing

A checkpoint dump may be requested by a checkpoint control card in the job stream, an executing program, or by a console message entered by the operator. An executing program may request that a checkpoint be taken at any point by issuing a checkpoint macro call to the supervisor—for example, upon an end-of-file condition, processing of a specified number of logical records completed, or a specified amount of time elapsing.

Checkpointing captures the total environment of a job on magnetic tape so that the job may be restarted from the same point in processing. Total environment includes local files associated with the control point of the job. For mass storage files (drum or disk), the complete file is captured, as well as the relative position within that file. For magnetic tape files, only the relative position on the tape is captured, so that the tape may be properly repositioned during restart.

1.3.2 Restarting

When a programmer takes a checkpoint dump during job execution, a file is written containing all information needed to restart the job at that point. In the event of machine malfunction, operator error, or program error, the job can be restarted from the last checkpoint rather than the beginning of the job.

Restarting is effected by a *restart* control card which directs the monitor to restart a job from its checkpoint tape. The checkpoint for restarting may be designated by name, number, or both. If a number is used and it is greater than the number of the last checkpoint taken, the restart attempt will be terminated.

After locating the proper checkpoint dump on the checkpoint tape, the restart program requests all tape files that were defined at checkpoint time, and repositions these files. The restart program also reestablishes all mass storage files from the copies appearing on the checkpoint tape, restores the central processor program, and restarts the user's job.

The restart job should not contain any request control cards; the restart facility requests all necessary files internally.

A checkpoint dump may not be restartable in the following cases:

1. A tape file necessary for restarting the program was overwritten after the checkpoint dump was taken;

2. A machine error propagated bad results but did not cause abnormal termination until after another checkpoint dump.

2.0 I/O CONTROL

The 6400/6500/6600 can control up to 12 I/O operations, one on each bi-directional data channel, and can control as many additional operations as there are additional data channels and/or multiplexing and buffering capabilities of individual I/O devices and controllers. When an I/O device becomes available, a data channel control flag so indicating is set.

The user performs I/O functions via file action requests. File action requests result in a return to the central program control subroutine. Subsequent actions depend on the state of the file. An *owncode* routine may be executed and/or a request to SCOPE 3 posted. When owncode routines are used, addresses of user-supplied routines may be given in the file environment table. These routines are executed by the central program control subroutine.

2.1 I/O Scheduling

SCOPE 3 queues I/O requests according to their priorities, which may be assigned by the system, system operator, or user. Automatic control is provided for I/O device assignment as physical units become available. I/O unit assignment may also be defined by the operator. Other I/O scheduling capabilities include system control of alternate routing and device reassignment; the latter may also be performed by the operator.

2.2 Data Transfer

All files within the SCOPE 3 system, regardless of type, are organized into logical records—for input files, through the ordering of control cards; for output files, through the language translator or other programs producing the output. Otherwise, logical record generation is the responsibility of the user.

Since the logical record concept is defined for all devices, files, may be transferred between devices without losing their structure. The physical format of a logical record is determined by the device on which the file resides. A physical record unit size is the smallest amount of information that may be transferred during a single physical read or write operation for each device within the system. Logical records are written as one or more physical record units, the last of which is short or zero length.

An area in core storage into which cards are to be read or from which cards are to be punched may be defined by a single instruction. As many cards as are necessary to satisfy the instruction are then read or punched under the supervision of the card reader/punch controllers.

SCOPE 3 provides the capabilities necessary to transfer data organized in the following tape file structures: single-reel file, multireel file, multifile reel, and multireel multifile. Reel swapping for a multireel file is automatic unless the user processor bit is set in the file environment table. When reading, if the file has a system label, it is read into the circular buffer and positioned at the first data record. If the file does not exist, an end-of-information status is returned. When writing, if the file has a system label, it is written using the parameters in the file environment table. The file remains positioned after the tape mark following the tape label. The file may be read and written until it is closed.

Random access files can be created on mass storage devices and their records can be read by direct addressing or sequential references. A disk address refers to pointers to system tables. When random file processing is requested, the disk address is returned when a logical record is written and gathered into an index. A disk address is accepted from the user when a logical record is read.

When files contain many logical records, multiple levels of indexes can be defined to conserve central memory space. When a multi-index file is written, logical record disk addresses are directed to a subindex buffer. When the buffer becomes full, the subindex itself can be written as a logical record in the file: the subindex disk address is directed to a main, or primary, index. The primary and subindexes can be supplied by a system service routine or by a user-supplied routine.

Extensive facilities are available for data communication. These include capabilities for connecting both vendor-manufactured and industry-standard terminal devices. In addition to terminal-to-computer and terminal-to-terminal communication, special single-speed multiplexing data set controllers designed for the 6000 series provide computer-to-computer communication.

The system provides facilities for rewinding, forward spacing, and backspacing magnetic tape. These are initiated by the applications program and then handled by the magnetic tape subsystem. Random access is achieved by positioning the disk arm at a designated track. Printer spacing and form positioning are under user control in conjunction with the format loop mounted by the operator.

2.3 Remote Terminal Support

Interactive time-sharing and remote batch processing capabilities are both provided under SCOPE 3 by the INTERCOM 1 package. Two types of terminals are available, teletypewriter and display. The display terminal is equipped with a cathode ray tube display screen, a display controller, and a keyboard. Neither type of terminal has off-line I/O equipment. Cards may be punched or read and output printed on central site peripheral equipment under control of commands issued from the terminals.

INTERCOM 1 support four types of files: user private, common, system, and permanent. User private files are created by the individual user and can be read, altered, or deleted only by their originator. System files exist in the SCOPE 3 library. They may be loaded by any user with an adequate access level, but they may not be modified or deleted. Permanent files are mass storage files, the location and identification of which are always known to the INTERCOM 1 system. Permanent files are protected from unauthorized access according to privacy controls specified by the creator of the files. They are also protectd from destruction; they are saved, even across deadstart (system startup), until the user decides to release them.

After logging-in to the system the user enters his user identification and password via the keyboard. Then he types the command corresponding to the mode in which he desires to execute his job. Time-sharing capabilities, which are provided by a utility program, allow the user to enter a program previously stored on disk, construct a program file line by line from the terminal, compile the program, correct compilation errors via line editing and resubmit the program, execute a correctly compiled program, and save a program file for subsequent compilation or execution. Users can communicate with other terminals if these terminals are logged-in and the user names are known. If a user does not desire to receive messages from other terminals, then he may lock his terminal out. When he again wants to receive messages from other terminals, he unlocks his terminal. Messages sent while a terminal is locked out are not saved.

In the remote batch mode, files are submitted one at a time to the SCOPE 3 batch processing queue. The user enters the file name of the file he wants placed in the batch queue. Only one name may be specified. The file may be of any type, but it must already exist on disk or the user cannot proceed. If the file is validated, the system responds and the user specifies the disposition of the file. A number of dispositions are permissable: place the file in the input queue, prepare it for card punching or line printing, rename it, or make it a common file or private file. After the user enters the disposition, the file is placed in the batch queue and processed according to the request. After the disposition has been entered, the system requests another file for batch processing. If the user has another file to process, he types the file name, and upon request, the disposition for that file. If he has no more files for batch processing, he exits from the batch mode and is thereupon returned to command mode.

2.4 File Handling

See 2.2 on data transfer.

3.0 DIAGNOSTIC ERROR PROCESSING

3.1 Hardware Error Control

Parity checking on data transferred to or from central memory is not a feature of SCOPE 3. Rapid software checks, however, may be performed by the user whenever he desires. Also, a memory diagnostic program can be periodically called and run concurrently with application programs to verify that the memory modules are functioning properly. Parity checks are performed on data transferred to extended core storage. Errors detected generate an error exit parity bit.

A 12-bit parity check word is automatically generated and recorded after each sector or disk storage is written. Data recovery from each sector is checked by instructions which automatically regenerate that sector's check word and compare it with the original. Error detection sets a testable indicator. Data recording and recovery for disk packs are handled similarly on a record basis by the use of a 16-bit word. An unsuccessful comparison results in a data transmission error signal. Telecommunication transmission errors are detectable in an analogous manner by the use of a 12-bit check word for each data block. Tape parity errors and errors arising from timing conflicts result in loss of data set indicators that can be tested by peripheral processor programs.

The user can supply an *owncode* routine, known as the end-of-information routine, for execution if an end-of-information mark is encountered after a forward operation, a beginning-of-information mark occurs after a backward operation, or an end-of-reel indicator is reached during a magnetic tape forward operation. These conditions are indicated by specific bit settings of the code and status field of the file environment table, which cause the end-of-information routine to be entered by the central program control subroutine. No other information was provided concerning specific hardware error control actions.

3.2 Program Error Control

System checks for program errors occurring in central memory are limited to those for handling a program memory reference to a location outside its boundaries, a reference to a locked area, and an invalid address. The first causes an interrupt, halts the central processor, and notifies the operator. In the case of the latter two, control is transferred to the peripheral processor monitor.

A reference to a protected area in extended core storage aborts the data transfer. Reference to an invalid address in disk storage or on a disk pack is prevented by system software.

Division by zero and overflow in the central processor set a flag and the result of the operation is set to the maximum value. Similarly, when an underflow occurs, a flag is set and the result is set to zero upon an underflow.

A user program may specify an error address in the file environment table to receive control if an error condition occurs after a request to initialize, position, or transfer data to or from a file. The file environment table code and status field will reflect the error condition. If processing can continue, the error routine should exit through its entry point; otherwise, an *abort* request may be issued. If the error address field is zero, the run continues normally. The file environment table code and status bits reflect the error condition upon normal return to the program. In the event that both end-of-information and error routine execution are needed, the error routine is executed.

3.3 Interface Error Control

Errors occurring in control cards and out-of-sequence control cards produce messages which are displayed on the console and stored in the system and job dayfiles. In both instances, the job is aborted.

4.0 PROCESSING SUPPORT

4.1 Timing Services

A job may ascertain the current reading of the system clock and the amount of central processor time it has used via system action requests to the supervisor. A job may also request the current date as entered by the operator or the data according to the Julian calendar.

4.2 Testing and Debugging Service

The system provides tracing, snapshot, and dump facilities. The user requests these services via control cards submitted with his job deck. When trace and snapshot control cards are inserted in the deck, coding is inserted into the user program which will transfer control to the appropriate system routines.

In tracing, instructions based on storage references, operand references, register usage, and branch instructions are analyzed. Trace output always includes a dump of the contents of all operand registers involved. An initial message indicates where tracing begins and the range involved. A terminal message is written when tracing stops. Tracing ranges can overlap and multiple outputs can be triggered.

The snapshot dump capability provides selective area printouts upon execution of specified instructions. Printing frequency is established by parameters on the snapshot control card. The dump may be provided in octal, octal with mnemonic op codes, integer, single or double precision floating point, or display code.

Upon normal or abnormal job termination, three dump formats are available: octal, labeled, change. Octal is the standard dump option.

The format of a labeled dump is the same as for the octal dump, except as the origin of a common block or subprogram is encountered, the associated name is printed. Also, a relative address counter indicates the position of the first word on the line relative to the last encountered subprogram or common block.

The change option provides a list of core locations which have changed from their initial values. When a job begins an execution phase, a core image of the entire field length is written on the DEBUG file. The image is compared with the contents of memory at the time of termination. The contents of changed locations are listed. A labeled dump always precedes a change dump.

4.3 Logging and Accounting

The system log is maintained as a file on mass storage. This chronological file—known as the dayfile—contains a running account of all control cards, equipment assignments, error diagnostics, central and peripheral-processor time used, and input/output routines used by the jobs in central memory. The dayfile can be accessed for accounting purposes. The information that it holds for a currently executing job is always printed at the end of that job's printout.

No mention is made in the documentation provided concerning the maintenance of any error statistics for hardware or software.

4.4 System Description Maintenance

A program may ascertain the type of I/O device that is currently assigned to a permanent file by interrogating the file environment table. No other information was provided regarding the capability of the system to provide executing tasks with information regarding current system status.

9
TIME-SHARING OPERATING SYSTEMS

OVERVIEW

This chapter uses the condensed outline format presented in Chapter 7 to summarize a selection of time-sharing operating systems. One time-sharing operating system was presented in Chapter 7 (the DEC PDP-8 TTS). All of the operating systems summarized in this chapter also are designed to serve as general-purpose multiprogramming operating systems as well.

The (Batch Time-sharing Monitor (BTM) for the XDS Sigma 5/7 computers is presented first for it is the simplest. It is in turn an extension of the Batch Processing Monitor (BPM) for these same computers.

The GECOS III for the Honeywell Information Systems 600 series of computers is summarized next. Time sharing is not the main focus of the GECOS III, but is an important additional attribute of the system.

The EXEC 8 operating system for the Univac 1108 computer is, like the GECOS III, an operating system of extensive capabilities. The time sharing is a part, but again is not the main focus, of the system.

The MCP (Master Control Program) for the Burroughs B6500 is an advanced version of the pioneering operating systems developed for the older B5000 series of computers by Burroughs. The operating system is an extensive one and clearly reflects in concept some of the hardware features of the computer, such as the use of stacks.

XDS SIGMA 5/7 BATCH TIME-SHARING MONITOR (BTM)

The Sigma 5/7 Batch Processing Monitor (BPM) is a disk-oriented multiprogramming system. The system can accommodate real-time foreground processing on a dynamic basis concurrently with both a background production job stack and peripheral processing symbionts. The batch time-sharing monitor (BTM) is an extension of BPM, which offers BPM services concurrent with conversational time-sharing.

1.0 JOB MANAGEMENT
1.1 Job Control
1.1.1 Scheduling

BTM supports real-time, time-sharing, and batch processing. Real-time programs are scheduled in response to interrupts and are executed in the system foreground with a priority corresponding to the hardware priority of the interrupt. Time-sharing and batch jobs may be run in the system background area. Time-sharing facilities are available to as many as 38 on-line terminal users. Batch jobs may be initiated at the computer site, through remote batch terminals or from any on-line terminal.

Real-time programs can either be installed permanently as extensions of the resident monitor or they can be dynamically loaded and initiated. For real-time programs requiring operation on a periodic time basis, the monitor offers a clock-watching service which activates the program when the appropriate time elapses.

Batch jobs can be run from a card reader stack in the simplest case or run under the rules of an installation's job scheduler by using the card-to-disk symbiont. The batch jobs may be loaded from a system input device or from job files which may be created by batch or time-sharing jobs. The job scheduler permits selective job operation based on job type or administrative priority to maximize throughput efficiency or environment needs. The computer operator maintains complete control over the job stack on secondary storage. Jobs can be suspended, initiated on a priority basis, or reorganized in sequence.

The time-sharing executive is called by the PTM at intervals governed by one of the hardware clocks.

The scheduling of on-line and batch jobs is performed in an asynchronous manner, with the clock enforcing certain maximum and minimum time intervals. The run control card for a batch program may specify that the program be executed after a certain time interval. It may also specify that the program execution be conditional upon receipt of a specific interrupt. Completion of console input may also be used to cause scheduling of a program.

System routines are provided to permit a program to schedule a succeeding program and link to it. Asynchronous execution of subtasks evidently is not provided by BTM. A value may be entered on the run card specifying the highest error severity level to be tolerated in accepting a program for execution.

1.1.2 Resource Allocation

Internal storage is allocated at system generation time into three fixed areas: a monitor area, a resident foreground area, and a background area. The monitor area contains the resident monitor, a buffer pool (for monitor and resident foreground tasks), and a monitor overlay area. The resident foreground area, as its name implies, includes all resident foreground tasks. The background area is dynamically allocated for several uses.

The background area is used for execution of nonresident foreground programs, symbionts, on-line (time-sharing) programs, and batch jobs. Programs may operate in a fixed amount of memory, or may expand dynamically, using subroutines which are provided both to request and to release additional pages of storage which may be required temporarily by a program. Foreground tasks may checkpoint and then restart background processes to make temporary use of the additional core memory.

Background programs are protected against access by foreground programs and foreground programs are protected against access by background programs. However, foreground programs *can* access other foreground programs. The monitor can access all areas.

I/O devices may be specified by device type, by device category, or by a specific reference to a device ID. The specification of the device may be made either in a control card submitted with the program or in pseudo-operations within the control program creating a data control block.

Files may be shared by several programs. The user is given the capability of preventing other users from accessing a record and/or a file until desired operations are complete. Temporary files may be allocated, which can be explicitly released at the end of a job step or automatically released at completion of a job.

1.1.3 Program Loading

Simple, overlay, and dynamic program structures are provided by the system.

A relocating loader brings load modules into core storage and then transfers control to the loaded program. An overlay loader generates programs consisting of a root segment with one or more overlays. The overlay may be so constructed that the overlays will be automatically called as needed, or the program may control the loading of overlays segments directly through use of a system subroutine.

Swapping is performed under control of the BTM resident executive. Time-slice lengths are determined at system generation time. An on-line task will run for the length of its specified quantum or until I/O completion, if it is in the middle of a random access device I/O operation.

Pages in a dynamic common storage area may be requested and released on a dynamic basis through calls to system subroutines.

1.1.4 Event Monitoring

In general, time-shared operations are given control at completion of each swap-in. Batch background jobs process during the input/output time interval required to transfer time sharing programs from core to random access storage and into core from random access storage. The minimum time slice for batch process monitor runs and the maximum time slice for on-line use are specified at system generation time.

Priority dispatching is dependent upon the interrupt system. A program operating on an interrupt level will continue to operate until it completes execution or until it is interrupted by a higher priority interrupt. The operator may also key-in commands to suspend a program and then restart it.

System hardware will support up to 224 interrupt levels. Each level can be individually disabled to prevent recognition of the interrupt or masked to defer recognition of the interrupt. Complete groups of interrupts may also be masked. Any individual interrupt may be triggered through programmed instructions.

Several executive subroutines are provided for use in connection with interrupts. Subroutines are provided to permit foreground programs to enable or disable interrupts, and to enter or leave mode or slave mode.

Another routine permits specifying interrupts as being in a trap or abort state. If an interrupt which is in the trap state occurs, control will be given to a user program. If an interrupt which is in the abort state occurs, control is given to a monitor subroutine.

The user has the option of specifying that console interrupts be handled directly by the user's program. This permits direct control of the program by the operator.

During execution, jobs are monitored to see that they do not exceed certain limits. Default limits are established during system generation time and any or all of them may be overridden by a limit control card. Limits which may be specified are execution time, pages of object listing, object cards, pages of diagnostic output, pages of output produced by the executing program, amount of temporary and permanent disk storage used, and number of scratch tapes which may be used.

1.1.5 Program Termination Processing

All time-sharing jobs may be terminated by the operator or individual jobs may be terminated by time-sharing users. Summary information is printed showing the amount of disk space, CPU time, I/O time, and CPU overhead time used.

Batch and foreground programs are normally terminated by calling on exit subroutine. A routine is provided to close input and output files and to specify files to be released or saved.

On control cards, the user may specify core dumps to be taken in the event an error exit is made instead of a normal exit. Two types of error exits are provided—one will discontinue execution of the current job step and proceed to the next job step, the other will cancel all steps within the current job.

1.2 System Communication

1.2.1 System Startup

The monitor may be bootstrapped from any available tape drive. Batch cards, if any, will be read from the system input device and control will be passed to a system initialization routine. Commands may be entered by the operator at this point to specify core size and device assignments, and to patch any desired areas of the monitor. The system then enters the wait state and is ready for normal job initialization.

Foreground initialization takes place during system initialization prior to entering the wait state. Specified interrupts are initialized and enabled or disabled. The operator may, at system generation time or at any time, key-in the current date and time.

The system may be saved by the operator if the system is "quiescent." The system is considered quiescent when the following conditions are met: no symbiont or time sharing program is active, no input or output symbiont files exist and all consoles are logged off (this can be assured through use of an operator command to terminate time sharing). When these conditions are met the monitor will print a message to that effect. The operator may then dump the system to tape or disk. If the system becomes inoperable due to an irrecoverable error during processing, it is possible to recover permanent files and symbiont output for all the jobs executing at the time of failure. The permanent file area for all currently open output files will be lost. Symbiont disk storage for symbiont files currently being output or being input will also be lost.

1.2.2 Job Control Communication

Noninteractive control may be provided through control cards which are read by the system from the system input device or are included in the job stream read from pre-stored job files. Operator commands are provided to suspend and restart job execution or to modify the priority of a job within the input job stream.

Control information may be passed between job steps through use of six program pseudo-sense switches. Subroutines are provided to set, reset, and test these switches. These switches may also be set or reset by operator key-ins.

1.2.3 Input/Output Stream Control

The input stream may be preprocessed by a system symbiont and loaded onto a random access device or it may be processed directly from the system input device. In either case, I/O is controlled by a *cooperative*. The cooperative is a monitor routine called as a result of the user's I/O request; the cooperative interfaces between user programs and (1) the specified I/O operation, in a nonsymbiont system, or (2) a random access device, in a symbiont system. In a symbiont system, the cooperative and the operator may control one or more symbionts concurrently.

Jobs may be input directly from the card reader's stack or under control of the system's job scheduler through use of a card-to-disk symbiont. A control command interpreter reads all control commands and performs specified functions. The console interpreter examines and processes all console messages and performs specified functions.

1.2.4 Resource Status Modification

The operator has the capability through a key-in to modify system device assignments.

1.2.5 System Status Interrogation

The operator may key-in a display command to request: information as to the currently available disk storage space, device names of all tape units currently available to the system, a list of outstanding system I/O files for a specified job, and the identity of any currently active background job. The status of any tape unit may be checked, or the operator may request that an unused tape unit be indicated. The operator may also request that system accounting information be output to a specified device.

An on-line user may at any time query the system to determine the current status (waiting, running, or completed) or any specified batch job.

1.3 Recovery Processing

1.3.1 Checkpointing

Checkpoint service can be requested by either a background program or a real-time foreground process. In both cases the background program is saved on secondary storage for reactivation at the checkpoint when appropriate. Thus a real-time foreground task can checkpoint the background if it requires additional core storage.

On-line time-sharing users are provided a save command which may be used to save the user's environment either temporarily or permanently.

1.3.2 Restarting

Restart subroutines are provided to resume processing of checkpointed programs. If a program is terminated due to a malfunction and restarted, data files are repositioned so that the program can then continue from the last checkpoint.

The on-line user may use a restore command to reload and restart a saved job. For on-line jobs, device repositioning is the user's responsibility; utility control commands are provided to position files.

2.0 I/O CONTROL

2.1 I/O Scheduling

The system supports up to eight input/output channels. The I/O supervisor program controls the queue of outstanding I/O requests. All background tasks performing any I/O functions must utilize the I/O control routines. Foreground tasks may also utilize these routines or may incorporate their own I/O routines. Device resolution is performed through use of device control blocks which are created at program generation or load time.

2.2 Data Transfer

I/O transfers are automatically buffered and I/O peripherals are serviced on a queue basis. The number and size of buffer pools are specified on a pool control card. Blocking and deblocking routines are provided under the monitor. To use these routines the user must indicate block size, record size, and location of the user's buffer. The user may specify any of several data codes for input or output. Among his choices are: BCD (which is assumed), binary, FORTRAN BCD, packed binary, or unpacked binary.

Data may be organized into sequential or keyed files. Each record of a keyed file has an identifying key associated with it which is stored in front of the record on tape, or in a key index on disk. Keyed files may be accessed either directly by key or sequentially by positioning the file. Records of a sequential file can only be accessed sequentially.

Teleprocessing communication control is provided by the system. Routines are provided to access messages input to the system or to initiate output of messages from the system. Programs can also request automatic activation upon receipt of teleprocessing messages.

Device manipulation subroutines are provided to rewind tapes or position volumes at a specified record or file.

2.3 Remote Terminal Support

Commands are provided for the time-sharing user to communicate with the system and control such operations as batch job initiation and file positioning. Additionally, the operator has the facility to communicate with on-line users.

2.4 File Handling

File catalogs are maintained by the system. The user has the ability to limit access to files and may specify account numbers of users who may write on a file, and account numbers of users who may read from a file. Write access implies read access. In addition to, or instead of, access controlled by user ID, the person creating a file may specify a password which must be used to access the file. The user also has the option of protecting specified records within a file without protecting the entire file.

Automatic label writing and reading facilities are provided by the system. In addition, the user may specify his own labels and check them himself.

3.0 DIAGNOSTIC ERROR PROCESSING

3.1 Hardware Error Control

When an I/O error is detected by the system, the system will retry the operation the number of times specified by the user. The user may specify an error return from I/O subroutines and may also use a subroutine to check the status of his I/O operations. When a preset number of error recovery retries have been attempted, a routine is entered to type out a message and read an operator key-in in response to the message. When the operator is notified of an I/O error, he may specify one of four options for monitor action: (1) continue, as is, (2) set an error flag associated with the I/O operation and continue, (3) continue, but lock-out the device from the system after completion of the current job, and (4) repeat the I/O operation.

3.2 Program Error Control

No information is available concerning system action upon the detection of a program error.

3.3 Interface Error Control

System detection of and recovery from interface errors is not discussed in the documentation provided.

4.0 PROCESSING SUPPORT

4.1 Timing Service

Sigma 7 can contain two or four real-time clocks. System subroutines are provided to request the time of day and date and to set and test interval timers.

4.2 Testing and Debugging Service

Postmortem dumps may be requested if an error is detected during execution of the program. Snapshot core dumps may be taken during program execution. Conditional snapshots may be controlled by special commands to test various conditions within the system. Another command may be used to initiate a dump if a certain instruction is executed more than a specified number of times.

Tracing is provided in connection with FORTRAN for time-sharing users.

The time-sharing user is provided with a "D" option of execution. Under this option, the user's program executes under control of a debug program. Some of its facilities are: the examination, insertion, and modification of elements of programs (instructions, numeric values, and coded information, etc.); control of execution, including the insertion of breakpoints into a program; tracing execution by displaying information at designated breakpoints; searching programs and data for specific values. The user may initiate execution at the normal location or at a specific instruction or may cause only a specific instruction to be executed. Execution will be halted at a breakpoint, by a user interruption, or by an error causing a machine interruption (illegal instruction, memory protect violation, etc.). Errors resulting in machine interrupts are reported to the user and control is returned to him to await further commands.

4.3 Logging and Accounting

The monitor provides for complete accounting of user job activity on the Sigma computer. Because of the system's multi-usage capability, the accounting information indicates both the elapsed time and actual machine utilization of each job. An operator key-in is provided to request the monitor to output the accounting file (normally to a card punch). The accounting records include account number, name, user identification, total time, CPU time, I/O statistics, and amount of secondary storage used.

4.4 System Description Maintenance

Monitor service routines are provided to permit a user program to determine the settings of six pseudo-sense switches, the boundary addresses of dynamic core (for dynamic page allocation), and to test the status of I/O operations.

HONEYWELL 600 SYSTEMS (615/625/635) GENERAL ELECTRIC COMPREHENSIVE OPERATING SUPERVISOR (GECOS III)

GECOS III is designed to operate in a multiprogramming/multiprocessing mode of operation. System throughput may be augmented by adding additional control processors (up to a maximum of four) to achieve simultaneous execution of user programs in the system. GECOS III is designed to provide local batch processing, remote batch processing, and time-sharing facilities.

1.0 JOB MANAGEMENT

1.1 Job Control

1.1.1 Scheduling

Programs may be entered onto an input queue from the local job stream or from a remote terminal. Each job on the queue is examined for resource requirements by the allocation program. If sufficient peripherals and core are available, the program is removed from the input queue and placed on the dispatching queue. If the resource requirements can be met only partially, the job is bypassed until all needs are satisfied. If a job does not obtain resources after a specified number of attempts, the operator is informed. He may raise the priority of the job to the point where peripheral allocation for other activities will be suspended until this job's requirements are met. For certain priority levels, executing tasks will be temporarily suspended (rolled-out) to make room in memory for the higher priority program.

Once a program is selected for execution, it is entered onto a dispatcher queue. This queue allows up to 63 entries. All of the time-sharing programs are treated as one entry.

Task execution can be conditional upon the results of preceding tasks, the setting of certain internal switches, and abort/no-abort conditions. Several kinds of job control cards are provided to conditionally bypass or execute tasks based on the above conditions.

1.1.2 Resource Allocation

The maximum amount of internal storage required by the job is contained in a parameter on the job control card. There are three levels of memory allocation. Jobs of normal priority are allocated memory only if a contiguous area large enough for the job is available. A higher level of priority will cause memory compaction to occur making noncontiguous areas of unused core contiguous. The highest level of priority will cause other jobs in execution to be removed from memory (rolled-out) to provide sufficient storage. Each time a job fails to obtain sufficient memory for execution, its priority level is increased. During program execution, internal storage may be dynamically allocated through requests for additional storage to the supervisor. The system also allows a common communications area for tasks within a job.

A program fault will occur if a user program attempts to address directly a part of storage outside of its range of assigned storage. Prior to initiating I/O operations the supervisor checks the parameters to see if locations outside the assigned storage limits are referenced. If so, the program is aborted.

I/O devices are normally allocated by device type (e.g., tape or disk); however, under certain circumstances, allocation may be by physical device identification. File sharing (on a *read only* basis) is permitted among any number of separate programs.

However, only one program at a time is permitted *write* access to the file.

Supervisor facilities exist that permit the problem program to dynamically request additional peripherals. Dynamic peripheral requests are limited to tape handlers and to existing files allocated on mass storage (disk and drum) devices. The implicit files used by the compilors and system routines (such as the files used to hold user jobs or those used as intermediate files during compilation) may also be allocated dynamically.

Resident system subroutines may be either reentrant or serially reusable. Though lock-out facilities are provided for the serially reusable routines, the system prefers to provide multiple copies when feasible to avoid the problem of task suspension due to a lock-out. For example, the subset of File Control routines required for program execution is appended to the problem program at program load time and maintained as a part of the user program.

1.1.3 Program Loading

GECOS III supports both simple and overlay structured programs. In addition, a certain amount of dynamic loading may be performed through the use of the resident loader within the supervisor. The load modules are all relocatable and storage compaction results when fragmented areas of core occur under certain priority conditions.

Programs of low priority may be swapped out to a mass storage device to permit the execution of high priority programs. Upon completion of the high priority program, the rolled-out program will be restored (rolled-in) and execution will resume.

GECOS III also features a time-sharing executive which performs the functions of selecting, allocating, dispatching, and swapping time-sharing user programs. The time-sharing executive is a single program activity as far as the main GECOS supervisor is concerned. Upon execution of the time-sharing executive, it in turn suballocates memory and subdispatches the time-shared user programs.

1.1.4 Event Monitoring

Time is allocated in time slices to the time-shared programs. The time-shared supervisor, however, competes with all of the other jobs in the system on a contention basis.

The dispatcher queue is maintained in priority order; consequently dispatching is a straightforward technique of selecting the top entry from the queue and executing it. Whenever a task is temporarily suspended, such as when it is waiting for I/O to complete, it is removed from the dispatcher queue. It is only reentered on the queue when the I/O operation is completed. At the completion of interrupt processing, control always returns to the dispatcher. Consequently, interrupts for I/O device completion, task completion, interval time, unsolicited inputs, and so on, always exit to the dispatcher. The interrupt-handling routine may either enter a program in the dispatcher queue or remove one.

Four types of I/O interrupts are recognized by the system hardware. Provision is made for up to 32 interrupt vectors which will route the interrupt to a preset-servicing routine.

An additional 16 interrupt vectors are provided for processing "faults." Fault processing covers such conditions as arithmetic overflow, timer runouts, and storage protect violations. One of these faults is reserved as a means for the problem program to request supervisor services (the master mode entry command).

The user may specify fault processing routines to handle certain program errors. If no fault processing routine is specified by the user, occurrence of these conditions will cause program abort.

Interrupts generated due to the successful completion of an I/O operation will cause the interrogation of a "courtesy call" address. Prior to initiating the I/O, the user has loaded this address with the location of his "I/O complete" routine. The user must return control to the system at the end of his routine so that his normal program execution may be resumed.

Total execution time for a program may be limited by a parameter specified on the job control card. Line limitation specifications are required for the system output device in order to detect abnormal output levels. Task termination occurs if the output level is exceeded.

1.1.5 Program Termination Processing

Normal program termination processing looks ahead to the next task to see if it is a compilation activity of the same type as the one terminating. If so, the new task is initiated immediately, using the same system resources. If the next task is not the same, the operator is notified of any files to be dismounted and an accounting record is written on the output file, itemizing the resources used by the task. The allocation phase is notified that the resources used by the task are available for reuse and the next task is made available for execution. If this is end of job, the job is removed from the job queue.

Abnormal termination permits a dump of allocated memory

to be written on the output device. Special programmer-defined abort tasks (dumping data files, etc.) are then scheduled for execution. As with normal termination, the resources used by the aborted task are released for reallocation. Compilation tasks following an aborted task are always executed; noncompilation tasks are executed only if specified by the programmer.

1.2 System Communication
1.2.1 System Startup

A startup package is provided, which is in itself a miniature operating system. This package initializes all system file devices, edits various files into the file system, and loads the system. The startup package generates the tables of module and file locations needed by the system and constructs a core resident monitor. Thus the startup package adapts GECOS III to the system at startup time without the requirement of a separate system generation run. On a system restart, a reboot of the system is permitted with the option of supplying various control sections of the startup package from the card reader. System restart provides recovery for incomplete jobs, interrupted system output, and in-core accounting information.

1.2.2 Job Control Communication

The job control language of GECOS III is the primary means of system control. The control cards are located in the input stream and may be submitted either locally or from a remote terminal. A third method of control card submission is through the use of a "JOB" tape that contains all of the control cards necessary for a number of jobs. Each job can be run by inserting a single control card in the input stream which causes the system to accept the necessary job control cards from the JOB tape.

Job control language is in a fixed format utilizing both positional and key word parameters. Default options are assumed for many of the parameters. Message formats for problem programs are not standardized. However, for problem program messages requiring an operator response, a special macro is used which causes the system to inform the operator that the message requires a response and inhibits any other typewriter commands until the response is received. If after 30 seconds the operator has not responded, the console terminates the read command with a status indication to the requesting program.

1.2.3 Input/Output Stream Control

The system input device consists of a tape or disk file which has been preprocessed by a system input symbiont. Similarly, the system output device is written onto tape or disk and processed later by a system output symbiont.

1.2.4 Resource Status Modification

The console operator may modify the status of the system and the status of jobs within the system by typing in appropriate messages on the console typewriter. He may also request that peripheral devices be exchanged with or moved to other devices. An operator may remove a device from the system by an appropriate console entry. He may not add a device to the system that was not originally defined; however, he may restore a previously defined device that was removed.

1.2.5 System Status Interrogation

The operator may request information on the status of all jobs within the system, devices available or unavailable to the system, and the status of remote terminals connected to the system. He may also request specific information on any single program or device by name.

1.3 Recovery Processing

1.3.1 Checkpointing

Checkpoints may be initiated by the supervisor or by a problem program. Supervisor initiated checkpoints are utilized under two conditions: the first occurs after an end of reel on a tape file when opening the subsequent reel; the second is required when a higher priority program requires the use of the core assigned to the program. In the first case, I/O device repositioning information is maintained, whereas in the second, I/O devices are not repositioned; consequently, repositioning information is not required. The problem program may request that a checkpoint be taken at any time by issuing a checkpoint call to the supervisor. The checkpoint file may be located on either tape or disk. If on tape, it may be imbedded with normal data records on an output file; if on disk, only one checkpoint record (the last) is maintained on a separate checkpoint file.

1.3.2 Restarting

A program that has been checkpointed by the supervisor due to the requirements of a higher priority program will automatically be restarted when facilities become available. As mentioned above, no device repositioning is required in this situation. A program checkpointed by a problem program or on an end-of-reel condition can only be reinitiated from the operator's console. In these situations, the following resources are repositioned: the input stream, sequential tapes, and direct access devices. Neither unit record devices nor the output stream are repositioned.

2.0 I/O CONTROL FUNCTIONS

2.1 I/O Scheduling

The input/output supervisor (IOS)—a part of the GECOS Supervisor—provides for the monitoring of input/output requests. Specifically, it provides for supervision of all input/output interrupts, the queueing of input/output requests, the monitoring of all peripheral channels, and the maintenance of an awareness of the status of each peripheral. Channel modules are provided to drive each type of I/O device. The modules handle all interrupts, I/O requests, error-processing functions, and channel queue selection strategies. In addition, IOS accounts for the time spent by the processor on all peripherals for each program executed. I/O request queues are maintained for each device. The length of the queue is dependent upon the entry space available in the program service area.

Priority I/O recognition is only available for magnetic tape files. A macro is provided to give a single tape file priority over all the other magnetic tape files for that particular I/O queue.

2.2 Data Transfer

The file and record control facilities of GECOS III permit the definition of fixed length, variable length, and mixed mode data records. All of these types may be either blocked or unblocked. Whenever the logical record blocking and/or deblocking facilities are to be used, one or two buffers must be defined and reserved. The system uses the simple buffering technique and does not provide exchange or dynamic buffering facilities.

Data record processing from a programming standpoint is on a logical basis. The programmer processes his files as a logical (not physical) entity either sequentially or randomly. The physical characteristics and restrictions of the device on which the file is physically located are handled by the supervisor.

Automatic code translation is provided for items in the input job stream through the use of a job control card specification. No mention is made of automatic code translation for other peripheral devices.

Nondata-transmitting calling sequences are provided to allow activities such as backspacing files, blocks, and records, forcing end-of-reel, rewinding, and so on. These functions are actually the software equivalents of the hardware commands that are executed to maintain the logical record control of the file.

GECOS III permits multiple remote devices and computers to communicate with the system. Control of these terminals is under the direction of the processing program. Up to three communication processors (Datanet-30 or Datanet-355) may also be controlled under GECOS III.

2.3 Remote Terminal Support

On-line terminal support within the GECOS III system is quite extensive. Supervisor facilities are provided for user programs to employ the remote terminal as an interactive I/O device. Whenever the terminal is not in use as an interactive device, batch processing jobs may be submitted through it. When used for remote batch processing, the terminal operator is also capable of specifying other terminals that are to receive the batch system output or any locally produced messages.

Remote terminals may communicate in a "direct access" mode with a processing program. In this mode, the remote terminal processing routines are bypassed and data is transmitted directly to and from terminal by a user program. This permits inquiry-type teleprocessing applications.

2.4 File Handling

File cataloging facilities are available as well as access limitation facilities. A file may be designated read-only and/or have its access restricted by passwords. Files may be shared among a number of separate programs simultaneously. However, only one program is allowed read/write access to the file; the remaining programs are restricted to read-only access. Label handling facilities are available and user coding may be included to supplement the system label-handling routines.

3.0 DIAGNOSTIC ERROR PROCESSING

3.1 Hardware Error Control

When an I/O device fails to perform properly, the system retries the operation in accordance with defined error-processing standards. In cases where the retry is successful, the failure is recorded on a permanent error file. This file is available for subsequent analysis by site support personnel to isolate units with higher than normal failure rates. In the event a peripheral failure becomes critical in the course of processing, the operator may utilize a "device interchange" feature. Utilizing this feature, the operator may remove the file from the failing device and place it on a new device and continue processing. The system keeps track of the number of files and records read from and written onto magnetic tape and uses this information to reposition the tape after the interchange has been accomplished.

Detection of a non-I/O hardware malfunction always causes an error message to be typed on the console typewriter and the registers at the time of the fault to be dumped. The control processor is notified of the fault (if the processor detecting the fault is not the processor executing the supervisory routines) and the control processor initiates a core dump. No information is provided as to whether system operation will continue in a degraded manner eliminating the failing device or whether processing is simply suspended.

GECOS III provides a comprehensive on-line peripheral test system. This system permits normal preventive maintenance testing of system peripherals concurrent with production processing.

3.2 Program Error Control

If a program fault is encountered in a user program, the user fault vector is interrogated to determine if user coding has been provided for this particular error. If so, control will be transferred to the user processing routine. If no routine is provided, the program is aborted. A limit is placed on the number of times a specific program fault may be executed by the user program. Subsequent tasks in the job may be executed conditionally on the user program either aborting or executing satisfactorily. Specifically, various file dump utilities can be scheduled on the basis of an abort having occurred and bypassed if execution is satisfactory.

3.3 Interface Error Control

A standard method of linking to the system supervisor programs from problem programs is employed through the use of a "master mode entry" command. This command transfers control, via an interrupt, to the supervisor. The command uses a coded number to indicate the specific supervisor function requested. Immediately following the master mode entry command in core is the formatted parameter list required by that function. Each command format has provisions for specifying both system error and normal return points. Invalid control codes cause a program abort.

4.0 PROCESSING SUPPORT

4.1 Timing Service

A real-time clock is maintained in the supervisor and the time of day, as well as the date, are available to the problem program via a supervisor calling sequence. Several interval timing facilities are also available. One of these facilities provides for program loop protection. This facility requires that a program loop be completed prior to the next interrupt, else the program is aborted. This is primarily a debugging aid, though it does have various real-time applications as well. Temporary task suspension may also be invoked through the use of the interval timer. By using this facility, a task may be suspended for up to five minutes at a time.

4.2 Testing and Debugging Service

Storage dumps, both terminal and intermediate, are available. The intermediate dumps may specify core limits, thus providing partial core dumps. A special service is also provided to conditionally execute subsequent tasks upon abnormal program termination. Consequently, various file dumps can be specified to be executed only when the program terminates abnormally.

4.3 Logging and Accounting

Detailed accounting records are produced at the termination of each task. The accounting information maintained includes processor time and core used, elapsed time, peripherals used, time used for each peripheral, lines of output produced on the system output device, and the number of records added or deleted from permanent disk or drum files. As mentioned previously, system error statistics are also maintained for I/O device failures.

4.4 System Description Maintenance

The capability of a problem program to request descriptive information is somewhat limited. One feature does, however, permit the problem program to request the total execution time it has used to the point of the request.

UNIVAC 1108 EXEC 8 OPERATING SYSTEM

The EXEC 8 is designed to operate as a master control program which establishes the multiprogramming environment for the UNIVAC 1108 Multiprocessor System. EXEC 8 permits concurrent batch, demand (interactive), and real-time processing operations.

1.0 JOB MANAGEMENT

1.1 Job Control

Jobs entering the 1108 system are sorted into information files by input symbionts, and these files are subsequently used by the supervisor for run scheduling and processing. Each job is composed of a series of tasks, where a task is defined to be a single operation of a system processor or the execution of a user program. All tasks for a given job are processed serially, while tasks of separate jobs are processed concurrently. The number of tasks executing concurrently is variable and dependent on the amount of core space available at any given time.

1.1.1 Scheduling

Separate scheduling philosophies are used for each job-processing mode. For batch job processing, all submitted jobs are collected in groups arranged by priority on disk queues. As facilities become available, these queues are examined to determine if a run may be initiated. All jobs in the group having highest priority must be initiated before jobs from a lower priority group will be selected. Within any group, the supervisor is free to choose the order of initiation based first on the facilities available at the moment, and second on the order of job submission. Batch jobs may also be assigned a time of day by which the job must be completed (called a deadline). Jobs with an impending deadline may be selected at any time regardless of priority.

The system defines demand processing as a demand and response type of activity (i.e., conversational). As demand jobs appear, they are initiated immediately. A priority is assigned to each demand job; however, this priority is not used for job scheduling. Rather, it is used when overload situations exist to resolve conflicts in gaining external facility assignments and to give certain privileges in CPU assigment. All demand jobs are therefore executed concurrently.

Real-time programs are submitted for processing in a manner similar to batch job processing. However, once initiated, real-time programs receive an execution priority directly below the interrupt processing priority. Once initiated, real-time programs remain core resident at all times, though they may be placed in a dormant state to be activated upon the receipt of selected external interruptions.

Batch processing jobs may be scheduled by two separate time-dependent methods. A start time can be specified indicating the time at which the job should be considered for execution. In the absence of a start time specification, the job is considered for execution immediately. A deadline parameter may be used by the programmer to specify a time of day or an elapsed time from the time of job submission by which his job must be completed. If a deadline cannot be met via normal scheduling, the system will take the necessary action to ensure the required completion time if possible. This action may degrade the general operation of the system as far as multiprogramming and system overhead are concerned. The estimated running time of active jobs is used to determine when a deadline job should be initiated.

Executing programs may also specify the initiation of a subtask to be executed concurrently with the main task. The subtask to be executed may be initiated immediately or delayed for a given increment of time depending on the form of the request.

Conditional control statements may be used to accomplish dynamic adjustment of the control stream as it is being executed. A control word is maintained by the system throughout the course of job processing. The value of the control word may be tested or set from within the control stream by conditional statements of the control language. This statement also permits portions of the stream to be bypassed, depending on the status of the control word. The control word is accessible to user programs and to the supervisor as well. Thus a user program may take different paths and/or set parts of the control word, so that portions of the control stream may be bypassed.

Two dispatching queues are maintained, one for batch job tasks and one for demand job tasks. For each job initiated, the scheduler prepares a program control table. This table contains certain fixed information such as run ID and estimated run time, as well as variable information such as the current facilities assigned and the core requirements of the particular task being executed. The control table is maintained by the dynamic allocator during the execution of the task and returned to the scheduler when the task terminates.

1.1.2 Resource Allocation

The facilities at the disposal of the executive system include the input/output channels, all peripheral equipment attached to these channels, and all core storage space. The supervisor assigns these facilities as needed to fulfill the facility requirements of all jobs entering the system. The system also maintains and continually updates inventory tables that reflect the facilities available for assignment and the jobs using the currently assigned facilities.

Internal storage is dynamically assignable by the executive system and dynamically releasable by the user. Storage is initially assigned to each task according to its immediate requirements. As these requirements change, the user may request additional core or he may release space to aid in optimizing system performance. Multiple requests for dynamic core allocation are satisfied in the following priority: executive system requests, real-time requests, deadline requests, and demand/batch requests (the latter based on respective individual job priorities). All program areas in main storage are locked-out from access by any other program in main storage. This lock-out safeguards all programs from an active program which may attempt to read, write, or branch into another program area.

All user files must be assigned prior to being referenced for I/O operations. The assignments may occur in one of three ways: (1) via a control statement, (2) via a supervisory request from within a user program, or (3) via a supervisory request from within a part of the executive system.

Statements to assign and free I/O devices may be placed anywhere within the control stream. However, programs may dynamically assign and free devices to avoid the problem of reserving files and/or facilities from the beginning of the job until completion.

Devices such as magnetic tapes are normally assigned before run execution since they cannot be shared by two or more runs and normally require operator set-up. Such devices are always released automatically at the termination of the run. However, they may also be released during the course of the run by the user. Magnetic tape units may be assigned for a particular channel or for a specific unit. When only the channel is selected, the supervisor will choose an available unit on the channel.

There is also an option for magnetic tape devices which will release a file while reserving the physical facility. The facility is placed in a pool for the job and is available for reassignment at any point within the job. The facility will not be returned to the executive facility pool (which is available to all jobs) until it is completely released or until the job terminates.

The supervisor routines allow assignment of a mass storage file to any number of jobs at one time, provided that no job has requested exclusive use of the file. If exclusive use is requested, the job is delayed until all other jobs have released the file; once the file is assigned exclusively, all other jobs requiring the file are delayed until the file is released.

All reentrant routines are so designated on the system library. When a reentrant routine is called by an executing task, the routine is loaded (if it is not already in core) and marked as unavailable for swapping. It remains unavailable for swapping until all calling routines relinquish control. The reentrant routine will still remain in core, but will be available for swapping when additional core space is needed.

All other routines are called as needed and are assigned to

the exclusive use of the calling task. A special instruction called "test and set" provides a capability for a core resident data base that may be used by a number of different executing tasks or jobs. The instruction provides a means of controlling access to the data base by a number of concurrently executing programs. Thus, common data may be temporarily protected from access while being modified.

1.1.3 Program Loading

All program elements are loaded from system or user files on a dynamic basis. Programs may be dynamically relocated in core storage in order to provide a more effective multiprogramming environment. Thus core storage may be rearranged periodically to provide contiguous blocks of unused core.

Two types of swapping control are available. First, demand programs that are in a wait state will be rolled-out whenever additional core is required for other demand programs. Second, inactive batch programs will be rolled-out whenever real-time or batch programs of a higher priority require additional core space.

1.1.4 Event Monitoring

Real-time programs receive priorities directly below executive I/O functions. Due to this high priority, they are allocated CPU time whenever they are in a position to use it. Since several programs with real-time requirements may have identical priorities, these programs must share control as required. Only when all activities of the higher priority levels have relinquished control is dispatching switched to the next lower level. If a program is interrupted due to an I/O completion that causes reactivation of a higher priority program, control will be switched to the higher priority program.

For batch jobs, when a task is ready for execution, it is placed in a core queue and executed in the general mix of batch tasks. For demand jobs a task is introduced into a special queue called a "core swap queue" and is given core space and CPU time as soon as its turn comes up. The basic philosophy of the dynamic allocator is to meet required deadlines for batch jobs, while at the same time maintaining the required response time for demand users. Within this dynamic operating environment the dividing line between demand and batch programs is subject to constant change as emphasis is placed on allocating time to batch runs approaching required completion time.

The allocator prepares a switching list used by the dispatcher in switching control among core resident programs as various events and contingencies arise. The allocator periodically adjusts the switching level of programs or classes of programs so as to force the CPU time to be used in a particular manner based on deadlines, priorities, and interaction rates, as well as certain overall constraints as to how CPU time should be shared among the different types of programs. The overall constraints (the portion of time to be spent between demand and batch processing) are specified at system generation.

A user program may synchronize its activities with the completion of an I/O operation via two supervisor requests. One request will allow the user program to suspend its activity until the completion of a particular I/O operation. The other supervisor request permits the user program to suspend its operation until any current I/O request has been completed.

The interrupt handling routines of EXEC 8 control all interrupts. These interrupts are received from the peripheral subsystem or from the control section of the central processor. The action taken in each case is dependent on which of the four interrupts was recognized—input/output, computer/core malfunctions, program contingency, or real-time channel interrupts.

The system permits run restrictions to be placed on each user job. At system generation time, installation maximums that apply to all jobs entering the system for running time, page count, and punch count are specified. At job submission time, the user has the capability of modifying these parameters for that particular job. The user can further specify whether or not that particular run should be terminated when a specification is exceeded. In the absence of termination, the operator is notified of overruns.

1.1.5 Program Termination Processing

Termination of the job is normally triggered by the completion of the last task within the job. At this point, space reserved for any temporary files on mass storage devices is released and the core storage occupied by the final task is released. Peripheral equipment such as tape units or paper tape equipment assigned to the job are returned to the pool of available facilities. An entry is also made in the system log indicating the completion time of the job.

The symbiont output processing of print files created by a job is initiated at job termination when facilities are available. If facilities are not available, such files are maintained on mass storage devices by the executive system and their processing is initiated whenever such facilities become free.

Abnormal termination may occur either in abort mode or error mode. Abort mode will cause the immediate termination of the job (if it is batch mode) or of the task (if it is demand mode). Core dumps are not available for programs terminating via the abort mode. For error mode, the user may request that various core and file dumps be provided when this condition occurs.

1.2 System Communication

1.2.1 System Startup

One of the outputs of the system generation routine is an output tape which contains the 1108 executive system and the system library. The tape is initially loaded by a manual hardware bootstrap method. Immediately after the bootstrap routine receives control, the current resident executive (if one is in core) is saved on an external mass storage device. After this area is saved, the routine reads the system tape to bring in each block of the system and copy it to a resident drum location. A fixed area of the drum is reserved for executive system usage only and is determined at system generation time. The user has the option of placing any of the executive processors on slower mass storage devices if they exist. An initialization routine finally places a copy of the resident portion of the executive system in core, initializes and/or reinstates the file directory and gives control to the system.

During the initial load various installation parameters may be temporarily modified.

1.2.2 Job Control Communication

Control of the operating environment is accomplished through a set of control statements. These statements direct the supervisor in scheduling, assignment of facilities, and in the disposition of program and data files. The basic format of the executive control statements, which is quite simple, is amenable to a large number of input devices. Statements may be of variable lengths and are not restricted to a card image format.

A unique feature of the EXEC 8 system permits an executing program to submit an executive control statement image for interpretation and processing. The image submitted must be a character string identical to what would be submitted as an executive control statement via the input stream.

All communications between the operator and the operating programs are handled via the communications section of the executive system. Communication takes place via the computer keyboard and on-line printer on the console channel. Neither the keyboard nor the console printer can be assigned to operating programs. The operator can change the priority, start time, and deadline time of any job; selectively hold the scheduling of jobs; obtain a summary of jobs that have not been opened; and remove a job from the job queue. These features, when used, can dynamically change the scheduling process.

1.2.3 Input/Output Stream Control

Submission of a job to the system for processing may be from either a primary input device or from a remote terminal. The system input symbionts control all primary input devices from which jobs can be submitted. All jobs in the stream are headed by a run statement. For each job submitted, the particular input symbiont will construct a file, place it on mass storage, and queue it for inspection by the storage scheduler. The symbiont extracts the job ID and priority specification from the run statement processed by the symbionts, an entry is made in the system log as to the time the job entered the system. Upon completion of every job, a symbiont is activated to process the print files that were created on mass storage devices and print them on the system printer.

1.2.4 Resource Status Modification

In addition to the control the operator has over the submitted job stream (see 1.2.2), he may also alter the status of various peripheral devices. Units may be suspended from the system or reactivated by appropriate operator messages. He may also alter the amount of CPU time that is to be allocated to demand processing and batch processing via minimum and maximum time parameters.

1.2.5 System Status Interrogation

The operator may request information on the status of any of the jobs in the dispatching queue, or request an overall system status report. A system status report indicates the percentage of time allocated to executive, batch, demand, idle, and real-time functions during the last six-second operating period. Overall system status also indicates the number of batch jobs in execution and awaiting execution.

1.3 Recovery Processing

1.3.1 Checkpointing

The EXEC 8 system incorporates a checkpoint restart facility that will function with any file format at any level of access. Checkpoints may be initiated by a user program, a control statement, or an unsolicited key-in. All jobs except real-time jobs may be checkpointed.

The checkpoint routine will automatically include all pertinent information necessary for restart except mass storage files being updated, which are cataloged or are to be cataloged. The user must specify whether the checkpoint routine should or should not dump such files. If they are dumped, the status of the original file remains unchanged. All temporary files will be automatically dumped and reloaded upon restart.

Checkpoint information may be recorded on tape or mass storage. If tape is chosen, the information can be interspersed with data or recorded on a nondata tape. Each checkpoint taken may be used as a restart point at some subsequent time. If checkpoint information is recorded on mass storage, only the last checkpoint is available for restarting. It is not possible to include file dumps within mass storage checkpoints.

1.3.2 Restarting

The EXEC 8 restart procedure restores a job to the status it had attained when the checkpoint was taken. The checkpoint file must be cataloged prior to restart. Requests for restart are similar to checkpoint requests in that they also can be initiated internally by a program and externally by a control statement or an operator key-in. Any checkpoint dump is capable of being reestablished by any restart request regardless of the type of checkpoint request used. For example, an internal checkpoint request may be restarted by an internal request, a control statement, or an unsolicited key-in.

2.0 I/O CONTROL

2.1 I/O Scheduling

Input/output operations are controlled by means of a central I/O routine, which accepts and queues requests and interrupts and gives control to the I/O device handler when appropriate. References to I/O control result in a transfer to the handler controlling the device referenced. The handler, in turn, considers the request and queues it for the particular I/O subsystem. When the subsystem becomes free, an entry is removed from the subsystem queue and the handler is entered at the appropriate point. Queueing is bypassed if the subsystem is initially free.

The executive system classifies an I/O request into one of three categories, depending on the activity that submitted the I/O request. The three categories are assigned priorities, and all requests in one category are completed before any request is honored from the next lower category. The order of priority is: real time, executive, and demand/batch. Look-ahead techniques are used within a category whenever appropriate, so that the average execution time for I/O requests may be reduced.

2.2 Data Transfer

The executive system provides a complex of routines called symbionts to interface the unit record equipment of the 1108 with the user program. These device routines are available for all standard terminals, card readers, card punches, printers, paper tape readers, and paper tape punches. Data to and from these devices is thus buffered on mass storage to provide an effective linkage to the asynchronous and relatively slow devices.

For magnetic tape, mass storage, and communication devices the system provides both single buffer and buffer pool capabilities. A buffer pool is a portion of the user's core storage area which is made available for use as an input/output area for one or more files. The pool can contain any desired number of buffers. The single buffer mode of execution is the most efficient, as there is little supervisor overhead involved. The single buffer mode will also use slightly less core storage per buffer because the pool mode requires additional storage areas for pool control information.

Separate buffer pools are maintained for data files and communication devices. For each cataloged file assigned to a job, there must be an associated buffer pool. A buffer pool may be assigned to one particular file or to many files. The size of each buffer must be equal to the maximum block size specified for the file plus three extra words for control purposes. A buffer pool for use with the communication handler may be established in any portion of the core storage area that the user may elect to set aside as an I/O area.

The data-handling routines are designed to process a wide variety of file formats. Few restrictions are placed on formats acceptable to the system. Files may be processed at the item, record, or block levels, with general disregard for the physical characteristics of the I/O device assigned. File access may be either random or sequential.

The data-handling techniques of EXEC 8 are very advanced, and encompass a great many of the functions that are normally associated with independent data management systems. Each file is defined by file format and item definitions. The item control table enables the user to access any item of a record on request.

A teleprocessing subsystem is available within the resident executive to handle all communications processing for a large number of independent terminals. The communications multiplexor handler is designed to present a common focal point between the multitude of available remote terminal devices and the programs to be executed on the Univac 1108. The diversity of available hardware dictates a general routine on which the variances of each application can be built. The communications handler supports two other modes of operation. The first level consists of a buffer-handling mode in which the handler supervises transmitting and receiving messages on a buffer-by-buffer basis, with no assumption concerning the content of each buffer. The second level of support assumes a system-defined format on devices capable of acknowledging transmission.

An extensive set of device manipulation functions is available through an independent file utility processor. This processor is called whenever a control statement referencing a file is recognized. The file utility processor permits file copying, positioning, and cataloging.

2.3 Remote Terminal Support

Demand mode processing is initiated and controlled by the executive control language. Commands are input via the user's remote console on a conversational basis. Provisions are also made for: (1) dialed communication connections in addition to leased lines and remote consoles on site; (2) paper tape input allowing pretyped command programs for high transmission efficiency; (3) user communications with the computer center, other consoles, and the executive system itself.

Input symbionts operating in the demand mode normally accept data input from a remote terminal. Thus the rate of input to the system is subject to the discretion of the remote operator. Command input from the terminal is buffered in main storage in the same manner as the input stream from an on-site card subsystem.

2.4 File Handling

The file supervisor controls the creation and maintenance of all program and data files. It also maintains an up-to-date master directory of files cataloged in the system and of the status of mass storage availability.

For each file known to the system, other than temporary files, an entry containing the identification and characteristics of the file is maintained by the system in a master directory of files. The process of entering a file into the master directory is referred to as cataloging and is effected by assignment control statement options. By referencing the master directory, the system remains cognizant of the current usage of mass storage and magnetic tapes.

File security is maintained by two keys which must be specified on an assignment statement to gain access to a cataloged file. The keys are initially obtained from the assignment statement which caused the file to be cataloged. The master directory also contains a count of the number of times the file is accessed and the time of last access. These fields, along with the system log, are available to the user to monitor file usage and to detect any encroachment on individual privacy.

3.0 DIAGNOSTIC ERROR PROCESSING

3.1 Hardware Error Control

EXEC 8 maintains a standard error recovery procedure for each possible I/O malfunction that may occur. When an abnormal status is returned from an I/O operation and the user has not suppressed error recovery, EXEC 8 will initiate the standard recovery procedure. In the event recovery is not successful, an error message is displayed on the console and the operator may issue specific error control instructions.

Computer/core malfunctions consist of I/O control memory parity errors, input/output data parity errors, core storage parity errors, and power failures. For I/O control memory parity errors, the executive determines whether the error is transient or permanent. If the error is transient, the I/O operation is reinitiated and control is returned to the interruption address. If the error is not transient, and equipment on another channel cannot assume the responsibility of this channel, the program assigned to this channel will be terminated and the channel declared down. If a transient error exists in certain registers and the recovery routine does not use the faulty register, automatic recovery is attempted.

System processing is identical for input/output data parity errors and core storage parity errors. When a transient error occurs, the user program is given control at a restart point, if one was provided. If a restart point was not provided, the program is terminated. If the error occurred within the executive and restart is impossible, the system will stop. If the error is not transient, the program interrupted is terminated and the block of memory involved is declared down. If the damaged coding was critical, the system will stop.

When a power failure occurs, the system initiates the following shutdown sequence: (1) upon occurrence of the interrupt, the interrupt address and control memory are saved; channels containing I/O action are flagged; (2) if the computer is restarted without clearing, the I/O action restart flags are cleared, control memory is restored, and a return is made to the interrupted address; (3) if the computer is restarted after clearing, the flagged I/O actions are requeued on the I/O request list, control memory is restored, and control is given to the interrupted program.

3.2 Program Error Control

A program contingency is a condition within a running program which causes a computer interrupt or pseudo interrupt. The user program may initially specify that it wishes to process such interrupts rather than accept the standard action provided by the system. The types of program contingencies recognized are: illegal operation codes, privileged instructions, core storage violations, floating point overflow and underflow, divide overflow, and test and set interrupts. The test and set interrupt occurs when a user program seeks access to common data that is currently protected by another executing program.

3.3 Interface Error Control

The control statement interpreter is responsible for interpreting the input control stream. Each control statement image presented to the control statement interpreter is checked for format accuracy.

A file interface error occurs when a user requests a file operation that violates prescribed procedures. For each occurrence of a file interface error, control will be returned to the user's specified error exit.

4.0 PROCESSING SUPPORT

4.1 Timing Service

An interval timing routine is used by the system for timing various activities such as I/O functions, operator response, and CPU usage. This routine is also used by the system to force interrupts after variable amounts of time, so that such events as nonresponding I/O devices and unbalanced CPU usage of time are detected. The user may also request interrupts based on time intervals.

A time of day routine is used by the system to maintain accurate standard time. This time is used by all processors for annotating listings, by the file control supervisor for maintaining historical information about all files and by the accounting and logging routines for time-tagging events. A supervisor request will supply the using program with the current date and time.

4.2 Testing and Debugging Service

A comprehensive diagnostic system is available within the EXEC 8 system to aid in the checkout of user programs. Commands are available which can trigger snapshot dumps. Postmortem dumps are also available through an executive job control statement.

Selected routines may be executed to conditionally control the occurrence of a dump or series of dumps. Other routines are available to record data in a diagnostic file; this data may range from individual messages to register dumps, core dumps, tape dumps, and drum and file dumps. Additional control routines are used to specify arbitrary print formats, core space for drum and tape file dumps, deletion of dumps not of interest, and activation or nullification of various diagnostic procedures.

4.3 Logging and Accounting

An extensive system is maintained for collecting information pertaining to each job and program. The information log is later used for accounting and post-execution processing. The basic types of information entered in the log are facility usage, job termination data, and the logging entries made by log control cards or executive requests. Within the master log, a record is maintained of the occurrence of I/O errors. Errors are counted for mass storage and magnetic tape devices.

A set of allowable account numbers is incorporated into the system at generation time. A job is not accepted if the account number is not known to the system, and the operator is notified. The operator may abort the job or accept the new account number. If he accepts the new number, it is added to the permanent set.

At each run termination a summary accounting routine is activated. The following information is provided: project identity, account number, total run time, pages of printing applicable to the job, number of cards read in and punched out, and time and date of job initiation. The accounting routine reads and updates all totals maintained. The accounting file is permanently assigned as a mass storage file. Continuing totals are kept until cleared by a billing routine or placed during system loading. A procedure for executing the billing routine must be established by the user.

Another special accounting file is also maintained by the executive system for the purpose of providing limited summary accounting information. The information is accumulated by account number at the time of job completion. The summary accumulates information on the following items: run time, time and date of first entry to the account number, time and date of last entry to the account number, number of pages printed, number of cards read, number of cards punched, and elapsed time an I/O facility has been assigned to the account. The summary accounting file is first constructed during system generation and includes the scheduling limitations for each account.

4.4 System Description Maintenance

All information stored in the control table used for job control is available to the user program via a supervisor request. The means for determinating the hardware description of any specified file is also available via a supervisor request.

BURROUGHS B6500 MASTER CONTROL PROGRAM

The Burroughs B6500 master control program (MCP) is a large-scale system which supports batch multiprogramming, time-sharing, and real-time operations. The system can also support multiprocessing by the addition of a second control processor. The fundamental system design concept is total hardware/software integration, which results in compiler-oriented hardware, thereby eliminating the requirement for assembly language programming.

1.0 JOB MANAGEMENT

The processor can operate in either of two states, control state under the MCP or normal state for user programs and certain MCP functions. In a dual-processor system each processor handles its own interrupts; that is, both processors may be in control state at the same time.

Entry into control state occurs when the processor is started and as a result of certain interrupt conditions. In control state the processor can execute privileged instructions not available in normal state, and various classes of interrupts can be inhibited or allowed programmatically. Exit from control state into normal state occurs whenever MCP initiates a normal state program or exits back to a normal state program following an interrupt. In the latter case, user program return may not be to the program in process when the interrupt occurred.

Normal state excludes use of privileged instructions required by the MCP, permits hardware detection of invalid operators, and enforces memory protect and security facilities. Exit from normal state occurs as a result of an interrupt condition or by a call to a control state program, for example, to execute I/O. Many MCP functions can be run in normal state. Interrupts to a normal state MCU function can be enabled.

1.1 Job Control

The MCP maintains job or process control through the use of stacks, description, and tables.

One stack is associated with each job in the system. The stack, a contiguous area of memory, is assigned to a job to provide storage for basic program and data references. It also provides for temporary storage of data and job history. When a job is activated, four high-speed registers are linked to the job's stack. This linkage is established by the stack-pointer register (S), which contains the memory address of the last word placed in the stack. The four top-of-stack registers extend the stack to provide quick access for data manipulation.

Data are brought into the stack through the top-of-stack registers according to the last-in, first-out principle. Total capacity of the top-of-stack register is two operands. Loading a third operand into the top-of-stack registers causes the first operand to be pushed from the top-of-stack registers into the stack. The stack-pointer register (S) is incremented by one as each word is placed into the stack and is decremented by one as each word is withdrawn from the stack and placed in the top-of-stack registers. As a result, the S register continually points to the last word placed into the job's stack.

A job's stack is bound, for memory protection, by two registers, the base-of-stack register (BOSR) and the limit-of-stack register (LOSR). The contents of BOSR define the base of the stack, and the LOSR defines the upper limit of the stack. The job is interrupted if the S register is set to the value contained in either LOSR or BOSR.

Descriptors are words used to locate data and program areas in memory and to describe these areas for control purposes. Descriptors are the only words containing absolute addresses which can be used by a normal state program; however, the normal state program cannot alter them. Descriptors are divided into three categories: data, string, and segment.

Data descriptors are used for referring to data areas, including input/output buffer areas. The data descriptor defines an area of memory starting at the base address contained in the descriptor. The size of the memory area in number of words is contained in the length field of the descriptor. For the purpose of initiating I/O operations, the data descriptor contains the unit number and the address of a buffer area. Data descriptors may directly reference any memory word address.

String descriptors refer to data areas organized as 4-, 6-, or 8-bit characters. The descriptor defines an area of memory starting at the base address contained in the descriptor. The size of the memory area is defined by the length field.

Segment descriptors are used to locate program segments. These descriptors contain either the main memory or disk file address of a particular segment. All programs are entered and exited through the segment descriptors common in the base stack; all references to those descriptors are relative. Entrance to or removal of any given program segment from memory is achieved by changing the "presencebit" in that segment descriptor. No stack search of any kind is required.

The MCP also maintains a series of tables which summarize system and process status. For each job awaiting execution, the schedule table contains its name, priority, and schedule index. The mix table contains the priority, status (active or suspended), and mix index of each job being executed. The job table contains the mix table entry, control card contents, and physical unit/file name correlation information for each job in the mix. The peripheral unit table has an entry for each peripheral unit in the system. Each entry contains the status of the corresponding unit and the file associated with that unit. Similarly, the label table contains an entry with status and content information for each I/O unit which is on-line. The disk directory table contains the names of the random access files in the system.

1.1.1 Scheduling

The scheduling routine determines the sequence of jobs to be run and the optimal program mix considering the priority ratings and system requirements of each object program, and the present system configuration. The MCP incorporates a dynamic scheduling algorithm, that is, one which reschedules the job sequence whenever a higher priority job is introduced into the system. Job priority may be programmer-defined via the *priority* statement. If no priority is specified, a default value of one-half the maximum allowable priority is assigned by the MCP.

The control card interpreting procedure *controlcard* makes an entry into the sheet queue to schedule each batch-mode process. The sheet queue is a linked list of processes which await execution. Each entry in the sheet queue is a partially built process stack. The information contained in the stack includes the estimated amount of main memory required by the process, priority, time of entry into the schedule, size and location of code segments, working storage stack size, and size and location of the process stack information. After *controlcard* completes its tasks, the entry is moved from the sheet queue to a queue called the ready queue.

The ready queue is divided into an active and a passive part. At the time the job is moved from the sheet queue to the ready queue, the resources required for efficient execution of the job are checked against the resources currently available to the system. If sufficient resources are not immediately available, then the job is placed in the passive part of the ready queue and temporarily assigned a priority of zero. If sufficient resources are available, then the job is placed in the active part of the ready queue.

The active and passive parts of the ready queue are ordered according to priority. The calculation of the priorities is performed in a well-isolated section of the MCP. Thus the user may easily tailor the Burroughs-supplied active and passive priority algorithms to his specific requirements.

Real-time and time-sharing applications entering the system via the data communication facilities merely become additions to the multiprogramming mix.

1.1.2 Resource Allocation

Central memory is composed of 1 to 32 modules, each containing 16,384 words. Each word is composed of 48 information bits, one parity bit, and three control bits which are used to provide memory protection, identify various types of data, and perform other control functions. Memory areas are classified as in-use or available according to their current state. The MCP maintains records of storage availability through the use of memory state records which are assigned within the areas they describe. Each type of state record is linked to form a list which contains sufficient information for a single hardware operator to find the next state record and all succeeding state records. Specifically, in-use state records contain the stack number of the requesting process, the length of the in-use area, an availability bit set in the "off" position, a code indicating the usage of the area, links to the last previously allocated and next in-use areas, and so on. Available memory state records contain the length of the area, an availability bit set in the "on" position, links to the next and last available areas, and so forth.

MCP performs dynamic storage allocation via the environment control routine for all system storage media: main memory, magnetic disk, and system library magnetic tape. As a result of considering the different system storage media as a hierarchy of memory, the MCP controls allocation and de-allocation of all system memory, regardless of the type. If the system has multiprocessing capabilities, the processors are also considered as allocatable resources. Each processor is considered to be assigned to a "logical" processor so that multiprocessing consists of the execution of a queue of logical processors on the physical processors available to the system.

Memory protection is provided for by a combination of hardware and software devices. One of the hardware features is automatic detection of an attempt by a program to index beyond its designated data area. Another is the use of one of the control bits in each word as a memory protect bit to prevent user programs from writing into words of memory which have the protect bit set. (The protect bit is set by the software.) Any attempt to perform such a write operation is inhibited, and an interrupt is generated, which results in termination of the program. Thus a user program cannot change program segments, data descriptors, or any program words or MCP tables during execution.

The MCP automatically assigns peripheral units to symbolic files whenever possible in order to minimize the amount of operator attention required by each process. Input files requested by a process cause the MCP to search its tables for the appropriate peripheral unit which contains the file requested. If the file name specified by the process is found on a particular unit, that unit is marked "in use" and assigned to the process. Output files requested by a process are automatically assigned by the MCP if a suitable unit exists for the file. In the case of disk files, a disk file directory entry is made and the required disk space is allocated for the file.

In order to allow dynamic specification of actual file names for a file, three tables are necessary, namely, a file parameter block, a label equation block, and a file information block. A file parameter block is created by *controlcard* for all files in a process. It contains the symbolic file name and any compilations or execution time label equation information specified for this process. The label equation block and the file information block are created by the compiler and maintained by I/O functions for each file in a process. The label equation block contains the current label equation and other file attribute information for a particular file, including any programmatic specification of file attributes. A file information block contains frequently used information concerning the file such as the type of access required, type of unit assigned, physical unit being used, and attributes which depend upon the type of unit assigned. Incorporation of the file attributes in the file information block and label equation block allows modification of file specifications such as buffer size and blocking factors, at program execution time, without recompilation of the program.

On some systems, especially those with a large number of system files, situations may arise where more disk space is required than is currently available. In such a situation the MCP will find or request a system scratch tape and unload the oldest access data file onto the system library tape until sufficient space is available. The MCP will then record the appropriate volume and reel number into the directory for each file. Subsequently, if one of the absent files is required, the system will automatically reload the file from the system tape.

Since each process on the B6500 System has a stack for data storage, and since the object program code is not modified by execution, both object programs and MCP routines on the B6500 are reentrant. References to the proper code segment for a process are established by executing an *enter* operator after an "indirect reference word" (IRW) is constructed which points to a "program control word" (PCW). The PCW contains the relative location in the segment dictionary of the object code segment descriptor, and the word index relative to the beginning of the code segment.

1.1.3 Program Loading

A program residing in memory occupies separately allocated areas, that is, each part of the program may reside anywhere in memory. The actual address is determined by the MCP. Also, the various parts are not necessarily assigned to contiguous memory areas. Registers within the processor indicate the bases of the various areas during the execution of a program.

The separately allocated areas of a program are: (1) the program segments—sequences of instructions performed by the processor in executing the program; (2) the segment dictionary, a table containing one word for each program segment; this word tells whether the program segment is in main memory or on the disk, and gives its corresponding main memory or disk address; (3) the stack, which contains all the variables associated with the program, including control words that indicate the dynamic status of the job as it is being executed; (4) the MCP stacks and segment dictionary, which contain variables pertinent to the MCP and the MCP segment dictionary entries.

In the B6500 system a reference to data or code through a data descriptor or a segment descriptor causes the processor to check the pressure bit in the descriptor. If the presence bit is off, an interrupt occurs which transfers control to *presencebit,* passing the nonpresent descriptor as a parameter. *Presencebit* reads the address field of the descriptor and calls the *getspace* procedure to allocate an area in main memory for the code segment. Parameters are supplied to *getspace* so that an adequate-sized contiguous area of memory may be reserved for a particular stack number. After *getspace* satisfies the request for core space, it returns the memory address of the area it has allocated and *presencebit* causes the information to be read from disk into memory. When the disk read is finished, *presencebit* stores the memory address of the information into the address field of the descriptor, turns the presence bit "on," and updates the descriptor in the process stack. *Presencebit* then returns control to the interrupted process, and the information is accessed again by the process. Now the information is present in memory; the information is obtained and the process execution continues in the normal manner.

The storage required for the referenced data or code may be allocated at the front or rear of an adequate-sized area and marked as overlayable or nonoverlayable. When an in-use area is allocated it is linked to the previously allocated in-use area by the left-off link and pointer fields in the memory links. These fields comprise the left-off list. A reference word pointing to the oldest entry in the left-off list allows the chronological history of in-use memory areas to be determined.

When there is insufficient available memory to satisfy a particular request, the overlay mechanism is invoked. The left-off list is searched, starting at the overlayable area that has been allocated for the longest period of time. If this area, combined with any adjacent available area, is adequate to satisfy the request, it is overlaid. Otherwise, allocated areas with lower starting addresses are considered.

If the request is satisfied and the area found is larger than the required size, the unused portion is made available by linking it to the available list. If the request is not satisfied, the next oldest overlayable area is obtained and the left-off list is searched as described above. This process is repeated until the left-off list has been exhausted. If the request cannot be satisfied, a No Memory condition exists.

It is convenient at this point to define the term "syllable," which is used in the description of some of the following functional areas. A syllable is the smallest component of a program operator (instruction). The length of a operator can range from 1 to 12 syllables, where each syllable is composed of 8 bits.

1.1.4 Event Monitoring

When sufficient system resources exist to allow another process into the mix, an independent runner process called *run* is started. *Run* unhooks the sheet queue and makes the system dictionary present in main memory. As soon as control is transferred to the new process, an interrupt occurs because the outer block code segment is not present in main memory. This interrupt is handled by the *presencebit* procedure of the MCP. *Presencebit* is entered and the following actions occur in order to bring the segment into memory: (1) *presencebit* calls *getspace* to allocate an area in main memory for the code segment; (2) after an area is allocated, *presencebit* calls *disk I/O,* the disk input/output procedure, and waits on an event which indicates that the segment has been read in; (3) *disk I/O* queries the request comes to the head of the queue, the disk I/O is performed. Upon completion of the disk I/O, the event is caused, thereby notifying *presencebit* that the segment is now available. *Presencebit* marks the segment descriptor present and exits back to the process at the point of interruption.

The MCP services two classes of interrupts, hardware interrupts and software interrupts. The hardware interrupts are generated automatically by the B6500 system and are handled by the MCP interrupt procedure. Software interrupts are programmatically defined for use by the MCP and object program processes. Software interrupts allow processes to communicate with each other and with the MCP.

Hardware interrupts may be subdivided into internal and external interrupts. For internal (syllable dependent and syllable independent) interrupts, each processor in a B6500 system is provided with a private, internal interrupt network. Internal interrupts associated with a processor are fed directly into this network and are stacked local to the processor. External interrupts, on the other hand, may be serviced by either processor.

Syllable dependent interrupts are detected by the processor operator logic. These include arithmetic error, *presencebit*, memory protect, and invalid operand interrupts. Except for arithmetic error interrupts, for which programmatic control may be supplied, and *presencebit* interrupts, this group of interrupts generally results in program termination. *Syllable independent* (alarm) interrupt conditions are not normally anticipated by the processor operator logic. They serve to inform the processor of some detrimental change in environment and can result from hardware failure as well as programming errors. These interrupts include those for a faulty read from memory, an invalid address, and an invalid program instruction word; all result in termination of the process involved. *External* interrupt conditions are similar to the alarm interrupts, in that they are not anticipated by the operator logic. However, they do not normally require immediate action and do not necessarily result in termination of the program. These include processor-to-processor and multiplexor interrupts.

When a hardware interrupt condition occurs, the interrupted processor enters the control state, marks the stack, and inserts three words in the top of the stack. The first entry is an indirect reference word which points to a register that contains a PCW which points to the MCP hardware interrupt procedure. The first entry is followed by two interrupt parameters, P1 and P2, which contain information indicating the nature of the interrupt condition. When the processor enters the MCP hardware interrupt procedure, it remains in control state in order to disable external interrupts. The processor execution state (control or normal) is determined by the control bit of the PCW. When the control bit is "on" the processor will execute a procedure in control state. Otherwise, it will execute in normal state.

Upon entry to the hardware interrupt procedure the parameter P1 is analyzed to determine the type of interrupt which occurred. For some interrupts such as *presencebit* interrupts, P2 contains additional information to be used by the interrupt procedure. Then the appropriate action is initiated.

After entering the interrupt procedure the program base register is pointing at the interrupt procedure, the program index register and the program syllable register are pointing at the interrupt procedure entry point, and the return control word for the interrupt procedure's exit is pointing back to the object program's code.

Software interrupts allow a process to stop running (thereby releasing the processor) until a specified event occurs, or continue running and be interrupted if the event does occur. A software interrupt occurs when a process is interrupted by the direct action of some other process. A process can be interrupted if it has an interrupt declaration (statement) within its scope.

A process may invoke the occurrence of an event via the *cause* statement. The MCP scans the event interrupt queue to determine if the interrupt has been enabled. If the interrupt is not enabled and the event is caused, no action is taken by the MCP on that process, and it looks at the next process stack in the queue.

If interrupts are enabled in the next stack, the MCP makes an entry in the software interrupt queue. This queue is ordered by stack number. If the stack is active, that is, another processor is working in the stack, the MCP will interrupt that processor with a processor-to-processor interrupt. Next, the MCP forces a transfer of control to the statement related to the interrupt declaration. Upon completion of this statement the process will return to its previous point of control unless a transfer of control is specified in the interrupt statement. In this case the process will not return the point of control before the interrupt, but will transfer control as specified in the interrupt statement.

As the MCP scans the event interrupt queue finding enabled interrupts in inactive stacks, it makes an entry in the software interrupt queue, doing nothing with that stack until it becomes active. Immediately after making the stack active, the MCP checks the software interrupt queue to see if there is an interrupt pointing to that stack. If an interrupt is found, the MCP forces a transfer of control to the statement referred to by the interrupt declaration. Upon completion of the statement, control is transferred as described above.

The programmer must specify the maximum amount of I/O time allowable for the object program or the compiler. If the I/O time exceeds that specified, the job is terminated.

1.1.5 Program Termination Processing

When a process execution is terminated the following actions occur: (1) any outstanding I/O requests are completed, if possible; any *open* files are closed, the units released, and the buffer areas are returned to the available memory table; (2) all overlayable disk areas allocated to the process are returned to the available disk table; (3) all process object code and data array areas of main memory are returned to the available memory table; (4) an end-of-job entry is made in the system log for the process; (5) the process stacks are linked into the Terminate Queue.

No information was provided concerning the outputting of process summary information or the availability of dump capabilities upon abnormal termination.

1.2 System Communication
1.2.1 System Startup

In order to place the MCP in control of the system, the MCP must be loaded onto disk and the option list must be initialized on the disk. These functions are performed by the system initialization program. The hardware disk load select function expects the MCP code file to be located at disk address zero. Therefore the initializer is used to load the MCP code file from tape (or elsewhere) onto disk, beginning at disk address zero. In addition, the MCP option list is written or revised on disk as indicated by initializer data cards.

The basic functions of the initializer are loading the MCP to disk address zero from tape or disk, writing or revising the MCP option list on disk, and specifying the status of the disk directory to the MCP. These functions may be specified individually or in various combinations by the data cards which the initializer reads. At the conclusion of initialization the first 8,192 words of the MCP are read from disk address zero into main memory, and control of the system is transferred to the MCP.

The type of initialization to be performed is specified to the initializer by the following types of control cards: (1) the *cold start* card which causes the MCP to create an empty disk directory when initialization is complete; (2) the *cool start* card which causes the MCP to retain the disk directory which currently exists—if neither cold start nor cool start are specified, cool start is assumed; (3) the *load* card which causes an MCP code file to be read from either tape or disk, whichever is specified, onto the disk beginning at disk address zero; (4) the option cards, namely, the *set* and *reset* option cards that set or reset all options. Individual options may be set or reset in addition to or instead of a universal specification. If a universal specification is not made, any option that is not specified remains unchanged from its previous setting. If no previous setting exists, which would be the case if no valid MCP option list exists on the disk, any unspecified options will be reset. The *stop* card indicates that the initializer has read all of the valid option specification cards. The *end* card signifies the physical end of the initializer control card deck. Any cards between the *stop* card and the *end* card are flushed through the card reader and ignored.

1.2.2 Job Control Communication

A user submits a job to the system as a set of control cards and a source language deck. Alternatively, the user may submit only a set of control cards if he has previously stored the programs on the disk and entered their names in the disk directory following an error-free compilation.

For a job requiring compilation, the first control card must be a compile statement, which specifies the compiler to be used and the type of compile to be made. There are three forms: compile and execute, compile for the library, and compile for syntax check. The other types of control cards may be used for all jobs whether they do or do not require compilation. These include an execute statement, process time statement, priority statement, core requirement statement, I/O time statement, and I/O unit statements which associate file labels with particular I/O units.

The time-sharing user controls his activities through the use of Command and Edit Language commands. Each command consists of a verb, that is, a directive, and in most cases, a list of parameters.

The operator communicates directly with the MCP through the use of input/output messages. The input messages include any control statement allowed on a control card, messages to enter jobs into and eliminate jobs from the schedule mix, and reactivate jobs suspended by certain operator output messages. Output messages pertain to other functional areas and therefore are not discussed here.

1.2.3 Input/Output Stream Control

As each process is read from the system input unit (card reader or "pseudo card readers," i.e., magnetic tape or disk) the *controlcard* procedure interprets the information contained in the first record of the process and makes an entry in the Sheet Queue to schedule the process.

When a process is terminated, the stack associated with the process is linked into the Terminate Queue. If a *terminate* independent runner is currently running, it is informed of the fact that another process has been introduced into the Terminate Queue. If *terminate* is not running, the MCP initiates a *terminate* independent runner.

1.2.4 Resource Status Modification

Control card statements are available for relabeling designated files and for removing specified file labels from disk storage subsequently releasing the associated disk space. The facilities for shutting down and disconnecting a unit are discussed under 2.1, Hardware Error Control.

1.2.5 System Status Interrogation

Communication with the MCP is accomplished with a combination of display units, control units (display units with associated keyboards), and control cards. The status of the system and of the processes in progress is presented on the display units. Specific questions requiring short answers may be entered via the keyboard. These questions and answers are displayed as they occur. Also, by entering the appropriate keyboard messages, various tables may be called for display. These tables include the job mix, schedule, peripheral unit, label, disk directory table, and job tables.

A data communications user may obtain his present status or that of his programs by the use of the *status* command. A *status* command with a file name is used to request information about a job which has been scheduled to run in the remote batch mode. This command returns either the length of time the job has been in the schedule or the amount of processor execution time it has used thus far. If the file has not been scheduled, an error message is provided.

If a file name is not included and the user is not running or compiling a program, the *status* command returns the date, the time of day, the time at which the user logged-in, the charge code being used, if any, the elapsed time since he logged in, the processor time he has used, and the status of any jobs he has submitted to run in the remote batch mode.

1.3 Recovery Processing

MCP provides a *breakstart* procedure which is used to perform breakouts (checkpointing) and restarts. The breakout records are written to magnetic tape. No other information was provided concerning this functional area.

2.0 I/O CONTROL

2.1 I/O Scheduling

All input/output operations on the B6500 system are performed by the MCP. The symbolic file name, the actual file name (file title), the peripheral type (disk, magnetic tape, card, paper tape, etc.), the access type (serial or random), the file mode (alpha, binary, etc.), the buffer size, the number of buffers, and the logical record size must be made available by the compilers. The actual file name is the file "title" which is associated with the unit that contains the file, or the "title" in the disk file header. The actual file name will be identical to the symbolic file name unless otherwise specified by *label equation* control statements.

There are two types of queues associated with I/O operations: the wait channel queues, one for each I/O channel; and the unit queues, one for each unit. I/O operations are requested by passing the address of an I/O buffer area to the MCP I/O request handling procedure *I/O request*. *I/O request* links the designated I/O buffer area into the appropriate unit queue. If this queue contains more than one entry, *I/O request* returns to the requesting process. Otherwise, *I/O request* calls *start I/O*. Start I/O constructs a unit word which specifies the unit channel. Then the hardware instruction which interrogates for an I/O path is executed. If a path (I/O channel) is available, *start I/O* calls *initiate I/O* which causes the channel to start transferring the information. *Initiate I/O* also records the initiate time which the I/O finish routine *I/O finish* uses to calculate I/O time for the process. Control is then returned to the process requesting the I/O action. If a path is not available, the unit word is entered into the wait channel queue and control is returned to the requesting process.

The channel handles the I/O request independently of the processor and builds a result descriptor as it performs the operation. Upon completion of the operation it generates an interrupt to the processor which activates *I/O finish*. *I/O finish* checks for errors that may have occurred. If no errors occurred, and additional I/O requests are pending, *I/O finish* checks the wait channel queue for the channel it used last and initiates the first I/O request in that queue. It then checks the unit queue for the unit it used last, removes the top entry from that queue, and inserts it in the wait channel queue. In order to prevent a conflict, a wait channel queue is not allowed to contain more than one I/O request for any given unit. If an I/O request occurs for a unit that is already in a wait channel queue (for any channel), then the request is entered in the appropriate unit queue.

2.2 Data Transfer

Object program I/O operations on the B6500 System involve the automatic transfer of logical records between a file and a process. A logical record consists of the information the process references with one Read or Write statement. The size of a logical record does not necessarily coincide with the size of the physical record or block accessed by the hardware I/O operations. When a physical record contains more than one logical record, the file is referred to as a blocked file.

When a file is accessed by a process, a physical record is written from or read to a memory area known as a "buffer" area for the file. If the file is blocked, the MCP maintains a record pointer into the buffer. This pointer is used by the process to access the current logical record. If the next record is not already present in a buffer, then the MCP automatically performs the required I/O operation.

The existence of parallel I/O multiplexor channels allows multiple buffers to effectively increase throughout for processes that require groups of physical records at one time. Since the MCP performs all object program I/O action, a process with multiple buffers allocated for a file allows the MCP to perform I/O operations independently of the status of the process. The determination of the number of buffers required for efficient execution of a process depends on the type of files being used, the particular hardware configuration being used, the processing characteristics of the process, the memory requirements of the process, and the mix of processes which are typically multiprocessing. The MCP attempts to keep all input buffers full and all output buffers empty for each process, regardless of status, thereby minimizing the time that a process is suspended waiting for an I/O operation to be completed.

Buffer areas are referred to by data descriptors. In order to initiate and coordinate all I/O operations, the executive routine maintains several tables in memory. Information about all the input/output descriptors for all programs in memory is recorded in these tables. Access through these tables enables the executive routine to reference a particular I/O descriptor when an I/O operation is to be executed. Thus the executive routine can evaluate the status of any descriptor at any time.

MCP provides facilities for forward spacing, backspacing, rewinding, and erasing magnetic tape. No disk arm positioning capabilities are necessary, as fixed read/write heads exist for every track. Reload/write operations are performed by electronic switching between tracks. Skipping and spacing operations are available for printer control.

2.3 Remote Terminal Support

MCP provides extensive data communication facilities, including time-sharing, remote computing, and remote inquiring. No terminal device interfaces directly with the control system. Instead, the necessary linkage is provided through a communications line, adaptor and multiplexing devices, and the data communications processor.

Those aspects of the data communications system that are oriented toward applications are handled by the message control system. These aspects include remote file maintenance and job control. In addition, the message control system coordinates interprogram communications and provides message-switching capabilities. A single remote station may communicate with other remote stations or more than one object job.

The MCS may (1) accept input from a variable number of remote stations through a program communication file in core; (2) react to the activation and deactivation of stations; for example, it may allow a dial-line, ring indicator to be answered and send the first message; (3) perform command and edit functions as required by the input data stream; (4) perform command functions upon occurrence of exception conditions, including controlling subsequent I/O of other processors attached to the line; (5) initiate object jobs as independent processes and handle certain command requests from object programs such as file open attachment of files to given lines; and (6) maintain file security restrictions and check remote user security.

2.4 File Handling

No summary is provided here.

3.0 DIAGNOSTIC ERROR PROCESSING

3.1 Hardware Error Control

Hardware failures such as memory parity errors generate alarm interrupts. Upon the occurrence of alarm interrupt conditions, the interrupt controller seizes control of the machine and the current operator is terminated prematurely.

Normally, system reconfiguration to eliminate a hardware module that has failed or must be shut down for maintenance is handled automatically by the MCP. The basic criterion for being able to shut down or disconnect a unit is whether it is currently in use by some process. If, for example, a memory module is shut down, an attempt to access data would almost certainly lead to an invalid address. However, if a unit which is not currently in use, such as a magnetic tape drive, is shut down, the system continues to function as if nothing has happened. It is possible to issue a command to the MCP indicating that a particular unit is to be shut down, and that the MCP is to respond by rearranging the system to avoid the use of the unit.

Certain major hardware modifications, however, require software modification of the MCP. This is due to the fact that the handling of the data communication processor interrupts and the general control adapter interrupts is dependent on the nature of the device involved. For example, if a data communication system or a substantially different data communication system is to be added, it is necessary to alter the MCP. Also, before connecting a device such as a plotter or analog interpreter, it is necessary to specify the nature of the general control adapter interrupt. Except for these two contingencies, however, reconfiguration of the system does not require modification of the MCP.

3.2 Program Error Control

Arithmetic errors generate interrupts that result in program termination unless programmatic control of these interrupts is specified. These errors include division by zero, exponent over/underflow, invalid indexing, and integer overflow.

Invalid addressing and invalid program instruction words cause alarm interrupts which result in program termination.

For each type of error that might occur while receiving input from a remote terminal station, a bit is reserved in the standard message header and is set if an error is detected. The user defines (via the *error action* statement) the action to be taken when any error flag is set. The specified action may continue with no recovery attempted, transfer and continue, or abort. The number of times error recovery is to be attempted is defined and after each recovery attempt, the retry value is automatically decremented by one. If the value reaches zero, error recovery is abandoned.

3.3 Interface Error Control

No information was provided concerning the editing of control cards for jobs submitted at the central site. However, it was noted that the processing of time-sharing commands is terminated upon error detection. Correction is effected by properly retyping the entire line which contains the rejected commands.

4.0 PROCESSING SUPPORT

4.1 Timing Service

The B6500 system contains a time-of-day register which may be set or read by the system processor(s). Information concerning software accessibility to this register was not provided.

The MCP for the B6500 makes use of two types of hardware clocks: the real-time clock and the interval timer. The real-time clock has a 1 microsecond resolution and counts up to 24 hours. It is used by the MCP logging routine and can also be read by application programs.

One interval timer is associated with each processor. The MCP uses the interval timer interrupt capability to provide a predetermined timed interrupt for loop hang-up and "time-slicing," that is, to distribute processor execution time among the processes according to their current priorities. The interval timer is activated by the set interval timer operator (the maximum interval is 1 second). The timer decrements every 512 microseconds until it is equal to zero. At this time, if the timer is still armed, the interrupt is set. However, the timer may be reset and the interrupt will not occur. The timer is disarmed whenever the processor handles an external interrupt.

4.2 Testing and Debugging Service

Information concerning dump facilities, tracing capabilities, or system test mode control was not provided.

4.3 Logging and Accounting

A record is maintained on disk of processing time for each program, including the time the job was started, elapsed running time, and the actual processor time.

System maintenance of error statistics was not discussed in the documentation supplied.

4.4 System Description Maintenance

The availability of system descriptive information to an applications program is not discussed in the documentation provided except for that described under 1.2.5, System Status Interrogation.

APPENDIX A

OPERATING SYSTEM FUNCTIONAL CLASSIFICATION SCHEME

Part I: Executive/Control Functions

1.0 Job Management
   1.1 Job Control
      1.1.1 Scheduling
         1.1.1.1 Algorithmic Scheduling
- Priority Recognition
- Resource Availability

         1.1.1.2 Time Initiated Scheduling
- Elapsed Interval
- Periodic Interval
- Time of Day

         1.1.1.3 Event Initiated Scheduling
- Interrupt Initiated
- Unsolicited Inputs

         1.1.1.4 Program Initiated Scheduling
- Subsequent Execution
- Asynchronous Execution

         1.1.1.5 Conditional Scheduling
- Prior Task/Job Completion
- Prior Task Error Code

         1.1.1.6 Scheduling Queue Maintenance
            1.1.1.6.1 Single Input Queue Control
            1.1.1.6.2 Multiple Input Queue Control
      1.1.2 Resource Allocation
         1.1.2.1 Internal Storage Allocation
            1.1.2.1.1 Fixed Block Allocation
            1.1.2.1.2 Dynamic Allocation
- Buffer Pools
- Free Pools of Internal Storage
- Program Expansion Area Pools

    1.1.2.1.3 Page Allocation
    1.1.2.1.4 Common (Shared) Storage Allocation
    1.1.2.1.5 Internal Storage Access Control
      • Storage Protection
  1.1.2.2 I/O Device Allocation
    1.1.2.2.1 Allocation by Specific Device
    1.1.2.2.2 Allocation by Device Type
      • Card Reader
      • Tape
      • Disk
    1.1.2.2.3 Allocation by Device Category
      • Sequential
      • Direct Access
    1.1.2.2.4 Shared Device Allocation
      • Operator's Console/Display
      • Common I/O Files
    1.1.2.2.5 Dynamic Allocation
      • Temporary Files
      • System Work Files
  1.1.2.3 Common Subroutine Allocation
    1.1.2.3.1 Reentrant Routine Control
    1.1.2.3.2 Serially Reusable Routine Control
      1.1.2.3.2.1 Lock/Unlock Facilities
      1.1.2.3.2.2 Request Queue Control
1.1.3 Program Loading
  1.1.3.1 Structure Control
    • Paged
    • Overlay
    • Dynamic
  1.1.3.2 Loading Control
    1.1.3.2.1 Program Relocating
    1.1.3.2.2 Storage Compacting
  1.1.3.3 Swapping Control
    1.1.3.3.1 Roll Out/Roll In Control
    1.1.3.3.2 Paging Control
      • Static
      • Demand
1.1.4 Event Monitoring
  1.1.4.1 Dispatching Control
    1.1.4.1.1 Time Slicing Control
    1.1.4.1.2 Contention (Priority) Dispatching
    1.1.4.1.3 Dispatcher Queue Maintenance
  1.1.4.2 Event Synchronization
    • I/O Device Completion

- Time Interval Interrupts
- Sub-Task Execution/Completion
1.1.4.3 Interrupt Processing Control
1.1.4.3.1 Interrupt Priority Recognition
1.1.4.3.2 Interrupt Masking/Disabling
1.1.4.3.3 Interrupt Stacking
1.1.4.4 Program Limit Monitoring
- Output Record Limits
- Execution Time Limits
1.1.5 Program Termination Processing
1.1.5.1 Resource Deallocation
- Closing Files
- Releasing Devices
- Releasing Core
1.1.5.2 Summary Information Outputting
- Record Counts
- Run Times
- Error Summarization
1.1.5.3 Abnormal Termination
- Core Dumps
- File Dumps
- Error Codes
- Program Recovery Initiation
1.2 I/O Control
1.2.1 I/O Scheduling
1.2.1.1 Device Resolution
1.2.1.2 Request Stacking
1.2.1.2.1 Device Queue Maintenance
1.2.1.2.2 Channel Queue Maintenance
1.2.1.2.3 I/O Initiation
- Priority Recognition
- Arm Optimization
1.2.1.3 Alternate Routine Control
- Alternate Channels to Device
- Alternate Devices
1.2.2 Data Transfer
1.2.2.1 Buffering Control
1.2.2.1.1 Buffer Pool Maintenance
1.2.2.1.2 Buffering Handling
- Simple Buffering
- Exchange Buffering
- Chained Segment Buffering
1.2.2.2 Data Code Translation
- Compressed Formats

- Character Code Conversion
- Paper Tape Formats
- Teleprocessing Code Conversion

1.2.3 Device Manipulation
- Tape/Disk Positioning
- Card Stacking
- Page Ejecting

1.2.4 Remote Terminal Support
    1.2.4.1 Interactive Communication Control
    1.2.4.2 Terminal-to-Terminal Communication Control
    1.2.4.3 Control of Remote Job Initiation

1.3 System Communication
  1.3.1 System Startup
    1.3.1.1 System Initialization
      1.3.1.1.1 Batch Job Initialization
      1.3.1.1.2 Foreground Initialization
      1.3.1.1.3 Standard Option Modification
      1.3.1.1.4 Resource Specification
- Peripheral Devices
- Partition Sizes
- Input/Output Symbionts

      1.3.1.1.5 Parameter Specification
- Date
- Time

    1.3.1.2 System Restart
      1.3.1.2.1 Suspended Queue Resumption
      1.3.1.2.2 Parameter Respecification

  1.3.2 Job Control Communication
    1.3.2.1 Non-Interactive Control
- Input Stream Control Cards
- Cataloged Procedures
- Operator Console Commands

    1.3.2.2 Interactive Control
- On-Line/Remote Terminal Dialogue
- Operator Console Dialogue

  1.3.3 Input/Output Stream Control
    1.3.3.1 Symbiont Processing
    1.3.3.2 Input/Output Queue Maintenance
    1.3.3.3 Control Command Analysis

  1.3.4 Resource Status Modification
    1.3.4.1 Addition/Deletion of System Resources
    1.3.4.2 Partition Size Modification
    1.3.4.3 Substitute Device Identification

  1.3.5 System Status Interrogation

                1.3.5.1 Current User Display
                1.3.5.2 Resource Status Display
                1.3.5.3 Job Status Display
  1.4 Recovery Processing
      1.4.1 Checkpointing
            1.4.1.1 Program Initiated Checkpointing
            1.4.1.2 System Initiated Checkpointing
                • Roll Out/Roll In
            1.4.1.3 Externally Initiated Checkpointing
                • Input Stream Control Card
                • Operator Console
                • On-Line/Remote Terminal
            1.4.1.4 Checkpoint Notification
                • Operator Console
                • Job Output Log
      1.4.2 Restarting
            1.4.2.1 Program Initiated Restarting
            1.4.2.2 System Initiated Restarting
                • Roll Out/Roll In
                • Error Detection Occurrence
            1.4.2.3 Externally Initiated Restarting
                • Input Stream Control Card
                • Operator Console
                • On-Line/Remote Terminal
            1.4.2.4 Device Repositioning
                • Input Stream
                • Output Stream
                • Peripheral Devices
                • Teleprocessing Devices
2.0 Diagnostic Error Processing
  2.1 Hardware Error Control
      2.1.1 Error Correction
            2.1.1.1 Fault Analysis
            2.1.1.2 Event Retry/Retransmission
                • Retransmission Threshold
            2.1.1.3 Controlled Linkage to User Error Routines
      2.1.2 Error Notification
            2.1.2.1 Operator Notification
            2.1.2.2 Program Notification
            2.1.2.3 Device Error Statistic Accumulation
            2.1.2.4 Diagnostic Logout of Permanent Errors
      2.1.3 Error Recovery
            2.1.3.1 System Reconfiguration
                2.1.3.1.1 Alternate Device Utilization
                2.1.3.1.2 Controlled System Degradation

2.1.3.2 Manual Reconfiguration
2.1.3.3 On-Line Diagnostic Testing Control
2.2 Program Error Control
 2.2.1 Error Correction
  2.2.1.1 Controlled Linkage to User Error Routines
  2.2.1.2 Simulation of Non-Hardware Implemented Operations
   • Non-Implemented OP Codes
 2.2.2 Error Notification
  2.2.2.1 Operator Notification
  2.2.2.2 Program Notification
  2.2.2.3 Diagnostic Error Log-Out
 2.2.3 Program Termination
2.3 Interface Error Control
 2.3.1 Operator Key-In Editing
 2.3.2 Control Command Editing
 2.3.3 Remote Terminal Communication Editing
 2.3.4 Program-to-System Link Verification
3.0 Processing Support
 3.1 Timing Service
  3.1.1 Real-Time Clock Service
   • Date
   • Time of Day
  3.1.2 Interval Timer Service
   3.1.2.1 Scheduling Periodic Interrupts
    • Loop Control
    • Timing Analysis
   3.1.2.2 Temporary Task Suspension Control
 3.2 Testing/Debugging Service
  3.2.1 Storage Dump Control
   3.2.1.1 Snapshot Control
   3.2.1.2 Partial Dump Control
  3.2.2 Tracing Control
   • Data Tracing
   • Instruction Tracing
   • Logic Tracing
   • Supervisor Entry Tracing
  3.2.3 System Test Mode Control
   3.2.3.1 I/O Simulation
    • Error Simulation
    • I/O Re-routing
   3.2.3.2 Abnormal Termination Service
    • Storage Dumps
    • File Dumps
    • Subsequent Task Execution

3.2.3.3 Interactive Testing Service
- Breakpoints
- Memory Searching
- Memory Modification
- Interrupt or Error Notification

3.3 Logging and Accounting
    3.3.1 Maintaining Job Charge Information
        3.3.1.1 CPU Time Recording
        3.3.1.2 I/O Channel and Device Time Recording
        3.3.1.3 Resource Utilization Recording
        3.3.1.4 Controlled Linkage to User-Supplied Accounting Routines
    3.3.3 Maintaining Error Statistics
        3.3.2.1 Hardware Error Summary Accumulation
        3.3.2.2 Program Error Summary Accumulation
        3.3.2.3 Hardware Log-out Storage and Maintenance
        3.3.2.4 Error Statistic Retrieval
    3.3.3 Maintaining System Utilization Statistics
        3.3.3.1 User Account Summary Recording
        3.3.3.2 File Access Summary Recording
        3.3.3.3 System Service Request Recording
        3.3.3.4 System Performance Monitoring

3.4 Program Accessible System Description Maintenance
    3.4.1 Current System Status Interrogation
- Number of Other Users
- Core Storage in Use
- Device Status
- Elapsed Program Execution Time

    3.4.2 System Definition Interrogation
- System Components
- Maximum Number of Users
- Generation Options Selected

Part II: System Management Functions

1.0 Operating System Management
    1.1 System Generation
        1.1.1 Initialization
            1.1.1.1 Program Media Transcription
- Bootstrap Loaders
- Magnetic Tape-to-Disk Copy Routines

            1.1.1.2 Workshop Allocation
- Volume Preparation

- 1.1.1.3 Generating Configuration Identification
- 1.1.2 Supervisor Generation
    - 1.1.2.1 Operating Configuration Identification
        - Memory Size
        - Partitions
        - Number of CPU's and I/O Controllers
        - I/O Devices
        - Console Devices
    - 1.1.2.2 Installation Parameter Specification
        - Memory Protection
        - Privacy Codes
        - Error Recovery Options
        - Accounting Options
    - 1.1.2.3 Foreground Processing Specification
        - Interrupt Assignments
        - Task Scheduling Priorities
        - Dynamic Storage Allocation Pool
    - 1.1.2.4 Background Processing Specification
        - Batch Processing Specifications
        - Time Sharing Options
    - 1.1.2.5 Resident/Transitional Module Determination
- 1.1.3 Operating System File Creation
    - 1.1.3.1 Support System Program Selection/Tailoring
        - Compilers
        - Data Management Systems
        - Utilities
    - 1.1.3.2 User-Developed Program Inclusion
- 1.1.4 Authorized User Declaration
    - User Identification
    - Passwords
    - Accounting Controls
    - Resource Limitations
    - Priorities
- 1.1.5 Default Specification
    - Standard Options
    - Priorities
- 1.2 System Maintenance
    - 1.2.1 Dynamic Maintenance
        - 1.2.1.1 System Reconfiguration Control
            - 1.2.1.1.1 Recognition of Added Processing Elements
            - 1.2.1.1.2 Recognition of Deleted Processing Elements
        - 1.2.1.2 Fallback (Degraded Operation) Mode Control
    - 1.2.2 System Software Modification
        - 1.2.2.1 System Regeneration

1.2.2.2 Module Addition/Replacement
- Permanent Usage
- Temporary Usage

1.2.2.3 Patching
- On-line Patching
- Permanent Patching
- Temporary Patching

1.2.3 User Maintenance
    1.2.3.1 Defining New Commands
    1.2.3.2 Renaming Commands, Operands, Expressions, Values
    1.2.3.3 Alteration of User Default Values

2.0 Program Maintenance
  2.1 Library and Directory Maintenance
    2.1.1 Dynamic Cataloging
- Load Modules
- Task/Procedure Definitions

    2.1.2 Static Cataloging
- Load Modules
- Relocatable Modules
- Source Modules
- Macro Routines
- Task and Job Procedures

    2.1.3 Utility Functions
      2.1.3.1 Copying
      2.1.3.2 Renaming
      2.1.3.3 Allocating/Deallocating/Repacking Library Space
      2.1.3.4 Punching/Listing/Displaying

  2.2 Load Module Generation
    2.2.1 Program Binding
      2.2.1.1 Program Element Relocating
        2.2.1.1.1 Dynamic Binding
- Relocatable Loaders

        2.2.1.1.2 Static Binding
- Linkage Editors
- Collectors

      2.2.1.2 Input Module Control
- Relocatable Modules
- Executable Modules

      2.2.1.3 Code Altering Facilities
- Patching
- Debug Support

    2.2.2 Linkage Resolution
      2.2.2.1 Program Control Reference Resolution
      2.2.2.2 Data Field Reference Resolution
      2.2.2.3 Library Scan for Unresolved References

2.2.3 Multiple Structure Support
- Overlay Programs
- Segmented Programs

3.0 Compiler Interfaces
  3.1 Executive Routine Support
    3.1.1 Recognition of Compiler Parameters on OS Control Cards
      - Listing Options
      - Conditional Compilation Parameters
      - Input Source
      - Output Form
    3.1.2 System Maintained Compiler Communication Tables
    3.1.3 Input and Output File Control
      - Compile File Maintenance
    3.1.4 Program Testing/Debugging Control
  3.2 Library Support
    - Source Program Libraries
    - Macro Libraries
    - Subroutine Libraries
  3.3 System Utility Program Support
    3.3.1 Sort/Merge Linkage Support
    3.3.2 Peripheral Conversion Linkage Support
    3.3.3 Data Management System Linkage Support

4.0 Management Support Utilities
  4.1 Peripheral Device Support
    4.1.1 Volume Preparation
      4.1.1.1 Record/Track Formatting
      4.1.1.2 Directory Creation
      4.1.1.3 Space Allocation
        - Dynamic Communication Buffer Areas
    4.1.2 Volume Maintenance
      4.1.2.1 Diagnostic Verification
        4.1.2.1.1 Surface Analysis
        4.1.2.1.2 Track Replacement
      4.1.2.2 File Purging
        - Clear Internal Storage
        - Clear Disk/Drum
        - Erase Tape
  4.2 System Simulation Routines
    4.2.1 System Facilities
      - I/O Device Activity
      - Real-Time Interrupts
    4.2.2 Communication Facilities
      - Message Transmission
      - Exception Processing

4.3 System Measurement Routines
- Sampling Routines
- Intercept Routines

4.4 Stand-Alone Utilities

    4.4.1 Status Display
- Storage and File Dumps
- Diagnostic Logout Displays

    4.4.2 Recovery Support
- Rebuild System Queues
- Rebuild Message Queues
- Reinitiate Suspended Processing

Part III: Data Manipulation Functions

1.0 Data Management

  1.1 File Management Facilities

    1.1.1 File Location Recognition

      1.1.1.1 File Cataloging Control
- Addition/Deletion of Cataloged Files
- Catalog Determination of File Location

      1.1.1.2 Label Recognition

    1.1.2 File Access Control

      1.1.2.1 File Security Control
- User ID Protection
- Password Protection
- Recognition of Hardware Keys

      1.1.2.2 Read/Write Access Control
- Read Access Only
- Selective Write Access

      1.1.2.3 Concurrent Access Control
- Multi-User Read/Single-User Write Access
- Record Lockout

    1.1.3 Backup and Restoration Facilities

  1.2 I/O Support Facilities

    1.2.1 Data Access Control

      1.2.1.1 Sequential Access Control

      1.2.1.2 Keyed/Indexed Access Control

      1.2.1.3 Random Access Control

      1.2.1.4 Teleprocessing Access Control

        1.2.1.4.1 Priority Message Control

        1.2.1.4.2 Message Queue Maintenance

        1.2.1.4.3 Input Message Decoding and Routing

        1.2.1.4.4 Output Message Routing

        1.2.1.4.5 Polling Control

1.2.2 Data Blocking/Deblocking Control
  1.2.2.1 Record Acquisition
    - Locate Mode
    - Move Mode
  1.2.2.2 Record Type Support
    - Fixed Length
    - Variable Length
    - Undefined Length
1.2.3 Label Processing
  1.2.3.1 Label Generation
    - System Standard Labels
    - User Standard Labels
    - User Non-standard Labels
  1.2.3.2 Label Checking
1.3 Data Management System Facilities
  1.3.1 Control Specification
    1.3.1.1 Specification Interpretation
      - File Description Tables
      - Query Descriptions
      - Report Descriptions
    1.3.1.2 Generation of Supporting Functions
      - Interpretative Tables
      - Executable Subroutines
  1.3.2 Data File Generation and Maintenance
    1.3.2.1 Structure Definition
      - Sequential
      - Hierarchial
      - Indexed
      - Ring
      - List
    1.3.2.2 Space Allocation
    1.3.2.3 Input Transaction Processing
      1.3.2.3.1 Input Format Definition
        - Pre-Defined Data
        - Self-Defining Data
      1.3.2.3.2 Input Validation
        - Range Verification
        - Specific Character Examination
        - Sequence Checking
        - Comparison Testing
      1.3.2.3.3 Input Alteration
        - Modification of Data Element Size
        - Encoding/Decoding of Data Elements
      1.3.2.3.4 Input Termination Recognition
        - Embedded Control Fields
        - Special Character(s)

1.3.2.4 Logical File Maintenance
- Single Value Updating
- Record Selectivity
- Subordinate File Updating

1.3.2.5 Interactive File Maintenance

1.3.2.6 File Reorganization
- Restructuring
- Merging

1.3.2.7 Data Error Procedures
- Interactive
- Predefined

1.3.3 Data Qualification and Retrieval
    1.3.3.1 Retrieval Mode Control
        1.3.3.1.1 Interactive Querying
- Programmed Queries
- Cue-Response Queries

        1.3.3.1.2 Batched-Mode Queries
- Prestored Queries/Skeletal Queries

    1.3.3.2 Query Processing
        1.3.3.2.1 Relational Operator Control
- Boolean
- Quantitative (Occurrence)
- Arithmetic or Statistical
- Application-Defined

        1.3.3.2.2 Term Resolution
- Constant Value
- Second Data Field
- Arithmetic Expression
- Interim Result

    1.3.3.3 Data Record Selection
- Single File Retrieval
- Multi-File Retrieval
- Inter-File Retrieval

1.3.4 Data Output
    1.3.4.1 Output Media Control
- Printed Listings
- Punched Cards
- Tape Files
- CRT Displays

    1.3.4.2 Output Mode Control
        1.3.4.2.1 User-Structured Report Control
        1.3.4.2.2 System Defined Report Control
        1.3.4.2.3 Interactively Defined Report Control

    1.3.4.3 Output Format Control

1.3.4.3.1 Labeling
- Data Labels
- Page Headings
- Trailer Information

1.3.4.3.2 Data Formatting
- Positioning
- Altering and Decoding
- Counting/Totaling

1.3.4.3.3 Pagination Control
- Printed/Typed Reports
- CRT Displays

2.0 Data Handling Utilities
  2.1 Display Facilities
    2.1.1 Unformatted Display
- Card to Printer
- Tape to Printer

    2.1.2 Formatted Display
- File Formats
- Formatted Tape/Disk Dumps
- Storage Dumps
- Directory Lists

  2.2 Peripheral Device Support
    2.2.1 Volume Positioning
      2.2.1.1 Forward/Backward Spacing
      2.2.1.2 Record/File Selection

    2.2.2 Media Copy Facilities
      2.2.2.1 Format Conversion
      2.2.2.2 Code Conversion
- BCD to Baudot Code
- Hollerith to Binary

      2.2.2.3 Field Insertion
- Constant Values
- Sequence Number

      2.2.2.4 Multi-Device Support
- Card
- Magnetic/Paper Tape
- Random Access
- Remote Terminal
- Main Storage

      2.2.2.5 Dump and Reload Facilities
- File/Storage Compaction
- Overflow Area Elimination
- Backup File Creation

292 Operating Systems Survey

- 2.2.3 Data Editing Facilities
  - File Compare
  - File Scanning
- 2.2.4 Test Data File Support
  - Test File Generation
  - Control Message Generation
- 3.0 Sorting and Merging
  - 3.1 Sort Module Development
    - 3.1.1 Control Card Editing/Interpreting
    - 3.1.2 Storage Requirement Determination
      - Internal Storage
      - Intermediate Storage
    - 3.1.3 Program Generation
      - Tailoring General Purpose Packages
      - Generating Unique Sort Modules
    - 3.1.4 Optional Support
      - Ascending/Descending Output Sequences
      - Single/Multiple Sort Control Fields
      - Field Type Recognition (Alphanumeric, Binary, Zoned/Packed Decimal, Floating Point, etc.)
      - User Specified Collating Sequences
      - Multi-Media Storage Devices (Magnetic Tape, Mass Storage, Random Access Devices)
  - 3.2 Sort Module Execution
    - 3.2.1 Input Data Control
      - User-Generated Records
      - Established Data Files
      - Internal Record Address Table
    - 3.2.2 Sort Block Creation
      - Full Data Records (Record Sort)
      - Sort Key and Record Address (Tag Sort)
      - Sort Key and Selected Fields (Field Select Sort)
    - 3.2.3 Sequenced String Creation
      - Replacement/Selection Sort
      - Tournament Sort
      - Balanced Merge
    - 3.2.4 Overflow Control
      - Develop Sort Subfields
      - Spillover to Spare Device
    - 3.2.5 Sequenced String Merge
      - Polyphase Sort
      - Oscillating Sort
      - Cascade Sort

3.2.6 Final Pass Control
    3.2.6.1 Multi-File Merging
    3.2.6.2 Final Pass Sequence Check
    3.2.6.3 Output Data Control
        3.2.6.3.1 Record Deblocking
        3.2.6.3.2 Record Address Table Creation
3.2.7 User Routine Linkage Control
- Label Processing
- Input Record Insertion/Modification/Deletion
- Output Record Insertion/Modification/Deletion
- I/O Error Processing

APPENDIX B

GLOSSARY OF OPERATING SYSTEM TERMINOLOGY

This Glossary is intended to provide the most commonly accepted definitions of operating system terminology. An Addendum, which follows the Glossary, discusses uncommon or conflicting definitions and terms. Relevant Addendum entries are referenced in the Glossary.

abnormal termination: Termination of a job or task due to an error condition (contrasted with *normal termination*).

address translator: A software or hardware feature which dynamically translates virtual instruction and data addresses to real main storage addresses. See *virtual address, real address*.

algorithm: A prescribed set of well-defined rules or processes for the solution of a problem in a finite number of steps.

algorithmic dispatching: Dispatching according to a series of rules and decisions.

algorithmic scheduling: Scheduling according to a series of rules and decisions.

allocate: To grant a resource to, or reserve the resource for, a job or task.

alternate routing:
1. Access of an I/O device via an alternate channel when an I/O device is connected to the CPU by more than one channel.
2. Transmission of output to a secondary device when the primary device is inoperable.

application software: Software oriented toward specific problem solution. See also: *problem program*.

arm (interrupt): To allow the occurence of an interrupt (opposite of *disarm*). See Addendum, *interrupt*.

assembler: A language processor which converts symbolic instructions into a form suitable for execution on a computer.

asynchronous: Without regular time relationships (opposite of *synchronous*); hence, as applied to program execution, unpredictable with respect to time or instruction sequence.

attach:
1. To reserve a system resource for the exclusive use of a single program.
2. To cause the execution of a dependent subtask.

automatic restart: A restart which is initiated by the system supervisor independently of either user or operator direction.

background: A partition or group of partitions used for processing batch jobs. The background is normally assigned the lowest priority in a multiprogramming environment. See also *foreground*; Addendum, *background*.

batch processing: Processing of jobs which are submitted to run independently of events outside the system (as opposed to real time or interactive jobs) and are normally processed on a deferred or time-independent basis (e.g., whenever the processing work load is light). See Addendum, *batch processing*.

batch query: A query processed in the batch processing mode. See *query*.

Baudot code: The standard five-channel teletypewriter code consisting of a start impulse and five character impulses, all of equal length, and a stop impulse whose length is 1.42 times all of the start impulse. This code is also known as the 1.42 unit code.

benchmark: A standard program used to evaluate the performance of computers relative to preselected criteria.

binding: Transforming one or more object modules into a composite program that is acceptable for execution Also called *collecting* (Univac), and *linkage editing* (IBM and RCA). See Addendum, *linkage resolution*.

block (*records*):
1. (v) To group records for the purpose of conserving storage space or increasing the efficiency of access or processing.
2. (n) A physical record so constituted, or a portion of a telecommunications message defined as a unit of data transmission.

blocking: The combining of two or more records into one block.

bootstrap: A technique for loading the first few instructions of a routine into storage, then using these instructions to bring in the rest of the routine.

breakpoint: A point in a computer program at which conditional interruption (to permit visual check, printing out, or other analyzing) may occur. Breakpoints are usually used in debugging operations.

buffer (*input/output*): A portion of storage into which data is read, or from which it is written. See also *chained segment buffer*.

buffering: A method of managing I/O buffers (e.g., *simple* or *exchange buffering*, *locate* or *move mode buffering*).

buffer pool: A group of buffers which may be allocated as needed to various jobs.

byte: A generic term used to indicate a measurable portion of consecutive binary digits; for example, an 8-bit or a 6-bit byte (most commonly, 8 bits). See also *word*.

---

catalog:
1. (n) A directory to locations of files and libraries.
2. (v) To enter an item in a directory.

cataloged procedure: A set of job control statements which has been placed in a special file and which may be used for job control by being named on a special control card.

chained segment buffer: A buffer composed of a chain of fragmented core areas with each area containing a pointer to the next area in the chain. Normally used to process records of varying lengths such as teleprocessing messages.

channel: A hardware device which connects a CPU and main storage or an I/O processor with I/O control units or devices.

channel queue: A queue of requests for service from a data channel.

channel scheduler: The part of the supervisory program which controls the movement of data between main storage and input/output devices.

character string (record): An unformatted record composed of a series of contiguous characters; usually applied to teleprocessing messages. See also *message*.

check: The occurrence of an error (e.g., *machine check, program check*). Usually causes an interrupt.

checkpoint:
1. A point at which information about a program is recorded which will permit subsequent resumption of processing from that point.
2. The recording of such information.

See also: *restart*.

collector: See *linkage editor/loader*.

command processing: The reading, analyzing, and performing of commands submitted via the console device or an input job stream.

common core: An area in main storage shared by two or more programs or program segments.

common page: A page allocated to more than one program, usually used for passing data between separate programs.

common subroutine: A subroutine which may be used by more than one executing task; only one copy of the subroutine resides in main storage.

communication region: An area of the supervisor set aside for interprogram and intraprogram communication.

compiler: A language processor which translates a problem-oriented language into a machine language.

compiler interfaces (operating system): Operating system functions that are oriented to providing supporting services to the system language compilers.

compressed format: A format for storing data in a minimum number of characters, generally achieved through the elimination of blanks.

concurrent: Existing or occurring during the same interval of time. See also *simultaneous*.

concurrent processing: Processing two or more programs (or tasks) on an interleaved basis.

console: The interface, or communication device, between a user or operator and the computer (e.g., *operator's console, remote terminal/console*).

contention: Rivalry for use of a system resource.

control block: A storage area through which a particular type of information required for control of the operating system is communicated (e.g., *message control block*).

control message: A finite sequence of letters, digits, symbols, etc., transmitted to convey regulatory information.

control program: A collective or general term for all routines or programs which are part of the operating system supervisor.

control specification: The act of defining to a set of routines the functions that they are to perform.

conversational: Synonymous with *interactive*.

core dump: To transfer the contents of all or part of main storage to a peripheral device.

core image library: A library of load modules.

core resident: The condition of a program or table which is in main storage.

core resident routine: A routine which executes from and remains permanently in main storage. Opposite of *transient routine*.

core storage: See *main storage*.

core storage access control: Preventing executing programs from retrieving and/or storing data in core storage areas not assigned to that program. See also *storage protection*.

CPU (*central processing unit*): The portion of a computer which directs the sequence of operations, interrupts the coded instructions, and initiates the proper commands to the computer circuits for execution. See Addendum, *CPU*.

cue-response query: A form of data management system interrogation in which the user participates in a question/answer dialogue with the system. See *query*.

data access control: Any of the data management techniques available to the user for transferring data between main storage and an I/O device (e.g., *direct, indexed, keyed, queued*, or *sequential access*).

data base:
  1. (generic) The entire collection of information available to a computing system.
  2. (specific) A structured collection of information as an entity or collection of related files treated as an entity.

data code translation: Translation of data from one symbolic representation to another; e.g., EBCDIC to USASCII-8.

data-handling utilities: Utility programs which provide a variety of independent services to manipulate and/or display various groupings of data elements.

data management: Comprehensive facilities which provide support for programmed access to the data files within the system. These facilities may be of two forms: routines supporting application program access to the data base, and the independent data management system supporting user access to the data base.

data management system: A group of integrated routines developed to create and maintain a large, organized, and structured collection of related data (known as the data base) and to interrogate the data base and produce various types of formatted reports.

data manipulation functions: The components of the operating system that permit the user to access and process data. These functions may be independent utility programs or subroutines incorporated within a user program.

data qualification: The process of isolating an element of a data file, usually for some purpose such as retrieval or file maintenance.

data set: A collection of related records treated as a unit (synonymous with *file*); or an item of equipment used in telecommunications (modem).

data transcription: The process of converting data from one peripheral medium to another (e.g., card to tape or mass storage to printer).

data transfer: The movement of data either within main storage, between main storage and secondary storage, or between main storage and input/output device.

deallocation: Restoring the availability of a system resource.

deblocking: Isolating the individual records within a block. See *block*; *blocking*.

dedicated memory: Main memory locations reserved by the system for special purposes, such as interrupts and real-time programs.

default option: An option which will automatically be assumed if not overridden by a parameter specification.

deferred restart: A restart which is initiated by operator or user action and usually involves resubmitting the job.

dependent program: Any user program or nonsupervisory system program.

device: A term used to refer to a computer component.

device category (I/O): A term used to collectively describe several different I/O devices having common *processing* characteristics, such as direct access devices and sequential devices.

device manipulation (I/O): Control functions that allow a physical I/O device to be positioned without involving data transfer. These functions typically include rewinding and/or unloading tapes, ejecting printer pages, stacking punched cards, and so forth.

device name: The general name for a device, specified at the time the system is generated and used for all symbolic references to the device.

device queue: A queue of requests for processing service from an I/O device.

device resolution: Determination of a specific physical device from a symbolic device name.

device type (I/O): A term used to describe collectively different I/O devices, such as magnetic tape and disk, having common *physical* characteristics.

diagnostic:
1. Pertaining to the detection and isolation of hardware or software malfunctions.
2. A message or record, recording the occurrence of a hardware or software error.

diagnostic error proccessing: The recognition of the occurrence of error conditions within the system, along with the corresponding corrective actions.

diagnostic logout: The detailed record of hardware status, including hardware registers, switches, etc., taken at the occurrence of a hardware or software failure.

direct access:
1. A method of accessing data records directly, without regard to the sequence in which they are recorded. See also *access control*.
2. A device oriented to support of this method of access, e g., disk, drum.

directory: See *catalog*

disarm (interrupt): To disallow the occurrence of an interrupt (opposite of *arm*). See Addendum, *interrupt*.

dispatcher queue: A queue of tasks ready for dispatching.

dispatching: Allocation of processor time by the supervisor to a specific task. Tasks that are eligible for dispatching have already been placed in an execution state by the scheduler and are not waiting for I/O activity, operator responses, etc.

driver: A program which controls the use of a peripheral device.

dynamic allocation: Providing resources (storage space, I/O devices, etc.) to a program or task in response to an actual demand by the program or task.

dynamic buffering: A buffering technique which provides buffers to a program or task in response to an actual demand for buffers by the program or task.

dynamic dump: A dump which is performed during the execution of a program.

dynamic program loading: The process of loading a program module into main storage, upon the demand for that program module by an executing program.

dynamic program relocation: Moving or relocating a program to another part of storage without modifying it, before it has completed execution, and still permitting subsequent execution.

dynamic storage: Storage which is dynamically allocated to tasks during program execution. It is normally used for subroutines, buffer pools, etc.

dynamic system maintenance: The on-line capability whereby a system reconfigures itself:
1. To adjust to operator addition or deletion of some of its processing elements;
2. To fallback into a degraded state of operation upon the failure of some of its processing elements. See also *system degradation*; *system maintenance*; *system reconfiguration*.

error recovery: Synonymous with *recovery processing*.

error severity code: A code indicating the severity of errors noted by an assembler or compiler, and used to determine subsequent processing of the resulting object module.

event: An occurrence of significance to a task, typically the completion of an asynchronous operation such as input/output.

event monitoring: Maintaining control over executing programs. Such control includes processing all interrupts, trapping all error conditions, notifying programs of external condition requiring attention, and, in a multiprogram environment, allocating CPU time among contending programs.

event synchronization: Delaying task execution until some specified event occurs, or triggering a task upon the occurrence of a specified event.

exchange buffering: A buffering technique which eliminates the need to move data in main storage by exchanging a system buffer area for a user buffer area.

execute: To carry out an instruction or run a program on the computer.

executing state: The state of a program during the time it is using the CPU.

executive/control functions: The components of the operating system that maintain real-time execution control over the system environment.

executing routine support (compiler interface): Special facilities that may be provided by the executive to the compiler, which are not available to other problem-oriented programs, for example, the use of communication tables within the resident executive. See also *compiler interfaces*.

fault analysis: The analysis of hardware or software malfunctions by the system for purposes of error recovery (including *system reconfiguration*).

file: A collection of related records treated as a unit. The records in a file may or may not be sequenced according to a key contained in each record. Synonymous with data set.

file access control: Preventing unauthorized access to a file. The protection may extend to read access, write access, or both.

file location recognition: The identification of a permanent data file via its system-assigned or user-assigned label.

file maintenance (interactive): The facility that provides for interactive updating of a data file from an on-line terminal.

file maintenance (logical): The facility that permits the conditional or programmed updating of a data file.

file management routines: The collection of operating system routines that are used to accomplish all the various file services provided by the system, such as file control, cataloging, file protection.

file purging: The act of destroying the contents of a file. The name of the file may or may not be removed from the system catalog.

file reorganization: The facility that supports the restructuring of one or more existing files.

file security control: Restricting access to a file or device to only those users who have been authorized to use it.

firmware: Software and hardware which interact so closely that the functions of both become intertwined.

fixed length record: A record having the same length as all other records in the same file. Contrasted with *variable length record*.

fixed logic query: A query in which the operands and operators cannot be altered by the user at execution time (as opposed to *skeletal* or *interactive queries*). See also *query*.

foreground: The partition or partitions which are normally used for real-time, communications, and time-sharing applications. The foreground is usually given priority over the background in a multiprogramming environment. See also *background*; Addendum, *background*.

foreground processing: Processing of programs in the foreground partitions.

foreground scheduler: A routine which analyzes processing requests and executes the appropriate foreground programs.

format: The arrangement of data.

free core pools: Areas of main storage which may be dynamically allocated as I/O buffers or program expansion areas.

generated code: The executable programs or subroutines produced from a set of specifications or commands.

hardware: Physical equipment, e.g., mechanical, electrical, or electronic devices. Contrasted with *software*.

header label: The record at the beginning of a file or volume containing control information about the file or volume. See also *trailer label*.

hierarchial file structure: A file structure in which the elements are classified and stored according to a ranking scheme.

I/O control: The initiation, execution, monitoring, and control of data transfers into and out of the system.

index:
  1. A table in the catalog structure used to locate files.
  2. A table used to locate the records of an indexed file.

indexed access: An access method in which record locations are determined from an index or table.

indexed file structure: A file structure in which one or more fields within the file are indexed. In addition to storing the individual records, indexed files maintain a directory of the values of indexed fields and the corresponding locations of all records containing each value.

initialize: To set various counters, switches, and addresses to prescribed starting values at the beginning of or at specified points in a computer routine.

input: Data transferred or to be transferred from an external storage medium into the internal storage of the computer.

input queue: The input data to a job or to the system.

input reader: A program which reads the input job stream and writes the information onto mass storage where it is kept until resources are available for execution of the program.

input (job) stream: The sequence of control statements and data submitted to the operating system on an input unit especially designated for this purpose at system generation time, or by the operator.

input transaction processing: A term which refers to the updating of designated records via a set of specific transactions. The updating may consist of the addition, deletion, or modification of one or more fields within each record. Each transaction contains the identification of the record it is to update.

inquiry: A technique whereby interrogation of a computer system or program may be initiated at a keyboard.

interactive: A conversational mode of processing which permits interaction or dialogue between a user and a time-sharing system. Contrasted with *non-interactive*; synonymous with conversational.

interactive query: A query formulated and posed on-line to a data management system. See *query*.

interface:
1. The place at which two different systems (or subsystems) meet and interact with each other.
2. The linkage and conventions established for communication between two independent elements, usually between a program and another program, computer operator, terminal user, etc.

interfile search: A multifile search in which the answers obtained from the results of querying one file are used to interrogate a second file. See also *multifile search*.

interleave: To arrange parts of one sequence of things or events so that they alternate with parts of one or more other sequences of things or events and so that each sequence retains its identity.

interrupt:
1. (n) A break in the normal flow of a system or routines such such that the flow can be resumed from that point at a later time. An interrupt is usually caused by a hardware-generated signal.
2. (v) To cause an interrupt.

See also *arm; disarm; mask; unmask;* Addendum, *interrupt*.

interrupt stacking: Recording the occurrence of one or more interrupts and allowing them to remain pending while processing continues.

interval timer: A counter which is automatically incremented or decremented at regular time intervals and which normally causes an interrupt when reaching zero. See also: *real-time clock*.

job: A total processing application comprised of one or more related processing programs, such as a weekly payroll, a day's business transactions, or the reduction of a collection of test data. See Addendum, *job*.

job class: A parameter which in some systems permits a measure of control over the sequence of program execution.

job control: A general term which collectively describes those functions of the

control program that regulate the use, by jobs, of the central processing unit and other resources except input/output devices.
job control language: The language used to provide job specifications to the job control routines.
job management: The real-time initiation, scheduling, monitoring, and control of normal system operations, together with the necessary allocation of resources.
job priority: A designation given by the user to each of his jobs to specify the relative sequence in which the jobs are to be executed.
job processing: The reading of control statements from an input stream, the initiating of job steps defined in these statements, and the writing of output messages.
job queue: The stack of jobs to be executed by an operating system.
job scheduler: The control program function which controls input job streams, obtains input/output resources for jobs and job steps, and otherwise regulates the use of the computing system by jobs.
job status: The status of a job at a given point in time, e,g., position within a job queue or state of activity.
job step: That unit of work associated with one processing program and related data. See also Addendum, *job*.

key:
  1. A data item which serves to uniquely identify a data record.
  2. A code used by a program to gain access to protected main storage areas, I/O files, or I/O devices. See also: *lock; password*.
keyed access:
  1. An access method in which record locations are determined algorithmically from keys.
  2. An access method dependent on hardware recognition of physically recorded keys.
keyed file structure: A file structure in which a data item is used to uniquely identify each data record. The search for a specific record by using the record key is implemented by hardware on some systems, by software on others.
key-in: Information entered by an operator via a keyboard.

label processing: Those facilities provided for writing and checking both standard and nonstandard labels when a data file is opened or closed.
language processor: A compiler, assembler, or program generator which transforms source modules into object modules.
library: In general, a collection of objects (e.g., files, volumes, card decks) associated with a particular use, and the location of which is identified in a directory of some type (e.g., *core image, private, public* or *system libraries*).
library and directory maintenance: The capabilities provided to create and update different types of libraries and directories.

library support (compiler interface): Support provided to maintain compiler-oriented libraries. These libraries may be compiler source program libraries, macro statement libraries, or compiler subroutine libraries. See also *compiler interfaces*.

linkage: The means by which communication is effected between two routines or modules.

linkage editor/loader: A program which produces a load module by transforming object modules into a format acceptable for execution and resolving all intermodule linkages. In some systems the resulting load module is located in main storage and may be immediately executed; in others, the load modules must be subsequently loaded for execution. See also Addendum, *linkage resolution*.

list file structure: A file structure wherein each data element incorporates a link which points to a successor element.

load: To read a load module into main storage preparatory to executing it.

loader: A program which takes load modules and places them in main storage.

load module: A program in a format suitable for loading into main storage for execution. See also *module; object module; source module*.

load module generation: The process of converting machine language program instructions into a format capable of being loaded directly into main storage and executed.

locate mode: A buffering technique in which data is pointed to rather than moved.

lock: A code used by an operating system to provide protection against improper use of main storage areas, I/O files, or I/O devices.

lockout: A programming technique used to prevent access to system resources when these resources are currently in use.

logical I/O: Conceptual I/O operations which are performed by user programs through use of the system and which may, in fact, involve no physical I/O, but only blocking or deblocking. Contrasted with *physical I/O*.

logical record: A record which is defined in terms of its use without regard to the way in which it is recorded.

logout:
  1. (v) To record the occurrence of an event
  2. (n) The documentation of the occurrence of an event.

machine check: An error due to hardware malfunction; usually causes an interrupt. See also *check*.

main storage: A digital computer's principal working storage, from which instructions can be executed or operands fetched for data manipulation. Also frequently referred to as memory or core storage, since magnetic cores often serve as the storage device. Contrasted with *secondary storage*.

management support utilities: Utility programs provided for the use of the system manager. These programs perform a wide variety of functions in support of initializing, testing, and monitoring the system.

manual reconfiguration: System reconfiguration performed through key-ins or control cards.

mapping device: A hardware address translator.

mask (interrupt): To suspend recognition of an interrupt (opposite of *unmask*). See also Addendum, *interrupt*.

mass storage: Secondary storage capable of holding large amounts of data; generally, a direct access device.

memory:
 1. Synonymous with *main storage*.
 2. A device in which data can be stored and from which it can be retrieved.

memory dump:
 1. The transfer of the contents of main storage to a secondary storage device.
 2. A print-out (generally edited or formatted) resulting from a memory dump.

message: A quantity of transmitted information that is physically continuous and processed as a unit.

message block: A set of characters transmitted as a unit to or from a remote terminal in a communications environment. A message block is usually variable in length.

message control: A function of the operating system which controls the transfer of data between programs and remote terminals.

message control block: Information generated for each incoming or outgoing message in a communications environment. The MCB governs the transfer and processing of the message. Included in the MCB is the identification of the remote terminal and the address of each block of the message to be processed. See also *control block*.

message queue. A list of communication messages.

message routing: Interpreting a code internal to a teleprocessing message and, on input, directing the message to the attention of the proper program, and on output, directing the message to the correct output device.

message time stamping: Appending the time of message receipt to the message.

module (programming): The input to or output from a single execution of a language, processor, or linkage editor; a source, object, or load module, hence, a program unit that is discrete and identifiable with respect to compiling and loading. See also *relocatable module*.

move mode: A buffering technique by which data is moved between the buffer and the user's work area.

multifile search: A data retrieval which interrogates several files.

multiprocessing: The employment of multiple interconnected processing units to execute two or more different programs or tasks simultaneously. See also Addendum, *multiprocessing*.

multiprogramming: A general term that expresses use of the computing system to execute two or more different programs or tasks concurrently. See also Addendum, *multiprogramming*.

noninteractive: Processing during which there is no dialogue between the user and the system. Contrasted with *interactive*.

normal termination: Termination of a job or a task upon successful completion of processing (contrasted with *abnormal termination*).

object module: The output of a single execution of a language processor, which either constitutes input to a linkage editor or is a load module. See also *module, source module*.

off-line: A generic reference to a device or operation which is *not* directly controlled by the computing system it is associated with.

on-line: A generic reference to a device or operation which is directly controlled by the computing system it is associated with.

on-line diagnostics: Diagnostic messages that are output to an operator or user console.

operating system: A set of programs and routines which guide a computer in the performance of its tasks and assist the programs (and programmers) with certain supporting functions.

operating system management: The generation and maintenance of the computer operating system.

operator: The individual who monitors the computer system and performs necessary physical actions such as mounting tapes, setting switches, etc., as required by the system.

operator command: A statement to the control program issued via a console device which causes the control program to provide requested information, alter normal operations, initiate new operations, or terminate existing operations.

operator's console: A console used by the computer operator, generally containing special manual controls not available on a user's console.

output: Data transferred or to be transferred from the internal storage of the computer to an external device or onto a permanent recording medium (paper, cards, etc.)

output stream: Diagnostic messages and other output data issued by the operating system or the processing program to output units especially designated for this purpose at system generation time or by the operator.

output work queue: A queue of control information describing system output files, which specifies to an output writer the location and disposition of system output.

output writer: A symbiont which transcribes specified output files onto an output unit independently of the program which produced such files.

overlap: To do something at the same time something else is being done; for example, to perform input/output operations while instructions are being executed by the central processing unit.

overlay program: A segmented program in which the segment currently being executed may use the same core storage area occupied by a previously executed segment.

overlay segment: The smallest functional unit which can be loaded as one logical entity during execution of an overlay program.

owner: The creator of a file, who may control access to the file by other users. See also *file access control*.

page: A program section of a convenient size for transmission between main storage and secondary storage.

paging: A technique of loading sections (pages) that are referenced during program execution.

parameter: A definable characteristic of an item, device, or system, which can be used to control or modify an algorithmic process such as a subroutine, a system generation program, etc.

parity check:
1. (n) A machine check which occurs due to the failure of a word or byte to contain an even number of bits (even parity) or an odd number of bits (odd parity.)
2. (v) To test a word or byte for proper parity.

partial dump: To transfer part of main storage to a peripheral device. See also *storage dump*.

partition: A subdivision of main storage which is allocated to a job or a system task for job or task execution. A partition may be fixed or variable in size. See also Addendum, *partition*.

password: A word used to allow the user access to protected storage, files, or I/O devices. Synonymous with *key*, definition 2; related to *file access control, storage*, and *volume protection*.

patch:
1. (n) A section of coding inserted into a routine to correct a mistake or alter the routine. It is often not inserted into the actual sequence of the routine being corrected, but placed somewhere else, with an exit to the patch and a return to the routine provided.
2. (v) To insert such corrected coding.

periodic interrupts: Interrupts scheduled to occur at a periodic interval.

peripheral:
1. A generic term referring to devices that are not a part of the computer main frame (e.g., card readers, printers, tape units, etc.).
2. Referring to an operation or device which is off-line.

physical I/O: I/O which takes place between main storage and on-line devices. Contrasted with *logical I/O*.

physical record: A record defined in terms of the way it is recorded without regard to its use.

polling: A technique by which each of the terminals sharing a communications line is periodically interrogated to determine if it requires servicing. See also *teleprocessing*.

pool: A collection of interchangeable peripheral devices or core storage locations. When the user requests a device or area from the pool, the system selects an available device or area to associate with the job (e.g., *buffer* or *free core pool*).

postmortem dump: A memory or file dump performed upon completion of program execution, frequently associated with abnormal termination.

pre-stored query: A query which has been stored in a system library. At execution time it may be loaded directly from the library. See *query*.

priority: An order of precedence established for competing events.

priority queue: A queue maintained in priority sequence.

priority scheduling: A form of job scheduling which schedules jobs by priority rather than by their sequence in the input job stream.

private library: A library which is accessible only by a restricted group of users.

privileged instruction: An instruction which can only be executed in supervisor mode. See also Addendum, *privileged instruction*.

problem mode: A hardware- or software-supported mode of operation in which certain privileged instructions cannot be executed by a program. Contrasted with *supervisor mode*. See also Addendum, *privileged instruction*.

problem program: Any of the class of routines or programs which perform processing of the type for which a computing system is intended, including routines that solve problems, monitor and control industrial processes, sort and merge records, perform computations, process transactions against stored records, etc. Similar to *user program*.

processing support: The routines within the supervisor which accomplish a variety of miscellaneous services for an application program.

processor:
1. From a hardware point of view, a device which performs one or many functions; usually means a central processing unit (*CPU*). See also Addendum, *CPU*.
2. From a software point of view, a processor is a program, usually an assembler or compiler, which transforms some input into some output.

program: The complete sequence of instructions and routines necessary to solve a problem (e.g., *control*, *problem*, *service*, or *user program*, or a *symbiont*).

program check: An error that occurs due to a programming error such as an invalid instruction or invalid address.

program expansion area pools: Areas of main storage which may be dynamically allocated to programs.

program generator: A language processor which combines and tailors general purpose object modules based on source control statements.

program library: A collection of available computer programs and routines.

program limit monitoring: Assuring that an executing program or task does not exceed certain system or user-specified limits. Limits are typically established for CPU time, main storage space, output cards/lines, and so forth.

program loading: The process of placing load modules in main storage. See also *loader*.

program maintenance: The support functions provided to the user for the maintenance and modification of application programs.

program termination processing: The processing functions that are executed when a program or task comes to either a normal or abnormal termination.

prompting query: An aid provided by some data management systems which assists a user in formulating meaningful retrieval statements by "leading" him through the interrogation process. See also *query*.

public library: A library available to all users of a system.

push-down list: A list which is constructed and maintained so that the next item to be retrieved is the most recently stored item in the list, i.e., last-in, first-out.

quantum: A limited or algorithmically specified interval of time.

query: A statement specifying the retrieval criteria necessary to locate specific information in a file. See also *batch query*; *cue-response query*; *fixed-logic query*; *interactive query*; *pre-stored query*; *prompting query*; *skeletal query*.

queue: A list of entries which identify things waiting for service or attention.

queue control: The system functions required to add elements to, remove elements from, and update elements within system queues.

queued access: An access method in which records are read prior to being requested and queued in main storage, thus eliminating a wait for transmission from an I/O device when a record is requested.

random access:
1. (v) A method of accessing data records without regard to the sequence in which they are recorded.
2. (n) A device oriented to support this method of access.

read only: An attribute of programs or files whereby they are not modified during execution of a program.

ready state: The condition of a task which is in contention with other tasks for use of the central processing unit and is awaiting assignment of the CPU. All requirements for its activation have been satisfied.

real address: An instruction address which refers to an actual location in main storage. Contrasted with *virtual address*.

real time:
1. Pertaining to the actual time during which a physical process transpires.
2. Pertaining to the performance of a computation during the actual time that the related physical process transpired in order that results of the computation can be used in guiding the physical process.

See also Addendum, *real time*.

real-time clock: A program-accessible clock which indicates the passage of actual time. The clock may be updated by hardware or software. See also *interval timer*.

record: A collection of related items of data, treated as a unit (e.g., *fixed length records*, *logical records*, *physical records*, *undefined records*, or *variable length records*).

recovery processing: Action performed by a user system program in response to the occurrence of an error. Synonymous with error recovery. See also *restart*.

recursive: Repetitive on a cyclical basis; a procedure which, while being executed, either calls itself or calls another procedure, which in turn calls the original one.

reenterable: Variation of reentrant.

reentrant: The attribute of a load module which allows the same copy of the load module to be used concurrently by two or more tasks. The attribute is attained by programming the load module in such a manner that it does not modify itself. See also *reusable*.

refreshable: A refreshable module can be replaced by a new copy during execution by a recovery management routine without changing either the sequence or the results of the processing. Thus it is a module that is never modified by itself or any other module during execution.

relocatable module: An object or load module which can be relocated in core.

relocation:
  1. Loading a program into main storage at an address other than that specified at assembly or compilation time.
  2. Moving a program module from one area of main storage to another.
  3. The modification of a program module required to effect relocation as defined above.

remote batch processing: The submission of jobs for batch processing from a remote terminal. See also *batch processing*.

remote terminal/console: An interface or communication device between a user and a computer, generally located away from the computer installation. See also *console*.

request stacking: Placing a request for processing (system service, I/O, etc.) in a queue which will be serviced at a later time.

resident supervisor: That portion of the supervisor which remains in main storage at all times.

resource: Any facility of the computing system or operating system required by a job or task. These include main storage, input/output devices, the central processing unit, files, and control and processing programs.

resource allocation: Assigning a system resource for the use of a partition, job, job step, or task.

resource deallocation: Removing a system resource from a partition, job, job step, or task.

resource status modification: Altering the availability or definition of system resources. Typically, I/O devices may be added or deleted from the operating environment, partition sizes may be modified, and so on.

restart: To reestablish the status of a system or job at some previous point in time (usually performed as a part of recovery processing). See also *automatic restart*; *checkpoint*; *deferred restart*.

retrieval (*data*): The act of locating and selecting specific information in a file.

return code: A code which is established by a program or subroutine to notify the system or calling program of its terminal status.

reusable: The attribute of a routine that permits the same copy of the routine to be used by two or more tasks. See also *reentrant*; *serially reusable*.

ring file structure: A circular list structure in which the last data element points back to the first. See also *list structure*.

roll-out, roll-in: A method of increasing available main storage by temporarily storing an executing program on secondary storage, using the area occupied by the program, and then returning the program from secondary to main storage and restoring its status.

root segment: That segment of an overlay program which remains in main storage at all times during execution of the overlay program.

round-robin scheduling: A technique for allocating CPU time to a number of contending programs (a type of time-slicing). The technique involves establishing a circular list of users and allocating a fixed amount of time to each user in turn without regard to priority.

routine: A set of instructions arranged in proper sequence to cause the computer to perform a desired task; usually part of, or executed as part of, a *program* (e.g., a *subroutine*).

scheduler: A system component which allocates all resources for a job and performs all necessary initialization operations prior to job execution.

scheduling: That system function which prepares a job for execution. See also *dispatching*.

scheduling algorithm: The rules and decisions by which a program is scheduled.

scheduling queue: A queue of jobs that are ready for scheduling.

secondary storage: Storage facilities not an integral part of the computer but directly connected to and controlled by the computer; e.g., magnetic drum and magnetic tapes. Contrasted with *main storage*.

segment:
1. The smallest functional unit of an overlay program which can be loaded as one logical entity.
2. As applied to telecommunications, a portion of a message which can be contained in a buffer of a specified size.

selective trace: A tracing routine wherein only instructions satisfying certain specified criteria are subject to tracing. Typical criteria are: (a) instruction type; (b) instruction location; (c) data location. For (a), where tracing is performed on transfer or branch instructions, the term "logical trace" is sometimes used.

sequential access:
1. A method of accessing data such that consecutive records are processed sequentially. See also *access control*.
2. An I/O device oriented toward the above method of access, e.g., tape drive, card reader.

sequential file structure: A file structure in which elements are stored serially.

serially reusable: The attribute of a routine such that, when in main storage, the same copy of the routine can be used by another task after the current use has been concluded. See also *resuable*.

serial processing: Processing which occurs on a sequential basis, i.e., execution of a task or program only upon completion of the preceding task or program.

service program: Any of the class of standard routines or programs which assist in the use of a computing system and in the successful execution of problem programs, without contributing directly to control of the system or production of results, and including utilities, simulators, test and debugging routines, etc.

session: The period of time during which the user engages in a dialogue with a time-sharing system.

shared device: A device which may be concurrently used by two or more users.

shared file: A file which may be accessed by two or more users.

shared routine: A routine which can be concurrently executed by several users.

simple buffering: A buffering technique which assigns buffers permanently to a program until the program is terminated.

simple program structure: A program structure consisting of one module which occupies a fixed amount of main storage.

simulation:
1. Use of a computer system to represent or model some other system, e.g., another computer system, a traffic situation, etc.
2. (*I/O*) A supervisory function which handles a problem program's I/O request without performing the actual data transfer. Used almost exclusively for testing/debugging.
3. (*system*) Routines which will simulate various operating system conditions or functions. These routines may be used to test and validate the operating system or application programs running under operating system control.

simultaneous: Existing or occurring at the same instant of time. See also *concurrent*.

skeletal query: A pre-stored query which is written in outline or skeletal form. The user may define the specific operators, operands, etc., at execution time. See also *pre-stored query*; *query*.

slave: An element of a computing system that is under the functional control of a similar element.

slave computer: A computer that is under the functional control of another computer.

slaved terminal: A terminal that functions as an I/O device for another terminal rather than as an independent terminal.

snapshot (*dump*): A memory dump performed during execution of a program; generally used as a debugging aid.

software: The collection of programs and routines associated with the computer (e.g., *application* or *system software*. Contrasted with *hardware*.

sorting and merging: Those routines that sequence strings of records according to keys within each record.

sorting technique: A scheme by which a set of data items are rearranged into a new sequence of records or strings.

sort module: The programming module that actually performs a sorting or merging function.

source module: A series of statements in the symbolic language of a language processor which constitutes the entire input to a single execution of the processor. See also *load module*; *module*; *object module*.

stacked job processing: A technique of automatic job-to-job transition with little or no operator intervention. See also *batch processing*; Addendum, *batch processing*.

stand-alone utilities: Routines which are not under operating system control during execution.

standard option: A system option for which a default was established during system generation. See also *default option*.

status display: The visible presentation of the current state of the system or of some component of the system.

storage compacting: A procedure for maximizing available main storage area by relocating active programs from fragmented to contiguous areas.

storage device: A device into which data can be entered, in which it can be held and from which it can be retrieved.

storage dump: To transfer the contents of all or part of main storage to a peripheral device.

storage protection: Protection of an area of main storage against unauthorized access (read, write, or both).

string: A connected sequence of elements, e.g., a bit string or a character string.

structure control: The capability of managing different program structures during the program loading process. Some representative program structures are: simple, overlay, and dynamic.

subroutine: A routine which is called by another routine to perform a specific function.

subtask: A task which is created by and is subordinate to another task.

supervisor: The programs which schedule, allocate, and control system resources rather than process data.

supervisor call (*monitor call, master mode entry, SVC*): A request by a program or task for a service to be performed by the supervisor.

supervisor mode: A hardware- or software-supported mode of operation in which all operations may be performed. Contrasted with *problem mode*. See also Addendum, *privileged instruction*.

surface analysis: A reliability check conducted to detect failing surface area. Normally, surface analysis is conducted for direct access devices, though it may also be performed on magnetic tape.

suspended: The state of a program whose execution has been halted pending the occurrence of some specified event.

swapping: A method of sharing main storage between several programs by maintaining each program and its status on secondary storage and loading each one into main storage for a limited time interval. See also *time-sharing*.

symbiont: A data transfer routine or program which executes concurrently with user and system programs.

symbolic I/O: Reference to an I/O device by a symbolic name.

synchronous: Occurring concurrently and with a regular or predictable time relationship. Opposite of *asynchronous*.

system: An assembly of software and hardware integrated to form an organized whole.

system communication: Information exchange between the user or operator and the operating system.

system definition: Creation of tables which determine the way in which general-purpose system programs will function; may be part of system generation.

system degradation: System reconfiguration (normally due to a malfunctioning unit) which results in poorer system performance.

system description maintenance: The operating system functions performed to maintain updated tables of the current state of the system. These tables may represent static conditions such as the parameters specified at system generation, or dynamic conditions such as the number of current system users.

system generation: A process which creates a particular and uniquely specified operating system. System generation combines user-specified options and parameters with manufacturer-supplied general-purpose or nonspecialized program subsections to produce an operating system (or other complex software) of the desired form and capacity.

system initialization: The process of loading the operating system into the computer and defining the processing environment.

system input device: An I/O unit specified as a source of an *input job stream*.

system interrogation:
  1. Operator-initiated communication requesting system status.
  2. Problem program-initiated interrogation of the supervisor requesting system status.

system library: A library available to all users of a system.

system maintenance: The process of updating the operating system in response to changes in the operating environment or changes and modifications to programs within the operating system itself. See also *dynamic system maintenance*.

system management functions: The nonreal-time components of the operating system which support and maintain both system and application programs.

system measurement routines: Those routines which enable the system manager to obtain various statistics about the operational use of the system. The system manager may use these statistics to better adapt the operating configuration to the actual processing environment.

system output device: An I/O unit to which system output is directed.
system reconfiguration: Modification of an operating system to recognize a change in system resources.
system residence device: The external storage device allocated for storing the basic operating system.
system service request: A request by an executing task for the operating system to perform a service function. Typical service functions are providing I/O services, timer services, scheduling services, storage dumps, etc.
system software: Software developed as a general purpose tool to supplement the computer hardware. Systems software normally include operating systems, compilers, assemblers, etc., but does not include application or problem oriented programs. Also referred to as basic software.
system startup: The process of loading and initializing an operating system.
system status: The status of an operating system at a given point in time, e.g., number of current jobs, status of system resources, etc.
system test mode: A distinct operating environment in which the executing program is being tested. Systems having this feature provide special debugging facilities which are not available to programs executing in *production mode*.
system utility program support (compiler interface): Linkage sequence generation capabilities provided by some compilers to users of the language so that they can reference various system utility programs. See also *compiler interfaces*.

task: A program subdivision which is treated as the basic unit of work by the supervisor. See also *subtask*; Addendum, *job*.
task suspension: Temporarily suspending the execution of a task while continuing to keep the task under system control. A suspended task is removed from the dispatching queue but is not treated as a terminated task.
telecommunication: A general term expressing data transmission between a computing system and remotely located devices via a unit which performs the necessary format conversion and controls the rate of transmission. See also *polling*.
teleprocessing: An IBM term for telecommunications.
terminal: See *remote terminal/console*.
third generation: A term used to characterize the general-purpose digital computers introduced in the late 1960s. The term is generally applied to three separate computer characteristics: electronic hardware components, logical organization, and software or programming techniques.
third-generation hardware: Hardware constructed from integrated circuits.
third-generation logical organization: Special features that provide the ability to handle many programs at the same time. Such features include: memory-protection circuits, hardware address modification, modular components (CPUs, memory, data channels), and telecommunication capabilities.
third-generation software: Software supporting an operating system that is indispensable to the normal functioning of the computer. Functions are divided between hardware and software logic so as to maximize joint efficiency.

time sharing:
1. The simultaneous utilization of a computer system from multiple terminals.
2. Performing several independent processes almost simultaneously by interleaving the operations of the processes on a single processor.

See Addendum, *time sharing*.

time slicing: The allocation of limited intervals of time (quantums) to programs in contention for use of the CPU (e.g., round-robin scheduling).

timing service: Service functions provided by the operating system to an executing program that utilize one of the system timers. Typical functions include providing the real clock time, providing notification of an elapsed interval time, and suspending the executing program for a specified interval.

trace: An interpretive technique which provides an analysis of each executed instruction and writes it on an output device as each instruction is executed.

track replacement: The substitution of an alternate track for a track determined to be defective during surface analysis. See also *surface analysis*.

trailer label: A record placed at the end of a file or volume which contains control information about the file or volume. See also *header label*.

transient area: A main storage area usually, but not necessarily, within the supervisor area used for executing transient routines.

transient routines: Routines permanently stored on the system resident device and loaded into a transient area when needed for execution. Generally, they accomplish selected supervisory functions, but are not executed often enough to merit inclusion in the resident supervisor.

turnaround time: The elapsed time between submission of a job to a computing center and the return of results.

undefined record: A record having a length unspecified or unknown to the system.

unmask (interrupt): To allow recognition of an interrupt. Opposite of *mask*. See also Addendum, *interrupt*.

user: Anyone who requires the services of a computing system.

user account: An account maintained within the system for each system user. This account typically contains user identification information, as well as accumulated charges and statistics of a computer system utilization.

user program: A program written by a user to solve a specific problem, i.e., not a supervisory or control program (similar to *problem programs*).

variable length record: A record having a length independent of the length of other records in the same file. Contrasted with *fixed length record*.

virtual address: An instruction address which refers to a relative or imaginary location in main storage and which must be algorithmically converted to a real address before the instruction is executed. Contrasted with *real address*.

virtual storage: A conceptual extension of main storage achieved via a software or hardware technique which permits storage address references beyond the physical limitations of main storage. Virtual addresses are equated to real addresses during actual program execution.

volume: All that portion of a single unit of storage media which is accessible to a single read/write mechanism, e.g., a reel of tape, removable disk pack, etc.

volume maintenance: Those functions which provide diagnostic information for, correct error conditions on, and remove unwanted elements from any volume in the system. See also *file purging*; *surface analysis*.

volume preparation: The functions invoked when a new volume is to be added as a system component. These functions include the writing of standard volume labels, formatting records and/or tracks, creating volume directory entries, etc.

volume protection: Protection of a volume against unauthorized access (read, write, or both).

waiting state:
1. The state of a program which is idle pending the occurrence of some event, e.g., completion of an I/O operation.
2. The state of a program on secondary storage which is waiting to be swapped into core for execution, e.g., a program in a time-sharing system.

word: A generic term used to indicate a measurable portion of consecutive binary digits; usually the equivalent of two or more characters or bytes.

ADDENDUM

This Addendum is a supplement to the Glossary and provides additional information about terms defined in the Glossary. It addresses three subjects: (1) conflicting definitions from various sources; (2) information which is pertinent to, but does not define, terms presented in the Glossary; and (3) collective discussion of interrelated terms.

Presenting these subjects as an Addendum, rather than including them in the main body of the Glossary, serves two purposes. First, the Glossary maintains its primary purpose, to provide commonly accepted definitions of OS terminology, and does not confront the reader with masses of text unnecessary to the definition of those terms. Second, the Addendum permits a freer format, more suited to the discussion of several terms as a group or the presentation of tables showing, for instance, variations in the terminology used by various manufacturers.

The following terms are discussed in the Addendum:

background, foreground
batch processing, stacked job processing
CPU (central processing unit), processor
interrupt (arm/disarm, enable/disable, mask/unmask, trap)
job (job step, task)
linkage resolution
multiprocessing, multiprogramming
partition (region, set)

privileged instruction (problem mode, supervisor mode)
real-time
time sharing

For comparison, the reader is referred to Martin H. Weik's *Standard Dictionary of Computer and Information Processing* (New York: Hayden Book Co., Inc., 1969).

background, foreground:

These terms apply to functionally oriented areas in main storage in a multi-programming system. The *background* area is normally used for batch or stacked job processing, while the *foreground* is used for real-time and time-sharing jobs, although in some systems time-sharing may also be considered a background operation. In general, high priority programs are foreground programs, and low priority programs are background programs. CDC, in fact, in its MSOS documentation, eliminates the definitions of background and foreground, and simply defines priorities. The terms background and foreground may also be used to refer to the types of programs run in these areas. Other definitions are as follows:

background: "on a time-sharing system, tasks that are executed non-conversationally; i.e., the batch processing workload." —IBM, 360 TSS.

background program: A "running program," i.e., not an interrupt servicing routine." —Digital, PDP-8.

"in multiprogramming, the background program is the program with lowest priority. Background programs execute from a stacked job input." —IBM, 360 DOS/TOS.

background area: "that area of core storage allocated to batch processing." —XDS, Sigma 5/7 BPM.

background processing: ". . . is the normal, stacked-job processing of the job stream in a communication or data transcription environment." —Honeywell, Series 200 Mod 2 (Extended) OS.

foreground: "A generic reference to tasks being executed by a time-sharing system, while there is a dialogue or conversational interaction between the user and the system." —IBM, 360 TSS.

foreground processing: "Processing of real-time programs in the memory area immediately following the resident control routines." —Honeywell, Series 200, Mod 2 (Extended) OS.

foreground program: "The interrupt service routine." —Digital, PDP-8.

"In multiprogramming, foreground programsare the highest priority programs." —IBM, 360 DOS/TOS. "a real-time program executed on the occurrence of a priority interrupt signal or an unsolicited key-in." —XDS, Sigma 5/7 BPM.

See also *batch processing*; *real time*; *time-sharing*.

batch processing, stacked job processing

Both terms are normally used to refer to processing jobs from a job stream, as opposed to real-time processing or time-sharing.

Historically, the technical definition of batch job processing referred to a technique that used a single program loading to process many individual jobs (such as a single compiler load to process many compilations). Honeywell distinguishes batch from stacked processing as follows:

"Stacked-job processing is a refinement of the batched-job approach. In batched-job processing, a single processing function, e.g., compilation, is applied to all jobs in the batch. In stacked-job processing, any number of processing functions, such as compilation, maintenance, and execution, can be successively applied to the same job. Thus, each job in the input stack is processed to completion before the next job is accepted."

However, the distinction between these two terms is no longer common and batch job processing has become synonymous with stacked job processing—a technique of automatic job transition with little or no operator intervention.

Other definitions of these terms are listed below:

batch: "... an object program running in a stacked job manner. Shares the central processing unit with the priority program when a priority program is present and executes only when the priority program is not in control of the processor." —CDC, 31/32/33/3500 MSOS.

batch processing: "a technique by which items to be processed must be coded and collected into groups prior to processing." —Datamation ADP Glossary.

"A mode of operation where several runs are grouped prior to processing. Transition from run to run is effected by the executive system." —UNIVAC, 1108 EXEC 8.

stacked job processing: "A technique that permits multiple job definitions to be grouped (stacked) for presentation to the system, which automatically recognizes the jobs, one after another. More advanced systems allow job definitions to be added to the group (stack) at any time and from any source, and also honor priorities." —IBM, 360 OS.

See also *real time*; *time-sharing*.

CPU (central processing unit), processor:

CPU is probably the most widely used term to describe the primary control unit of a computing system. The term processor (or variants, e.g., processor module, central processor) is also widely used. However, "processor" may also be used to refer to a variety of control units in a modular system. For instance, some common types of processors are central processor modules (program control and operations units), memory modules (main storage and memory control), and input/output control (IOC) modules (controlling data transfer between memory modules and I/O devices). The GE 600 system is an example of a modular system with several types of processors.

Listed below are terms used to describe the unit (or units, in a multiprocessing system) containing the major control circuitry in a variety of computing systems.

central processor: Burroughs (B8500), CDC (31/32/33/3500), GE (615/-635), Honeywell (Series 200)
computer: CDC (1700)
CPU (central processing unit): Digital (PDP-8), IBM (360), XDS (Sigma 2, Sigma 7), SEL (Systems 86)
mainframe section (of computer): IBM (1800)
processor: Burroughs (B2500/B3500, B6500), HP (2116B), Honeywell (Model 8200), RCA (Spectra 70)
processor module: Burroughs (B8500), GE-615/635

interrupt (arm/disarm, enable/disable, mask/unmask, trap):

Systems which provide an interrupt feature provide the capability of *masking* interrupts (to defer recognition to them) and *unmasking* interrupts (to allow immediate recognition of them). The XDS Sigma 2 and 7 systems have this capability, but refer to masking and unmasking as *disabling* and *enabling*, respectively. The Sigma 2 and 7 also provide the additional capability of preventing any recognition of interrupts. *Disarmed* interrupts will be totally ignored; *armed* interrupts will be held pending if they are masked or recognized if they are unmasked. The word trap is frequently used synonymously with interrupt; it may also be used to refer to status information trapped (saved) when an interrupt occurs.

job (job step, task):

Work submitted to an operating system in a job stream can be classified at one of three levels. At the highest level is a *job* encompassing all the programs required for the execution of a given application. In extended multiprogramming systems, several jobs may be scheduled to execute concurrently. However, the individual programs within each job are processed serially.

At the intermediate level is the *job step*, an individual program to be scheduled for loading and execution. Job steps are specified by separate execute cards within the job.

At the lowest level is a *task* which is the smallest independently executable block of coding. This block may be a separate program or part of a program. The execution of a task is directed by an internal command from another executing program. The following table shows the terms used in various systems to describe these levels. Note that all three levels are not defined in all operating systems.

	Job	*Job Step*	*Task*
Burroughs (MCP)	—	Job/Program	—
CDC: SCOPE			
MASTER	Job	Task	Task
MSOS	Job	Run	—
Digital (Multiprogramming			
and Swapping Monitors)	—	Job/Program	—
GE (GECOS III)	Job	Activity	—
Honeywell:			
Mod 1 (TR) OS	Job	Program	—
Mod 2(Extended) OS	Job	Program Step	—
Mod 4 OS	Job	Job Step	—
IBM:			
DOS/TOS	Job	Program	—
OS	Job	Job Step	Task
SDC (ADEPT)	Job	Program	—
SEL (810A/810B OS)	—	Job/Program	—
RCA (POS, DOS, TDOS)	Job	Program	—
UNIVAC:			
EXEC-8	Run	Task	Activity
494 OS	Job	Task	Activity

linkage resolution: In most systems capabilities exist to combine the object modules produced by various language compilers with subroutines and other object modules to produce a single program or task. In order for this to occur, the subroutines and object modules (with the possible exception of the base module) must be *relocatable* with respect to assigned storage addresses. When these modules are combined, the assigned storage addresses of the relocatable modules are modified so that no two modules are assigned the same core area; instead the modules are normally assigned to contiguous storage locations. Once these locations are determined, the intermodule linkages (whereby one object module transfers control and data to another) are resolved by determining the newly assigned storage locations of the respective modules and inserting these addresses into the linkage sequence.

Many systems also offer an additional capability that will permit an automatic search of a system library for any object modules or subroutines with a name the same as that in an unresolved linkage sequence. These systems will then load and relocate these additional modules.

The program that performs this function occurs in two different forms, depending on the system. In some systems it is an independent job step that must be scheduled explicitly. In others it is a supervisor service that may be dynamically invoked by an executing task. Furthermore, the resulting load module may, in some systems, be immediately executed, while in others it may require subsequent loading as part of a separate job step.

The names assigned to this process and to the program that performs the process are:

	Process	*Program Name*
Burroughs	binding	binder
CDC	linking	loader, relocatable loader
DEC:		
PDP-9 Keyboard Monitor	linking	linking loader
PDP-10 Multiprogramming Monitor	linking	relocatable loader
GE	linking	loader
Honeywell	linking	linkage loader
IBM:		
S/360	linkage-editing	linkage-editor
1800	building	builder
RCA	linkage-editing	linkage-editor
XDS:		
Sigma 2 BCM	linking	linking (relocatable) loader
Sigma 5/7 BPM	linking	loader
SEL	linking	relocatable loader
UNIVAC:		
1108 EXEC-8	collecting	collector
418-III OS	collection phase	job loading
494 Omega OS	collection	loader
9400 OS	collecting	linkage-editor

multiprocessing, multiprogramming:

The Glossary defines multiprocessing and multiprogramming as simultaneous and concurrent execution of programs, respectively. *"Multiprocessing"* is almost always used to mean simultaneous execution of programs by multiple processing units. *"Multiprogramming"* is normally used to mean interleaved execution of programs, but may be used in a more general sense to refer to any method of concurrently executing programs, including multiprocessing.

The *USA Standard Vocabulary for Information Processing* (1966), on the other hand, defines multiprocessing as concurrent and multiprogramming as interleaved execution. Thus according to USASI, multiprocessing subsumes multiprogramming. However, most sources agree with the definition presented in the glossary.

Several definitions of multiprocessing and multiprogramming follow:

multiprocessing:
> "The use of two or more computers to logically or functionally divide jobs or processes and to simultaneously execute various programs or segments of programs asynchronously." —CDC, 33/3500 MASTER

> "Two or more processors simultaneously executing programs in memory to gain greater throughput." —GE, GECOS III

> "Two or more processes running simultaneously in one computer system." —Honeywell

> "The simultaneous use of two or more processing units in the same computing system." —IBM, 360 TSS

> ". . . employing two or more interconnected processing units to execute programs simultaneously." —IBM, 360 OS

multiprogramming:
> ". . . a technique for processing two programs simultaneously by overlapping or interleaving their execution." —CDC, 31/32/33/3500 MSOS

> "The concurrent processing of many programs residing in core memory to maintain the highest possible amount of simultaneous input/output, and to maximize processor utilization." —GE, GECOS III

> "Two or more programs operating simultaneously in one computer system." —Honeywell

> "A processing technique whereby more than one program coexists in computer memory, simultaneously contending for system resources." — Honeywell, Series 200 MOD 2 (Extended) OS

> "A general term that expresses use of the computing system to fulfill two or more different requirements concurrently." —IBM, 360 OS

> "A technique by which a computing system can be used to execute two or more unrelated programs, parts of which reside in main storage." —IBM, 360 TSS

> "The concurrent execution of several programs which occupy main storage. This is accomplished by sharing the attentions of the central processor." — UNIVAC, 1108, EXEC 8

partition (region, set):

In most multiprogramming systems, the user area is divided into partitions; each partition can be used for the execution of one program (a time-sharing controller and the programs swapped in and out of an area are usually treated as one program by the multiprogramming supervisor). These partitions may be fixed size (determined at system generation time or by the operator) or variable size (expanded or contracted dynamically by the system in response to calls from the problem program).

The Honeywell Mod 4 system also defines a *set* which is a fixed area of core containing one fixed partition or two variable partitions. IBM OS documentation uses the term partition to mean fixed size partition (MFT) and defines *region* as a variable size partition (MVT).

privileged instruction (problem mode, supervisor mode):

Many current computing systems provide two operating modes: a *problem mode* in which certain *privileged instructions* cannot be executed and, a *supervisor mode* in which all instructions can be executed. The purpose of these modes is to prevent the problem programmer's mistakes from disrupting system operation by disallowing his use of instructions vital to the integrity of the system. I/O, interrupt handling, and storage protection instructions are typically privileged.

Computing systems which include this feature and the terms used to designate each state are listed below. Note that not all systems having this feature have terms associated with the states.

	Supervisor Mode	*Problem Mode*
Burroughs (B2500/B3500)	control state	normal state
CDC (3300/3500)	monitor state	program state
GE (600 Systems)	master mode	slave mode
Honeywell (Series 200)	—	standard processing mode
IBM (360)	supervisor state	problem state
RCS (Spectra 70)	privileged mode	nonprivileged mode
XDS:		
Sigma 2	—	—
Sigma 7	master mode	slave mode
SEL (810B)	privileged state	unprivileged state
UNIVAC (1106/1108)	—	guard mode

real-time

Several definitions are listed below.

real time:

> "Pertaining to a program for which time requirements are particularly stringent; that is, the data processing must keep up with a physical process within a time period of seconds or less."   —CDC, 33/3500 MASTER

> "Pertaining to computation performed while the related physical process is taking place so that results of the computation can be used in guiding the physical process."   —Digital, PDP-8.

"(1) Pertaining to the actual time during which a physical process transpires. (2) Pertaining to the performance of a computation during the actual time that the related physical process transpired in order that results of the computation can be used in guiding the physical process." —Honeywell

"The actual time during which a physical process transpires, especially if that process is monitored or controlled by a computing system." —IBM, 360 TSS.

real-time processing:

"An environment in which communications data is received from remote terminals, processed, and returned to these terminals within a reasonable time frame. Each user appears to have sole possession of the system while, in fact, system resources are time-shared among the users demanding service." —Honeywell, Series 200 Mod 2 (Extended) OS. (Note: This definition corresponds with the Glossary definition of time sharing rather than real time.)

"An operating environment in which the response to external stimuli is sufficiently fast to achieve a desired objective. Depending upon the application, the response time may vary from seconds to microseconds. Generally, real-time processing is under the influence of asynchronous inputs from one or more devices." —Univac, 1108, EXEC 8.

See also *batch processing*; *time-sharing*.

time-sharing:

Time-sharing usually implies real-time use of a computing system by several users, concurrently. Unlike multiprogramming, where several programs reside in main storage simultaneously, time-sharing is generally accomplished by swapping programs into main storage from a high-speed secondary storage device. Several definitions of time-sharing are provided below.

time-sharing:

"the use of a device for two or more purposes during the same overall time interval, accomplished by interspersing component actions in time." — Datamation ADP Glossary.

"The capability of a computing system to accommodate more than one user during the same interval of time without apparent restriction by the existence of other users. In time-sharing, a given device is used in rapid succession by a number of other devices or various units of a system are used by different users or programs." —CDC, 33/3500 MASTER "a method of allocating central processor time and other computer services to multiple users so that the computer, in effect, processes a number of programs simultaneously." —Digital, PDP-8 Family

"the interleaving of the time of a device." —Digital, PDP-8/1.

"Using a device, such as a computer, to work on two or more tasks, alternating the work from one task to another. Thus, the total operating time available is divided among several tasks, using the full capability of the device." —Honeywell

"A method of using a computing system that allows a number of users to execute programs concurrently and to interact with them during execution." —IBM, 360 TSS.

"Pertaining to the interleaved use of the time of a device." Univac, USASI

See also *multiprocessing*; *real time*.

BIBLIOGRAPHY

References on the various operating systems summarized in this book are available from each of the respective computer manufacturers. For detailed supporting data, we recommend that the interested reader consult the reference list published by the manufacturer of the computer for the operating system in which he is interested.

Abel, V. A.; Rosen, S.; and Wagner, R. E. "Scheduling in a general purpose operating system." *Proc. AFIPS 1970 Fall Joint Computer Conference,* Vol. 37, Houston, Tex., November 1970, 89-96.

Atkinson, M. P.; Lister, A. M.; and Colin, A. J. T. "Multi-access facilities in a single stream batch processing system." *Computer Bulletin, 14,* 3 (March 1970), 75-78.

Batson, Alan; Ju Shy-Ming; and Wood, David C. "Measurements of segment size." *Comm. ACM, 13,* 3 (March 1970), 155-159.

Belady, L. A.; and Kuhner, C. F. "Dynamic space-sharing in computer systems." *Comm. ACM, 12,* 5 (May 1969), 282-288.

Bouvard, J. "Perspective on operating systems." In *Comparative Operative Systems: A Symposium.* Brandon/Systems Press, Princeton, N.J., 1969, 43-56.

Campbell, D.; Cook, W.; and Heffner, W. "Three dimensional operating system." In *Comparative Operating Systems: A Symposium.* Brandon/Systems Press, Princeton, N.J., 1969, 71-83.

Chapin, Ned. "Operating systems." *Computers.* Van Nostrand Reinhold Co., New York, 1971, 460-483.

Coffman, E. G.; and Muntz, R. R. "Models of pure time-sharing disciplines for resource allocation." *Proc. ACM 24th National Conference,* Vol. 33, San Francisco, Calif., August 1969, 217-228.

Cohen, Leo J. *Operating System Analysis and Design.* Spartan Books, New York, 1970, 182 pp.

Coleman, Don. "Operating systems: development for a computer family." In *Comparative Operating Systems: A Symposium.* Brandon/Systems Press, Princeton, N.J., 1969, 57-70.

Corbato, F. J.; and Vyssotsky, R. A. "Introduction and overview of the MULTICS system." *Proc. AFIPS 1965 Fall Joint Computer Conference,* Vol. 27, Las Vegas, Nev., November, 1965, 185-196.

Cuttle, G.; and Robinson, P. B. *Executive Programs and Operating Systems.* American Elsevier Inc., New York, 1970, 116 pp.

Denning, Peter J. "Thrashing: its causes and prevention." *Proc. AFIPS 1968 Fall Joint Computer Conference,* Vol. 33, San Francisco, California, December 1968, 915-922.

——— "Virtual memory." *Computing Surveys, 2,* 3 (September 1970), 153-189.

Frank, H. "Analysis and optimization of disk storage devices for time-sharing systems." *J. ACM, 16,* 4 (October, 1969), 602-620.

Habermann, A. N. "Prevention of system deadlocks." *Comm. ACM, 12,* 7 (July 1969), 373-377, 385.

Hansen, Per Brinch. "The nucleus of a multiprogramming system." *Comm. ACM, 13,* 4 (April 1970), 238-250.

Jamison, Floyd L. (ed.). *Comparative Operating Systems: A Symposium.* Brandon/Systems Press, Princeton, N.J., 1969, 124 pp.

Jones, Robert M. "Factors affecting the efficiency of a virtual memory." *IEEE Trans. Computers, C-18,* 11 (November 1969), 1,004-1,008.

Katzan, H. "Operating systems architecture." *Proc. AFIPS 1970 Spring Joint Computer Conference,* Vol. 36, Atlantic City, N.J., May 1970, 109-119.

Kellington, Myrtle R. (ed.). *Second Symposium on Operating System Principles.* ACM, New York, October 1969, 181 pp.

Kilburn, T.; Payne, R. B.; and Howarth, D. J., "The Atlas supervisor." In *Programming Systems and Languages.* McGraw-Hill Book Co., New York, 1967, 661-682.

Lampson, Butler W. "Dynamic protection structures." *Proc. AFIPS 1969 Fall Joint Computer Conference,* Vol. 35, Las Vegas, Nev., November 1969, 27-28.

Mealy, George H. "Operating systems." *Programming Systems and Languages.* McGraw-Hill Book Co., New York, 1967, 516-534.

Randall, Brian (ed.). "Proc. of the ACM symposium on operating system principles" ("Gatlinburg Symposium"). *Comm. ACM, 11,* 5 (May 1968), 295-377

Randall, Brian; and Kuehner, C. J. "Dynamic storage allocation systems." *Comm. ACM, 2,* 5 (May 1968), 297-306.

Rosin, Robert F. "Supervisory and monitor systems." *Computing Surveys 1,* 1 (March 1969), 37-54.

Selwyn, L. "Computer resource accounting in a time sharing environment." *Proc. AFIPS 1970 Spring Joint Computer Conference,* Vol. 36, Atlantic City, N.J., May 1970, 119-130.

Smith, John L. "Multiprogramming under a page on demand strategy." *Comm. ACM, 10,* 10 (October 1967), 636-646.

Weizer, Norman; and Oppenheimer, G. "Virtual memory management in a paging environment." *Proc. AFIPS 1969 Spring Joint Computer Conference,* Vol. 34, Boston, Mass., May 1969, 249-256.

INDEX

Absolute address 8, 37, 101
Access methods 55, 61-64, 66, 83
Access queue 23-24
Accounting 30, 41
Address priority 45
Addressability 8
Algorithms 47, 59, 98
Allocation 17, 29, 37-43, 66
Arm/disarm 320
Assistance to personnel 10-11
Attach 80
Auxiliary storage 55-56

B2500/B3500/B5500/B6500 92
Background processing 16, 73, 99, 318-319
Backup 130
Badge reader 73
Base register 8
Basic access method 60-61, 63
Basic multiprogramming systems 88-90, 92-93, 97
Basic program level 66
Batch processing 13, 17, 81, 88, 90, 92, 96, 99, 111, 129, 319
Binding 125, 322
Bit switches 51
Branching 6, 8
Buffering 22, 62
Burroughs: see B5500; MCP
Busy channel 40

Card punch or reader 60-61

Catalog 64-65
CCWS 64
CDC 3100, CDC 3200, CDC 3300, CDC 3500, CDC 3600 92, 182
CDC 6400/CDC 6500/CDC 6600 92, 211
CDC Master Operating System 167, 182-200
CDC Scope 3 Operating System 167, 211-228
Central processing unit: see CPU
Chained program access method 60-61
Channel 4, 7, 8, 10, 40-41
Channel availability 40
Channel commands 65
Channel control words 64
Channel hardware 50
Channel program 59, 61-64, 66
Checkpoint 114-115, 150, 157, 163, 171-172, 179, 196, 207, 221, 235, 243, 255, 272
Checkpoint restart 10, 52, 67-68, 111, 130
Clock 3, 21
Clock-time scheduling 97
Collecting 135, 322
Commands 21, 64
Common program 11
Communication 8, 26-29
  see also Telecommunications
Compile step 28
Compiler 28
Compiler communication table 125
Compiler interfaces 94, 125-126

Compiler source program libraries 125-126
Compiler subroutine libraries 126
Computer applications 2, 78
Computer speeds 14
Conditional scheduling 97
Console communication 20, 26-27
Control blocks 63
Control cards 23, 27-29, 31, 43, 49, 80, 111, 123
Control Data Corp. *see* headings beginning CDC
Control field 79
Control language 21, 80, 86, 132
Control program 3, 5, 74, 79-80
Control state 324
Conversational entry 79-80
CPU (Central processing unit) 5, 8, 9, 12, 15, 20, 42-43, 77-78, 320
CPU to I/O speed differential 7, 9, 14, 24
CRBE 79
CRJE 79
CRT 72-73
Cylinder 65

Data access control 130-131
Data banks 71-72
Data blocking/deblocking control 131-132
Data card 28
Data entry 60, 71
Data file generation and maintenance 132-134
Data formatting error 48
Data handling utilities 94, 136-137
Data management 17, 18, 21, 55, 64, 66, 94, 128-136
Data manipulation 94, 128-139
Data output 135-136
Data protection 66, 82
Data qualification and retrieval 134-135
Data records 55-60
Data set protection 10

Data sets 28, 55-60, 65
Data transfer 107-108, 141, 145, 151-152, 158, 164, 172-173, 180, 188-189, 197-198, 208, 223-224, 236, 244-245, 256-257, 273-274
Deblock 62-63
Debugging programs 11
DEC Time Sharing System 141, 146-153
Default options 30-31
Define a job 20
Deletion 69
Device availability 41
Device independence 11
Device manipulation 109
Diagnostic error processing 94, 115-117, 141, 145, 152-153, 158, 165-166, 173-174, 181, 189-190, 199-200, 209-210, 225-227, 237, 245-246, 258-259, 275-276
Digital data 76
Direct access 23, 56, 60, 63, 66, 71
Direct space management 59, 65-66
Directory 57-58
Disadvantages of operating system 13
Dispatching control 98, 103
Displacement 38
Display facilities 17, 73, 136
Documentation 1
DOS 167, 175-182
Double buffering 108
Dumps 118, 136
Dynamic allocation 99, 108
Dynamic buffering 108
Dynamic cataloging 124
Dynamic maintenance 122

Enable/disable 320
Entry/inquiry/update applications 75
Errors 48-52, 66
Event monitoring 103-106, 140, 143, 148-149, 156, 161-162, 169-170, 177, 185-186, 193-194, 204-205, 217, 232-233, 240-241, 251-252, 267-269

Index   331

Event synchronization 103, 105
Exchange buffering 108
Execution-interruption 6
Executive/control functions 17, 94, 96-120
Executive routine support 125
Executor 34, 64
Extended multiprogramming systems 88-90, 92-93, 96, 104
External symbolic references 8

File handling 128-130, 141, 145, 152, 158, 164, 173, 180, 189, 198-199, 209, 225, 236, 245, 257-258, 275
File management facilities 128-130
File reorganization 134
File updating 134
First generation 3, 85-86
First-in, first-out 36
Flow of work 9
Foreground processing 73, 76, 99, 318-319
Free space 65, 99
Functional classification 91-92

GECOS III 229, 238-247
General Electric 600 Series 92, 320
Go step 28
Grandfather files 130
Guard mode 324

H 200 Series 92
H 8200 92
Hard copy 73
Hardware and software 4, 72-76
Hardware data entry 72
Hardware error control 116-117, 141, 152, 158, 165, 173-174, 181, 189-190, 199, 209, 225-226, 237, 245-246, 258-259, 275-276
Hardware errors 48-51
Hashing 59
Hierarchial data structure 132-133

High speed storage 37
HIS G.E. Comprehensive Operating Supervisor 229, 238-247
Honeywell: *see* GE 600 Series; H 200 Series
HP 2000A 92

IBM 159-166
IBM 360 93, 201
IBM 1800 73
IBM 1800 Multiprogramming Executive Operating System 141
IBM Disk Operating System 167, 175-182
IBM Operating System MFT/MVT 167, 201-211
Index 58
Indexed access methods 130
Indexed data structure 132-133
Indexed sequential data set 58, 62-63
Indirect addressing 59
Information retrieval 17
Initiating the job 29-30
Input job stream 43, 96-98
Input queue 21, 24, 26
Input unit record devices 60
Input/output 2, 17, 18, 22, 35, 49
Input/output allocation 28-29
Input/output assignment 100-101
Input/output bound 9, 24, 30, 32, 81
Input/output control 5, 96, 106-110, 141, 144-145, 151-152, 157-158, 163-164, 172-173, 179-181, 188-189, 197-199, 207-209, 222-225, 235-236, 244-245, 255-258, 273-275
Input/output devices 60-61
Input/output error 49, 57, 64, 66-68
Input/output interrupts 35, 106
Input/output operation 22, 40-41, 43, 62-63, 67, 75, 79
Input/output programs 22, 55
Input/output queues 106-107
Input/output requests 21, 34, 36, 38-39, 52, 58, 62, 74

Input/output scheduling 15, 16, 27, 63, 107, 141, 144, 151, 157, 163, 172, 179, 188, 197, 207-208, 222, 235-236, 244, 255-256, 273
Input/output space 29, 31, 44
Input/output stream control 112-113, 141, 144, 150, 157, 163, 171, 178, 187-188, 195-196, 206, 220, 234, 243, 254, 271-272
Input/output supervisors (IOS) 55, 66
Input/output support facilities 128, 130-132
Inquiry 71
Instruction loop 41
Interactive maintenance 134
Interface error control 117, 141, 153, 158, 166, 174, 181, 190, 200, 210, 226, 237, 246, 259, 276
Intermediate data sets 69
Intermediate storage 23, 26, 28
Internal priorities 35, 36-37, 45, 47, 81
Internal processing speed 3
 see also CPU to I/O
Internal storage: see Main storage
Interrupt 6, 8, 15, 20, 34-36, 42, 74, 79, 81, 104-105, 127, 320
Interrupt handling 35-37, 103-104
Interrupt levels 34-37, 121
Invalid key 63

JCL 21, 26, 80
Job 9, 20-23, 26, 28, 96, 320-321
Job card 28, 65
Job classes 24
Job control 96-106, 140, 142-143, 146-149, 154, 156, 159-162, 168-170, 175, 182-187, 191-194, 201-205, 213-218, 230-233, 238-242, 247-253, 261-270
Job control communication 111-112, 141, 144, 149-150, 157, 162-163, 170-171, 178, 187, 195, 206, 219-220, 234, 243, 253-254, 271

Job control language: see JCL
Job initiation 29
Job management 17, 20-32, 80, 94-115, 140, 142-144, 146-151, 154-157, 159-163, 168-172, 175-179, 182-188, 191-197
Job Control 201-207, 211-222, 230-235, 238-244, 247-255, 261-272
Job mix 24
Job queues 23, 26
Job scheduling 21-24, 26, 28, 96
Job step 21, 28-29, 43, 320-321
Job stream 47
Job throughput 24, 32, 47

Key words 82
Keyed access methods 130
Keys 58-59

Label processing 86, 132
Library 30-31, 58
Library and directory maintenance 31, 123-124
Library support 125-126
Linkage editor 8, 28, 30, 125, 322
Linkage resolution 321-322
Link-edit 28
Linking loader 322
List data structure 132-133
Load module 8, 28, 124
Load module generation 124-125
Load module libraries 123
Loader 8, 28, 322
Local entry equipment 60
Logical data path 41
Logical record 62, 134
Logging and accounting 9, 119, 141, 145, 153, 159, 166, 175, 182, 191, 200, 211, 227-228, 238, 247, 260, 277
Machine check interrupt 35, 49
Machine errors 48-51
Macro libraries 123, 126
Magnetic disks 55, 60
 see also Direct access

Index   **333**

Magnetic tape   13, 55, 60
Main storage   5, 21, 27, 37, 39, 51, 99
Main storage allocation   36
Management support utilities   94, 126-128
Mask/unmask   35, 320
Master Control Program   229, 261-277
Master index   58
Master mode   324
Master operating system   167, 182-200
MCP: *see* Master Control Program
Media conversion facilities   137
Message queues   131
Message switching   71, 75-76
MFT   167, 201-211
Microwaves   77
Monitor state   69, 324
Mother task   45
Multiprocessing   47-48, 73, 88, 322-323
Multiprogrammed time-sharing system   90, 93
Multiprogramming   5, 6, 8, 13, 17, 23, 34, 43-45, 73, 75-76, 79-81, 86, 88-90, 98, 114, 127, 129, 322-323
Multitasking   45-46
MVT   167, 201-211

NCR 100/NCR 200   93
Nonprivileged mode/state   324
Nonsequential operations   56
Normal state   324

Offset (displacement)   8
On-line systems   73, 81
Operating systems characteristics   13, 88-90
Operating systems development   2-3, 20-21, 28
Operating systems functions   91-95
Operating systems levels   90-91
Operating systems management   94, 120-122

Operating systems types   17
Operations   3
Operator set-up time   4
OS   167, 201-211
Output   26
Output equipment   60
Output job stream   112-113
Overhead   12, 67

Packs   55
Paging   39, 99-100, 103
PDP-8/PDP-10/PDP-15   92
Parameters   31
Parity errors   116
Partition   16, 39, 42, 45, 47, 89, 99, 121, 323-324
Partitioned data set   56-58, 63
Passwords   66, 82
PCI   35
Peripherals   12
   see also Input/Output
Peripherals device support   126, 137
Polling   74
Power failures   116
Predictable interrupts   74
Printer   61
Priority   9, 21, 23, 81
Priority queue   36
Priority scheduler   22-23, 26
Privileged mode/state   8, 35, 324
Problem mode/state   3, 6, 8, 324
Problem program   3, 4, 6
Process control   16, 76-77
Processing support   94, 117-120, 141, 145, 153, 159, 166, 174-175, 181-182, 190-191, 200, 210-211, 227-228, 237-238, 246-247, 259-260, 276-277
Program controlled interrupt (PCI)   35
Program error control   117, 141, 153, 158, 165-166, 174, 181, 190, 199, 210, 226, 237, 246, 259, 276
Program errors   48-49
Program initiated scheduling   97

Program interrupt 35
Program libraries 1, 30-31, 43
Program loading 101-103, 105, 140,
Program loading 101-103, 105, 140, 143, 147-148, 155-156, 160-161, 169, 176, 185, 193, 203-204, 215-217, 231-232, 240, 251, 266-267
Program maintenance 94, 122-125
Program mode/state 324
Program termination processing 106, 140, 143, 149, 156, 162, 170, 177, 186-187, 194, 205, 217-218, 233, 241-242, 252-253, 269-270
Programs 17, 21, 29-30, 34-35
Protection 13, 40, 100

Queue 7, 23-26, 29, 36, 45, 47, 83
Queue priority schemes 45-47
Queue request 36
Queued access methods 60-63, 66
Query 135

Random access 56, 59
Random methods 59, 131
RBE 79
RBM system 154
RCA Spectra 70, 93
RCA Tape-Disk Operating System 167-175
Real time 16, 17, 41, 44, 71, 75-77, 82, 92, 94, 96-97, 99-100, 105, 111, 116, 121-122, 126, 128, 130, 324-325
Real-time clock 118
Records 56, 60, 71
  see also Data sets
Records blocking/deblocking 86
Recovery processing 96, 114-115, 141, 144, 150-151, 157, 163, 171-172, 179, 188, 196-197, 207, 221-222, 235, 243-244, 255, 272
Redundant circuits 51
Reenterability 7, 10, 101

Refreshable module 111
Region 323-324
Relocatable loader 322
Relocatable program libraries 123
Relocatability 4, 5, 8, 28, 30
Remote batch entry (RBE) 79
Remote data entry 60-61, 71-78, 81
Remote data equipment 61, 72-73, 80
Remote data processing 74, 82
Remote inquiry 71
Remote job entry (RJE) 79-80, 109
Remote processing 63, 71, 73-74, 76, 81, 83
Remote program entry 74-75, 78-80, 81-82
Remote terminals 15, 16, 17, 42, 71-73, 77-78
Remote terminals support 108-109, 141, 145, 152, 158, 164, 173, 180, 189, 198, 208, 224-225, 236, 245, 257, 274-275
Resident input/output error recovery module 66
Resident supervisor 310
Resource allocation 36-45, 98-101, 140, 143, 147, 155, 160, 169, 176, 183-185, 192-193, 202, 213-215, 231, 239-240, 249-251, 263-265
Resource queues 35-36, 41, 44-45, 47
Resource status modification 113-114, 141, 144, 150, 157, 163, 171, 178, 188, 196, 206, 220-221, 234, 243, 254, 272
Response time 81
Restarting 10, 68, 115, 150-151, 157, 163, 172, 179, 190-197, 207, 221-222, 235, 243, 244, 255, 272
Retrying the input/output operation 67
Return interrupt 74
Ring data structure 132-133
RJE 79-80, 109
Roll-out, roll-in 95, 103, 115
Routine 21
  see also Type of routine
Routing 76

Scheduling 5, 20, 23, 95-98, 140, 142, 146-147, 154, 159-160, 168, 175, 182-183, 191-192, 201, 213, 230-231, 238-239, 248-249, 263
Scope 3, 167, 211-228
Search 55, 65
Second generation 3
Secondary storage 10, 16, 21, 23, 28, 38-39, 52, 58, 63, 65, 71-72
Security data sets 66-67, 83
Seek 55, 65
Segments 38
SEL 810A/810B 93
SEL Operating System 141-145
Sequential access 56, 62
Sequential methods 130
Sequential data structure (set) 56-57, 60, 132-133
Serial batch systems 16
Serial processing systems 86, 88-90, 92-93, 96, 98, 114
Serial scheduling 22-23, 26
Serial tasking 44
Serial time sharing systems 88-90
Serially reusable routines 101
Service interrupt 35
Service program 8, 69
Servomechanisms 76
Set 323-324
Set up time 3
Sigma 2/5/7 93
Sigma Operating System 141, 154-159, 229-238
Single buffering 107-108
Slave mode 324
Sort module 138-139
Sorting and merging 94, 137-139
Source program libraries 10, 123
Space 66
    see also Storage
Spectra 70, 93
Stacks 23, 26, 36, 319
Stand-alone utilities 127-128
Standard error routines 63
Standard processing mode 324

Standardized programs 2
Starting the job 29-30
Static cataloging 124
Storage 5, 10
Storage dumps 51, 118, 136
Storage pools 99
Storage of program modules 57
Storage protection 10, 40
Subroutine libraries 11
Supervisor 8, 64, 96
Supervisor call interrupt 6, 35
Supervisor mode/state 3, 6, 34-35, 324
Swapping 103
Symbionts 112-113
Symbolic name/address 8
Synchronous interrupt 74
System 20, 114
System communication 96, 110-114, 141, 143-144, 149-150, 156-157, 162-163, 170-171, 178-179, 187-188, 194-196, 205-207, 218-221, 233-235, 242-243, 253, 254, 270-272
System description maintenance 119-120, 141, 145, 153, 159, 166, 175, 182, 191, 200, 211, 228, 238, 247 260, 277
System error recovery 48-52
System generation 52, 81, 120-121
System initialization 110
System maintenance 121-122
System management functions 20, 94, 120-128
System measurement routines 127
System resource management 17, 20
System restarting 48-52, 110
    see also Errors
System startup 110-111, 141, 143, 149, 156, 162, 170, 178, 187, 194, 205, 218-219, 233-234, 242, 253, 270-271
System status interrogation 114, 141, 144, 150, 157, 163, 171, 179, 188, 196, 207, 221, 235, 243, 254, 272

System stimulation routines 126-127
System timer or clock 41
System utilities 126

Tape-Disk Operating System 167-175
Tapes 10
Task control card 28
Task management 17, 20-21, 34-54
Task priority 34
Task queue 45, 47
Task supervisor 44-48
Tasks 21, 23, 26, 28-29, 34-35, 43-45, 47, 320-321
Telecommunications 44, 61-62, 71-83, 110, 126
Telephone lines 15, 72, 77
Terminal 14, 16, 71
  see also Remote terminals
Testing/debugging service 118-119, 141, 145, 153, 159, 166, 174, 181-182, 190-191, 200, 211, 227, 237-238, 247, 259-260, 277
Third generation 4-18, 86
Throughput 24
Time out 41
Time sharing 14-17, 42, 71, 79, 80, 88-90, 92, 96, 98-99, 103-104, 109, 113-114, 119, 122, 129, 141, 146-153, 325-326
Timing circuits 74
Timing service 117-118, 141, 145, 153, 159, 166, 174, 181, 190, 200, 210, 227, 237, 246-247, 259, 276-277
Time slice or quantum 16, 42, 89
Track 56, 65
Track index 58
Transaction data files 130

Transfer of control 10
Transmission media 77-78
Trap 320
TSS/8 141, 146-153
Turnaround 74

Univac 418/494/1100 series/9000 series 93
Univac 1108 Multiprocessor System 247
Univac Exec 8 Operating System 229, 247-260
Unit record equipment 60-61
Unprivileged state 324
Unsupported 83
Update 71
Use of storage 12-13
User implications 3, 5, 30-32, 52-53, 68-69, 81-83
User program errors 48
User program mode 34
Utility programs 10, 69, 127-128

Virtual memory 37-40, 79
Voice receiver 82
Volume 31, 36, 55-56, 65
Volume positioning 109
Volume table of contents (VTOC) 65

Wait state 51, 67
Wait loop 31

XDS Batch Time Sharing Monitor 229-238
XDS Real Time Batch Monitor 141, 154-159
XDS Sigma 2/5/7 93

OHIO UNIVERSIT
Please return this bo
have finished with
fine it must

6 1982